In the Wake of War

Democratization and Internal Armed Conflict in Latin America

D0048011

Edited by

Cynthia J. Arnson

Woodrow Wilson Center Press
Washington, D.C.

Stanford University Press
Stanford, California

EDITORIAL OFFICES

Woodrow Wilson Center Press
One Woodrow Wilson Plaza
1300 Pennsylvania Avenue, N.W.
Washington, DC 20004-3027
Telephone: 202-691-4029
www.wilsoncenter.org

ORDER FROM

Stanford University Press
Chicago Distribution Center
11030 South Langley Avenue
Chicago, IL 60628
Telephone: 800-621-2736; 773-568-1550

Library of Congress Cataloging-in-Publication Data

In the wake of war : democratization and internal conflict in Latin America / edited by
Cynthia J. Arnson.
    p. cm.
  Includes index.
  ISBN-13: 978-0-8047-7667-7 (cloth)
  ISBN-10: 0-8047-7667-9 (cloth)
  ISBN-13: 978-0-8047-7668-4 (pbk.)
  ISBN-10: 0-8047-7668-7 (pbk.)
  1. Democratization—Latin America—History. 2. Peace-building—Latin America—History.
3. Nation-building—Latin America—History. I. Arnson, Cynthia.

  JL966.I5 2012
  320.98—dc23

                                                                2011053431

In loving memory
Arthur David Arnson
Carlos Iván Degregori

Contents

ix

Tables and Figures

Tables

Figures

Acknowledgments

This book represents the culmination of the Woodrow Wilson Center Latin American Program's fifteen-year Project on Comparative Peace Processes in Latin America. Over the years of inquiry, the program has published dozens of reports in English and Spanish, frequently in conjunction with partner institutions in the region. An earlier book, *Comparative Peace Processes in Latin America,* was published by the Woodrow Wilson Center Press and Stanford University Press in 1999 and is now in its third printing.

Many colleagues have been more than generous with their time and insights as this manuscript was in preparation. I am particularly indebted to Dinorah Azpuru of Wichita State University for unflagging support, assistance, and critical comment. I am grateful as well to Diego Abente, Mariano Aguirre, Ariel Armony, Frances Hagopian, Cynthia McClintock, Shelley McConnell, Ramón Tasat, and two anonymous reviewers for detailed and helpful comments on all or part of the manuscript. Felipe Agüero, Blanca Antonini, Ariel Armony, Charles T. Call, Cristina Eguizábal, Pablo de Greiff, Gonzalo Sánchez Gómez, Ana Sojo, Alexander Segovia, and Teresa

Whitfield participated in the conference that launched this book, and it is enriched by their contributions. Thanks as well to Shep Forman of New York University for sharing his insights early on about the relationship between state building and democratic transitions.

This book would not have been possible without the hard work and collaboration of numerous colleagues and interns at the Woodrow Wilson Center. Over a period of several years, Jonathan Carver, Julián Casal, Adam Drolet, Angela Granum, Lisa Kraus, Alyssa Pardo, Kristen Smith, Smith Monson, and Camilo Zambrano provided outstanding research and editorial support. In the final stages, no one was as critical to the book's progress and success than Lisa Hartland. I am grateful to my colleagues in the Latin American Program, especially Andrew Selee and Adam Stubits, for providing the stimulating and collegial environment in which the book took shape. Superb editorial assistance was given by Joe Brinley, Yamile Kahn, and Cherie Worth of the Woodrow Wilson Center Press and by the copyeditor, Alfred Imhoff. Michael Van Dusen and Robert Litwak offered support and encouragement over the many years of this book's gestation. My husband, Gerry Serotta, and children, Zack, Jeanne, and Micah, deserve, now and always, my gratitude for their love and indulgence.

Finally, this book would not have been possible without the generous financial support of the Royal Norwegian Ministry of Foreign Affairs and the Ford Foundation. To them and to everyone mentioned above, my deepest thanks.

Cynthia J. Arnson
December 2011

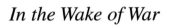

In the Wake of War

Chapter 1

Introduction:
Conflict, Democratization, and the State

Cynthia J. Arnson

This book is about internal armed conflict and its relationship to postwar democratization in Latin America. The book takes as its starting point a theme developed in a previous volume: that for a subset of Latin American countries, guerrilla insurgency—its settlement and aftermath, or its continuation—have had a decisive impact on the nature and quality of democratization and on the possibilities for establishing effective democratic governance.[1] Our earlier volume, *Comparative Peace Processes in Latin America,* led us to the general conclusion that there was a positive and mutually reinforcing relationship between democratization and peace processes to end guerrilla war: Processes of democratic opening tended to precede peace negotiations, and negotiations themselves advanced processes of democratization, both during peace talks and during periods of implementation of peace accords. With some important qualifications, this conclusion has stood the test of time. We also noted that the multiple challenges faced by postwar regimes, which paralleled but exceeded the challenges of achieving a transition from military authoritarianism to

1

democracy—left very much open the question of "transition toward what?" As we will discuss below, the transitions metaphor itself has been questioned; it also has proved limited in explaining how the legacy of internal armed conflict shapes and limits the possibilities for democratization in the postwar period, and how postconflict democratization differs from democratization in nonconflict settings.

This inquiry focuses on seven countries—Colombia, El Salvador, Guatemala, Haiti, Mexico, Nicaragua, and Peru. With the exceptions of Mexico and Haiti, these countries have distinguished themselves from others in Latin America to the degree that insurgency or counterinsurgency war[2] was a, if not the, dominant aspect of political life during and immediately after the end of the Cold War. In the case of Mexico, the phase of direct military confrontation in the state of Chiapas was measured in days rather than years and affected relatively small numbers of people, but the political effect of the indigenous uprising reverberated for the better part of a decade. In the case of Colombia, the conflict continues, even though the insurgents have been dramatically weakened since 2002. The inclusion of Haiti in this collection reflects the multiple ways that, even in the absence of outright war, chronic political instability, acute poverty, and rampant political and social violence have challenged the viability of the Haitian state, even before the devastating earthquake of January 2010 that killed hundreds of thousands of people and left the capital city, and much of the country's capacity for governance, in ruins.

The chapters in this book seek to deepen the analysis of the relationship between democratization and war. We adopt a liberal definition of political democracy,[3] for two reasons endogenous to Latin America itself. First, in the Southern Cone, a return to representative forms of government constituted the explicit goal of a generation of Latin Americans struggling against repressive military rule. Second, and more important for the cases considered in this book, the insurgencies themselves were a product of deep crises of political exclusion, reinforced in most instances by patterns of socioeconomic marginalization and exclusion. Therefore, the very processes to negotiate an end to internal armed conflict established democratization and reform of the political system as a central objective of postwar transformation. (For a number of reasons discussed in subsequent chapters, addressing the sources of socioeconomic exclusion were not accorded the same primacy as political reform.) We are thus less concerned with normative judgments regarding the appropriateness of Western-style liberal democracy to postwar settings than we are with assessing the ability of postwar regimes to address questions of political inclusion within the parameters of an explicitly agreed-upon political architecture.[4]

How, then, has war shaped, influenced, or otherwise affected the nature of political democratization in these Latin American countries? Does the course of postwar political change allow us to further refine the distinction between transitions that take place during or after armed conflict and other transitions from authoritarianism in Latin America? What, if any, new issues, themes, or patterns have emerged during the past decade that might be particular to this set of countries? Does the conflict resolution literature concerning weak states, fragile states, state failure, and state collapse— a literature drawn from case studies of Africa, Southeast Asia, Eastern Europe, and now Iraq and Afghanistan—offer new ways of understanding prospects for democratization in postwar settings?[5]

In *Comparative Peace Processes,* we posited that achieving and maintaining peace—defined both as preventing a relapse into war and creating a functioning polity capable of processing conflict without violence[6]— involved a complex array of political, socioeconomic, and technical processes set against a backdrop of frail or nonfunctioning institutions of the state. Armed conflict left regimes fortified in their military and/or repressive dimensions, but typically weak in their capacity to engage in the interrelated political, economic, and social tasks that would prevent future violence or address root causes of conflict. Peace accords to end wars in several Latin American countries—and at times even the negotiations themselves—had a positive impact on democratization and respect for human rights; these accords broadened the political space to allow for the participation of previously excluded groups, expanded civil liberties and media freedoms, and launched processes of broad institutional reform. Engagement by the international community in monitoring the implementation of the accords added resources along with pressure for compliance. Nowhere has this political evolution been more dramatically illustrated than in El Salvador, where twenty years after the war's end, the candidate representing the political party of the former guerrillas won the presidential election in 2009 and took office in an orderly transfer of power.

However, it is evident that in other cases the end of conflict and the advance of democratization are less clearly, if at all, related. The manner in which conflicts end—not just whether they end—is a decisive influence on postwar political development. In some cases, military victory has served to validate authoritarian practices and the concentration of executive and military power, while root causes of conflict go unattended. Elsewhere, "reserve domains" of power held by active-duty or retired members of the armed forces, the intelligence apparatus, and the police have been strong and resilient enough to block security-sector reforms, stunt the acquisition of civilian authority, and keep civil society in a state of fear and uncertainty; parallel structures operate as a "state within the state," unaccountable to legally constituted authority. In several of the cases discussed in this book, underlying conditions of state weakness during and after conflict have been exploited by predatory networks of organized crime that have penetrated and corrupted state institutions, deforming or arresting their democratic potential.

As much as we attempt to draw generalizations about the impact of internal armed conflict on democratization, we must also point out the ways that the case studies developed in this book defy comparison. The history and origins of armed conflict in Latin America may be rooted in common patterns of political and socioeconomic inequalities, but the dynamics and duration of conflict, the nature of preexisting state institutions, and of the state response to conflict have varied greatly. To name a few of these differences:

- *The duration and geographic reach of conflict:* The wars in El Salvador, Guatemala, Nicaragua, and Peru collectively claimed hundreds of thousands of civilian victims. War was the dominant fact of life for at least a decade, and, in the case of Guatemala, several decades. In Colombia, the historic absence of the state from large portions of the national territory left openings for illegal armed actors—guerrillas, paramilitaries, and drug traffickers—to flourish. These groups undermined state authority over a period of several decades and established parallel sources of political, economic, military, and social power. By contrast, in Chiapas, Mexico, the armed conflict itself lasted less than two weeks and was quite localized, even though its political effects reverberated nationally over a period of many years.
- *The salience of the Cold War and the role of the United States:* With the exception of the cases of Mexico and Haiti, some form of Marxist-Leninist or Maoist ideology has permeated the armed conflicts in Latin America. Throughout the period of the Cold War, the United States provided substantial levels of military aid, equipment, and training to Latin American armed forces for the purposes of defeating the insurgencies and justified them in the name of fighting Communism. The Central American conflicts of the 1980s, waged in close geographic proximity

to the United States, were deeply permeated by a Cold War logic; in the 1980s, the United States spent billions of dollars on overt and covert support for counterinsurgency efforts in El Salvador and to support a counterrevolutionary army fighting Nicaragua's Sandinista government. (Because of extensive human rights abuses in Guatemala, the U.S. Congress prohibited most military aid to the Guatemalan army.) The end of the Cold War—marked by the fall of the Berlin Wall in 1989 and the subsequent collapse of the Soviet Union—created openings for a change in U.S. policy and, hence, for negotiated settlements to the Central American wars to prosper. In contrast to Central America, the U.S. role in Colombia and Peru has been shaped principally by counternarcotics objectives and their blending over time with counterinsurgency strategy. U.S. military assistance to Colombia in the late 1990s and 2000s was a critical element of a successful military campaign to extend the state's presence throughout the countryside and weaken the insurgents. As of this writing, in mid-2011, it was too early to tell whether and in what manner these efforts would contribute to an end of the conflict in Colombia.

- *The nature of settlement and the role of the international community:* In only two cases—El Salvador and Guatemala—did wars come to an end through a negotiated political settlement between the parties, mediated by the United Nations and leading to the signing of a formal peace accord. Third-party mediation by the United Nations and the Organization of American States was also critical to the achievement of a cease-fire in Nicaragua and the subsequent demobilization of the counterrevolutionary army fighting the Sandinistas. Although the international community has been critical to the achievement of peace settlements in Central America, its success in fostering accord compliance in the postwar period has been much more limited. The United Nations also played a significant, and ultimately unsuccessful, role in attempting to broker a peace settlement in Colombia between the government and two remaining guerrilla organizations. (Smaller insurgent organizations demobilized in the 1980s and early 1990s through direct talks with the Colombian government.) By contrast, Peru achieved a "strategic victory" over the Shining Path (*Sendero Luminoso*) guerrilla movement in the early 1990s. Unlike in Central America, where the end of armed conflict was linked to political opening and the expansion of civil liberties, the end of war in Peru served to validate the authoritarian practices of the regime of President Alberto Fujimori. Subsequently,

Peru's postauthoritarian governments failed to adopt measures to consolidate peace. The lack of state attention to neglected areas that had served as the cradle of conflict created conditions for the emergence of antidemocratic "outsiders" in the political arena. In the 2006 and 2011 presidential elections, a former military officer, Ollanta Humala, drew his greatest strength from same remote areas of the country where Shining Path had been most active.

- *The role of natural resource income for the insurgents:* Insurgencies typically finance their activities through a wide range of illegal pursuits—including kidnapping, extortion, and robbery—which take place through clandestine networks for the movement of weapons, money, and fighters. The production and trade in illegal narcotics, however, has introduced financial resources of a different order of magnitude. In the Colombian case, the income from illicit drugs has transformed the nature of the conflict along with the objectives of the multiple armed actors involved.[7] Narcotics production and trafficking and overlapping issues of criminality have contributed to the intractability of the Colombian conflict, despite major military setbacks for the guerrillas. In Peru, by contrast, insurgent income from coca did not prevent its "strategic defeat" in the early 1990s, even though drug-producing regions of Peru have seen a resurgence of Shining Path activity.

- *The role of ethnicity:* Questions of ethnic discrimination and exclusion were central characteristics of the uprising in Chiapas and also of the conflicts in Peru and Guatemala. In Nicaragua, the Miskito Indians living on the country's Atlantic Coast joined the anti-Sandinista rebellion, but ethnic claims were peripheral to the principal dynamic of war between the Sandinista government and the U.S.-backed National Resistance, or "contra," counterrevolutionary army. Questions of ethnicity were for the most part absent in El Salvador; and though not irrelevant in Colombia, they have been tangential to the central dynamic of the armed conflict.

- *Conflict-related versus postwar violence:* In countries such as El Salvador and Guatemala, postwar violence and the number of homicides now exceed the levels experienced during most years of the conflict, underscoring the degree to which the terms "postwar" and "postconflict" are not interchangeable. Yet contemporary Central America also demonstrates that there is no neat and simple correlation between armed conflict and surging rates of criminality. War in Nicaragua spanned the entire decade of the 1980s, but postwar levels of crime and violence there are a small fraction of what exists elsewhere in Central America and the rest of the region. Honduras, meanwhile, did not experience the protracted armed conflicts of its neighbors, even though it was deeply affected by the use of its own territory for the waging of war in bordering countries, particularly El Salvador and Nicaragua. A "quasi-conflict" case, Honduras by 2010 and 2011 had levels of criminal violence equal to or higher than those of El Salvador and Guatemala.

Because these variations among the case studies are so profound, one may well ask whether there are grounds for meaningful comparison. Indeed, recent comparative work on democratic governance in Latin American has raised renewed questions about the utility of broad generalizations, arguing that particular contexts or settings are the major determinants of democratic outcomes and possibilities.[8]

Without negating the highly distinctive histories of each of the countries discussed in this book—the different patterns of conflict as well as natures of settlement—we nonetheless answer the question posed above with a tentative yes. In all the countries discussed in this book, some aspect of state weakness—the absence of a state monopoly on force, the inability to uphold a legal order, and the inability or unwillingness to provide basic services to the population—interacted with one or more forms of political or social exclusion to serve as a fundamental structural underpinning of conflict. The state response to this existential threat to its existence takes a variety of forms, some of which strengthen the ability of the state to perform certain functions, while others undermine its legitimacy. The process of state reconstruction or reconfiguration in the postwar period has a decisive impact on the nature, extent, and possibilities for democratization.

This book thus goes beyond earlier works that have sought to distinguish how cases of postwar democratization in Latin America differ from nonwar transitions from authoritarianism to democracy. In other words, we transcend the previous focus on the multiple and simultaneous transitions in conflict countries (from war to peace, from authoritarianism to democracy, from militarization to demilitarization, etc.)[9] to suggest that the nature of the state and its capacity to fulfill basic functions constitute more useful concepts for exploring postwar democratization. Hence, we draw attention to the importance of "state-ness"—a concept at the center of the literature on conflict resolution but, until very recently, less prominent in theories of democratic transition or democratization—as key to understanding postwar democratization in Latin America.[10]

In his commentary on chapters 1 and 2, Stewart Patrick highlights many of the ways that the literatures on conflict resolution and on democratization do not speak to each other. Studies of democratization in Latin America, a rich and extensive literature born initially of concern for the destruction of democracy by bureaucratic authoritarian military regimes, have evolved over several decades. The original focus on the breakdown of democracy in the 1970s developed into a concern with transitions away from authoritarian rule and the subsequent consolidation of democratic systems in the 1980s and 1990s. More recent work in the 2000s has focused primarily on questions of democratic quality, performance, and the variations among subtypes of democratic regimes, with growing attention to the nature of the state as a determinant of the possibility for a democratic outcome.[11] Studies of conflict resolution and postconflict peace building, meanwhile, have always taken as their central unit of analysis the state: the relationship between state fragility or collapse and internal armed conflict, and strategies for state strengthening, construction, or reconstruction. The relationship of democratization to state strengthening is a subject of debate among conflict resolution specialists. As we will explore below, however, the concern with *governance* serves as a theoretical and practical bridge between students of Latin American democratization and those concerned with conflict resolution.[12]

Although an extensive discussion of theories of the state is beyond the scope of this inquiry, it is nonetheless important to define the concept of the state as used here. "The state" is fundamentally an abstraction, understood as performing certain roles and possessing certain attributes fundamental to social order. For centuries, political philosophers, political scientists, economists, sociologists, and, now, policy practitioners have debated the precise nature of the state and its importance for maintaining order, for promoting economic development and collective and individual well-being, and for mediating relations between social classes.[13] In the early twentieth century, the German sociologist Max Weber defined the state as a "compulsory political organization" with an administrative staff capable of upholding "the claim to the *monopoly* of the *legitimate* use of physical force in the enforcement of its order" (emphasis in original).[14] Weber's emphasis on the monopoly of legitimate violence within a defined territory stands at the core of contemporary scholarship regarding the state, but its reductionism has been challenged and refined. Thus, the political theorist Margaret Levi offers the following, more comprehensive definition:

A state is a complex apparatus of centralized and institutionalized power that concentrates violence, establishes property rights, and regulates society within a given territory while being formally recognized as a state by international forums. All states share some common characteristics: a legal structure and coercive apparatus that creates and enforces property rights; a system of laws and norms that regulates interactions among those who live in the state; a mechanism for trading with, defending against, and attacking those in other states; and procedures and agencies for taxing and policing the population.[15]

According to Levi, the roles and functions of the state are fulfilled by multiple institutions and actors both in and out of government; that is, the state itself is different from state institutions, which are more functional in nature.[16] The state as an apparatus is thus distinct from a particular regime (whether democratic or authoritarian) and from the particular government operatives who exercise authority (with or without legitimacy and/ or legality).

It is certainly true that many states in Latin America and throughout the developing world lack a number of the characteristics enumerated by Levi, and state institutions are thus unable to fulfill core roles. Moreover, state weakness limits the quality of democratic governance in many countries of Latin America, not just those that have emerged out of war. The coercive, legal and juridical, and service-providing aspects of state presence are uneven throughout the region, even in states with strong central authority and institutional capacity. In situations of relative weakness, however, not all states spawn armed conflict. What concern us here are less the particular paths through which state weakness give rise to conflict (that is, we are not attempting to create new theory regarding the origins of revolution), but rather the impact of prolonged political violence on the state and its institutions such that the prospects for democracy are diminished, distorted, or altogether absent.

Two initial caveats are necessary. First, if the state has received less consistent attention by scholars of democratic transition in Latin America, it has hardly been ignored. In 1993, Guillermo O'Donnell identified an effective state as critical to the exercise of citizenship in a democracy.[17] The state, in his view, could only ensure the legitimate exercise of its authority through a legal system regulating both public and private life. He also viewed a strong—as opposed to "big"—state as critical to the implementation of social policies to address poverty and inequality.[18] The social

scientist Adam Przeworski and other scholars of democratic transitions in
Latin America and Eastern Europe took issue with the antistate bias of
neoliberal structural reforms advocated by international financial institutions in the 1990s. Though such reforms sought to shrink or dismantle
state involvement in the market and in other areas such as the provision of
services, Latin American scholars noted the centrality of state institutions
in performing a broad range of functions critical to the sustainability of
democracy.[19] Juan Linz and Alfred Stepan viewed modern democracy as
impossible without a state, a prior condition for the creation of democratic
institutions.[20] Theories of the state have also been central to the critique of
democratic "sequencing," which held that democracies evolved on a more
or less predictable path from transition to consolidation and that democratization itself had to await the construction of a well-functioning state.[21]
International organizations such as the United Nations Development
Program and the Organization of American States have similarly called
attention to the need for a capable and effective state, with resources, institutional capacity, and concrete mechanisms for promoting human development, combating poverty and inequality, and ensuring citizen security.
Latin American democracies are impoverished, in their view, because "the
state is poor, limited and dependent," incapable of exercising its functions
and thereby incapable of representing the majority or guaranteeing the
broad exercise of citizenship.[22]

Second, scholarship on democratization concerning all of Latin America—not just countries conditioned by armed conflict—has focused for
some time on questions of democratic quality, and particularly its limitations, "deficits," and shortcomings. Today, the essential requirements for
political, procedural democracy—based on free, competitive elections and
universal suffrage within a basic framework of civil rights[23]—exist in most
countries of the hemisphere. Yet even in those liberal democracies with a
basic framework for electoral alternation and civil rights, scholars have
emphasized that fundamental aspects of democratic quality are missing or
severely compromised.[24]

Deficiencies at both the national and subnational levels are evident in
the uneven application of the rule of law,[25] the absence of mechanisms of
either vertical or horizontal accountability, the lack of respect for human
rights, the weakness of channels of representation and participation, patterns of de facto discrimination against ethnic and racial minorities, and so
on. Scholars thus have adopted a number of qualifiers, such as "hybrid,"[26]
"delegative,"[27] and "illiberal"[28]—that is, "democracy with adjectives"[29]—to

capture the variety of ways that formal democracies that emerged in the so-called third wave[30] of democratic transitions around the world fell short of the liberal ideal envisioned in the consolidation literature. Scholars have identified authoritarian regimes that held periodic elections as "competitive authoritarian," thus delinking the holding of elections with democracy.[31] More recent scholarship has emphasized the lack of citizen security and high levels of inequality, along with asymmetries in the way political power is held and exercised, as fundamental issues compromising and limiting democratic quality.[32]

Recent scholarship on democracy in Latin America has also focused on levels of public support for democratic regimes and the responsiveness of governments to citizen demands; these studies have noted widespread disillusionment (*desencanto*) with the performance of democratic regimes and distrust of political leaders, parties, and institutions.[33] In some countries, surging rates of violence, crime, and organized crime have undermined public trust in institutions and made daily life a misery for significant segments of the population.[34] Indeed, annual public opinion surveys in Latin America have revealed that crime and unemployment are the major public concerns in most countries of the hemisphere, with crime overtaking unemployment by the end of the decade.[35] Less known but the subject of wide debate among practitioners is the extent to which crime, violence, and organized crime—beyond constituting threats to democratic quality—have hollowed out and penetrated state institutions to such an extent that they have become threats to the very survival of democratic regimes. History may provide a sobering antecedent. In an analysis of the breakdown of democracy in Europe before World War II, the political scientist Nancy Bermeo has argued that crime, not economic depression or inflation, was the key ingredient distinguishing democracies that survived from those that did not.[36]

Public opinion surveys conducted by the polling firm Latinobarómetro and the Americas Barometer demonstrate that citizens in Latin America for the most part have reacted to failures of democratic performance in the economic, political, and security realms without abandoning faith in democracy itself.[37] In 2009, for example, the results were especially striking. Despite a global recession, support for democracy reached its highest level since polling began in the mid-1990s, rising 11 percentage points since the beginning of the decade, an upward trend that continued in 2010.[38] Nonetheless, as indicated in chapter 2, a further breakdown among countries shows that satisfaction with democratic performance in countries that have undergone internal armed conflict is lower than in the rest of Latin America.

In a number of countries, however, most prominently in the Andean region, systems of representative democracy have imploded. The chronic weakness of democratic institutions, failures of democratic representation and incorporation (particularly vis-à-vis large indigenous populations), and long-standing patterns of socioeconomic exclusion have given rise to populist forms of government, some with overtly authoritarian overtones, that have sought to supplant the institutions of representative democracy with unmediated forms of "direct" or "participatory" democracy.[39] The rise of radical populism in such countries as Bolivia, Ecuador, and Venezuela differs from the cases discussed in this book, however, in that institutional weakness was not a product of prolonged political violence represented by war.[40] What the populist cases share with the cases of internal armed conflict, however, is a profound crisis of political inclusion and incorporation. Indeed, the Colombian historian Marco Palacios, the author of chapter 6 in this book, has suggested that revolutionary warfare in such countries as El Salvador, Guatemala, Nicaragua, and even Colombia erupted when populist experiments failed or were absent altogether.[41]

If Latin American citizens have shown increasing levels of support for democracy, it is also true that not all scholars of Latin American democracy have accepted or shared the overall pessimism about the state of democracy in the hemisphere. Philippe Schmitter, for example, has objected to an ever-expanding set of criteria used to assess democratic quality, indicating that "all real existing democracies are based on compromises." Evaluating new democracies by standards that took older democracies decades or even centuries to attain leads to unwarranted negativity about the achievement and potential of political democracy throughout the hemisphere.[42] Others have pointed to examples of public policy innovation, creative leadership at the local and national levels, the emergence of vibrant civil societies, new forms of citizen participation, and institutional reform as reflections of democracy's resilience and creative potential.[43]

Attempts to characterize the quality of democracy as well as citizen satisfaction point to an overarching concern with the concept of *governance* as critical to the deepening and sustainability of democracy.[44] Definitions of governance abound, combining technical and political aspects as articulated by the United Nations Development Program in 1997. The program described governance as "the exercise of economic, political, and administrative authority to manage a country's affairs at all levels."[45] Common to definitions of governance is the notion of *capacity,* the ability to get things done. These "things" range from providing basic security to ensuring the provision of social services to the establishment and functioning of a framework for orderly political, economic, and social life.[46] Hence, a broad definition of governance calls forth many attributes of the state. Democratic governance, in turn, was based on transparent and accountable public institutions, the rule of law, and popular participation in decisionmaking, viewed as central to achieving not only sustainable development but also sustainable peace.[47] The notion of governance and its corollaries—"good" governance[48] and democratic governance—thus provide a conceptual bridge linking the study of democratization, on the one hand, to the study of building peace in conflict or postwar settings, on the other.

"Bringing the State Back In"[49]

The study of governance as it relates to conflict resolution and efforts to rebuild postconflict societies developed largely in the 1990s and in areas of the world for the most part unrelated to Latin America. In the decade following the end of the Cold War, the international community grappled with how to respond to the civil wars and genocide erupting in Africa and Central Europe—widespread expectations that the end of the Cold War would usher in a period of greater global harmony collapsed as "new wars" broke out in such places as the former Yugoslavia, Rwanda, Sierra Leone, and Afghanistan. These conflicts were distinguished not only by the virulent political manipulation of ethnic and national identities but also by the sheer magnitude of human suffering; by the 1990s, some 90 percent of the victims of armed conflict were civilians, not soldiers, reversing the ratio from the beginning of the twentieth century.[50] These new conflicts also evidenced the role of globalization in blurring the distinction between war and organized crime and in fostering war economies—built on looting and black market transactions—that benefited from a more open international trading regime and the weakening of market regulation.[51]

Attempts to understand and resolve these "new wars" centered on the role of weak or collapsed states in fostering armed conflict and impeding its resolution.[52] Concepts such as state failure or collapse and state weakness or fragility were relative terms describing conditions along a continuum; they were also dynamic processes rather than static conditions. But the core definition of a failing or collapsed state centered on the loss of the ability to perform basic state functions.[53] According to The Hague, these functions included the ability to control or administer territory, provide security to citizens through a monopoly on the legitimate use of force, provide essential public services or create conditions for their provision, and uphold an internal legal order.[54] Virtually all the definitions of state weakness and/or failure emphasized the territorial, security, administrative, and economic (social welfare) dimensions of statehood.[55] In attempting to reconstruct failed states, practitioners accorded a central role to political democracy as essential to solidifying the legitimacy of governing authorities and institutions.

The United Nations led the international community in the post–Cold War years in assuming a wider role in resolving conflict and creating the conditions for stable peace. The multiple international peacekeeping operations that were launched in the early 1990s and that cost billions of dollars gave rise to a renewed and in many respects unprecedented attention to questions of the state. How could states be rebuilt to perform basic functions in the security, political, and economic realms? What institutions needed to be created or reformed? How could peacekeepers restore national authority in order to leave once they had entered?

The early 1990s version of state building had humanitarian and developmentalist underpinnings. The "human security" agenda embraced by the United Nations and advanced by Canada and several European governments substituted the promotion of collective and individual well-being for more conventional military notions of security.[56] The terrorist attacks of September 11, 2001, and subsequent interventions in Iraq and Afghanistan, served to highlight the international security dimension of weak states, and identified the United States as an explicit breeding ground for terrorism and, hence, a major security concern.[57]

Numerous studies have pointed to the clashes of priorities among international agencies and donors involved in postconflict state building, along with failures of coordination and long-term commitment.[58] Yet what the Africa scholar Marina Ottaway called a "prevalent model of state reconstruction" emerged, aimed at restoring the functions of a de facto state.[59] This required actions in the security, economic, and political arenas, ranging from initial programs to demobilize combatants and provide relief to war-affected populations to longer-term efforts to transform the security forces, develop a viable political infrastructure, and create the conditions for a functioning economy. The importance of Western-style democratization to the postwar framework for state building grew out of an implicit or explicit emphasis on constructing new political institutions and carrying out political reforms; drafting or revising constitutions; writing electoral laws and developing electoral oversight bodies; creating or strengthening political parties and the judicial system; and enhancing the capacity of civil society to provide meaningful input to and monitoring of governmental actions. Democracy was closely tied to the restoration of postconflict political legitimacy to governmental authorities, based on the principles of participation and inclusion.[60]

Critiques of the democratization–peace building nexus abound, zeroing in on the presumptive liberal, Western bias of democratization theory along with the assumption that peace and democracy are mutually reinforcing.[61] The Africa scholar and diplomat Howard Wolpe noted, for example, that democracy involves competition based on a shared understanding of the underlying rules of the game. In many postconflict societies, however, leaders view politics in zero-sum terms, knowing how to compete but not how to collaborate. The key task in divided postwar societies, therefore, is to build a consensus on procedures, rebuilding the trust and confidence necessary for leaders to believe in agreements over how power will be shared and organized.[62] This process may not be helped by a move toward early democratic elections. Other analysts have urged that "dilemma analysis" be built into a framework for state building after internal armed conflict. As experience with postwar state building has accumulated, many scholars have pointed to the many contradictions among various priorities in practice, requiring trade-offs and the balancing of hard choices.[63]

A second area in which opinions diverge has to do with the role played not by elites but by civil society in building democracy and peace. Actors in civil society can build a culture of peace and mechanisms for nonviolent conflict resolution at the local level, expanding grassroots participation. Scholars have increasingly disagreed, however, over the precise relationship between civil society and democracy and over the impact of subnational civil society initiatives on democratization and peace building at the national level. What is critical, some have argued, is not civic participation per se, but rather the building of a culture of tolerance in the postwar setting.[64]

Outline of the Book

The chapters of this book explore in detail a number of key topics stemming from the themes delineated above. In chapter 2, Dinorah Azpuru uses a number of quantitative indicators to assess the state of democracy and the "state of the state," exploring how individual countries have performed vis-à-vis their own past, how they compare with one another, and—most significantly—how countries that have undergone internal armed conflict compare with postauthoritarian, nonconflict countries in Latin America.

Azpuru argues that since the early 1990s, the conflict and postwar countries addressed in this book (with the exception of Haiti) have made significant strides in terms of procedural democracy but still face serious shortcomings in aspects related to the rule of law and in the socioeconomic arena. With only a few exceptions, measurements of political democracy and public satisfaction with democracy are lower in conflict and postwar countries than in other Latin American countries, although support for and levels of trust in institutions are uniformly low throughout the region. Moreover, on the social, economic, and political indicators used to measure vulnerability to violent conflict and societal deterioration, conflict and postwar countries in Latin America in general scored worse than nonconflict counterparts in the region. Human development indicators overall were also worse, as were percentages of the population living in poverty or extreme poverty. Azpuru concludes that overall, the conflict and postwar countries face political challenges similar to the rest of the Latin American countries with respect to institutional strengthening and the broadening of social inclusion. She notes, however, that countries such as Guatemala, Colombia, Haiti, and, more recently, Mexico, face additional challenges—particularly those related to high levels of crime and violence and the penetration of state structures by organized crime, especially narcotrafficking—which undermine the very essence of democratic governance. Again, Stewart Patrick's commentary on the introduction and chapter 2 delineates areas of overlap as well as divergences between the transitions and conflict resolution literatures.

In the case of El Salvador, Ricardo Córdova Macías and Carlos G. Ramos argue in chapter 3 that the 1992 peace agreement between the government and the guerrillas provided the foundation for the political and institutional modernization and democratization of the regime. El Salvador's multiple transitions—from war to peace, from militarism to democratization, and from authoritarianism to democracy—redistributed power to political parties that were shaped by the war and whose transformation and modernization was not contemplated in the peace accords. Hence, these parties were ill equipped to assume the central roles ascribed to them in El Salvador's transition. Two dominant parties—the Nationalist Republican Alliance (Alianza Republicana Nacionalista, ARENA) on the right and the Farabundo Martí National Liberation Front (Frente Farabundo Martí para la Liberación Nacional, FMLN) on the left—represent the extremes of the ideological spectrum, producing polarization at the national level that has made dialogue and consensus difficult. The 2009 presidential elections showed greater moderation by both parties, culminating in a landmark for the peace process: the election of the candidate of the FMLN and the peaceful transfer of power from ARENA to the opposition. Although greater pluralism has been manifest at the local level, Salvadoran voters since the war have demonstrated low levels of trust in political parties, and both high and increasing dissatisfaction with the way democracy functions. Spiraling violence and crime in the postwar era have had a significant impact on levels of support for the political system. Public opinion polls also demonstrate that support for authoritarian values has risen in tandem with the perception of insecurity. Meanwhile, economic reforms undertaken by successive ARENA governments have led to a reconcentration of economic power, a countervailing process to the peace accords' provisions for broader political inclusion. This asymmetry between the political-institutional and socioeconomic aspects of the peace accords constitutes a central tension in El Salvador's postwar development, and may help explain the FMLN's victory at the polls in the March 2009 presidential elections, at a time of deep global and regional economic crisis. The chapter authors argue that additional political reforms would help depoliticize key electoral institutions and reinforce the modernization and independence of the judiciary.

Like El Salvador, Guatemala suffered decades of military dictatorship and counterinsurgency war before the signing of peace accords in 1996 ushered in a period of formal peace. In chapter 4, Edelberto Torres-Rivas argues that the duration and extent of the repression in Guatemala—a postwar truth commission found that about 60,000 indigenous people were murdered by the army between 1980 and 1983 alone—left the weakness of civilian state institutions as their central legacy. State terrorism preceded guerrilla activity, he indicates—it actively undermined the system of justice; limited the capacity to develop social programs to address deep poverty, inequality, and ethnic discrimination; compromised and undermined citizen participation; and hindered the development of parties as articulators of citizens' interests rather than as personalistic vehicles to win elections. Against this powerful backdrop, Torres-Rivas notes significant progress in making Guatemala's electoral system more competitive and inclusive, curbing military influence, broadening indigenous rights and participation, enhancing freedom of expression, and creating a culture of dialogue. He reminds us that democratization is a process lasting generations, and that the "interplay of light and shadow" makes the future of Guatemala uncertain at this point in history. Indeed, the state's continuing weakness in confronting surging violent crime and rooting out institutional corruption has left it vulnerable to penetration and co-optation by organized criminal structures.

In both El Salvador and Guatemala, limited democratic openings during the time of armed conflict predated peace processes that provided a basis for renegotiating the design of core democratic institutions and procedures. By contrast, Nicaragua's transition was carved against a backdrop of military dictatorship throughout most of the twentieth century, followed by revolutionary and then counterrevolutionary war. In chapter 5, Shelley McConnell illustrates how, in the absence of preexisting democratic institutions, the transfer of conflict in Nicaragua to the political arena—a desired outcome of most peace processes—polarized the country's politics along an enduring Sandinista/anti-Sandinista cleavage. Important progress was made in the 1990s in key areas of democratic strengthening, including the consolidation of civilian control over the armed forces, the expansion of civil liberties, and the growth of civil society. Yet in the absence of mechanisms of horizontal accountability across branches or institutions of government, corruption and opportunism flourished. Nowhere were these qualities more in evidence than in "the pact," a secret political agreement reached at the end of the 1990s between the Sandinistas and the ruling Liberal Party to share power at the expense of other, smaller political forces.

According to McConnell, *el pacto* allowed the two dominant parties to establish a "virtual duopoly on institutions of state." Through an alliance regarding legislative and constitutional reforms, the Liberals and the Sandinistas achieved dominance of such key institutions as the Supreme Electoral Council and the Supreme Court. By controlling the design of the electoral regime, the two parties raised almost insurmountable barriers to democratic competition, and Nicaragua's electoral system became the most exclusionary in all Latin America. In addition, a key change to the Constitution made it possible for a presidential candidate to win with as little as 35 percent of the vote, a principal factor behind the 2006 electoral victory of the Sandinista leader Daniel Ortega, who had been defeated in four earlier presidential races. The embedding of Nicaragua's postwar political cleavage in the very architecture of the state did not deepen democracy. Rather, McConnell demonstrates how it created the conditions for a stable yet illiberal regime, which continued the personalistic and clientelistic patterns of rule of prerevolutionary Nicaragua.

Unlike the countries where political settlements to internal conflict advanced a process of democratization, Colombia's armed conflict and the government's responses to it underscored the chronic failure of the country's political class to construct an inclusionary, democratic state. In chapter 6, the historian Marco Palacios argues that a weak state in Colombia gave rise to complex political, economic, and social relationships based on large landholdings (latifundism) and clientelism. He dates Colombia's contemporary armed conflict to the 1980s, not forty or fifty years ago when the guerrilla groups first emerged, pointing to the massive concentration of land ownership in the latter part of the twentieth century and the take-off of "mafia-driven modernization" impelled by narco-trafficking. The drug trade accelerated an expansion of the armed conflict, accentuating the weakness of the state and providing vast means for the corruption and intimidation of politicians, the security forces, and the judiciary. For the guerrillas, Palacios argues, income from protection and extortion related to drug trafficking makes up for their lack of a mass social base. Paramilitary groups achieved rapid territorial expansion through the enormous financial resources linked to the drug trade, and, since their formal demobilization, have resurfaced as criminal actors still deeply involved in narco-trafficking.

Taking issue with other scholars of the Colombian conflict, Palacios argues that war and peace are not central national issues; only 5 percent of the population lives in "territories of de facto power" that are the heart of the armed organizations. Another two-thirds live in metropolitan areas that constitute "islands of legitimacy" for the government, and the rest of the country goes back and forth between the two. Efforts to negotiate a political settlement with guerrillas of the Revolutionary Armed Forces of Colombia (Fuerzas Armadas Revolucionarias de Colombia, FARC) failed during the administration of President Andrés Pastrana, due to internal factors such as the autarchic nature of the FARC and its growing isolation along with the exponential growth in the size and territorial reach of the paramilitaries. Palacios argues that the aid program known as Plan Colombia "narcotized" U.S.-Colombian relations; it strengthened the state only in the military arena, forcing the FARC into retreat but leaving the state weak vis-à-vis electoral democracy and social policies directed to the country's interior. Paramilitary demobilization under President Álvaro Uribe—including the extradition of top paramilitary leaders to the United States—left the group's fortunes largely intact. Some paramilitary groups have rearmed, while land, bank accounts, and illegal businesses serve as an ongoing basis of political and electoral power in the country. President Juan

Manuel Santos, who was inaugurated in August 2010, has taken bold steps to reverse the concentration of landownership and provide restitution to the victims of armed conflict; although the implementation of these measures is fraught with difficulties, the efforts themselves represent a sea change in government attitudes toward the roots and consequences of Colombia's conflict. Ana María Bejarano offers a commentary on chapter 6, highlighting several reasons that future peace talks to resolve the conflict will be more difficult than those in the past.

The relationship between a weak state, armed conflict, and the general deterioration of political democracy is also key to understanding recent Peruvian political history. In chapter 7, Carlos Basombrío discusses how the authoritarian legacy of the war against the Shining Path guerrillas—coupled with a failure to address the extreme poverty, racism, and exclusion that fueled the insurgency—have undermined the effort to construct a democratic system with broad-based support. President Alberto Fujimori, who staged a 1992 "self-coup" (*autogolpe*) that dissolved the institutions of representative democracy, engaged in further manipulations of the law and the electoral apparatus to run for an unprecedented third term. He was elected in 2000 amid allegations of massive fraud, only to watch his regime implode in a corruption scandal sparked by the leaking of videotapes showing the head of his intelligence service delivering a cash bribe to a member of Congress. He fled the country (he was later extradited, tried, and convicted of human rights abuse and corruption), and the transitional regime that replaced him ushered in a brief era of democratic opening. Basombrío chronicles how reform efforts—including the convening of a Truth and Reconciliation Commission, and steps to reform and modernize the armed forces and police—represented important advances, only to be undermined by minimal continuity and a lack of support from the highest political authorities, including President Alejandro Toledo.

Peru's 2006 presidential elections brought into sharp relief the twin legacies of authoritarianism and armed conflict. A former army commander, Ollanta Humala, whose combination of ultranationalism and xenophobia proved repugnant to Peruvian elites, won the first round of the elections, drawing his strongest support from the poor and marginalized regions of Peru most devastated by the war with the Shining Path. Following the defeat of the guerrilla movement, and particularly under the elected governments that succeeded Fujimori, Peruvian elites had failed to consolidate peace by enacting structural reforms to address the country's centuries-old problems of racism and inequality. Although the economy grew at robust rates, an inefficient and incompetent state proved incapable of improving the quality of life for the majority of Peruvians. The state, moreover, remained unable to control all the nation's territory, a weakness that permitted remnants of armed groups to resurface in traditional areas of the illicit coca economy. Basombrío shows how both sources of weakness and illegitimacy kept "authoritarian impulses" alive in Peruvian society, where support for democracy was the lowest in all Latin America. The neck-and-neck race in the June 2011 presidential elections between Humala and Keiko Fujimori, the daughter of the imprisoned former president, was a direct product of this authoritarian legacy and also of the failure of past administrations to redistribute the fruits of Peru's rapid growth. Humala, who was inaugurated in July 2011, promised to redress the country's social deficits while respecting the rules governing a market economy. What his government will mean for political democratization remains to be seen.

In Mexico, where the military confrontation between Zapatista insurgents and government troops lasted less than two weeks, Raúl Benítez Manuat, Tania Carrasco, and Armando Rodríguez Luna locate the roots of the conflict in the historic failure of the Mexican state to overcome centuries of discrimination against the indigenous population. In chapter 8, these authors identify as a central backdrop to the 1994 Zapatista uprising the structural dualism between Mexico's urban, developed North and its rural, poor South, a dichotomy reproduced in the state of Chiapas itself. For the first time, the uprising put the issue of indigenous rights on the broader national agenda for democratization: Social and political forces embraced the Zapatista cause as part of the effort to end close to seventy years of one-party rule in Mexico; at the same time, the existence of "two Mexicos" called into question the notion that democracy meant only a change in government through elections.

When the opposition candidate Vicente Fox won the presidential elections in 2000, he made the political resolution of the Chiapas crisis a centerpiece of government policy. But a subsequent indigenous rights law promoted by his administration and approved by Congress failed to address key Zapatista demands for the recognition of collective rights and control over natural resources. The Zapatistas refused to accept the government's legitimacy or recognize the evolution of Mexican democracy, instead focusing on the building of alternative political structures at the local level. The convocation of alternative forms of social organization has contributed to increasing tensions within and among communities in Chiapas. The failure to complete the transition from military to political actors and participate openly in the political system has led to the Zapatistas' increased isolation in Mexico and to open conflict with the organized left. At the same time, their continued presence at the local level has testified to the Mexican state's inability to create legal or political mechanisms to relate to emerging social movements or to resolve in a comprehensive fashion centuries-old patterns of discrimination against indigenous peoples.

The issue not only of state weakness but also of state failure has arisen in Latin America only in the case of Haiti, the poorest country in the Western Hemisphere. In chapter 9, Johanna Mendelson Forman describes Haiti's chronic instability and economic decay resulting from decades (if not centuries) of rule by tyrants and rent-seeking elites. Spiraling violence by youth gangs and former military personnel, human rights violations, and state weakness—though not open armed conflict—provided the backdrop for a series of United Nations–led interventions to develop institutions of security, governance, and economic development. Mendelson Forman considers Haiti a test case for international efforts at state building in the name of postconflict reconstruction to overcome state failure. She notes, among a variety of factors, how the international community's initial failure to commit to long-term engagement, but especially the exit of the UN in 2000, led to only limited success in the effort to create a functioning state. When the UN did return in 2004, it confronted problems that combined underdevelopment with insecurity and economic decay—which were only exacerbated by the devastating earthquake in January 2010. At the same time, Mendelson Forman emphasizes that progress toward even limited goals was not possible without the engagement and buy-in of Haitian political leaders and key elites.

An initial decision by international actors to disband the Haitian armed forces in 1995 had created pools of angry, unemployed former soldiers capable of disrupting the stabilization effort. The creation of a Haitian National Police did not resolve the security problem. As competing Haitian political leaders and parties continued to jockey for power, they turned to armed gangs to threaten or engage in violence at times of political stalemate. The election of President René Préval in 2006 marked a turning point; efforts at political reconciliation among political leaders and civil society gained traction alongside a UN effort to engage in "developmental peacekeeping," a holistic approach to enhancing security, building the capacity for democratic governance, and spurring economic growth. The ambitious attempt by the international community—led by Latin American nations—to engage in state building in Haiti is ongoing, particularly in the post-earthquake setting. The state remains very fragile, and the potential for renewed violence in the context of Haiti's deep and enduring poverty remains high, although there is some hope after the presidential elections of 2010 that the situation might improve. Mendelson Forman indicates that an important lesson for the international community has already been learned: Progress in overcoming state failure requires long-term engagement, and improving the government's capacity to deliver basic services to the citizenry depends on assistance in maintaining security. Also required are strong partnerships with local governments, so that initial gains can be sustained over time and the state's role in governance can be gradually legitimized. It is this latter aspect of state building in Haiti that remains a central challenge as the country recovers from the destruction after the earthquake.

A far less extensive form of international involvement in peace processes and peace building relies on the traditional instruments of diplomacy and foreign assistance. In chapter 10, Markus Schultze-Kraft analyzes how and why the countries of Europe—individually or collectively, under the umbrella of the European Union—became engaged in peace processes in Central America and Colombia, in the absence of any broader European strategic or economic interest in the region. In Central America in the 1980s, a number of socialist or social democratic governments in Europe viewed U.S. policy as both misguided and dangerous. In countries such as France, Germany, Spain, and Sweden, leaders believed not only that the roots of antiregime violence in Nicaragua, El Salvador, and Guatemala were political and socioeconomic but also that the Reagan administration's insistence on external factors—meddling by the Soviet Union and Cuba—threatened European security by potentially provoking Soviet military intervention in Western Europe. According to Schultze-Kraft, "soft intervention" on the part of European governments served as a brake on military escalation by the United States and lent international legitimacy to regional peace initiatives. These included a Costa Rican–devised plan that ultimately served as the blueprint for dismantling the contra war in Nicaragua. European actors ultimately were secondary players in the settlement of the Central American wars—national and regional actors and the United Nations played the dominant roles—but foreign assistance in the 1990s made a significant contribution to postwar reconstruction.

In the Colombian case, Schultze-Kraft indicates how European integration transformed the EU into a more powerful international actor, even if the bloc is still far from speaking with a single voice. European involvement in Colombia went through distinct stages, paralleling not only advances in European integration but also changing circumstances within Colombia itself. Several European countries actively supported the peace process undertaken by President Andrés Pastrana. They were motivated not only by a long-standing preference for ending conflict through political negotiations but also by opposition to the emphasis of Plan Colombia on military and counternarcotics assistance. The EU's alternative strategy for Colombia focused on tackling the socioeconomic roots of the crisis, supporting human rights and institutional strengthening, and building a "culture of peace," especially at the local level. Given that the stakes for Europe in Colombia are low, European policy has not sought to take the lead in fomenting peace or in serving as a counterweight to U.S. policy. Rather, the EU has attempted to map out its own multilateral strategy commensurate with the continent's growing role on the world stage and consistent with its long-standing emphasis on building democratic institutions, fostering dialogue between the government and civil society, and alleviating humanitarian crisis.

Finally, this book explores two central aspects of the postconflict environment. One, the establishment of truth commissions in Guatemala and Peru, aimed to contribute to social and political reconciliation by assigning responsibility for the pervasive human rights abuses during the war and thereby establish norms, albeit not necessarily legal remedies, to prevent their recurrence. Second, we deepen the understanding of why the terms "postwar" and "postconflict" are not synonymous,[65] by tracing the violence of youth gangs and organized crime in Central America and Mexico to the defects of institutional transformation and to the very nature of the state response to crime.

In chapter 11, on social and criminal violence, José Miguel Cruz, Rafael Fernández de Castro, and Gema Santamaría Balmaceda acknowledge the role of poverty, social exclusion, migration, and lack of opportunity as partial explanations for the emergence and growth of Central American youth gangs (*maras*). But they situate the phenomenon of violence, including the growing menace of organized crime, more squarely within the nature of the political transitions in Central America's "Northern Tier" (El Salvador, Guatemala, and Honduras) along with Mexico. The authors reject what many have posited as an explanatory linkage between internal armed conflict and the subsequent emergence of gangs; they note that Honduras has a significant gang problem without having had a prior civil war, whereas Nicaragua suffered close to a decade of armed conflict but has escaped a significant gang problem. The decisive causal factors, the authors argue, relate to the failure during the transition to establish effective public security institutions, which instead remained plagued with internal corruption, links with organized crime, and human rights violations rooted in the authoritarian past. The subsequent adoption of *mano dura* (iron fist) policies to combat crime in El Salvador, Guatemala, and Honduras, at times for expressly political and electoral purposes, only worsened the situation. Such tactics opened the door to extralegal responses, made it possible for armed groups (including state agents) to engage in "social cleansing" targeting young people, and created a permissive environment for the private financing of illegal groups. Government-sponsored preventive programs such as those adopted in Nicaragua have offered an alternative, integrated, and ultimately more effective policy based on crime prevention.

According to the three authors, the Mexican transition of the 1990s also contributed to violence, but through a different process of institutional transformation. They point to the 1994 economic crisis and the gradual loss of hegemonic control of the state apparatus by the Institutional Revolutionary Party (Partido Revolucionario Institucional, PRI), which signified the loss of corporative practices of co-optation that had served for decades to resolve conflicts and prevent crises of governance. The reshuffling of power relationships leading to the defeat of the PRI in historic 2000 presidential elections, along with the decentralization and fragmentation of the coercive apparatus, created conflicts within state public security institutions. This left power vacuums that were exploited by organized crime, including drug trafficking syndicates. As much as Mexico's democratic transition itself may have been linked in part to the crisis in Chiapas in the mid-1990s, political violence there had very little impact on the subsequent wave of violence unleashed by organized crime in the early years of the twenty-first century. As in Central America, severe violence in Mexico threatens the consolidation of a democratic state.

The way governments and societies deal with human rights violations committed over the course of armed conflict also has a bearing on the nature of postconflict democratic rule. Although knowing the truth and prosecuting those responsible for abuses have at times been viewed as trade-offs, in chapter 12 the anthropologist Victoria Sanford argues that official truth commissions such as Guatemala's Commission for Historical Clarification (Comisión de Esclaricimiento, CEH) can enhance the possibilities for future justice. The CEH, formed under the peace accords and operating under United Nations auspices, placed the number of those murdered or disappeared during the country's thirty-six-year conflict at more than 200,000, and attributed 93 percent of the abuses to the Guatemalan military. Notably, the CEH ruled that the armed forces had committed "acts of genocide" against Guatemala's largely rural, indigenous Mayan population, marking the first time in recent Latin American history that such a term was used to describe mass killings. Among the conflict's urban victims—students, professors, union leaders, priests, and nuns—the CEH found a disproportionate number of human rights activists.

Although the claim of genocide was subsequently disavowed by the Guatemalan government, Sanford shows how communities affected by violence took advantage of the space created by the CEH's work to push for court cases against those responsible and for exhumations of mass graves. The international community also took a number of steps to help reverse the long history of impunity, including the establishment of a joint UN-Guatemalan government commission to dismantle clandestine organizations that continue to threaten human rights and the rule of law. Nonetheless, Sanford comes to the sobering conclusion that "there is no more justice today" in Guatemala than there was twenty years ago. Homicide rates continue to rise, violence against human rights defenders continues unabated, and "parallel powers" continue to infiltrate and undermine state institutions, posing a threat to the survival of democracy.

The Peruvian case also demonstrates that the mere existence of a truth commission—whatever the quality or authoritativeness of its work—cannot itself produce reconciliation, reparation, or justice in the absence of government and societal will. In a commentary on chapter 12, Carlos Iván Degregori, a member of Peru's Truth and Reconciliation Commission (Comisión de Verdad y Reconciliación, CVR) shows that, even when insurgent groups themselves are found to have borne the major responsibility for wartime atrocities, the government's failure to adopt measures to "win the peace" has profound political consequences for the future. Violence does not disappear but mutates, and the lack of political will to redress the injustices, racism, and discrimination identified by the CVR meant that a key opportunity offered by the transition was lost. Nonetheless, Degregori sees the CVR as contributing to accountability in Peru—of which the most extraordinary example was the extradition, trial, and sentencing of former president Alberto Fujimori for human rights and other crimes.

Conclusion

The chapters in this volume illustrate the uneven patterns of state strengthening and democratization during the past decade. The specificity of each case, and of the conditions under which war was waged and brought to an end (or not), cannot be overstated. The historical roots of conflict, the degree of prior state and institutional weakness, the kind of settlement, the relative strength of political and social forces involved in negotiating a settlement (to the extent that it exists) and overseeing its implementation, and the commitment of postwar governments to fundamental transformations vary from country to county.

That said, the nature of postwar societies in Latin America cannot be understood in terms of the dominant democratization paradigms developed for other countries of the region. The relationship between prolonged political violence and democratization requires attention to the state and its institutions. Depending on its intensity and duration, internal armed conflict distorts the nature of the state, posing more severe limits on the potential for postwar democratization. This distortion takes place "from above," via state institutions that are incapable or compromised in their ability to promote the rule of law and ensure social well-being through social policy and regulatory frameworks. But the distortion also occurs "from below," in terms of the impact of war on the capacity of members of an autonomous civil society to exercise the rights of citizenship. "Problematizing" the international community in terms of its role in seeking and building peace—in essence, exploring the roles of international organizations or individual nations—now more aptly directs us to view the international dimension also in terms of *nonstate* actors that have prospered through globalization, particularly organized crime.

As the chapters that follow demonstrate, issues of the state are not separable from the less abstract issue of political agency: Human beings, not structures or institutions, make choices that have an impact on whether politics evolves in a democratic direction. Both during and after armed conflict, opportunities can be used or squandered by political elites. In other words, actors make choices that can, for example, address chronic underlying problems, derail reforms, amass political power and personal fortunes, or promote reconciliation. These choices then have consequences for institutions and, ultimately, for the strengthening of the state.

Notes

1. See Cynthia J. Arnson, ed., *Comparative Peace Processes in Latin America* (Washington, D.C., and Stanford, Calif.: Woodrow Wilson Center Press and Stanford University Press, 1999).

2. These conflicts cannot be described as civil wars, but rather as insurgencies or uprisings (in the case of Chiapas) against the state.

3. Liberal democracy is grounded in the notion of divided power (checks and balances), institutionalized channels of citizen participation and representation, and consistent "rules of the game" that nonetheless produce uncertain outcomes. Most scholars of political democracy point to the defining works of Joseph A. Schumpeter, *Capitalism, Socialism, and Democracy* (New York: Harper, 1947), 269; and Robert A. Dahl, *Polyarchy: Participation and Opposition* (New Haven, Conn.: Yale University Press, 1971).

4. In addition, we do not equate democracy with the holding of free elections, but rather consider a far broader range of aspects of democratic quality and governance.

5. For an earlier treatment of this relationship, see, e.g., the special issue of the journal *Global Governance* 9, no. 2 (2003), and especially the article by Charles T. Call and Susan E. Cook, "On Democratization and Peacebuilding," 233–47.

6. Michael Doyle and Nicholas Sambanis, "International Peacebuilding: A Theoretical and Quantitative Analysis," *American Political Science Review* 94, no. 4 (December 2000): 779–801, quoted by Cynthia J. Arnson and Dinorah Azpuru, "From Peace to Democratization: Lessons from Central America," in *Contemporary Peacemaking: Conflict Peace Processes and Post-War Reconstruction,* 2nd ed., edited by John Darby and Roger MacGinty (New York: Palgrave Macmillan, 2008), 271–88.

7. There is an extensive literature on the role of economic resources in fueling and transforming internal armed conflict. See the extensive writings on the subject by the former World Bank economist Paul Collier, e.g., Paul Collier, "Doing Well Out of War: An Economic Perspective," in *Greed and Grievance: Economic Agendas in Civil Wars,* edited by Mats Berdal and David Malone (Boulder, Colo.: Lynne Rienner, 2000); Paul Collier and Anke Hoeffler, *Greed and Grievance in Civil War,* Policy Research Working Paper 2355 (Washington, D.C.: World Bank, 2000); Paul Collier et al., *Breaking the Conflict Trap: Civil War and Development Policy* (New York: Oxford University Press for the World Bank, 2003); and Paul Collier, *Wars, Guns, and Votes: Democracy in Dangerous Places* (New York: HarperCollins, 2009). Also see Karen Ballentine and Heiko Nitzschke, *Profiting from Peace: Managing the Resource Dimensions of Civil War* (Boulder, Colo.: Lynne Rienner, 2005); Karen Ballentine and Jake Sherman, eds., *The Political Economy of Armed Conflict: Beyond Greed and Grievance* (Boulder, Colo.: Lynne Rienner, 2003); Cynthia J. Arnson and I. William Zartman, eds., *Rethinking the Economics of War: The Intersection of Need, Creed, and Greed* (Washington, D.C., and Baltimore: Woodrow Wilson Center Press and Johns Hopkins University Press, 2005). On Colombia, see Cynthia J. Arnson and Teresa Whitfield, "Third Parties and Intractable Conflicts: The Case of Colombia," in *Grasping the Nettle: Analyzing Cases of Intractable Conflict,* edited by Chester A. Crocker, Fen Osler Hampson, and Pamela Aall (Washington, D.C.: U.S. Institute of Peace Press, 2005).

8. Scott Mainwaring and Timothy R. Scully, *Democratic Governance in Latin America* (Stanford, Calif.: Stanford University Press, 2010), 381–83.

9. Interview with Rubén I. Zamora, "La izquierda en la encrucijada," *Revista Tendencias* (San Salvador), February 15, 1992; Ricardo Córdova Macias, "El Salvador: Transition from Civil War," in *Constructing Democratic Governance: Mexico, Central America and the Caribbean in the 1990s,* edited by Jorge I. Domínguez and Abraham F. Lowenthal (Baltimore: Johns Hopkins University Press, 1996), 26–49. Also see the essay by Terry Lynn Karl in *El Salvador's Democratic Transition Ten Years after the Peace Accord,* Latin American Program Report on the Americas 6, edited by Cynthia J. Arnson (Washington, D.C.: Woodrow Wilson International Center for Scholars, 2003), 37–43.

10. The relationship between building peace and building the state, and the contradictions between the two, are treated extensively by Charles T. Call with Vanessa Wyeth, *Building States to Build Peace* (Boulder, Colo.: Lynne Rienner, 2008).

11. For an extensive discussion of the importance of the state to "posttransition" Latin America, see Organización de los Estados Americanos y Programa de las Naciones Unidas para el Desarrollo, *La Democracia de Cuidadanía: Una Agenda para la Construcción de la Ciudadanía en América Latina* (Washington, D.C., and New York: Organization of American States and United Nations Development Program, 2009).

12. One of the first extensive treatments of this connection is given by Ballentine and Sherman, *Political Economy of Armed Conflict,* especially in the introduction by Ballentine.

13. See Theda Skocpol, *States and Social Revolutions* (Cambridge: Cambridge University Press, 1979); Margaret Levi, "The State of the Study of the State," in *Political Science: The State of the Discipline,* edited by Ira Katznelson and Helen V. Milner (New York: W. W. Norton, 2003), 33–55; Atul Kohli, "State, Society, and Development," ibid., 84–117. See also Michael J. Sodaro et. al., *Comparative Politics: A Global Introduction* (Boston: McGraw-Hill, 2001), 124–33.

14. Max Weber, *Economy and Society: An Outline of Interpretive Sociology,* translation edited by Guenther Roth and Claus Wittich (New York: Bedminster Press, 1968), 54. The slight variations in the way this statement appears in various works can be attributed to different translations of the original German. Speaking to a group of students in 1918, Weber referred to the modern state as "institutionally a domination entity that has successfully attempted to monopolize the legitimate physical violence as a means of domination within a territory and which to that end has concentrated the material means of administration in the hands of the leaders." Max Weber, *The Profession of Politics* (Washington, D.C.: Plutarch Press, 1989), 8. In other collections of Weber's writings, this lecture is referred to as "Politics as Avocation."

15. Margaret Levi, "State of the Study," 40.

16. Political theorists such as Joel Migdal have taken issue with the notion that the state is "a fixed ideological entity" with a one-dimensional bureaucratic or "rule enforcing" character. Rather, "it embodies an ongoing dynamic, a changing set of goals, as it engages other social groups." Joel Migdal, "The State in Society: An Approach to Struggles for Domination," in *State Power and Social Forces: Domination and Transformation in the Third World,* edited by Joel Midgal, Atul Kholi, and Vivienne Shu (Cambridge: Cambridge University Press, 1994), 11–12.

17. Guillermo O'Donnell, *On the State, Democratization and Some Conceptual Problems (A Latin American View with Glances at Some Post-Communist Countries),* Working Paper 192 (Notre Dame, Ind.: Helen Kellogg Institute of International Studies, University of Notre Dame, 1993).

18. Guillermo O'Donnell, "Poverty and Inequality in Latin America: Some Political Reflections," in *Poverty and Inequality in Latin America: Issues and New Challenges,* edited by Víctor E. Tokman and Guillermo O'Donnell (Notre Dame, Ind.: University of Notre Dame Press, 1998), 49–71.

19. Adam Przeworski, *Sustainable Democracy* (Cambridge: Cambridge University Press, 1995), 11–12, 34–52.

20. Juan J. Linz and Alfred Stepan, *Problems of Democratic Transition and Consolidation: Southern Europe, South America, and Post-Communist Europe* (Baltimore: Johns Hopkins University Press, 1996), 2–37.

21. See Thomas Carothers, "The 'Sequencing' Fallacy," *Journal of Democracy* 18, no. 1 (January 2007): 18–20.

22. Organización de los Estados Americanos y Programa de las Naciones Unidas para el Desarrollo, *La Democracia de Cuidadanía,* 61; and Organización de los Estados Americanos y Programa de las Naciones Unidas para el Desarrollo, *Nuestra Democracia* (Mexico City: Fondo de Cultura Económica, 2010).

23. See Samuel H. Barnes, "The Contribution of Democracy to Rebuilding Post-conflict Societies," *American Journal of International Law* 95, no. 86 (January 2001): 86–101; the citation here is on 86, 88–89.

24. The Paraguayan scholar Diego Abente Brun identifies three central aspects of democratic quality: legitimacy (levels of public support for the system), effectiveness (the quality of governance), and efficacy (involving socioeconomic performance). See Diego Abente Brun, *The Quality of Democracy in Small South American Countries: The Case of Paraguay,* Working Paper 343 (Notre Dame, Ind.: Helen Kellogg Institute of International Studies, University of Notre Dame, 2007). For an extensive discussion of the various dimensions of democratic quality, see Guillermo O'Donnell, Jorge Vargas Cullell, and Osvaldo M. Iazzetta, eds., *The Quality of Democracy: Theory and Applications* (Notre Dame, Ind.: University of Notre Dame Press, 2004).

25. Scholars are not in agreement as to whether the rule of law is an aspect of the quality of democracy or one of its defining elements. In addition, some scholars consider the rule of law an attribute of the state rather than the democratic regime. See Abente Brun, *Quality of Democracy,* 6–7; and Guillermo O'Donnell, "Why the Rule of Law Matters," *Journal of Democracy* 15 (October 2004): 32–46.

26. Hybrid regimes combine democratic elements (e.g., elections) with authoritarian ones (e.g., military domination of politics and widespread human rights abuses). See Terry Lynn Karl, "The Hybrid Regimes of Central America," *Journal of Democracy* 6 (July 1995): 72–86; and Larry Diamond, "Thinking about Hybrid Regimes," *Journal of Democracy* 13, no. 2 (April 2002): 21–35.

27. As defined by Guillermo O'Donnell, delegative democracies "rest on the premise that whoever wins election to the presidency is thereby entitled to govern as he or she sees fit, constrained only by the hard facts of existing power relations and by a constitutionally limited term of office." Mechanisms of horizontal accountability are typically weak or nonexistent. See Guillermo O'Donnell, "Delegative Democracy," *Journal of Democracy* 5, no. 1 (January 1994): 59.

28. See Fareed Zakaria, "The Rise of Illiberal Democracy," *Foreign Affairs* 76, no. 6 (November–December 1997): 22–43.

29. See David Collier and Steven Levitsky, "Democracy with Adjectives: Conceptual Innovation in Comparative Research," *World Politics* 49, no. 3 (April 1997): 430–51. The authors draw the title of their article from the title of a book by the Mexican writer and intellectual Enrique Krauze, *Por una democracia sin adjectivos.*

30. Samuel P. Huntington, *The Third Wave: Democratization in the Late Twentieth Century* (Norman: University of Oklahoma Press, 1991). According to Huntington, democracy's "third wave" began in 1974 with the demise of dictatorship in Portugal. The "first wave" of democratization, rooted in the American and French revolutions, took place between approximately 1828 and the late 1920s. The "second wave" took place as a result of World War II and lasted through the 1950s. Huntington also called attention to periods of democratic reversal that followed each wave.

31. See Steven Levitsky and Lucan A. Way, "The Rise of Competitive Authoritarianism," *Journal of Democracy* 13, no. 2 (April 2002): 51–65.

32. The political scientists Ariel Armony and Hector Schamis labeled the various qualifications a "terminological Babel" that has contributed little to greater precision in democratization studies. The adjectives, they argue, have clouded the distinction between democracy and autocracy and concealed fundamental aspects of new as well as old democracies. See Ariel C. Armony and Hector E. Schamis, "Babel in Democratization Studies," *Journal of Democracy* 16, no. 4 (2005): 113–28. See also Organización de los Estados Americanos y Programa de las Naciones Unidas para el Desarrollo, *La Democracia de Cuidadanía,* 12–17.

33. See, e.g., Frances Hagopian, "Conclusions: Government Performance, Political Representation, and Public Perceptions of Contemporary Democracy in Latin America," in *The Third Wave of Democratization in Latin America,* edited by Frances Hagopian and Scott P. Mainwaring (Cambridge: Cambridge University Press, 2005), 319–62; and Jorge I. Domínguez and Michael Shifter, eds., *Constructing Democratic Governance in Latin America,* 3rd ed. (Baltimore: Johns Hopkins University Press, 2008).

34. See Marcelo Bergman and Laurence Whitehead, *Criminality, Public Security, and the Challenge to Democracy in Latin America* (Notre Dame, Ind.: University of Notre Dame Press, 2009).

35. See the annual *Informe* produced by Corporación Latinobarómetro, Santiago, 2005, 2006, 2007, 2008, 2009, and 2010. The concern about crime exceeded the concern about unemployment in 2007 and 2010.

36. Cited by Mitchell Seligson, "Democracy on Ice: The Multiple Challenges of Guatemala's Peace Process," in *Third Wave,* ed. Hagopian and Mainwaring, 225.

37. See Marta Lagos, "A Road with No Returns," *Journal of Democracy* 14, no. 2 (April 2003): 163–74; and Mitchell Seligson and Amy Erica Smith, eds., *The Political Culture of Democracy 2010: Democratic Consolidation in the Americas in Hard Times, Regional Report* (Nashville: Vanderbilt University Press, 2010).

38. Corporación Latinobarómetro, *Informe 2009* (Santiago: Corporación Latinobarómetro, 2009), 19; "The Latinobarómetro Poll: The Democratic Routine," *The Economist,* December 2, 2010.

39. See Scott Mainwaring, Ana María Bejarano, and Eduardo Pizarro Leongómez, *The Crisis of Democratic Representation in the Andes* (Stanford, Calif.: Stanford University Press, 2006); and Paul W. Drake and Eric Hershberg, eds., *State and Society in Conflict: Comparative Perspectives on Andean Crises* (Pittsburgh: University of Pittsburgh Press, 2006). For a series of essays on "populism of the twenty-first century," see http://www.wilsoncenter.org/index.cfm?topic_id=1425&categoryid=34E9B83A-CB57-C5AF-D903BC09B555E2CE&fuseaction=topics.events_item_topics&event_id=553905.

40. Nonetheless, Venezuela suffers one of the highest rates of criminal violence in all of Latin America.

41. Marco Palacios, "Presencia y ausencia de populismo: Para un contrapunto colombo-venezolano," in *Populistas: El poder las palabras—Estudios de política,* edited by Marco Palacios (Bogotá: Universidad Nacional, 2011), 117–42.

42. See Philippe C. Schmitter, "Defects and Deficits in the Quality of Neo-Democracy," in *Democratic Deficits: Addressing Challenges to Sustainability and Consolidation around the World,* edited by Gary Bland and Cynthia J. Arnson (Washington, D.C.: Woodrow Wilson International Center for Scholars and RTI International, 2009), 19–35.

43. Leonardo Avritzer, *Participatory Institutions in Democratic Brazil* (Washington, D.C., and Baltimore: Woodrow Wilson Center Press and Johns Hopkins University Press, 2009); Andrew Selee and Enrique Peruzzotti, eds., *Participatory Innovation and Representative Democracy in Latin America* (Washington, D.C., and Baltimore: Woodrow Wilson Center Press and Johns Hopkins University Press, 2009); and Gary Bland, "The Transition to Local Democracy in Latin America," paper presented at Annual Meeting of the Southern Political Science Association, New Orleans, January 4–6, 2007.

44. Initially, scholars of the transition from authoritarianism to democracy emphasized the concept of democratic consolidation, something which is said to have occurred when democratic norms and practices had taken root such that democratic rule would not end and democracy was "the only game in town." See Linz and Stepan, *Problems of Democratic Transition,* 3–15. See also Barnes, "Contribution of Democracy." A later critique of the transitions metaphor argued that it was mistaken in assuming that movement away from authoritarianism was movement toward democracy; that transitions proceeded according to a relatively predictable sequence, with consolidation as an end point; that elections had determinative power; that transitions were built on coherent, functioning states; and that underlying structural factors—such as economic development or political history—were not major determinants of the potential for democratization. Instead of democracy being the logical end point of a transition, many regimes had come to occupy a "political gray zone," in which "serious democratic deficits"—low levels of participation and of confidence in the state, poor representation, and a lack of accountability of government officials—had become the norm, not the exception. See Thomas Carothers, "The End of the Transition Paradigm," *Journal of Democracy* 13, no. 1 (2002): 5–21.

45. United Nations Development Program, "Governance for Sustainable Human Development (New York: United Nations Development Program, 1997), cited by Derick W. Brinkerhoff, "Rebuilding Governance in Failed States and Post-Conflict Societies: Core Concepts and Cross-Cutting Themes," *Public Administration and Development* 25 (2005): 5.

46. Brinkerhoff, "Rebuilding Governance," 5–7.

47. Mark Malloch Brown, "Democratic Governance: Toward a Framework for Sustainable Peace," *Global Governance* 9, no. 2 (special issue) (2003). At the time, Malloch Brown was director of the United Nations Development Program.

48. A World Bank study assessed the quality of governance along six dimensions: voice and accountability, political stability, government effectiveness, regulatory quality, the rule of law, and corruption control. See Daniel Kaufmann, Aart Kraay, and Massimo Mastruzzi, *Governance Matters IV: Governance Indicators for 1996–2004* (Washington, D.C.: World Bank, 2005), cited by Abente Brun, *Quality of Democracy,* 6.

49. The title of this section echoes the title of the book by Peter B. Evans, Dietrich Rueschemeyer, and Theda Skocpol, *Bringing the State Back In* (Cambridge: Cambridge University Press, 1985).

50. Roland Paris, *Building Peace after Civil Conflict* (Cambridge: Cambridge University Press, 2004), 1.

51. Mary Kaldor, *New and Old Wars: Organized Violence in a Global Era* (Stanford, Calif.: Stanford University Press, 1999, 2001). See also note 4 above.

52. The dynamics and different trajectories of state collapse and its relationship to violence are explored by Martin Doornbos, "State Collapse and Fresh Starts: Some Critical Reflections," *Development and Change* 33, no. 5 (2002): 797–815.

53. I. William Zartman, ed., *Collapsed States: The Disintegration and Restoration of Legitimate Authority* (Boulder, Colo.: Lynne Rienner, 1995), 5.

54. Advisory Council on International Affairs, *Failing States: A Global Responsibility* (The Hague: Advisory Council on International Affairs, 2004), 11, cited by Mariano Aguirre, "Violencia y Estados (frágiles?) en América Latina, Fundación para las Relaciones Internacionales y el Diálogo Exterior, Madrid.

55. Stewart Patrick emphasized the relative nature of a state's strength, based on its ability and willingness to provide physical security, legitimate political institutions, economic management, and social welfare. The Failed States Index devised by the Fund for Peace, a nonprofit research group, examined twelve indicators of risk—including extensive corruption; the inability to collect taxes; large-scale, involuntary displacement of the population; sharp economic decline; and group-based inequality. See Stewart Patrick, "Weak States and Global Threats: Fact or Fiction?" *Washington Quarterly* 29, no. 2 (2006): 29; and Fund for Peace, "The Failed States Index 2008," *Foreign Policy,* http://www.foreignpolicy.com/story/cms.php?story_id=4350&page=8.

56. Human security encompassed not only individual protection from political violence and human rights violations but also "people-centered development" to protect from a range of threats including disease, hunger, environmental degradation and natural disasters. See United Nations Development Program, *Human Development Report 1994* (New York: Oxford University Press, 2004), http://hdr.undp.org/en/reports/global/hdr1994/; Amartya Sen, ed., *Resources, Values and Development* (Cambridge, Mass.: Harvard University Press, 1984); and Human Security Centre of University of British Columbia, *The Human Security Report 2005: War and Peace in the 21st Century,* http://www.humansecurityreport.info/index.php?option=content&task.

57. According to the 2002 U.S. National Security Strategy released by the George W. Bush administration, "the events of September 11, 2001, taught us that weak states, like Afghanistan, can pose as great a danger to our national interests as strong states. . . . Poverty, weak institutions, and corruption can make weak states vulnerable to terrorist networks and drug cartels within their borders." White House, September 17, 2002, http://georgewbush-whitehouse.archives.gov/nsc/nss/2002/nssintro.html.

58. Shepard Forman and Stewart Patrick, *Good Intentions: Pledges of Aid for Postconflict Recovery* (Boulder, Colo.: Lynne Rienner, 2000); Jeroen de Qeeuw and Krishna Kumar, *Promoting Democracy in Postconflict Societies* (Boulder, Colo.: Lynne Rienner, 2006).

59. Marina Ottaway, "Rebuilding State Institutions in Collapsed States," *Development and Change* 33, no. 5 (2002): 1001–23.

60. De Zeeuw and Kumar, *Promoting Democracy,* 1–21, 275–90; Malloch Brown, "Democratic Governance"; Brinkerhoff, "Rebuilding Governance," 5–7.

61. See Call and Cook, "On Democratization."

62. See Howard Wolpe and Steve McDonald, "Democracy and Peace-building: Rethinking the Conventional Wisdom," *The Round Table* 97, no. 394 (February 2008): 137–45.

63. Roland Paris and Timothy D. Sisk, *The Dilemmas of Statebuilding: Confronting the Contradictions of Postwar Peace Operations* (London: Routledge, 2009); Call with Wyeth, *Building States,* 365–88; Susan Woodward, "Economic Priorities for Successful Peace Implementation," in *Ending Civil Wars: The Implementation of Peace Agreements,* edited by Stephen John Stedman, Donald Rothchild, and Elizabeth M. Cousens (Boulder, Colo.: Lynne Rienner, 2002), 183–214; the citation here is on 7.

64. See Mariano Aguirre, "Failed States or Weak Democracies? The State in Latin America," http://www.opendemocracy.net/democracy-protest/state_violence_3187.jsp; Francine Jácome, Paz Milet, and Andrés Serbín, *Conflict Prevention, Civil Society and International Organizations: The Difficult Path for Peace Building in Latin America and the Caribbean,* Policy Paper FPP 05-05 (Ottawa: Canadian Foundation for the Americas, 2005); Ariel Armony, *The Dubious Link: Civic Engagement and Democratization* (Stanford, Calif.: Stanford University Press, 2004); and Bernardo Sorj and Miguel Darcy de Oliveira, *Sociedad Civil y Democracia en América Latina: Crisis y reinvención de la política* (São Paulo: Instituto Fernando Henrique Cardoso y Centro Edelstein de Pesquisas Sociais, 2007).

65. See Alejandro Bendaña, "Reflections," in *Comparative Peace Processes,* ed. Arnson, 65–68.

Chapter 2

Democracy and Governance in Conflict and Postwar Latin America: A Quantitative Assessment

Dinorah Azpuru

The case study chapters in this book provide an in-depth discussion of the challenges that exist in conflict/postwar countries in Latin America today and the major political issues and developments in those societies in recent years. The goal of this chapter is to provide an overarching vision that allows for some initial comparisons. Through the use of a variety of quantitative indicators, this chapter presents an overview on the state of democracy and the "state of the state" in the seven countries covered in this book. Throughout this chapter, three types of comparisons are made: (1) How the countries in this volume are doing vis-à-vis their own recent past; (2) how they compare with each other at the present time, and (3) how they compare with other postauthoritarian countries in Latin America that did not experience civil war or internal armed conflict.

This chapter is particularly concerned with the fate of democratization in these seven countries, most of which were part of the sweeping wave of political change that occurred in Latin America in the 1980s and 1990s. In 1999, the first volume on these issues, *Comparative Peace Processes in*

Latin America, noted that the transition to democracy was likely to be more challenging in countries that, in addition to experiencing ruthless military rule as in other countries in Latin America, also underwent a bloody internal strife and the destruction of social and economic infrastructure.[1] After a brief conceptual discussion, the first section of this chapter makes a quantitative assessment of the state of democracy in these countries using indicators such as the Freedom House Index and the Global Democracy Ranking. These measures help compare the situation of democracy today to the situation that prevailed during the transitions (both the transition to democracy and the transition from war to peace), and to compare the state of democracy in these conflict/postwar countries with that of the postauthoritarian nonconflict countries in the region. Additionally, selected public opinion data (drawn from the Americas Barometer) tapping on citizens' perceptions of democracy are also included.

The chapter's second section focuses on the state of the state, a key issue raised by Cynthia Arnson in chapter 1, the introduction to this book. Beyond the establishment of a democratic regime, it is essential to assess to what extent have these conflict/postwar countries been able to build a state that delivers effective policies, notably security and the application of justice; indicators such as the World Bank's rule-of-law governance indicator provide a quantitative perspective on the existing differences in these aspects.

It is important to remember that political and social exclusion were at the core of many of the armed conflicts in the countries covered in this chapter, and therefore that building state capacity to address these issues is crucial to ensure long-term stability. The ability of the state to foster political inclusion is discussed in depth in the country-specific chapters of this book; in this chapter, political inclusion is evaluated using the World Bank's voice and accountability governance indicator. The state's capacity to foster social inclusion is assessed through the examination of the Human Development Index and the levels of poverty and inequality existing in the different countries. Additionally, two indicators that directly address state policy are explored: the amount of social expenditures, and the overall effectiveness of state policies (using the World Bank's government effectiveness indicator).

The literature on postconflict societies often points out the fragility of the state in countries that have experienced armed confrontation.[2] Through the use of the State Fragility Index and the Failed State Index, this chapter rounds out the discussion on the state of the state in Latin American conflict and postwar countries, trying to assess to what extent the state in these countries is fragile or at risk.

The quantitative assessment presented in this chapter complements the in-depth analysis made in the country-specific chapters. Each of those societies faces highly complex issues that cannot be simply reduced to numbers, but the overarching perspective can provide an overview of the current challenges they face.

Before discussing the state of democracy and the state of the state in conflict/postwar Latin America, two caveats are important. As Arnson stresses in chapter 1, there are important differences among the countries included in this book; the cases of Mexico and Haiti, in particular, need to be qualified. On the one hand, whether Mexico is altogether a postconflict society can be questioned, given that the conflict there was geographically limited, that the time span of the conflict was short-lived, and that the death toll and destruction derived from the conflict were low in comparison with the other countries analyzed in this book. The case of Haiti, on the other hand, is also atypical vis-à-vis the other conflict/postconflict countries, given that no armed opposition group was directly challenging the state with the goal of installing a revolutionary government, and the death toll and destruction of infrastructure were also below those in the other countries. Nonetheless, both countries deserve to be included in this analysis because they do represent cases of violent contestation by nonstate groups. In any case, the indicators presented here for Mexico and Haiti should be interpreted while taking into account the contextual differences with the other conflict countries.

The second caveat relates to the indicators themselves. Readers who are not familiar with quantitative analysis may find that numbers do not do justice to the complexity of the reality on the ground, and that they may not necessarily reflect the dimensions that they claim to measure. Quantitative researchers constantly debate issues related to the reliability and the validity of their measurements, but most agree that in spite of the limitations, indicators are an important approximation to reality. They are particularly important for comparative researchers trying to assess multiple countries at the same time.

This chapter endeavors to present indicators from the same source for all countries in order to make the analysis truly comparative. The most recent indicators available in late 2010 were selected, but in some cases (i.e., poverty) the figures represent different years. Finally, it is important to mention that cross-country indicators always represent national-level data.

Reliable comparisons of countries can only be done using measurements that have been compiled using similar methodologies, and therefore it is not appropriate to use data produced or compiled by diverse local institutions; this chapter uses indicators compiled by international organizations, using similar methodologies for all countries.[3] None of these global indicators includes subnational-level data.

The State of Democracy in Conflict/Postwar Latin America

The current wave of democratization has been the most durable and widespread in Latin America's political history. Democracy has advanced significantly in the last two decades, but the region's third wave democracies are still seeking ways to ensure the stability of democracy in the long term. Even what had been some of the longer-standing democracies in the region, like Venezuela, have faced serious challenges. The trajectory of democracy has been uneven in many of the third wave democracies of Latin America, not only for the conflict countries. In fact, several of the nonconflict postauthoritarian countries have experienced deeper political crises than the countries included in this book,[4] and consequently one cannot automatically categorize the conflict/postwar cases as less democratic or unstable than other postauthoritarian cases.

However, democracy building may be especially complex for countries that have endured or are still undergoing violent civil conflicts. Those societies, among other things, have to deal with particular issues, such as the insertion of former combatants and refugees in the political, economic, and social dynamic of the country; the lingering violence, polarization, and intolerance that may pervade society—both elites and the mass public—as a result of years of armed confrontation; the subsequent process of reconciliation between different sectors of society and the provision of moral and economic compensation to families victimized by the conflict; the modernization and demilitarization of state institutions that were shaped by the war; and the fact that social and political leadership at all levels may have been decimated by the conflict.[5]

Zürcher analyzes the difficulties of building democracy in postwar societies, noting that United Nations peace building operations have been relatively successful in maintaining peace but not so successful in establishing democratic regimes.[6] His analysis does not take into account the three cases in Latin American in which peacekeeping and peace building missions have been launched—El Salvador, Guatemala, and Haiti. But several of the arguments he makes about countries in other regions of the world can be applied to these three cases.

More than a decade has passed since *Comparative Peace Processes in Latin America* was published in the late 1990s.[7] At that time, most of the countries considered in this book were in the early stages of multiple transitions, especially from authoritarianism to democracy and from conflict to peace. Mexico was only starting the political opening that would conclude with the democratic elections of 2000, and the conflict in Chiapas had attenuated to such an extent that it was no longer an issue on the national agenda. Guatemala, El Salvador, and Nicaragua had recently signed peace agreements that, among other things, were aimed at deepening the formal democracy established in those countries in the mid-1980s. Peru had been a democracy for more than a decade but was undergoing a reversal of democracy under the administration of Alberto Fujimori. Haiti was formally still under constitutional rule, but in practice instability and violence between opposing groups were rampant. Of all the countries analyzed in this volume, only Colombia had been a formal electoral democracy for several decades, but its internal armed conflict was the longest running in all Latin America.

In retrospect, since then, most countries have been able to maintain the formal structure of democracy. With the exception of Haiti, all the rest have continued holding uninterrupted, fair, and free elections according to their respective constitutional frameworks. Yet in spite of these advances in procedural democracy, democratic regimes in all these countries face multiple problems and challenges—some may be similar to those faced by other postauthoritarian democratizing societies in Latin America, but others may be specific challenges derived at least in part from the fact that they are conflict or postwar societies.

The examination of the state of democracy in conflict/postwar Latin American countries needs to begin by assessing what type of democracies they are. From a conceptual perspective, an initial difficulty is that there is no consensus among academics on what "democracy" means. As Arnson indicates in the introduction, hundreds of adjectives have been added to the word "democracy" over the years, creating a large variety of "subtypes" of democracy.[8] In spite of this ambiguity, one useful approach is Diamond's fourfold typology of political regimes:[9]

1. Authoritarian regimes (or nondemocracies), which may vary in their level of freedom and may even hold competitive elections;

2. Pseudo-democracies, which tolerate legal alternative parties that constitute at least some real and independent opposition to a ruling party
and provide space for organizational pluralism, but still have important
restrictions, including the lack of an arena of contestation sufficiently
fair that the ruling party can be turned out of power;

3. Electoral, (mid-range) democracies, which are civilian, constitutional
systems in which public offices are filled through regular, competitive,
multiparty elections with universal suffrage. These regimes usually
comply with the minimalist definition of democracy and are sometimes
equated with procedural democracy; and

4. Liberal democracies, which in addition to the elements of an electoral
democracy have ten components of their own, namely, the control of the
state and its key decisions in the elected officials; constitutional constraints to the executive power; uncertain electoral outcomes and significant opposition; participation of minority groups; the existence of
multiple channels of expression for citizens; the existence of alternative
sources of information; substantial freedom of belief, opinion, speech,
publication, assembly, demonstration, and petition; political equality
under the law; effective protection of individual and group liberties;
and the existence of a rule of law that protects citizens from unjustified
actions by the state and other organized nonstate or antistate groups.

Using this framework of analysis, it can be said that none of the seven
countries discussed in this volume is to be categorized as authoritarian or
pseudo-authoritarian. They can all be considered as mid-range democracies,[10] and some may even show traits of liberal democracy.

Several indicators could be used to measure democracy or partial dimensions of democracy, but for the purposes of this chapter I focus on composite indicators that integrate different aspects of democratization and can
also be traced over time.[11] To assess the cross-time development of democratization in conflict/postconflict countries in Latin America, the most
useful indicator is the Freedom House Index, which is often considered a
proxy for democracy and has been consistently published every year since
1973.[12] This index assesses the extent of political rights and civil liberties
in countries around the globe.

The Freedom House Index results for conflict/postwar Latin America
are shown in figure 2.1. To facilitate the understanding of these results,
the original scale was recoded to a positive range, in which 1 is negative and 13 is the best score possible.[13] In 2010, three of the postconflict

Figure 2.1. Cross-Time Freedom House Index for Conflict and Postwar Countries in Latin America

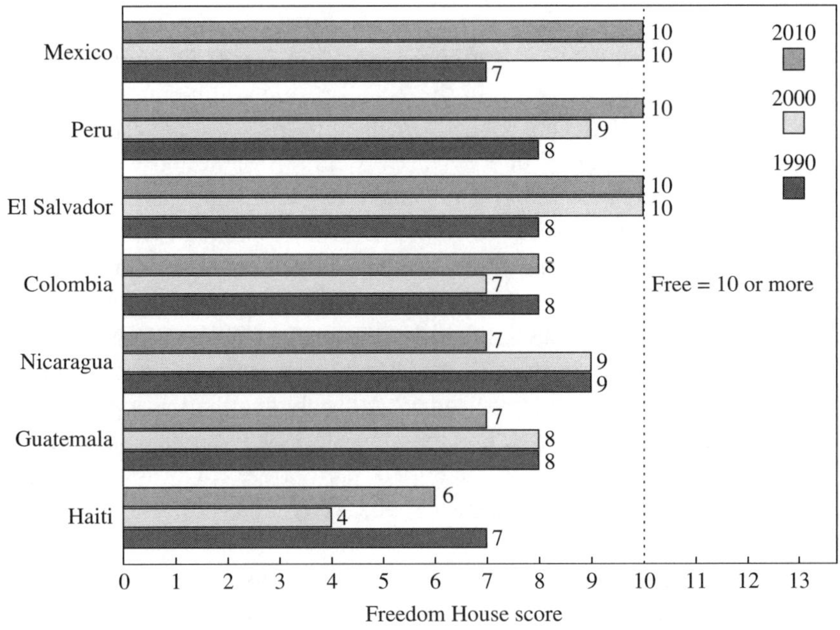

Source: Prepared by the author with data from Freedom House (www.freedomhouse.org).

countries—Mexico, Peru, and El Salvador—qualified as "free" by Freedom House standards. None of them, however, attained the perfect score of 13, which means that in spite of being free (a.k.a. democratic), they still displayed some flaws in terms of political rights and civil liberties. The remaining four countries—Colombia, Nicaragua, Guatemala, and Haiti—were all considered partly free countries, with scores that range from 8 for Colombia to 6 for Haiti. Their status as partly free countries indicates that they have shortcomings in civil liberties and political rights, the core indicators of the Freedom House Index.

With regard to the progression of democracy, during the past twenty years (from 1990 to 2010), these countries have had a great deal of fluctuation in their democratization process, and though some have shown an upward trend, the process has been erratic or downward in most.[14] Over time, the countries that in 2010 were located in the "free" category have overall performed better than the rest. Thus, El Salvador went from a score of 8 in 1990 to 9 in 1995 and to 10 in 2000, and has remained there ever since. As Ricardo Córdova Macías and Carlos G. Ramos indicate in chapter 3 of this volume, since the signing of the 1992 peace accords, the political environment has improved steadily. The victory of the former armed opposition, the Farabundo Martí National Liberation Front (Farabundo Martí para la Liberación Nacional), in the 2009 presidential elections showed how much it has advanced.[15] Peru has also progressed almost in a linear way, except for the period under Alberto Fujimori; it started with a score of 8 in 1990, went down to 6 in 1995, and then picked up again, attaining a score of 9 in 2000 and a score of 10 in 2005 and remaining there since. We should remember that after Fujimori, and in spite of the unpopularity of the sitting presidents, there has been relative stability in the country. Mexico was the last country in Latin America (except for Cuba) to join the third wave of democratization in 2000, but it moved quickly into the league of free countries. Whereas in 1990 and 1995 it only qualified as a partly free country, by 2000 it had moved into the free category. It remained there until 2011, when it went back to the category of partly free. This was due largely to the violence and other problems derived from narco-trafficking in some regions of the country.

The most erratic Freedom House scores in the past twenty years are for the partially free countries. It is noticeable that most of these countries, except Colombia, actually had a higher score in 1990 than in 2010. Colombia had a score of 8 in 1990, but went down to a score of 7 for several years, until 2010, when it again attained a score of 8. Even though it is the longest-standing formal democracy of the seven countries under analysis, its ongoing armed conflict has evidently had an impact on respect for civil liberties and political rights. Next is Nicaragua, which has shown great variation; it began with a relatively high score of 9 in 1990, but by 1995 it had gone down to 7. It regained its score of 9 between 2000 and 2005, but in 2010 it dropped to 7 again. These scores are a reflection of the growing restrictions for the opposition and the irregularities in the electoral processes after Daniel Ortega took office in early 2007.

Guatemala and Haiti are at the bottom of the group. Guatemala achieved its highest score of 8 in 1990—oddly, when the peace accords had not been signed but a democratization process had already been initiated. By 1995 its score had declined to 6, and then, after the peace accords were signed in 1996, it went up to 8 again. By 2000, however, it had gone down to 7 and has remained there since. The profound crisis of the justice system in that country, together with the rampant levels of crime, have probably exacerbated this relapse. Finally, Haiti has been the country with the most dramatic variation in Freedom House scores. It started with a score of 7 in 1990, when its first free elections took place. However, its score plunged steadily after the 1991 coup and the subsequent instability, reaching its lowest point in 2005, when it became a "not free" country with a score of only 2 points. After the 2006 elections, it reversed the downward trend and obtained a score of 6 by 2010.

An analysis of these Freedom House scores gives a broad perspective of the trends in democratization in the countries included in this volume. It shows that two of them have fared better than the others, namely El Salvador and Peru; but it also shows that some—Guatemala, and particularly Haiti—have had the least advancement. The Freedom House Index can also be useful for comparing how the countries in this book fare with respect to other postauthoritarian countries in Latin America that did not experience civil strife. Figure 2.2 is similar to figure 2.1, but it presents the Freedom House scores for nonconflict postauthoritarian countries for 1990 and 2010. It is beyond the scope of this chapter to discuss the development of democracy in each of these countries over time, but some general comparisons that can be useful. Three things stand out. At the beginning of the period under analysis, 1990, most of the nonconflict countries had higher scores than those of the conflict countries, to the extent that they were considered "free" countries by Freedom House standards, whereas none of the conflict countries was considered "free." Only Panama and Paraguay were considered partly free, but even they had relatively high scores, of 9 and 8 points, respectively. In the twenty-year period under consideration, the nonconflict countries, unlike the conflict countries, have never scored lower than 8, except for Honduras, which obtained a score of 7 after the coup d'état in 2009.

Another distinction is that whereas the conflict/postwar countries endured significant fluctuation in their scores during two decades, most of the nonconflict societies experienced relative stability. The only relevant fluctuations occurred in Ecuador and Bolivia, where there were a series of constitutional crises and removals of elected presidents, but the relatively quick fixes to these crises got them back on track. In 2010, these two countries were considered partly free; but throughout the period under analysis, they have been able to score beyond 10 points and have been considered free at times, a point that most of the conflict countries have never attained.

Figure 2.2. Cross-Time Freedom House Index for Postauthoritarian Nonconflict Countries

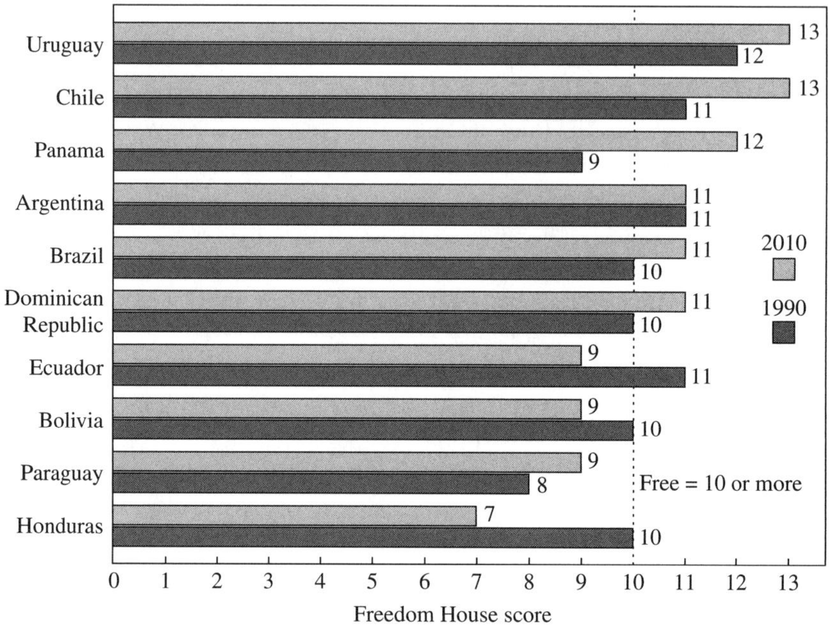

Source: Prepared by the author with data from Freedom House (www.freedomhouse.org).

A notable difference emerges when we look only at the 2010 scores: it is evident that as a group, the postauthoritarian nonconflict countries were doing much better than the postauthoritarian conflict/postwar ones. None of the countries that experienced internal armed conflict scored above 10 points in 2010, but several of the nonconflict ones have scores of 11 (Brazil, Argentina, and Dominican Republic), 12 (Panama), and even 13 (Uruguay and Chile). Using this converted Freedom House scale, the average score for the conflict/postconflict countries in 2010 was 8.29, while the postauthoritarian nonconflict countries obtained an average of 10.4.

To corroborate if the results produced by Freedom House in 2010 are consistent, we examine another global democracy indicator. The Global Democracy Ranking (headquartered in Vienna) uses a conceptual formula that includes the quality of democracy (freedom and other characteristics of the political system), plus performance on nonpolitical dimensions (gender, economy, knowledge, health, and the environment). Democracies around

Figure 2.3. Democracy in Latin America: Freedom House Index vs. Global Democracy Ranking, 2009–2010

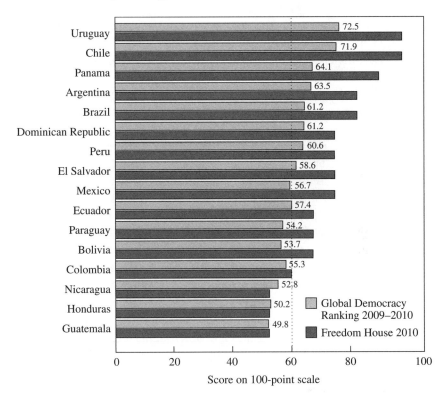

Source: Prepared by the author with data from Freedom House (www.freedomhouse.org) and Global Democracy Ranking (www.democracyranking.org).

the globe are given a score between 1, worst, and 100, best. Figure 2.3 shows the positioning of Latin American conflict and nonconflict countries according to the Global Democracy Ranking, comparing it with the results of the Freedom House Index (for the purpose of comparison in this figure, the Freedom House scores were converted to a 100-point scale).[16] The over-all pattern is similar for most countries, regardless of the indicator, with the exception of Mexico, Bolivia, and Paraguay, which ranked higher in the list using Freedom House standards. It is noticeable that three of the conflict/ postwar countries covered in this volume (Colombia, Nicaragua, and Guate-mala, in that order) are in the lower or bottom part of the list for both indica-tors. Haiti is not included in the Global Democracy Ranking, but it would probably fall at the end, as it does with Freedom House. By contrast, Peru and El Salvador fall in the upper half for both indicators.

The positioning of Mexico and Colombia is particularly interesting. Whereas Mexico fares much better than Colombia in the Freedom House ranking (which only measures political aspects), both countries appear much closer when policy performance measures are included, in the Global Democracy Ranking.

Several other indicators of democratization have been developed over the years,[17] but it is not the purpose of this chapter to compare how the countries under analysis perform in all of them; the idea is to show only a few of the most relevant indicators, particularly those such as Freedom House, that can be tracked over time. However, it is worth mentioning that Polity IV, another commonly used indicator of democracy among academics, produces contrasting results. The Polity IV scores for most of the conflict/postwar countries have been fairly stable during the past ten years. In addition, the results place most countries on the high end of the 10-point scale (7, 8, or 9) since 2000. According to the categories used by Polity IV, the only country that was not considered a democracy in 2009 was Haiti, with 5 points. The next-lowest score in 2009 is Colombia's, with 7 points, followed by several countries with 8 points (Mexico, El Salvador, and Guatemala). Only Peru and Nicaragua scored 9 points. The contrast between Polity IV and the other two indicators stems from the fact that unlike Freedom House—which focuses on civil liberties and political rights—Polity IV is an indicator of institutional democracy composed of six measures related to executive recruitment, constraints on executive authority, and political competition.[18]

This first section included indicators of democracy that help to assess how the conflict/postwar countries considered in this book fare with regard to their own past, with regard to each other, and vis-à-vis other postauthoritarian nonconflict countries in the Latin American region. Beyond what these aggregate indicators may portray, it is important to know how citizens in these countries feel about their own democracy. Do citizens in these conflict/postwar societies trust the political regime and the democratic institutions that emerged in the aftermath of the war? How do they rate the democratic system prevalent in their country?

One perspective on the state of democracy in conflict/postwar societies in Latin America can be obtained through the use of public opinion data. Events in Latin America in recent years have shown that democracy is no longer solely a game of the political, social, or economic elites or organized civil society. Unorganized citizens—often referred to as the mass public—can play a crucial role in deepening or weakening democracy in their own country. In consequence, it is increasingly important to understand the attitudes, perceptions, values, and behaviors of ordinary citizens. This is particularly important for conflict and postwar societies, where citizens may still carry scars from the past, may not be accustomed to engaging in dialogue to solve social and political conflicts, and may have become habituated to living under authoritarian or pseudo-authoritarian governments.

A critical aspect of democracy is legitimacy.[19] Linz and other political scientists have argued that the legitimacy of democracy is essential for its survival in the long run. According to Linz and Stepan, there is legitimacy when political competitors regard democracy as the only viable framework for governing their society and advancing their own interests. At the mass level, there must be a broad consensus on the existing democratic system—however poor or unsatisfying its performance may be at any point in time.[20] In this chapter, I assess the legitimacy of democracy as an abstract idea, the satisfaction with the actual performance of democracy, and the legitimacy of democratic institutions.[21] The data come from the Americas Barometer 2010 survey. Table 2.1 shows the results for conflict/postwar countries as well as for other postauthoritarian but nonconflict countries in the region. Results above 51 points can be considered desirable on the scale of 0 to 100 used as the reference.

In terms of public support for the idea of democracy (as an abstract concept), some of the conflict countries (namely, Colombia and Nicaragua) display relatively high levels of support, but most countries are in the range of 60 points, with Peru being the lowest. The situation is similar in nonconflict countries, with several countries obtaining results in the range of 60 points and others in the range of 70. The overall average is higher for nonconflict countries.

With regard to the satisfaction with the performance of democracy, the second column in table 2.1 shows that citizens of Latin American conflict/postwar nations are only partially satisfied with the performance of democracy in their own countries. Once again, only Colombia and Nicaragua are above the 50-point reference line. Satisfaction is particularly low in Mexico, Guatemala, and Haiti, which is the only country whose result is in the range of 30 points. The results contrast sharply with those for nonconflict Latin America. The average satisfaction score among the postwar countries is 47.3, whereas it is 55.2 for the nonconflict countries. Among the nonconflict countries, only Paraguay and Argentina have scores in the 40s.

*Table 2.1. The Legitimacy of Democracy in Conflict/Postwar versus
Nonconflict Countries of Latin America, 2010 (average; scale: 0–100)*

Country	Support for the Idea of Democracy[a]	Satisfaction with Democracy[b]	Support for Democratic Institutions[c]
Conflict/postwar countries			
Colombia	72.3	54.7	51.1
El Salvador	64.1	48.6	52.8
Guatemala	62.8	44.7	38.2
Haiti (2008)	66.6	38.9	36.4
Mexico	66.8	44.6	60.7
Nicaragua	71.3	51.9	39.6
Peru	60.1	47.8	34.5
Average for conflict countries	66.3	47.3	44.8
Postauthoritarian/nonconflict countries			
Argentina	79.6	45.3	34.8
Bolivia	70.3	56.7	45.7
Brazil	73.7	56.1	47.5
Chile	76.1	53.9	50.8
Dominican Republic	68.6	50.7	47.4
Ecuador	68.4	51.3	40.8
Honduras	62.6	57.8	55.7
Panama	75.5	62.5	49.8
Paraguay	63.3	49.9	37.6
Uruguay	86.2	67.9	62.4
Average for nonconflict countries	72.4	55.2	47.3

[a]Respondents were asked their opinion on the following statement: Democracy may have its problems, but it is better than any other form of government. Scale 1–100, in which 1 means strongly disagree and 100 strongly agree.
[b]Respondents were asked: In general, would you say you are very satisfied, satisfied, unsatisfied or very unsatisfied with the way democracy works in your country? They could choose one of those options.
[c]Respondents were asked how much do they trust five democratic institutions and a composite index summarizing the results was created. The five institutions are Congress, the national government, the local government, the Supreme Court, and political parties.
Source: Prepared by the author with data from the Americas Barometer, 2010 (www.lapopsurveys.org).

The legitimacy of democratic institutions is usually assessed using questions that ask citizens how much they trust specific institutions. The support must remain at a certain point that reflects the fact that citizens support and respect those institutions more than others that could be created. The last column in table 2.1 shows the results of a composite index of institutional legitimacy that measures public trust in Congress, the national government, the local government, the Supreme Court, and political parties. Mexico has a particularly high score among the conflict countries, which as mentioned at the beginning, should not be surprising given that these are national-level results and the conflict in Mexico was localized in Chiapas; thus the effect of the conflict on the trust in institutions is minimal. (As José Miguel Cruz, Rafael Fernández de Castro, and Gema Santamaría Balmaceda point out in chapter 11, however, at the subnational level, the areas of Mexico hardest hit by narco-trafficking violence may diverge considerably with respect to trust of public institutions such as the judiciary and police.) Colombian and Salvadoran institutions obtain a middle-of-the-road result in terms of public trust. However, the trust is rather low (in the 30-point range) in Guatemala, Nicaragua, Haiti, and Peru. In comparison with the conflict countries, nonconflict Latin American nations fare better overall; only Argentina and Paraguay obtain results that can be considered low (in the 30-point range), but most obtain more than 45 points. Notably, Uruguay and Honduras obtain results above 51. The average of institutional support is slightly higher in the nonconflict countries (47.3 vs. 44.8 in the conflict countries).

In summary, citizens in nonconflict countries display higher levels of support for the idea of democracy and higher levels of satisfaction with democracy vis-à-vis citizens in the conflict countries, but when considering levels of institutional support, the differences are not as pronounced.

The State of the State in Conflict/Postwar Latin America

According to the conceptual framework presented in the previous section, all the countries included in this volume could be considered electoral democracies in 2010, although quantitative indicators show that their level of democratic development varies significantly. Beyond democratization, it is also important to assess to what extent these countries have been able to build a capable state: one that fosters political and social inclusion and delivers the basic functions of a state, particularly with regard to providing security to its citizens and enforcing the rule of law.

Theorists of the state from the days of Max Weber to the present agree that maintaining territorial integrity and providing security to citizens are essential traits of any state, a fact that is recognized in the constitutions of most nation-states. To fulfill these functions, states need to enforce the rules contained in a legal framework that governs a given polity, in other words, ensure the application of the rule of law.[22] During the Cold War, most conflict countries in Latin America developed states that suppressed armed (and often unarmed) opposition and dissent through violent means and created a setting in which those who held positions in government were for the most part beyond the reach of the law. Consequently, one of the key issues in the postconflict period was to dismantle the structures that were created within the state to repress the population, turning them into structures that are capable of the fair application of the law (without recurring to unnecessary violence) that could ensure that no one—including those in positions of authority—is above the law, and that could guarantee that citizens are protected rather than threatened by the state.

The inability to fulfill the essential functions of providing security and ensuring the application of the rule of law has often been associated with weak or failing states. Aguirre contends that a minimum definition of a fragile or failing state is one that

- is unable to control its territory or large parts of its territory and guarantee the security of its citizens, because it has lost its monopoly on the use of force;
- is no longer able to uphold its internal legal order; and
- is no longer able to deliver public services to its population or create the conditions for such delivery.[23]

From a conceptual viewpoint, a country could be an electoral democracy and at the same time be a failed or failing state. In other words, it could hold regular and fair elections and respect political rights, but might simultaneously be facing problems such as internal violence, institutional weakness, and a lack of state capacity to address its citizens' deteriorating quality of life.

The Rule of Law

Although it is difficult to find indicators that tap into the capabilities of the state in terms of providing security to citizens, maintaining the rule of law, and exercising a monopoly of force within its territory, Skaaning identified seven indicators that attempt to measure the rule of law.[24] Most of these indicators are not regularly updated; therefore, like Mainwaring and Scully,[25] this chapter uses the rule-of-law governance indicator developed

Figure 2.4. The Rule of Law in Latin America: Conflict/Postwar versus Nonconflict Countries

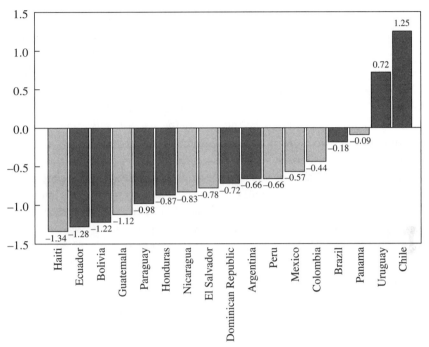

Source: Prepared by the author with data from the World Bank's rule-of-law governance indicator, 2009 (www.worldbank.org).

by the World Bank. This composite indicator "captures perceptions of the extent to which agents have confidence in and abide by the rules of society, and in particular the quality of contract enforcement, property rights, the police, and the courts, as well as the likelihood of crime and violence."[26] The results of this measure for conflict/postwar and nonconflict Latin America are shown in figure 2.4. The differences between conflict and nonconflict countries in this measure are not as evident. Haiti obtains the worst score of all 17 countries, with –1.34 on a scale ranging from +2.5 to –2.5, but is followed relatively closely by two nonconflict countries, Ecuador, –1.28, and Bolivia, –1.22. Next in line is Guatemala, with –1.12. All the rest of the countries received scores above –1.0, although Paraguay

was close, with –0.98. Conflict countries—such as Colombia, with a surprising –0.44; Mexico, –0.57; and Peru, –0.66—fare relatively well with
respect to this indicator. Peru actually had the same result as Argentina in
2009. Of the whole group of countries, only Uruguay and Chile obtained
a positive score for the World Bank's rule-of-law indicator: +0.72 and
+1.25, respectively.

The problems related to the rule of law, particularly crime and insecurity, are likely to have an impact on the legitimacy of democracy in the eyes
of the public; therefore, it is worth examining the salience of these issues
in each society. The surveys conducted by the Americas Barometer asked
citizens in 2010 to identify the most important problem in their country.
Economic-related problems were by far the most important ones in Nicaragua and Haiti, although also in Mexico and Peru about 50 percent of
the population considered them the most relevant problems. In Colombia,
El Salvador, and Guatemala, about one-third of the respondents considered
economic problems a priority. Conversely, violence-related problems were
named the country's most pressing problem by important proportions of
the population in certain countries. The extreme cases were El Salvador
and Guatemala, where a huge proportion identified violence as the main
problem—61 and 48 percent, respectively. It is notable that only 12 percent
of citizens in Peru and only 3 percent in Nicaragua said that violence and
crime were the most important problems. In the nonconflict societies, the
distribution of the responses was more balanced. Economic issues were
the main concern in Ecuador and Dominican Republic, but in the rest only
about a third of respondents consider them the priority. What is intriguing
is that violence-related problems were also mentioned as the most important ones by 58 percent of the population in Panama and 44 percent in
Uruguay; in most countries, crime-related problems were mentioned by
about a fourth of the population. Only in Bolivia did fewer than 15 percent
considered violence the most important problem.

These figures could give the impression that violence and crime have
the same magnitude in several countries (i.e., Uruguay and Guatemala);
however, that is not the case. Table 2.2 shows the number of homicides per
100,000 inhabitants in most of the countries mentioned above. It is evident
from the staggering figures that the levels of violence are much greater in
El Salvador, Guatemala, and Colombia than in any of the other countries.
By contrast, Uruguay, where almost half the population identified violence and crime as the most pressing problem, had only 6.1 homicides

Table 2.2. Homicides per 100,000 inhabitants in Latin America, 2009–2010

Country	Homicides per 100,000 inhabitants
Conflict/postwar countries	
El Salvador	66.0
Guatemala	41.4
Colombia	33.4
Mexico	18.1
Nicaragua	13.2
Haiti	6.9
Peru	5.2
Nonconflict countries	
Honduras	82.1
Dominican Republic	24.9
Brazil	22.7
Panama	21.6
Ecuador	18.2
Paraguay	11.5
Bolivia	8.9
Uruguay	6.1
Argentina	5.5
Chile	3.7

Source: Prepared by the author with data from the United Nations Office on Drugs and Crime, *Global Study on Homicide 2011* (www.unodc.org).

per 100,000 in 2010. In other words, Uruguayans may be as concerned as Guatemalans with crime, but the extent of crime is much greater in Guatemala. In most countries, the aggregate data on homicides coincide with the perception of crime.

Political and Social Inclusion and Public Policy

Beyond the application of the rule of law, it is important to assess the extent to which states in conflict/postwar Latin America have been capable of fostering political and social inclusion. This is particularly relevant because political and social exclusion were among the factors that triggered the conflicts in many of these countries. The countries analyzed in this volume are part of the most unequal region in the world. The *2010 Regional Report*

on Human Development for Latin America and the Caribbean points out
that social and political exclusion go hand in hand. The report suggests the
following in order to reduce inequality in the region:

> The state has the potential to intervene to broaden and guarantee, for
> example, access to education and health in order to promote equal access
> to quality services. In addition, it must guarantee equality in political
> participation through institutional channels. . . . The inequality of power
> and influence among individuals and groups tends to be detrimental to
> the most vulnerable sectors, leading to the persistence of their situation
> of relative disadvantage.[27]

In terms of political inclusion, the indicators of democracy discussed
above indirectly tap into this issue, particularly the Freedom House Index,
which measures civil liberties and political rights; thus, in countries that
have a higher degree of freedom, citizens are more likely to be part of
the decision-making process beyond the act of voting. Another one of the
World Bank's governance indicators can also tap into the degree of political
inclusion in the different countries. The voice and accountability measure
captures "perceptions of the extent to which a country's citizens are able
to participate in selecting their government, as well as freedom of expression, freedom of association, and a free media." The results for conflict and
nonconflict Latin America are shown in figure 2.5.

In comparison with the rule-of-law governance indicator (figure 2.4), it
is evident that in general all countries in the region fare better in terms of
political inclusion than in terms of establishing the rule of law. More countries obtained scores that fell above the world mean in 2009. Among the
countries included in this book, Mexico, El Salvador, and Peru score at the
positive end, whereas Colombia, Guatemala, Nicaragua, and Haiti (in that
order) score at the negative end.

Another measure of political inclusion is the range of ideologies that
are allowed to compete for power. In all postconflict countries, there is no
longer a ban on the participation of certain parties, such as those that profess
Communism or are located on the left of the ideological spectrum; left-wing
guerrillas have in fact become political parties in Guatemala, El Salvador,
and earlier in Colombia. Furthermore, the left has made important inroads
into power in several of these countries: In Mexico, the center-left was close
to winning the 2006 elections; in Nicaragua, the left regained power in
2006; in Guatemala, for the first time in several decades, a center-left party

Figure 2.5. Political Inclusion in Latin America: Conflict versus Nonconflict Countries

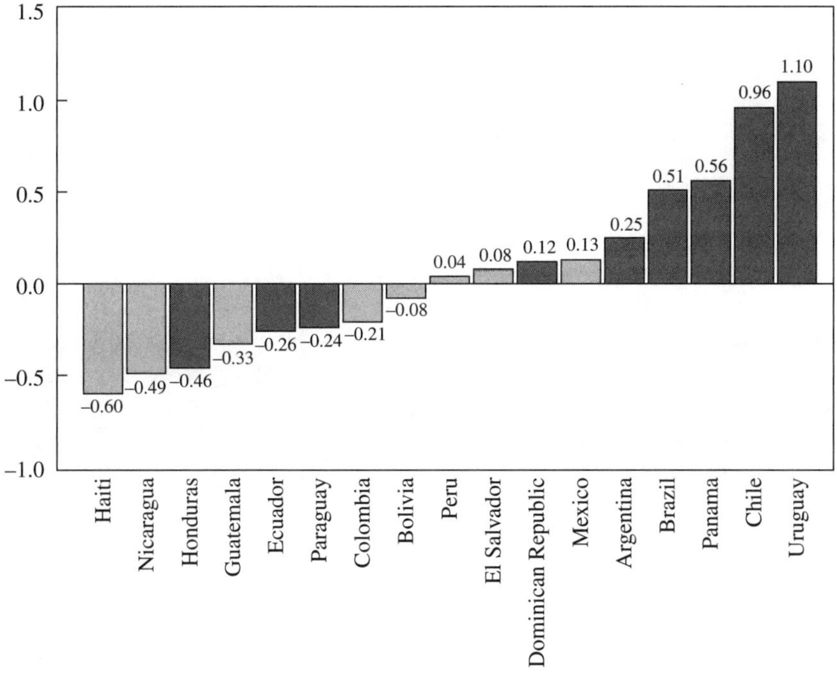

Source: Prepared by the author with data from the World Bank's voice and accountability governance indicator, 2009 (www.worldbank.org).

won the 2007 elections; and in El Salvador, the left won the presidential elections in 2009. In fact, in two of the postconflict countries, El Salvador and Nicaragua, the former parties of the guerrillas were in power; in 2011 and in Guatemala, prominent leaders who were once linked to the guerrillas occupied important positions in the Álvaro Colom government.

In terms of social inclusion, the discussion about the role of the state in Latin America as a promoter of social inclusion is often an ideologically charged issue. But it is increasingly acknowledged that, in view of the persistent levels of inequality, the state must get involved.[28] Using the most common indicator of inequality, the Gini Index, figure 2.6 shows that two of the postconflict/conflict countries, Haiti and Colombia, are among the most unequal societies in the region, but certainly not the only ones. At the other extreme, Peru, El Salvador, and Mexico have some of the lowest levels of

Figure 2.6. Income Inequality in Latin America: Conflict and Nonconflict Countries, 2006 (Gini Index)

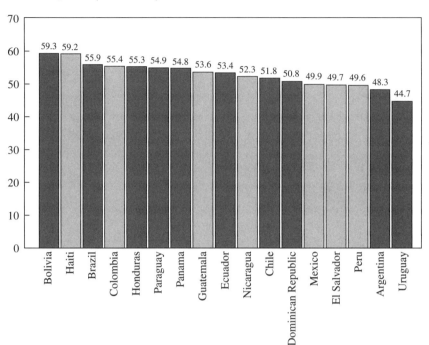

Source: Prepared by author with data from *Informe Regional de Desarrollo Humano para América Latina y el Caribe 2010* (New York: United Nations Development Program, 2010).

inequality in the Latin American region, although they are highly unequal in comparison with most countries in the rest of the world.

Assessing the quality of life in the conflict/postwar societies included in this volume can help to determine their shortcomings or successes in promoting social inclusion; rather than using a variety of indicators, the Human Development Index (HDI) provides an all-encompassing measure of quality of life that includes life expectancy, educational attainment, and income (measured in terms of purchasing power parity to account for income distribution within each country). The HDI groups countries in four categories according to their degree of development: very high development, high development, medium development, and low development. None of the Latin American countries is in the very high development category.

Table 2.3. Quality of Life in Latin America: Conflict versus Nonconflict Countries Measured by the Human Development Index (HDI)

Country	HDI 1990	Level of Development	HDI 2010	Level of Development and World Rank, 2010	HDI Growth Rate 1990–2010 (Percent)
Conflict and postwar countries					
Mexico	0.635	High	0.750	High (56)	0.83
Peru	0.608	Medium	0.723	High (63)	0.85
Colombia	0.579	High	0.689	High (79)	0.83
El Salvador	0.511	Medium	0.659	Medium (90)	1.27
Nicaragua	0.454	Medium	0.565	Medium (115)	1.10
Guatemala	0.451	Medium	0.560	Medium (116)	1.08
Haiti	N.A.	Low	0.404	Low (145)	N.A.
Average 2010 score			0.622		
Postauthoritarian non-conflict countries					
Chile	0.675	High	0.783	High (45)	0.74
Argentina	0.682	High	0.775	High (46)	0.56
Uruguay	0.670	High	0.765	High (52)	0.67
Panama	0.644	High	0.755	High (54)	0.79
Brazil	0.649[a]	Medium	0.699	High (73)	N.A.
Ecuador	0.612	Medium	0.695	High (77)	0.64
Dominican Republic	0.560	Medium	0.663	Medium (88)	0.85
Bolivia	0.593[a]	Medium	0.643	Medium (95)	N.A.
Paraguay	0.557	Medium	0.640	Medium (96)	0.69
Honduras	0.495	Medium	0.604	Medium (106)	0.99
Average 2010 score			0.702		

Note: The highest possible score is 1.000. As a parameter, Norway was ranked as number 1 in 2010, with a score of 0.938. The lowest score was for Zimbawe, with 0.140 in position 169. N.A. = not available.
[a]HDI for 2000.
Sources: Prepared by the author with data from the *Human Development Reports* (New York: United Nations Development Program).

Table 2.3 shows the results of the HDI for Latin America. Three of the conflict/postwar countries (Mexico, Colombia, and Peru) are in the category of high development, whereas three smaller countries (Guatemala, El Salvador, and Nicaragua) are in the medium development category. Haiti is the only country in the low development category. With respect to their own past, table 2.3 shows that all the countries in this volume improved their HDI score in the period under analysis, which spans two decades.

El Salvador, followed by Guatemala and Nicaragua, experienced the highest growth; however, they continued in the same medium development category; Peru, however, moved to the high development category in this period and was ranked second among the conflict/postwar countries. In comparison with other postauthoritarian but nonconflict societies, the HDI also rose in all the nonconflict countries during the period under analysis, in some more than others. The majority of these countries were in the medium development category in 1990, but two of them moved up to the high development category (Ecuador and Brazil). Overall, the countries have similar scores to the conflict/postwar countries, except for Guatemala, Nicaragua, and particularly Haiti, which are the three countries with the lowest scores in all Latin America. In 2010, the overall average HDI for the nonconflict countries was higher (0.702) than that of the conflict/postconflict ones (0.564).

Beyond the HDI, one measure that usually serves as a proxy for social exclusion/inclusion is poverty. Accurate and updated poverty rates, as well as same-year data, are difficult to obtain, but figure 2.7 shows some comparable results. It can be observed that in all countries in the Latin American region, poverty has decreased in the past ten years. The darker bars show the data for 2009 (or the closest date available), and the lighter bars indicate how much poverty existed in about 1999 (or the closest year available). Several conflict/postwar countries (Nicaragua, Guatemala, El Salvador, and Colombia) fall in the lower half of the graph, which means that they display higher levels of poverty than nonconflict countries. In all these, nearly half or more than half the population lived in poverty in 2009. Haiti is not shown in figure 2.7, but the only data available show that more than 65 percent of the population lives in poverty. Mexico and to some extent Peru are exceptions, both with poverty in the 30 percent range. The comparison with postauthoritarian nonconflict countries shows that some of them also display high poverty rates, particularly Honduras, Paraguay, and Bolivia. It is notable that these countries, together with the Central American postconflict countries, also tend to have low scores in the indicators of political democratization examined in the first section of this chapter.

Social policy can be crucial in helping to reduce the development gap within countries with such high levels of poverty. On the one hand, governments can invest important amounts of money in social issues such as health, education, and housing. On the other hand, the delivery of policies should be effective in order to have a real impact. Two final indicators need to be noted in this section to help us focus on these two issues: the

Figure 2.7. Cross-Time Poverty in Latin America:
Percentage of the Population under the Poverty Line

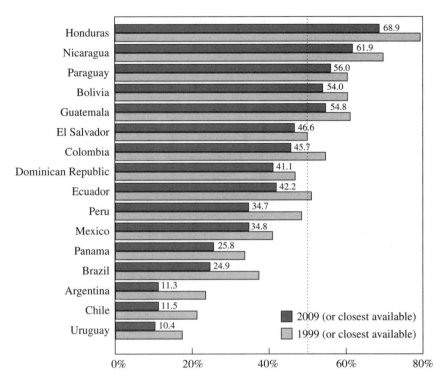

Source: Prepared by the author with data from Badeinso/CEPAL (www.cepal.org).

percentage of the gross national product devoted to social expenditures, and the effectiveness of the policies themselves. Table 2.4 compares social expenditures in conflict and nonconflict countries, as well as the rate of change of poverty levels (first column). Some of the conflict countries—Mexico and Peru—and some of the nonconflict countries—such as Argentina, Panama, Brazil—seem to be reducing poverty at faster rates than the rest of the countries in the region, but most display similar rates of change as conflict countries. El Salvador had the slowest rate of decrease of poverty between 1999–2009.

All conflict/postwar countries have increased their levels of social investment, but it still represents a relatively small share of national wealth, especially when compared with some postauthoritarian nonconflict

Table 2.4. Changes in Poverty Rates and Social Expenditures in Conflict and Nonconflict Countries of Latin America, 1999–2009

Country	Change in Poverty Levels in Ten Years (percent)	Social Expenditures in 1999, or Closest Year Available (percent of gross national income)	Social Expenditures in 2009, or Closest Year Available (percent of gross national income)
Conflict and postwar countries			
Mexico	−12.1	9.42	12.52
Colombia	−9.2	11.44	12.59
Peru	−13.8	7.32	7.82
El Salvador	−2.3	8.52	11.07
Guatemala	−6.3	6.85	7.03
Nicaragua	8.0	9.26	12.30
Haiti	N.A.	N.A.	N.A.
Postauthoritarian nonconflict countries			
Chile	−10.2	14.16	14.22
Argentina	−12.4	21.80	23.23
Uruguay	−7.3	20.38	21.65
Panama	−8.2	8.73	9.44
Brazil	−12.6	21.52	26.05
Ecuador	−9.0	4.37	6.39
Dominican Republic	−5.8	5.85	8.11
Paraguay	−4.6	9.58	8.87
Honduras	−10.8	8.27	11.38
Bolivia	−6.6	16.67	16.24

Note: N.A. = not available.
Source: Prepared by the author with data from Badeinso/CEPAL (www.cepal.org).

countries—such as Argentina, Uruguay, Brazil, and Bolivia, which invest more than 15 percent of their gross national income. None of the conflict/postwar countries spends above 13 percent on social issues, and some, such as Guatemala and Peru, invest less than 10 percent.

The final measure noted in this section is the World Bank's governance indicator called government effectiveness, which captures the perceptions of the quality of public services, the quality of civil service and the degree of its independence from political pressures, the quality of policy formulation and implementation, and the credibility of the government's commitment to such policies. Figure 2.8 shows that, overall, there is not a discernible pattern in this indicator among the conflict/postwar countries,

Figure 2.8. Government Effectiveness in Conflict and Nonconflict Countries of Latin America, 2009

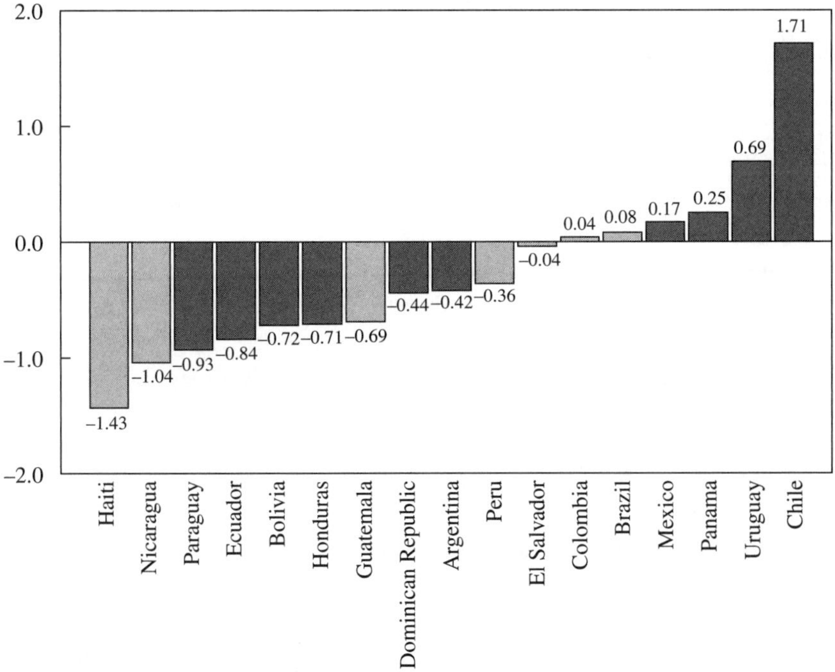

Source: Prepared by the author with data from the World Bank's government effectiveness governance indicator, 2009 (www.worldbank.org).

except for Haiti and Nicaragua, which obtain the lowest scores out of the seventeen countries included in the analysis. Among the conflict/postwar countries, only Mexico, Colombia, and El Salvador obtain positive scores; but they are only slightly above the world mean. Some of the nonconflict countries, particularly Uruguay and Chile, score well above the mean, but the rest of nonconflict countries are scattered in different positions. Several nonconflict countries have negative scores, including Argentina, the Dominican Republic, and Ecuador; and some nonconflict governments—such as Bolivia, Paraguay, Ecuador, and Honduras—seem to be less effective than most postwar countries, except Nicaragua.

It is important to point out that the indicators presented throughout this chapter for Mexico reflect the situation at the national level, but we should remember that the armed conflict in that country was localized in the southern state of Chiapas. When one analyzes domestic sources that provide subnational-level statistics for Chiapas, it is evident that the levels of social exclusion are greater there than in most of the Mexican territory. As Raúl Benítez Manaut, Tania Carrasco, and Armando Rodríguez Luna indicate in chapter 8, the state of Chiapas has the second-highest level of marginalization in the whole country. For instance, though in Mexico the overall maternal mortality rate is 51 per 100,000 births, in Chiapas it is 117. Likewise, infant mortality is higher in Chiapas (31.9) than in the rest of the country (24.9). Chiapas also has the highest level of income inequality in Mexico.[29]

Chiapas has one of the highest concentrations of indigenous population in Mexico, and the statistics show this group's poorer quality of life:

- The income of the indigenous groups represents only 32 percent of the total income of the state population.
- Agriculture is the occupation of 83 percent of the indigenous population, while only 58.3 percent of the nonindigenous population is in that sector.
- A total of 85.7 percent of the indigenous population cooks with wood or charcoal.
- Although 21.4 percent of the state population (15 years or more) is illiterate, this number increases to 39.2 percent among the indigenous population. The situation is worse among indigenous women: Though 27.9 percent of indigenous men are illiterate, illiteracy among indigenous women is 50.1 percent.
- In 2008, 71.6 percent of the indigenous population was malnourished.

In this section, we have examined some indicators that reflect on the state of the state in conflict/postwar Latin America by looking at the performance of those states in maintaining the rule of law and fostering political and social inclusion. Among the group of conflict/postwar countries, Mexico and Peru seem to have better indicators in all these areas, whereas Nicaragua, Guatemala, and Haiti (in that order) are usually at the bottom. In comparison with other postauthoritarian nonconflict countries in the region, most of the conflict countries appear to have more critical problems with regard to security and the application of the rule of law. In terms of political and social inclusion, however, the situation varies; some postauthoritarian nonconflict countries, such as Bolivia, Ecuador, and Paraguay, show indicators that are lower than several of the conflict/postwar countries.

State Fragility or State Failure?

This last section focuses on a critical issue: Are conflict/postwar societies in Latin America more likely to become failed states? This issue is particularly relevant for Mexico and Guatemala, which some have alleged were prone to becoming failed states in recent years, mostly because of the widespread penetration of narco-trafficking in certain parts of their territory. The authorities in both countries have rejected the label.[30] The extent of the fragility of the state in the region can be evaluated using two indicators: the Failed States Index and the State Fragility Index.

According to the Failed States Index (table 2.5), the only country in Latin America considered under "alert" conditions in 2010 was Haiti, ranked as the number 12 failed state in the world. To get a better idea of which countries are considered failed states, it is useful to note that Somalia, Zimbabwe, and Sudan are in the first three places. The remaining six conflict/postwar Latin American countries are ranked as states under "warning" conditions. Colombia was in the alert category in 2006 but improved, and in 2010 it was ranked 41. The next country is Nicaragua, in position 64, surprisingly in a worse position than Guatemala, which in 2010 was ranked number 75. The better ranked among this group of conflict/postwar countries was Mexico, which in 2010 placed in position 98, followed by Peru, in 92, and El Salvador, in 91. It is surprising to see that two of the postauthoritarian nonconflict countries, Bolivia (ranked 51) and Ecuador (69), fare worse than several conflict/postwar countries for this indicator. At the other extreme, nonconflict countries such as Chile and Uruguay are ranked among the least failed states in the world, in positions 155 and 154, respectively.

The Failed States Index is a composite measure formed by 12 different indicators.[31] It is important to note that when the Failed States Index is disaggregated, the specific weak areas of the state in conflict and postwar Latin America can be identified. This group of countries shows lower scores on the indicators of criminalization/delegitimation of the state, the suspension or arbitrary application of the rule of law, and particularly in the indicator that measures to what extent the security apparatus operates as a "state within a state."

Finally, again to confirm the reliability of the Failed State Index for Latin America, figure 2.9 shows the comparison between the results of the Failed States Index and the State Fragility Index.[32] In figure 2.9, both were converted to a 100-point scale. They produce overall similar results. Clearly,

Table 2.5. The Failed States Index and Latin America:
Conflict versus Nonconflict Countries

Country	Failed State Index, 2010	World Position as a Failed State (of 177 countries)	Status
Conflict and postconflict countries			
Haiti	101.6	12	Under alert
Colombia	88.2	41	Under warning
Nicaragua	82.5	64	Under warning
Guatemala	81.2	75	Under warning
El Salvador	78.1	91	Under warning
Peru	76.9	92	Under warning
Mexico	76.1	98	Under warning
Postauthoritarian nonconflict countries			
Bolivia	84.9	51	Under warning
Ecuador	81.7	69	Under warning
Dominican Republic	76.8	88	Under warning
Honduras	80.0	90	Under warning
Paraguay	72.1	106	Under warning
Brazil	67.4	113	Under warning
Panama	59.3	132	Under monitoring
Argentina	45.8	149	Under monitoring
Uruguay	41.3	154	Under monitoring
Chile	38.0	155	Under monitoring

Source: Prepared by the author with data from the Fund for Peace (www.fundforpeace.org). The composite Failed States Index ranges from 1 (best score) to 120 (worst score). Countries with scores of 1–30 are considered as sustainable (S); countries with scores of 31–59 are considered under monitoring (M); countries with scores of 60–89 are considered under warning (W), and countries with scores of 90–120 are considered under alert (A). The composite index includes twelve social, political, and economic indicators.

Haiti is at the top as the most fragile state in Latin America; and at the other end, Uruguay, Argentina, and Chile are the least fragile. However, there are some differences: The Failed States Index places Colombia below Guatemala, whereas the Fragile State Index gives them basically the same score. Nicaragua, conversely, fares a little better than Colombia and Guatemala vis-à-vis the State Fragility Index. Mexico, Peru, and El Salvador actually perform much better on the State Fragility Index than on the Failed States Index. But overall, several conflict/postconflict countries appear to be more fragile than the postauthoritarian nonconflict countries (with the exception of Ecuador and Bolivia).

Figure 2.9. State Fragility in Conflict and Nonconflict Countries
of Latin America, 2009–2010

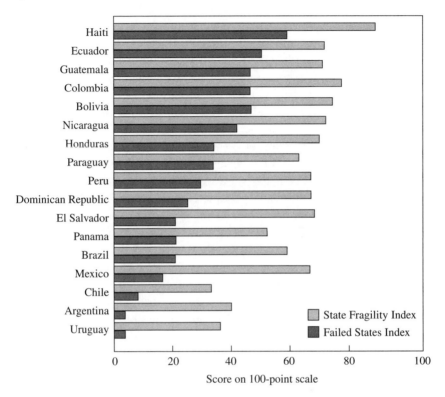

Source: Prepared by the author with data from the Fund for Peace (www.fundforpeace.org) and Systemic Peace (www.systemicpeace.org).

Conclusion

The quantitative indicators used in this chapter can help us to assess the state of democracy and the state of the state in the conflict and postwar societies of Latin America. Although it is not possible to make a thorough analysis in these pages, the different types of data show that these societies have made improvements in several areas but are still facing numerous problems and challenges on different fronts.

In comparative perspective, we observed that there is great disparity in the level of democratic development both within and between countries, and that the degree of variation is largely related to what aspects of democracy are being measured by the different indicators. In spite of this, some general trends appear across the board: In all conflict and postwar countries, formal aspects of democracy—such as regular free and fair elections, participation, and even the respect for civil liberties—have come a long way. However, when indicators related to the rule of law and social and political inclusion are incorporated, the results are not as encouraging for most countries. In general, Peru and to some extent El Salvador and Mexico tend to come at the top and Guatemala and Haiti at the bottom of the countries included in this volume.

In terms of the comparison between the set of conflict/postwar countries analyzed in this volume and the postauthoritarian nonconflict countries in Latin America, the analysis has shown that some of the nonconflict societies (i.e., Uruguay, Chile, and to some extent Panama and Brazil), fare better than most conflict/postwar societies in this book in most indicators. In contrast, Paraguay, Ecuador, and Bolivia obtain very similar or in some cases worse results than the conflict countries.

Overall, the individual analysis of countries shows that although some nonconflict countries are doing better than the conflict societies, there is no clear pattern in the comparison. Noticeable differences emerge, however, when the analysis compares the whole group of conflict/postwar to the group of nonconflict countries. When group averages are compared, the conflict/postwar Latin American countries have lower Freedom House scores than the region's postauthoritarian nonconflict countries. They are also more likely to have states that have been criminalized or delegitimized and more likely to have a security apparatus that operates as a state within the state. In addition, the comparison of averages shows that they have higher scores in terms of the fragility of the state as a whole.

One important thing that also stands out from the comparison of means (averages) is that the conflict/postwar countries do not differ significantly from the nonconflict countries in terms of the indicators of political or social inclusion. Some conflict countries, such as Haiti and Guatemala, show dismal indicators, but so do some nonconflict countries, such as Bolivia and Paraguay.

All things considered, many of the political challenges and social problems of conflict and postconflict Latin American countries seem to be similar to those faced by other Latin American nations that made the transition from authoritarianism to democracy in the mid-1980s. Some problems, however, seem particularly acute in conflict/postwar countries, namely, excessive levels of crime and violence, and particularly the lack of state capacity to curtail them. Furthermore, the penetration of state structures by organized crime and narco-trafficking call into question the very essence of governance in countries like Guatemala, and more recently Mexico. Colombia still struggles with these issues but has made some headway vis-à-vis its own past.

None of the countries in this study can take democracy for granted. Democratization, even in its restricted political dimension, should be understood and addressed as a process that is still ongoing. More important, in addition to working on the political challenges, Latin American countries and in particular their elected governments—on the right or on the left—must improve the quality of democracy and therefore confront the structural problems of pervasive poverty, inequality, and a lack of access, all of which are increasingly playing a role in the delegitimation of political democracy.

Notes

1. Cynthia J. Arnson, ed., *Comparative Peace Processes in Latin America* (Washington, D.C., and Stanford, Calif.: Woodrow Wilson Center Press and Stanford University Press, 1999).

2. See Charles T. Call with Vanessa Wyeth, eds., *Building States to Build Peace* (Boulder, Colo.: Lynne Rienner, 2008).

3. A database in SPSS (Statistical Package for the Social Sciences) was created by the author with all the different indicators in order to conduct the analysis and create the figures included in this chapter.

4. González classified the countries in three groups, according to their political stability: (1) three consolidated democracies, Chile, Costa Rica, and Uruguay; (2) seven countries experiencing acute political crises during the years 2000–2007, Paraguay, Peru, Ecuador, Argentina, Venezuela, Bolivia, and Nicaragua; and (3) an intermediate group, neither consolidated nor experiencing acute crises, including Colombia, Brazil, El Salvador, Panama, Mexico, Guatemala, and Honduras. Since then, Honduras can be added to group 2 because of the coup d'état in 2009. In addition, Haiti, which is not included in González classification, can also be added to group 2. According to this arrangement, four of the cases in this book have not experienced acute political crises in the period under analysis. Guatemala, however, experienced an executive coup d'état in 1993. See Luis E. González, *Political Crises and Democracy in Latin America since the End of the Cold War,* Working Paper 353 (Notre Dame, Ind.: Kellogg Institute, 2008).

5. See Cynthia J. Arnson, "Introduction," in *Comparative Peace Processes,* ed. Arnson.

6. See Christoph Zürcher, "Building Democracy while Building Peace," *Journal of Democracy* 22, no. 1 (January 2011): 81–95. In this article, Zürcher analyzes the cases of Namibia, Bosnia, Timor-Leste, Kosovo, Tajikistan, Macedonia, Mozambique, Afghanistan, and Rwanda. According to Zürcher, a democratic outcome is likely only

when democracy offers local elites expected benefits that are greater than the expected costs of adopting democratic ways.

7. Arnson, *Comparative Peace Processes.*

8. In 1997, David Collier and Steven Levitsky identified more than 550 subtypes of democracy used in the literature. See David Collier and Steven Levitsky, "Democracy with Adjectives: Conceptual Innovation in Comparative Research," *World Politics,* 49, no. 3 (1997): 430–51.

9. Larry Diamond, *Developing Democracy: Toward Consolidation* (Baltimore: Johns Hopkins University Press, 1999), 10–17.

10. Mid-range is a better word because Freedom House designates as an "electoral democracy" any country that holds fair elections; this includes advanced democracies such as the United States and France and developing democracies such as Colombia and Thailand. By 2012, Tunisia joined the ranks of electoral democracies. By contrast, Nicaragua was dropped from the list but continued to be considered a partly free country.

11. Other indexes, such as the Transparency International Corruption Perceptions Index, are more specific and do not necessarily measure democracy or single features of democracy.

12. While recognizing that the Freedom House Index has a bias toward Western-style democracy, Burnell notes that it is the most commonly used indicator of democratization among academics and practitioners. Peter Burnell and Vicky Randall, *Politics in the Developing World* (Oxford: Oxford University Press, 2008).

13. The Freedom House index ranges from 1 to 7. Countries with scores between 1.0 and 2.5 are considered free (F); countries with scores between 3.0 and 5.0 are categorized partially free (PF), and countries with scores between 5.5 and 7.0 are considered not free (NF). The composite index includes a series of indicators that measure civil liberties and political rights. In this chapter, for the purposes of better understanding, those scores have been recoded to a positive 13-point scale.

14. Figure 2.1 only shows intervals of ten years for clarity, but the text discusses significant changes that may have taken place in 1995 or 2005.

15. See Dinorah Azpuru, "The Salience of Ideology: Fifteen Years of Presidential Elections in El Salvador," *Latin American Politics and Society* 52, no. 2 (Summer 2010).

16. These results reflect the Freedom House scores for 2010 and the Global Democracy Scores for 2009–2010.

17. See Gerardo L. Munck, ed., *Regimes and Democracy in Latin America: Theories and Methods* (Oxford: Oxford University Press, 2007).

18. Polity IV does not divide the countries into categories according to their score, but the project suggests that scores can be converted to regime categories: "autocracies" (–10 to –6), "anocracies" (–5 to +5, and the three special values: –66, –77, and –88), and "democracies" (+6 to +10).

19. Among these ongoing projects are the Afrobarometer, the Americas Barometer, the Arab Barometer, the New Democracies Barometer, the Russia Barometer, Latinobarómetro, and the World Values Survey.

20. Juan Linz and Alfred Stepan, *Problems of Democratic Transition and Consolidation: Southern Europe, South America, and Post-Communist Europe* (Baltimore: Johns Hopkins University Press, 1996).

21. David Easton, and later other scholars such as Pippa Norris, have argued that the legitimacy of democracy is multidimensional and multileveled and should therefore be measured by items that tap into support for different levels of democracy.

22. See Daniele Carmani, *Comparative Politics* (Oxford: Oxford University Press, 2008).

23. See Mariano Aguirre, "Failed States or Weak Democracies? The State in Latin America," Open Democracy, January 2006, http://www.opendemocracy.net/democracy-protest/state_violence_3187.jsp.

24. See Svend-Erik Skaaning, "Measuring the Rule of Law," *Political Research Quarterly* 63, no. 2 (June 2010). He mentions rule-of-law indicators in the following databases: Bertelsmann Transformation Index, Freedom in the World, Countries at the Crossroads, Nations in Transit, Global Integrity Index, International Country Risk Guide, and World Bank Worldwide Governance Indicators.

25. See Scott Mainwaring and Timothy R. Scully, *Democratic Governance in Latin America* (Stanford, Calif.: Stanford University Press, 2010).

26. Daniel Kauffman, Aart Kraay, and Massimo Mastruzzi, *Worldwide Governance Indicators: Methodology and Analytical Issues,* Policy Research Working Paper 5430 (Washington, D.C.: World Bank, 2010). Mainwaring and Scully indicate that the score for the rule of law (and the other five governance indicators) is equal to the number of standard deviations a country is away from the mean score for all countries in a given year. A positive score indicates that a country ranked above the world mean, whereas a negative score indicates that a country ranked worse than the world mean.

27. See United Nations Development Program, *Informe regional sobre desarrollo humano para América Latina y el Caribe 2010* (New York: United Nations Development Program, 2010), 35.

28. Ibid.

29. See "Chiapas en Datos," http://www.sipaz.org/data/chis_es_02.htm.

30. In an interview with the Associated Press, Mexico's president, Felipe Calderón, said that the idea that Mexico is in danger of becoming a failed state if violence continues is "absolutely false." He insisted that his government has not "lost any part of the Mexican territory" to organized crime. A Pentagon report in November 2008 singled out Mexico and Pakistan as countries where state control is at risk. See Associated Press, "Mexican President Rejects 'Failed State' Label," elpasotimes.com, February 27, 2009.

31. The Failed States Index (FSI) ranks 177 states in order of their vulnerability to violent internal conflict and societal deterioration. According to the FSI Web site (www.fundforpeace.org), the index is compiled using the Conflict Assessment System Tool to assess violent internal conflicts and measure the impact of mitigating strategies. In addition to the risk of state failure and violent conflict, it assesses the capacities of core state institutions and analyzes trends in state instability. The twelve indicators are mounting demographic pressures, massive movement of refugees or internally displaced persons, legacy of vengeance-seeking group grievance or group paranoia, chronic and sustained human flight, uneven economic development along group lines, sharp or severe economic decline, criminalization and/or delegitimation of the state, progressive deterioration of public services, suspension or arbitrary application of the rule of law and widespread violation of human rights, the security apparatus operating as a "state within a state," the rise of factionalized elites, and the intervention of other states or external political actors.

32. The State Fragility Index is also a composite and multidimensional score. It lists all independent countries in the world in which the total country population is greater than 500,000. According to the *Global Report 2009: Conflict, Governance, and State*

Fragility, the Fragility Matrix scores each country on both effectiveness and legitimacy in four performance dimensions: security, political, economic, and social. Each of the matrix indicators is rated on a 3-point fragility scale: 0, "no fragility"; 1, "low fragility"; 2, "medium fragility"; and 3, "high fragility"—with the exception of the economic effectiveness indicator, which is rated on a 4-point fragility scale, including 4, "extreme fragility." The State Fragility Index, then, combines scores on the eight indicators and ranges from 0, "no fragility," to 25, "extreme fragility." A country's fragility is closely associated with its *state capacity* to manage conflict, make and implement public policy, and deliver essential services; and its *systemic resilience* in maintaining system coherence, cohesion, and quality of life; responding effectively to challenges and crises, and continuing progressive development. See Monty G. Marshall and Benjamin R. Cole, *Global Report 2009: Conflict, Governance, and State Fragility* (Vienna, Va., and Arlington, Va.: Center for Systemic Peace and Center for Global Policy, 2010).

Commentary: Democratic Consolidation in Postconflict States in Latin America— Insights from the Peace Building and Fragile States Literature

Stewart Patrick

The nature of and prospects for democratization may be quite different in countries with a legacy of violence and conflict. Yet, as Charles Call and Susan Cook have pointed out, there has been little cross-fertilization between scholarship on democratic transitions and on postconflict peace building.[1] The transitions literature does not generally address the question of the legacy of conflict. Likewise, democratization is rarely the central question for students of peace building; it is presumed to be an objective, but only insofar as it contributes to—or results from—peace. Yet despite these differences, scholars of peace building and democratic transition may have some things to learn from one another.

To date, the two streams of scholarship have been largely self-contained. This is partly due to geographic focus. The transitions literature is largely based on the experiences of the shift from authoritarian (or totalitarian) rule in Southern Europe, the former Soviet Bloc, and the Southern Cone. The peace building literature has a more global scope, encompassing not only conflict zones in Africa but also experiences elsewhere ranging from

71

Afghanistan to Cambodia, and from Bosnia to East Timor. The question for this group is whether the broader peace building literature is relevant to democratic transitions in Latin America. Or is the Western Hemisphere's experience unique?

There are at least three notable differences between the Latin American cases under discussion in this volume and recent peace building experiences around the world. The first pertains to the relative degree of underdevelopment. With the exception of Haiti, the countries considered in this book rank in the middle or (in a few cases) lower middle of the Human Development Index. They thus do not reflect the absolutely grinding levels of poverty found in many of the African cases. This has significance for the potential reemergence of violent conflict, given that the econometric evidence of Paul Collier and his colleagues shows that prospects for peace improve greatly as per capita income increases.[2]

The second difference concerns the scale of destruction. Although levels of violence in some Latin American cases have been (and remain) quite startling, they do not in general reach the magnitude of devastation experienced in places such as Afghanistan, Cambodia, and Liberia. This makes the transition from violent conflict in the Latin American cases more promising.

The third important difference relates to the capacities of the state. Again, with the partial exception of Haiti (which obviously is an outlier in the hemisphere), the predicament in Latin America is not one of state failure. Unlike in Africa, there are few "quasi-states" that lack functioning institutions or whose legitimacy or borders are contested.

What of the two literatures themselves? Generally speaking, the focus of recent writing on transitions from violent conflict differs from scholarship on transitions from authoritarian rule in several fundamental ways. First, the overriding preoccupation of the peace building literature is how to ensure sustainable peace and recovery from conflict, with a special emphasis on bolstering the institutions of state and society needed to avoid a relapse into violence. Consolidating democracy is at best a secondary consideration. Indeed, one of the most hotly debated questions is whether the requirements of peace and democracy are congruent: There is broad agreement that they are mutually enforcing in the long run, but also that they may be in tension in the short run, with the pursuit of peace requiring some postponement of competitive electoral politics.

Second, whereas the democratization literature is modest regarding the role of outsiders in the democratic transition, the peace building literature emphasizes (and no doubt exaggerates) the role of external actors in help-ing to drive the peace process.[3] This focus on outsiders reflects the typically heavy involvement of the international community in multidimensional UN peace operations and reconstruction efforts and the often low-level domes-tic institutions, physical infrastructure, and human capital in the aftermath of protracted internal violence. The peace building literature starts from a general presumption that the international community, having intervened, has become a custodian of the peace process and, therefore, has a legiti-mate stake in its outcome. (This international presence is often at odds with the simultaneously espoused goal of creating "local ownership" in recovering societies.)

Third, the literature suggests that postconflict environments have dis-tinctive attributes that distinguish them from "normal" transitions from authoritarian rule. They are often awash in arms, lacking in infrastructure and social capital, and habituated to high degrees of violence. Moreover, they are often undergoing not just one transition but several simultane-ously.[4] Beyond making the political shift from an authoritarian regime to a more participatory, democratic system, they are also transitioning from war to peace; from a wartime (and sometimes command) economy to a peacetime, market one; and from an atmosphere of impunity to one gov-erned by the rule of law. But if the preceding conflict leaves a sad legacy that cannot be wished away, it can also present an opportunity for rapid change, a fluid environment in which underlying institutional structures can be transformed.

What can the peace building literature contribute to our understanding of the requirements for democratic transition and sustainable peace in post-conflict states in Latin America? One insight is that context is absolutely critical in guiding external interventions. The nature and scale of the con-flict and the means of its "resolution" will influence prospects not only for an enduring peace but also for democratization.

A second insight from the peace building literature is that democratic transition cannot be considered in isolation but must be embedded in a more general strategy of conflict transformation.[5] International actors seeking to assist local actors in building a sustainable peace must adopt a multidimensional response—with four main pillars. The first pillar of conflict transformation is the establishment of basic physical security for the inhabitants, including through the disarmament and demobilization and reintegration of former combatants; the marginalization of extremists and potential "spoilers"; and the completion of a broad-based program of security-sector reform, including the purging of the military and police of corrupt and abusive elements. It also requires addressing the human insecurity that often breaks out following the end of formal hostilities, as some former combatants turn to lives of crime. As the experience of Central America over the past two decades suggests, "postconflict" does not necessarily mean "postviolent."

The second pillar of conflict transformation, after establishing physical security, is moderating political conflict, or an effort to move from zero-sum conflict to governance where the competition for power is conducted by the ballot and not the bullet. However, the peace building literature underlines that the pace of democratization must be set by the requirements of peace. And whereas the transitions literature emphasizes the importance of preelection "pacts," scholars of postconflict peace building suggest that such arrangements are most sensible after an election, when the relative distribution of power among groups has been established.[6]

The third pillar of conflict transformation is the establishment of a vital economy to foster licit private-sector growth and generate revenues for the government, which can permit the delivery of basic social services and welfare. The challenge is to move beyond the gray and black markets, or the "shadow economy," that often develop during warfare, by cutting revenue streams and incentive structures of those who benefit from conflict. As several analysts have noted, donors often face a dilemma between their desire to restore a functional economy as quickly as possible through orthodox policy prescriptions and the reality that these policies may undercut critical investments in the peace process and social welfare.[7] For example, there is a tendency among the Bretton Woods institutions to want to downsize the civil service, yet this sector often provides valuable outlets for people who may otherwise take matters into their own hands through violent means.

The fourth pillar is the rule of law. Like democratization experts, students of peace building are increasingly aware that advancing the rule of law is fundamental in making the shift from a political system based on oppression and impunity to a system of impartial justice and equal rights. As in the transitions literature, scholars of peace building emphasize the importance of accounting for crimes, although they continue to debate the relative merits of truth and reconciliation commissions versus more punitive tribunals. In practice, all four pillars of the postconflict transition are linked to one another, raising complex issues of sequencing and prioritization.

A third emerging insight from the peace building literature is that *state building* is a critical dimension of enduring peace and sustainable recovery in war-torn countries, where state institutions are often terribly weak or absent entirely. At the same time, the peace building literature recognizes that the espoused donor goal of nurturing indigenous institutions—a painstaking and protracted undertaking—often collides with a parallel set of donor imperatives and incentives to deliver services as rapidly as possible using their own providers.[8] Even more problematic, the literature raises questions about whether donors actually know how to go about nurturing indigenous state capacities.[9]

A fourth insight, of direct relevance to the transitions literature, is growing skepticism about what has been termed the "democratic reconstruction"[10] or "liberal peace building"[11] model, which emphasizes the prompt creation of formal democratic institutions and the rapid move to elections, usually within two years of a peace agreement. Although this model is still favored by the international community as part of an "exit strategy" for UN peace operations, many specialists regard the move to competitive elections as imprudent in highly divided societies lacking a political culture of—and incentives for—political restraint. Recent experience, suggesting that a large proportion of such elections lead to authoritarianism,[12] would tend to argue for a more protracted political timetable.

Thus, a recommendation emerging from much postconflict writing is to adopt a longer transition period—and experiment with various forms of transitional governance—before making the shift to electoral democracy. Postponing the movement toward electoral politics through interim power sharing and other arrangements may provide critical breathing space to ensure that politics has been demilitarized and to allow national actors to begin building democratic institutions, including at the local level.[13] Similarly, on the economic front, there is a growing recognition that precipitous movement toward economic liberalization can be dangerous, because again this process entails injecting a competitive dynamic into a volatile situation. What is more, the traditional neoliberal model requires structural adjustment and rigid macroeconomic conditions that often undercut the constituencies needed for peace.[14]

Finally, there are areas in which the democratization and peace building literatures may inform one another. Most important, the peace building literature emphasizes that the nature of the preceding conflict and the manner and degree of its resolution should inform the pacing of democratization efforts. In reciprocal fashion, the peace building literature may be better informed by the democratization literature's focus on alternative electoral models. Indeed, scholars of postwar transition are only beginning to consider the various trade-offs of consociational democracy, other power-sharing arrangements, and majority-rule democracy.[15]

Another area of potentially fruitful cross-pollination is the consideration of particular types of states. In chapter 2 of this volume, Dinorah Azpuru creates a fourfold typology of democratic states. In a parallel fashion, experts on state fragility have begun to develop typologies of their own, distinguishing among weak states, shadow states, captured states, failing states, and collapsed states. It would be interesting to compare these two sets of typologies to see if there are any correlations, and to investigate whether or not the degree of state weakness has any bearing on the degree of success in terms of democratization. As Call and Cook note, the issues of peace building and democratization also raise dilemmas of centralization versus decentralization—although the literatures tend to pull in different directions.[16] Given the danger of fragmentation in many war-torn environments, and the limits on the resources of external interveners, the temptation is often to centralize political authority. And yet true democratization may require a measure of decentralization, as an antidote to a recrudescence of the unchecked power that stimulated violent conflict in the past.

There is a growing recognition that peace building, like democratization, is an ongoing process, rather than a discrete event marked by a peace treaty (or, in the case of democratization, by an election), and that it can be marked by setbacks and recidivism.[17] Just as the democratization literature now focuses on protracted processes of transition and consolidation, so scholars of peace building are increasingly focusing on the determinants of successful "peace implementation."[18]

In closing, one might offer a comment on the selection of cases for this volume. Viewed through a conflict lens, the seven countries represent an extremely heterogeneous cohort. Certainly, the three Central American cases share some similarities: The conflicts unfolded in a Cold War context; they each ended through negotiated settlements and the presence of a UN mission, yet without large peacekeeping operations; and they were all influenced by a strong U.S. presence. Then there is the case of Haiti, a truly failed state, where there has not been war but an endemic history of violence. Colombia, a country that has evolved significantly but where conflict still endures, possesses a unique dynamic regarding the linkage to the narcotics trade. Peru is an example of a defeated rural insurgency with a strong ethnic element. Finally, there is Mexico, where the conflict was highly localized to the specific region of Chiapas, and there was no real sense that the country was at war. The inclusion of such diversity in this volume brings out the richness of democratic transitions in "postconflict" Latin America. But from a comparative perspective, it may also narrow opportunities to make broad generalizations of an empirical or policy nature.

Notes

1. For an excellent overview of points of convergence and divergence, on which this commentary draws, see Charles T. Call and Susan E. Cook, "On Democracy and Peacebuilding," *Governance after War: Rethinking Democratization and Peacebuilding,* special issue of *Global Governance* 9, no. 2 (Spring 2003), coedited by Charles Call and Susan Cook.

2. Paul Collier et al., *Breaking the Conflict Trap: Civil War and Development Policy* (Washington, D.C.: World Bank, 2003); Lael Brainerd and Derek Chollet, eds., *Too Poor for Peace? Global Poverty, Conflict, and Peace in the 21st Century* (Washington, D.C.: Brookings Institution Press, 2007).

3. Call and Cook, "On Democratization and Peacebuilding."

4. Shepard Forman and Stewart Patrick, "Introduction," in *Good Intentions: Pledges of Aid for Post-Conflict Recovery,* edited by Shepard Forman and Stewart Patrick (Boulder, Colo.: Lynne Rienner, 2000), 1–33, esp. 5–6.

5. For a thorough discussion of these pillars, see Jock Covey, Michael J. Dziedzic, and Leonard R. Hawley, eds., *The Quest for Viable Peace: International Intervention and Strategies for Conflict Transformation* (Washington, D.C.: U.S. Institute of Peace Press, 2005).

6. Terrence Lyons, "Transforming the Institutions of War: Post-Conflict Elections and the Reconstruction of Failed States," in *When States Fail: Causes and Consequences,* edited by Robert I. Rotberg (Princeton, N.J.: Princeton University Press, 2004), 269–301, esp. 289–91.

7. Susan Woodward, "Economic Priorities for Successful Peace Implementation," in *Ending Civil Wars: The Implementation of Peace Agreements,* edited by Stephen John Stedman, Donald Rothchild, and Elizabeth M. Cousens (Boulder, Colo.: Lynne Rienner, 2002), 183–214. James K. Boyce, "Beyond Good Intentions: External Assistance and Peacebuilding," in *Good Intentions,* ed. Forman and Patrick, 367–82.

8. Ashraf Ghani, Clare Lockhart, and Michael Carnahan, *Closing the Sovereignty Gap: An Approach to State-Building,* ODI Working Paper 253 (London: Overseas Development Institute, 2005). http://www.odi.org.uk/publications/working_papers/wp253.pdf.

9. Francis Fukuyama, *State-Building: Governance and World Order in the 21st Century* (Ithaca, N.Y.: Cornell University Press, 2004).

10. The label, which is Marina Ottaway's, is cited by Call and Cook, "On Democracy and Peacebuilding." See also Ottaway, "Rebuilding State Institutions in Collapsed States," in *State Failure, Collapse, and Reconstruction: Development and Change,* edited by Jennifer Milliken (New York: Wiley-Blackwell, 2003).

11. Roland Paris, "Wilson's Ghost: The Faulty Assumptions of Post-Conflict Peacebuilding," in *Turbulent Peace: The Challenges of Managing Internal Conflict,* edited by Chester A. Crocker, Fen Osler Hampson, and Pamela Aall (Washington, D.C.: U.S. Institute of Peace Press, 2001), 765–84.

12. Call and Cook, "On Democracy and Peacebuilding."

13. Lyons, "Transforming the Institutions of War."

14. Boyce, "Beyond Good Intentions."

15. Timothy D. Sisk, "Democratization and Peacebuilding: Perils and Promises," in *Turbulent Peace,* ed. Crocker, Hampson, and Aall, 785–800.

16. Call and Cook, "On Democracy and Peacebuilding."

17. Ibid.

18. Stedman, Rothchild, and Cousens, *Ending Civil Wars.*

Chapter 3

The Peace Process and the Construction of Democracy in El Salvador: Progress, Deficiencies, and Challenges

Ricardo Córdova Macías and Carlos G. Ramos

El Salvador's twelve-year civil war in the 1980s pitted a left-wing political-military alliance composed of the Farabundo Martí National Liberation Front (Frente Farabundo Martí para la Liberación Nacional, FMLN) and the Democratic Revolutionary Front (Frente Democrático Revolucionario), against the Salvadoran government, the armed forces, and right-wing parties, which had strong political and financial backing from the U.S. government.[1] The Salvadoran civil war was one of the most intense internal armed conflicts in Latin America.[2] Estimates of casualties, including civilians and

Some ideas in this chapter have been developed from ideas initially expressed by Ricardo Córdova Macías, Carlos Guillermo Ramos, and Nayelly Loya, "La contribución del proceso de paz a la construcción de la democracia en El Salvador (1992–2004)," in *Construyendo la democracia en sociedades posconflicto: Un enfoque comparado entre Guatemala y El Salvador,* edited by Dinorah Azpuru et al. (Guatemala City and Ottawa: F&G Editores and IDRC Publishers, 2007). We would like to thank Cynthia Arnson, Orlando J. Pérez, and Leslie Quiñónez for their comments on an earlier version of this work.

79

combatants, run as high as 75,000; the human cost was such that 1 in 66 Salvadorans died in the war.[3] At the same time, the massive internal displacement of entire populations reshaped the country's demographic map; this period was also marked by a significant increase in migration—primarily toward the United States—which became and continues to be a central factor in the country's economy.[4] The government of El Salvador calculated the direct economic cost of the conflict at $328.97 million, with indirect costs of an additional $1.25 billion, for a total of $1.58 billion. The costs of reconstruction were approximately $1.62 billion. Thus, adding direct, indirect and reconstruction costs, the total cost of the armed conflict stands at more than $3.2 billion.[5]

The sheer amount of economic and military aid provided by the United States to the government of El Salvador during the course of the conflict serves to underscore its importance in the context of the Cold War. From 1980 to 1985, the war's first half decade, U.S. assistance totaled $1.74 billion. Thirty percent consisted of military aid directly related to the prosecution of the war, whereas another 44.1 percent constituted indirect war aid, including cash transfers to sustain the Salvadoran government. Only 15.4 percent of U.S. assistance went to reform and development, and 10.5 percent to food aid.[6] By the end of 1991, the United States had spent about $6 billion in El Salvador, making it—until the outbreak of the first Persian Gulf War— the most expensive U.S. military endeavor since Vietnam.[7]

From its onset, the Salvadoran conflict involved a double logic that entailed intensifying the armed confrontation at the same time that political negotiations were under way. At different stages of the conflict, one or the other logic prevailed. Initially, negotiation efforts were tactical in nature, used to improve the combatants' political and diplomatic positions while the search for a military solution to the conflict prevailed. The break with the tactical approach to negotiations and the move to a strategic approach resulted from the conviction by actors on both sides that it would not be possible to win the war by military means. In the case of El Salvador, serious negotiations to end the war responded to a classic case of military stalemate or equilibrium, in which neither the guerrillas nor the armed forces could be defeated or vanquish their adversaries. This deadlock provided the framework in which the logic of a negotiated, political solution to the conflict could take hold.[8]

The Salvadoran peace negotiations took place in two phases. The first, from 1984 to 1989, can be characterized as a dialogue without negotiation. The second unfolded between 1990 and 1992, in which there was a time frame for reaching an accord, an intense negotiating agenda, and a process of rapprochement that culminated in the signing of the January 16, 1992, peace accords at the Chapultepec castle in Mexico City.

The 1992 peace accords and the processes they set in motion are undoubtedly the most important historical events of the twentieth century in El Salvador. The accords paved the way for the simultaneous development of three transitions: from war to peace, from militarism to demilitarization, and from authoritarianism to democracy. The peace accords ended the armed conflict; they initiated an important process of demilitarization; they ended the Salvadoran political regime's century-long cycle of authoritarianism; and they established the political and institutional foundations for the modernization and democratization of the political regime for the coming century.

The peace process in El Salvador thus displays the special characteristics and unique challenges that are inherent to constructing democracy in countries emerging from armed conflict.[9] These processes can be referred to as war transitions, "pacted" transitions,[10] or negotiated transitions to democracy.[11]

The peace accords included a vast blueprint for institutional reform; this chapter, written eighteen years after their signing, reflects on the progress made in constructing political democracy and on the shortcomings and challenges that lie ahead.[12] The election of Mauricio Funes in the March 2009 presidential race marked a transcendental moment in El Salvador's history: The political party formed out of the former coalition of guerrilla organizations, the FMLN, concluded a journey from armed insurrection to electoral triumph. Mauricio Funes, a former television journalist, led the FMLN to a narrow victory with 51.3 percent of the vote, defeating former police chief Rodrigo Ávila of the conservative National Republican Alliance (Alianza Republicana Nacionalista, ARENA), who won 48.7 percent. The elections brought an end to twenty consecutive years of rule by ARENA. Notably, neither Funes nor Ávila had been historic leaders of their parties. Instead, both ARENA and the FMLN demonstrated moderation when they reached beyond their ranks to put forward a candidate seen as having greater appeal across the Salvadoran electorate. Funes finally made the FMLN acceptable—albeit by a slim margin—to the elusive Salvadoran independents and those undecided voters that the FMLN until that time had failed to captivate.

Despite fears from certain sectors, the 2009 elections and the resulting transfer of power took place in an orderly fashion. The succession constituted the clearest signal that the cycle of political transition launched with the signing of the peace accords had satisfactorily overcome one of its greatest tests.

This chapter is divided into five sections that explore in depth the relationship between the Salvadoran peace process and the country's advance toward democratization. The first section discusses the design of the peace accords and the proposal to institutionalize democracy. The second focuses on the operational aspects of the agreement itself. The third section analyzes the main contributions the peace process has made to the construction of democracy; and the fourth highlights and reflects on the sociopolitical challenges facing the nation almost two decades after the end of the war. The fifth section offers some general conclusions.

Important members of the international community, notably the United Nations, accompanied the process of negotiation and the implementation of the peace agreements. Although the importance of the international community's presence is incontrovertible, this chapter focuses on the domestic factors shaping the Salvadoran political process.

The Peace Accords and the
Proposal to Institutionalize Democracy

Arriving at a negotiated settlement of the Salvadoran conflict was prolonged and difficult, marked by a nonlinear dynamic of dialogue and negotiation between the armed conflict's contenders for power. The process of negotiation consisted of two clearly differentiated periods. The first was an extended period of tactical negotiations between the Salvadoran government (then headed by President José Napoleón Duarte of the Christian Democratic Party) and the FMLN, which began in 1984 in the town of La Palma and lasted, in on-and-off fashion, until the rebel offensive in November 1989. During this first period, negotiations were characterized by meager results, born of a logic that subordinated dialogue to a military solution. By contrast, the second was much shorter. It formally began with a meeting between the Salvadoran government (by then headed by Alfredo Cristiani of ARENA) and the FMLN in April 1990, in Geneva. This second, intense phase took place under the active mediation of the United Nations and focused on issues that were significant and relevant for peace; the second phase concluded with the signing of the final peace accords on January 16, 1992.

The difference between the first and second phases of the negotiations was that by 1990, conditions had amply demonstrated that the war had reached a stalemate. On November 11, 1989, the FMLN launched the strongest military offensive of the war, entering and holding significant parts of the capital city for several days, but ultimately retreating. In the midst of the offensive, members of an elite army unit murdered six Jesuit priests from the José Simeón Cañas Central American University (Universidad Centroamericana "José Simeón Cañas," UCA). The offensive, and the international outcry that followed the assassination of the Jesuits, proved to be a breaking point.[13] The political scientist William LeoGrande described it this way:

> Like the 1968 Tet offensive in Vietnam, the FMLN's offensive was less a military success than a political one. Although it did not fundamentally alter the military balance, it mocked conventional wisdom in Washington. The strength and tenacity of the offensive shattered the illusion that the Salvadoran army was winning the war, and the army's brutal response shattered the illusion that the Salvadoran trappings of democracy constrained the men in uniform.[14]

Once it was acknowledged that a military solution was not viable in any foreseeable future—something the parties had long refused to accept—the path to peace through a political settlement was opened. The new international context—the fall of the Berlin Wall and the end of the Cold War—helped make this possible.

The peace accords and the unprecedented institutional transformations they embodied marked the beginning of the democratic transition; the accords were thus foundational for the new democratic regime and defined the contours of a pacted transition.[15] The content and processes laid out in the peace accords aimed at solving the problem of political exclusion in three ways: (1) by demilitarizing the political system, (2) by promoting legal-institutional transformations, and (3) by supporting the political parties as key protagonists in the new postwar political arena.

As many scholars have noted, the peace accords did not seek to address the socioeconomic causes of the war; according to the political scientist Elisabeth Wood, for example, "the insurgents accepted political inclusion in exchange for moderation of their economic agenda."[16] Others have indicated that conditions at the time of the negotiations made the inclusion of socioeconomic issues unfeasible.[17] Indeed, the precise wording and formulation of the political-institutional and security issues in the accords contrasts markedly with the lack of specificity regarding economic issues, and this asymmetrical relationship is fundamental to understanding the political nature of the entire process of accord implementation.[18] The relatively limited socioeconomic provisions that were included in the agreement were viewed primarily as a stabilizing element that would enhance the viability of the political process overall.[19]

The near-absence of provisions to address socioeconomic exclusion in El Salvador immediately set up a fundamental contradiction with the political aspects of the accord. Economic reform and structural adjustment policies launched by the conservative government of President Alfredo Cristiani in 1989, based on the principles of the free market, trade liberalization, and privatization,[20] constituted a dynamic parallel but unrelated to the political reforms discussed in the peace negotiations. The processes of economic and political reform shared no common ground,[21] and neither the content nor the timing and rhythm of implementation of political and economic measures were coordinated. Specifically, the design of the economic reforms never envisioned that they would be carried out in a flexible fashion within the framework of the political and institutional transformation generated by the peace accords; at the same time, the political reform itself was unable to affect or redefine measures associated with the economic reform. This led to surging tensions between the logic of political inclusion derived from the peace accords and the orientation of the economic reform process that was under way. This "collision course" was described by the UN assistant secretary-general for political affairs, Álvaro de Soto, who brokered the accords, and his assistant, Graciana del Castillo, early in the process of accord implementation:

> El Salvador now faces a very real dilemma: Should it sacrifice economic stabilization to proceed with implementing the peace accords, or should it strictly carry out its stabilization and structural adjustment program, perhaps endangering peace? Neither path is independently sustainable. There is an overriding need to harmonize the two processes so that they support, rather than counteract each other.[22]

The economist James Boyce put it a different way:

> During the post-conflict transition the goals of economic policy cannot be limited to macroeconomic stabilization and conventional structural adjustment. Economic policy must also promote adjustment toward peace. . . . Two broad sets of economic issues arise in adjustment toward

peace. The first concerns the problem of financing the immediate costs of peace, including the establishment of new democratic institutions, the reintegration of ex-combatants into civilian life, and the repair of physical infrastructure. The mobilization of resources for the peace process is a political problem as well as financial problem. . . . The second set of issues concerns the longer-term interrelationships among economic growth, income distribution, and the consolidation of peace.[23]

In other words, socioeconomic issues and the economic reforms already under way were not addressed or affected by the peace accords. The multiple socioeconomic challenges that have arisen since the signing of the peace agreement are closely related to the postagreement social and economic dynamics, or are the result of specific economic policies that have been implemented. Thus, these challenges do not represent failures of the peace accords because the accords were not aimed at addressing these socioeconomic issues.

The Operational Design of the Peace Accords

Four aspects characterize the design for peace accord implementation. First, the process was condensed into a very short period of time. Except for a few tasks, execution was to be completed in one year (February 1992–February 1993). Considering the scope and breadth of the accords, the timeline for implementation required concentrated and intense political activity, not only on the part of the individuals responsible but also for the political system in general.

Second, the schedule for implementation remained faithful to the priorities established in the accords. Out of a total of 118 provisions with established deadlines, 81, or 68.6 percent, corresponded to the demilitarization of the state (the cease-fire, armed forces, and National Civilian Police), whereas state institutions (the justice system; the electoral system; the establishment of a National Peace Commission [Comisión Nacional para la Consolidación de la Paz, COPAZ], to oversee accord implementation; and political participation by the FMLN) made up 18.6 percent. Only 12.7 percent was dedicated to economic and social issues. The number of deadlines for specific goals, grouped by category, provides one indication of the priority accorded to these tasks within the implementation schedule (see table 3.1).

Table 3.1. Number of Deadlines for Specific Goals in El Salvador, by Issue

Issue	Number
National Peace Commission (Comisión Nacional para la Consolidación de la Paz)	2
Armed Forces	40
National Civil Police	25
Justice system	9
Electoral system	5
Economic and social issues	15
Political participation by FMLN	6
Cessation of hostilities	16
Total	118

Source: Ricardo Córdova Macías, Carlos Guillermo Ramos, and Nayelly Loya, "La contribución del proceso de paz a la construcción de la democracia en El Salvador (1992–2004)," in *Construyendo la democracia en sociedades posconflicto: Un enfoque comparado entre Guatemala y El Salvador,* edited by Dinorah Azpuru et al. (Guatemala City and Ottawa: F&G Editores and IDRC Publishers, 2007), 75.

Third, the implementation process required the development of simultaneous processes in which compliance by one of the parties depended upon compliance with commitments made by the other party. This simultaneity and mutual conditionality were aimed at limiting possible delays or unilateral adjustments of the accord's terms and processes and, in turn, served as a safeguard to counteract the lack of trust between the parties.

Finally, the parties themselves were guaranteed a direct role in the implementation of priority issues. This way, the process of peace implementation was characterized by a kind of "permanent negotiation" between the parties over issues of compliance.

The Contribution of the Peace Process to the Construction of Democracy

This section does not review the implementation of the various reforms outlined in the peace accords. Rather, it focuses on the five main contributions of the peace process to the construction of political democracy. Just as accord implementation did not follow a linear process with a definitively established direction, the fundamental factors that constitute its contribution to democracy have also evolved at different rates and in diverse directions. Each of the contributing factors, as well as its development and current status, is briefly described here: the successful end of the armed conflict, the demilitarization of politics, the justice system and human rights, bolstering the system of political parties, and the institutionalization of electoral democracy.

The Successful End of the Armed Conflict

The peace process had great initial success in separating the warring forces. This came about through a cease-fire aimed at bringing the FMLN's military structure to an end, and occurred without delays or interruptions. The twelve-year war was formally brought to an end. In contrast to other cases around the world, the cease-fire in El Salvador held and the warring parties did not return to the battlefield.

The Demilitarization of Politics

The implementation of the peace accords allowed for the profound demilitarization of the state and of the political process, launching an institutional transformation of the armed forces and redefining the role of the military in the political system. As a consequence of these reforms, the armed forces were excluded from the political control of the state, laying the foundation for the subordination of the military to the constitutionally elected civilian authorities.[24]

The principal measures underlying the process of demilitarization were: a doctrinal and legal reform that separated the functions and institutions of national defense from those of public security; a reform of the armed forces' educational system; a significant reduction in the military's number of troops and budget; a reorganization of the governmental intelligence service; a reform of the draft; the dissolution of the existing internal security forces; and the creation of the new National Civilian Police (Policía Nacional Civil, PNC).

In separating the functions of national defense and public security, the peace accords assigned to the armed forces the mission of "defend[ing] the sovereignty of the state and the integrity of the territory," and placed it within the Ministry of Defense. The PNC, meanwhile, was charged with ensuring public security and became part of the new Ministry of Justice and Public Security. The importance of this achievement lies in the fact that the 1983 Constitution had assigned multiple roles to the armed forces. In the past, the armed forces had been a "suprainstitution" above all others. It had the power to make decisions on a broad range of issues and exhibited a high level of autonomy relative to other branches of the state.[25]

The constitutional reform of 1992, which was necessary to implement several aspects of the peace agreement, modified the legal principles governing the armed forces, going beyond the simple redefinition of its mission. A text known as the "Armed Forces Doctrine" contained six basic principles defining the role and function of the military institution in a democratic society.[26]

In the years immediately following the signing of the peace accords, the Legislative Assembly passed or reformed several important laws in order to adapt the armed forces to El Salvador's new political landscape. The armed forces' educational system was reformed and the number of active duty soldiers shrank by half, from 63,175 in 1991 to 31,000 in February 1993. A decade later, by 2003, that number had been further reduced to 15,500. The defense budget was reduced from 13.7 percent of the nation's budget in 1992 to almost half that in 1995 (7.4 percent); by 2004, its share of the national budget had shrunk to 3.80 percent. Just as important as the reductions in their size and budget, the armed forces went through a purge of their ranks and an investigation of past acts of violence, carried out by two separate entities: an Ad Hoc Commission and a Truth Commission. Not without difficulty and controversy, officers cited in the reports of these institutions were removed from their positions. The National Intelligence Bureau was dissolved. A new law set up a State Intelligence Agency administered by civilians and answering to the office of the president.

Despite these significant advances in reform of the defense and security apparatus, some researchers have pointed to the high degree of institutional autonomy still enjoyed by the armed forces.[27] Challenges that have been identified include the responsibility that the civilian leadership of the executive branch and Congress has in defining the armed forces' specific missions; and the need to strengthen the legislature's capacity to effectively oversee the military budget.[28]

As noted above, the central purpose of the reform was to separate the functions of national defense and public security, and to place the responsibility for them in separate institutions. The doctrine and organization of the new police force (PNC) were redefined, new mechanisms established for hiring, educating, and training its personnel. A legal framework for its operations was developed. Sweeping in scope, the police reform process nevertheless encountered serious difficulties: limited financial resources and equipment; conflicts over the nature of the new model for public security; weaknesses in internal control mechanisms; and enormous institutional pressure generated by the rise in crime and related security issues, such as gangs. The PNC was forced to give precedence to the quantity rather than quality of trained agents, in order to deploy the force throughout the national territory in the shortest period of time possible. Decisions about how to confront rising crime and violence were affected by these imperatives.[29]

The Foundation for the Study of the Application of Law (Fundación de Estudios para la Aplicación del Derecho), a legal studies institute, has identified a number of major problems regarding the PNC since 2000. These include accusations of human rights violations, problems with the process of promotion in the force, changes in legislation that modified the requirements for hiring the PNC director, and the force's weak system of internal control.[30] In addition, the National Academy for Public Security suffered an identity crisis, and lost some of its independence to the PNC.[31] Following a restructuring of the PNC in 2001, the internal affairs investigation unit known as the Inspector General (Inspectoría General) was placed under the PNC's director, thus also reducing the body's independence.[32]

The reform of the defense and public security sectors in the postconflict period was heavily affected by an increase in crime and an overall deterioration in the perception of security among the population. This posed a number of significant challenges for both the government and society. A 2008 study revealed that 34.5 percent of Salvadorans considered the country's main problems to be violence, crime, and security, whereas 61.2 percent worried more about economic factors.[33] By 2010, those numbers were almost entirely reversed. A total of 59.3 percent considered the country's main problems to be violence, crime, and security, whereas 35.5 percent were concerned about economic factors.[34] Meanwhile, a study by the United Nations Development Program earlier in the decade revealed that the economic costs of violence were staggering, totaling about $1.7 billion in 2003, a figure equal to 11.5 percent of gross domestic product.[35]

The army's involvement, under the PNC's direction, in operations to combat crime has generated public debate regarding the army's renewed role in public security tasks.[36] The concern is that the progress made in separating defense and public security institutions—a core provision of the peace accords—could be severely compromised.

The Justice System and Human Rights

The peace accords included numerous provisions to overcome impunity, improve the application of the rule of law, and protect against the grave human rights violations of the past. Constitutional reforms modified the process for the selection of Supreme Court magistrates. A total of 6 percent of the government budget now goes to the judicial branch, and the Office of the Human Rights Ombudsman was created, although this entity has not received sufficient support to carry out its operations. In addition, a qualified majority of members of Congress is needed to elect the attorney general (the *procurador general de la república*), and the human rights ombudsman.

In general, the observance of human rights, along with civil and political rights, has improved in the postconflict period. The Salvadoran social scientist Roberto Turcios has noted that

> never in the country's political history has there been such broad respect for personal freedom—the right not to be detained arbitrarily; for freedom of expression and of the press—the right to dissent and to express criticism publicly, which has allowed for the formation of a political opposition and for the control of those in power; freedom of assembly, equivalent to the right to collective protest, and freedom of association, which opens the way for effective political alternatives. These freedoms have enjoyed a golden era in the period opened by the Chapultepec Accords.[37]

Bolstering the System of Political Parties

The peace accords have been instrumental in the "redistribution of power and the reassigning of political functions," principally from the military to the political party system.[38] However, according to the Salvadoran political analyst and political figure Rubén Zamora, the peace accords "accepted the political parties as they were at the time, without requiring any modifications of them other than their being assigned an even greater share of power and responsibility." According to Zamora, the lack of party reform was certain to have consequences, reflected primarily in a widening gap between the country's needs and realities and the capabilities of the parties themselves. Tensions arose as the political life of the country changed significantly, without corresponding changes and adaptations in the political parties that would have reviewed their operational assumptions, legal structures, and methods of operation.[39] Paradoxically, important shares of power were transferred to institutions that developed during and were shaped by the war, without consideration being given to measures for transforming, modernizing, and democratizing political parties.[40] This caused them to fall behind in facing the new situations and challenges that have presented themselves.

Some analysts have argued that a crisis of representation exists in the party system, which is reflected in the relationship between the representatives and those they represent and, thus, in how the parties fulfill their basic functions of aggregating and representing interests. Public opinion surveys have revealed the difficulties parties have experienced in connecting with citizens and gaining their trust. This acquires special relevance for political parties, which, according to the Constitution, have a monopoly on political representation. Overall, one of the shortcomings in the postwar democratic regime has to do with the way in which political parties function.

The Institutionalization of Electoral Democracy

A critical aspect of the peace accords has been their role in establishing elections as the sole means to legitimately access government power. One of the most fundamental aspects of the transformation of the electoral landscape has been the reconfiguration of the FMLN from a guerrilla group to a political party. This entailed opening political competition in the postwar period to include the entire political-ideological spectrum, something that had never existed before. Other important reforms were the creation of the new Supreme Electoral Tribunal (Tribunal Supremo Electoral, TSE), and the 1993 enactment of a new Electoral Code.

The electoral calendar in the postwar period has been quite intense: presidential, legislative, and municipal elections in 1994; legislative and municipal elections in 1997; presidential elections in 1999; legislative and municipal elections in 2000 and 2003; presidential elections in 2004; legislative and municipal elections in 2006; and again, presidential, legislative, and municipal elections in 2009. This signifies that the fifteen years between 1994 and 2009 witnessed a total of ten electoral processes: four presidential and six legislative and municipal elections. Although some technical problems have been reported, these elections have been regular, competitive, and free, and have allowed for the institutionalization of electoral or representative democracy.[41] The March 2009 elections gave rise to a first-ever postwar alternation in power; the FMLN triumphed over ARENA, ending the right-wing party's twenty-year rule. This was the first time a left-wing government had been elected in the postwar period.

Competitive and free elections in the postwar period have not, however, motivated mass participation. The rate of electoral participation—in terms of total votes cast compared with the number of registered voters—reveals two trends. In the 1994 presidential elections (the first postwar elections),

52.7 percent of the population voted. After that, the number of voters started to decline—to 39.2 percent in the 1997 legislative elections, 38.6 percent in the 1999 presidential elections, and 38.4 percent in the 2000 legislative elections. This trend changed during the 2003 legislative elections with a slight increase to 41 percent, and an important expansion during in the presidential elections of 2004 (67.3 percent),[42] although the figure fell off once again for the 2006 legislative elections (54.21 percent), and then rose again in the March 2009 elections (62.9 percent).[43] The main characteristics of the postwar electoral processes are as follows.

PRESIDENTIAL ELECTIONS

Although several parties and coalitions have participated in presidential elections, only five have participated continuously: ARENA, the FMLN, the National Conciliation Party (Partido de Conciliación Nacional, PCN), the Christian Democratic Party (Partido Demócrata Cristiano, PDC), and the Democratic Convergence/United Democratic Center/Democratic Change (Convergencia Democrática/Centro Democrático Unido/Cambio Democrático, or CD/CDU/CD). Despite the participation of these five, however, competition has taken place principally between ARENA and the FMLN. The voting shares of these two parties increased from 74.1 percent in 1994, to 81 percent in 1999, to 93.9 percent in 2004, and to fully 100 percent in 2009. In the 2009 elections, the PDC and PCN candidates withdrew from the race, and the CD registered no candidates. Therefore, the competition was reduced to the candidates of ARENA and the FMLN.[44] The postwar political system has been characterized as multiparty, but it has been dominated by two parties that are on opposite extremes of the political spectrum.

Another interesting characteristic has been the less competitive nature of presidential elections. The first three postwar presidential elections were decided by a vote margin of more than 20 percent. In the 2004 elections, when ARENA won its fourth consecutive presidential term, ARENA obtained 57.7 percent of the votes, followed by the FMLN in second place with 35.68 percent, whereas the CDU-PDC coalition won 3.9 percent, and the PCN won just 2.71 percent.[45] By 2009, the electorate was more evenly split; Funes of the FMLN party won with slightly more than 51 percent of the vote.

LEGISLATIVE ELECTIONS

Six legislative elections took place between 1994 and 2009, and a wide variety of parties has been in the running: nine in 1994, thirteen in 1997, ten in 2000, eleven in 2003, six in 2006, and six in 2009. However, only five parties participated in all six legislative elections: ARENA, FMLN, PCN, PDC, and CD/CDU/CD.

Compared with presidential elections in the postwar period, legislative elections have been much more competitive. Beginning in 1997, the two major parties were in close competition. By the 2003 elections, the FMLN obtained a higher percentage of votes than ARENA, and became the leading electoral force in the legislative elections. The narrowing of the margin of electoral victory in legislative elections is reflected in the following statistics: 23.6 percent in 1994, 2.4 percent in 1997, 0.8 percent in 2000, 2.1 percent in 2003, 0.1 percent in 2006, and 4.1 percent in 2009—for an average of 5.5 percent during this period.[46]

Table 3.2 shows the percentage of valid votes as well as the number of legislative deputies from various parties that were elected to the legislature between 1994 and 2009. Of the two major parties, ARENA won 39 seats in 1994, slid to 28 in 1997, then rose to 29 in 2000, and stepped back to 27 in 2003, before moving up to 34 in 2006, and dropping to 32 in 2009. On the other hand, the FMLN went from holding 21 seats in 1994, up to 27 in 1997. Then it climbed again to 31 in 2000 and 2003, and went further to 32 in 2006, then up to 35 in 2009. In the case of ARENA, however, there has been a noticeable weakening in its parliamentary wing. In the wake of Funes's victory in the 2009 presidential elections, internal conflicts within ARENA intensified, leading to a split in October 2009 in which 12 elected deputies left the party.

Although legislative elections have been marked by the involvement of multiple parties, the two major parties still dominate the competition. At a legislative level, the combined votes for ARENA and the FMLN have been 66.4 percent in 1994, 68.4 percent in 1997, 71.3 percent in 2000, 65.9 percent in 2003, 78.5 percent in 2006, and 81.2 percent in 2009. Thus, while the post–civil war political party system has been characterized as multiparty, its configuration has been essentially bipolar, marked by polarized competition and structured partisanship. Some observers have described the system as a polarized pluralism, in which political competition exhibits a centrifugal tendency.[47] Bipolarity has intensified over time—in the 2009 presidential elections, ARENA and the FMLN together accounted for 100 percent of the vote; and in the legislative elections that same year, the two parties together garnered 81.2 percent of the vote.

The concentration of votes in the two largest parties reduces the space available for the remaining political forces; and the polarization places the

Table 3.2. *Percentage of Valid Votes and Number of Legislative Deputies per Party in El Salvador, 1994–2009*

Party	1994		1997		2000		2003		2006		2009	
	% Valid Votes	No. of Deputies	% Valid Votes	No. of Deputies	% Valid Votes	No. of Deputies	% Valid Votes	No. of Deputies	% Valid Votes	No. of Deputies	% Valid Votes	No. of Deputies
ARENA	45.03	39	35.40	28	36.04	29	31.91	27	39.20	34	38.55	32
FMLN	21.39	21	33.02	27	35.22	31	33.96	31	39.29	32	42.60	35
PCN	6.21	4	8.70	11	8.82	14	12.95	16	11.42	10	8.79	11
PDC	17.87	18	8.36	10	7.19	5	7.28	5	6.93	6	6.94	5
CD/CDU/CD	4.45	1	3.50	2	5.38	3	6.37	5	3.05	2	2.12	1
MU	2.49	1	2.25	1								
PRSC			3.58	3								
PLD			3.15	2								
PAN					3.71	2						
PNL									0.1	0		
FDR											1.0	0
Total	100	84	100	84	100	84	100	84	100	84	100	84

Source: Prepared by the authors based on Tribunal Supremo Electoral data.

postwar political system in a bind. Political/electoral polarization has been accompanied by a reduction in the capacity for dialogue and for the building of bridges between the two dominant political forces.

Although progress toward free and competitive elections has been significant during the postwar era, the behavior of political actors and of electoral institutions has given rise to a number of key concerns. In 2004 and 2006, for example, the TSE did nothing to prevent and sanction the early start of electoral campaigning. It failed to rule on a number of complaints filed over the course of the electoral campaign, and did not control the use of inappropriate campaign materials.[48] The TSE's performance was marked by the partisan nature of its composition.

The two major parties have also exhibited scant regard for the rules. In 2004, ARENA did not respect the legal deadlines for beginning and ending its campaign, under the pretext that it was not soliciting votes. The party's adherents destroyed its adversary's campaign advertising, and verbally and physically attacked its supporters, making the 2004 campaign the most violent since 1993–94. The FMLN also violated electoral regulations, albeit to a lesser extent. Like ARENA and under the same pretext, the FMLN began campaigning before the legal starting date; party supporters also destroyed the campaign advertisements of their opponents.[49]

The 2006 electoral campaign, according to the political analyst Álvaro Artiga, brought to light "the serious institutional deterioration in the country." The TSE, the political parties—particularly ARENA and the FMLN—and the Office of the President all contributed to serious institutional deterioration.[50] Artiga took aim especially at then-president Antonio Saca's "full participation" in the electoral campaign, behaving "as if he were president of only one section of the population: the ARENA party," rather than president of all Salvadorans.[51]

The 2004 presidential race and the 2006 legislative elections were marked by the deterioration of electoral institutions that still had not been remedied by 2009. Indeed, one of the major conclusions in a preliminary report by the European Union's 2009 Elections-Observer Mission was that "the legal framework that governs electoral processes in El Salvador makes it possible for democratic elections to take place, but there are large voids. Despite having been amended on numerous occasions, it still lacks legislation in terms of political parties, campaign financing, and media access."[52]

The 2004 presidential race and 2006 legislative elections showed evidence of deterioration in the electoral institutions, which had been brought about by the behavior of the political actors. Among the shortcomings in the democratic process are core problems with the parties, the party system, and the electoral institution. However, the peaceful transfer of power from ARENA to the FMLN in 2009 showed that electoral institutions had progressed and were capable of managing El Salvador's first alternation at the presidential level since the signing of the peace agreements.

Challenges for the Construction of Democratic Governance

The implementation of measures included in the peace accords has led to the institutionalization of the new postwar political system. In this sense, the accords provide the foundation for political democracy. However, in spite of the progress made in democratizing the country, we believe it is premature to conclude that the Salvadoran democracy has been consolidated. The way some institutions operate and the behavior of political actors in the postwar period constitute important deficits in the democratic process. These deficits can no longer be understood in light of the content of the peace accords themselves; rather, they should be understood in terms of the manner in which the newly constructed institutions operate, and the needs that are endogenous to the deepening of democracy.[53]

The challenges to deepening democratization following the inauguration of President Mauricio Funes and beyond are diverse and complex. These challenges fall in four principal areas.

Issues of Violence, Crime, and Security

As discussed in chapter 11, different forms of crime and violence have become a constant in the daily life for Salvadorans, to a degree far beyond the levels experienced during the war. The political transition has failed to create acceptable conditions of security and peaceful coexistence, dashing many of the expectations generated at the end of the armed conflict.[54] The trends in homicide rates, reflected in figure 3.1, provide one indicator of the burden of crime on society. The homicide rate over a period of several years ranged from 40 to 70 homicides per 100,000 inhabitants, one of the highest rates in the entire world among countries formally at peace. Figure 3.1 presents an alarming finding: 31,774 murders in the ten-year period between 1999 and 2009, when the country was formally at peace. Crime and violence constitute one of the greatest challenges to democratic governance in El Salvador.

Figure 3.1. Reports of Homicides Made at Police Stations in El Salvador, 1999–2009

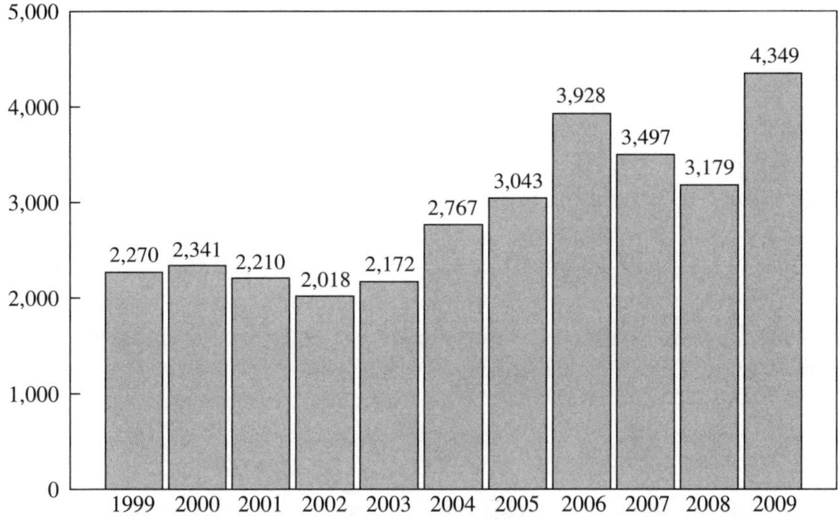

Note: Before 2005, the data are from the National Civil Police. Starting in 2006, several institutions agreed to unify the process of statistics-gathering for homicide data. This agreement became operational through the creation of the Technical Roundtable (National Civilian Police, Attorney General's Office, and Legal Medicine Institute).
Source: Carlos G. Ramos, "Construcción democrática y violencia en el proceso político salvadoreño," paper presented at International University Symposium for Development and Peace, Universidad Católica de Pereira Carrera, Risaralda, Colombia, September 2010.

From 1994 to 2009, successive ARENA governments responded to the problem of violence and crime with markedly coercive policies, leaving little room for programs of prevention or rehabilitation. Policies implemented were tardy and reactive and had unsatisfactory results, leading to heightened tension between the demand for improved security and the need to advance respect for citizens' rights, as mandated in the peace accords. Recurring disputes over the last decade between the executive branch and the judicial system over issues of due process are simply one expression of this tension.

The security challenges are numerous, including the institutional strengthening of the PNC and the Office of the Attorney General. Other challenges include improving the technical capacity to investigate crime, improving the quantity and quality of resources, and strengthening mechanisms for internal control. It is also essential to make crime prevention part of a comprehensive approach to confronting the challenge of violence. A 2007 report by the National Committee for Public Security and Social Peace (Comisión Nacional para la Seguridad Pública y la Paz Social) called for comprehensive, national, and sustainable policies in such areas as violence prevention; improving the functioning of institutions, improving information, transparency, and accountability; obtaining more and better resources, including financial resources; improving institutional coordination; and adopting coherent criminal laws and procedural regulations to ensure the effective enforcement of the law.[55]

The degree to which crime victimization and a sense of insecurity have a negative effect on support for the political system and on the levels of interpersonal trust cannot be overstated. In addition, rates of victimization and perceptions of insecurity increase levels of support for extralegal solutions that undermine the rule of law.[56]

The Impact of the Economic Crisis

Beginning in 2007—and considerably more than a year before the global economic crisis of 2008—the Salvadoran economy was deeply affected by worldwide increase in prices of food and energy, particularly oil. According to the United Nations Development Program, El Salvador's oil bill rose from $500 million in 2000 to $1.4 billion in 2007, and then to $1.86 billion in 2008. Simultaneously, the cost of the basic food basket (*canasta básica*) increased, leading to a rapid decline in purchasing power for large segments of the population. The United Nations Development Program estimated that between June 2007 and June 2008, the cost of the *canasta básica* rose by 22 percent in urban areas and 20 percent in rural areas.[57]

These global factors worsened the already sluggish growth rates of the Salvadoran economy. During the first half of the decade of the 2000s, El Salvador's economy grew at modest levels, from 3.3 percent in 2005 to 4.2 and 4.3 percent in 2006 and 2007, respectively (figure 3.2). Growth fell to a meager 2.4 percent in 2008. And as the combined effects of the domestic and international economic crises grew in intensity, El Salvador's growth rate was a dismal negative 3.5 percent by 2009.

Although our focus in this chapter is on political developments in the period following the signing of the peace accords, consolidating democracy and confronting the sociopolitical challenges that have arisen in the nearly two decades since the end of the war require dealing with socioeconomic issues that were addressed only marginally in the accords. This

Figure 3.2. Annual Growth of El Salvador's Gross Domestic Product, 2000–2009 (in 1990 constant prices)

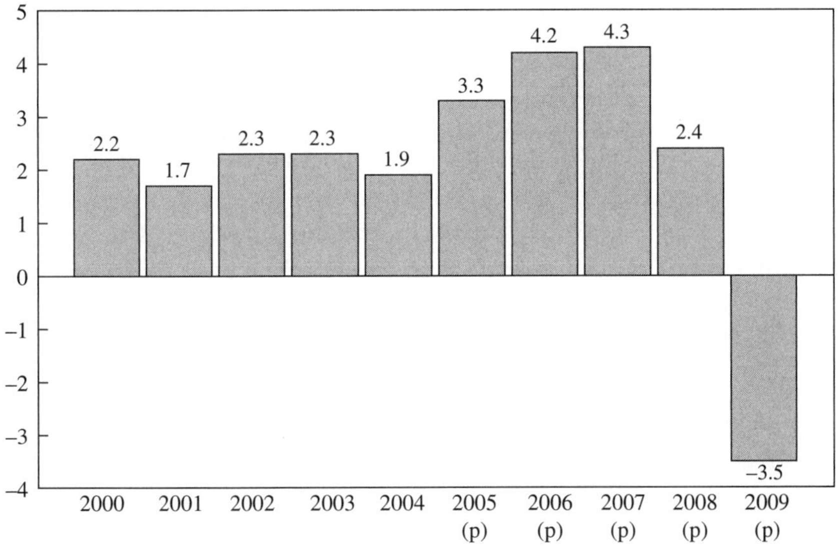

Source: Compiled by the authors with data from the Central Reserve Bank of El Salvador.

challenge has proved even greater given that the postconflict era has witnessed a noticeable increase in the tension between the peace accords' effort at greater political inclusion and the tendency toward socioeconomic exclusion resulting from economic reforms.[58]

Overall, in recent years El Salvador has tended toward a redistribution of political power, or the opening up of spaces for citizen participation, while at the economic level it has experienced "a reconcentration of economic power that is narrowing spaces for participation in the wealth generated by the economy."[59] Placing socioeconomic issues on the agenda and establishing channels for citizens' social and economic demands are some of the main challenges in order to strengthen governance in El Salvador.

Promoting Political Reform

Various initiatives in recent years have aimed to deepen democratization by promoting reform in the political-electoral system. This pending agenda constitutes, without a doubt, a second generation of political reforms, in that they go beyond the transformations possible at the time the peace accords were signed. The basic agenda for electoral reform includes ending the partisanship of the TSE and separating its administrative from its jurisdictional functions. The agenda also includes reinforcing the linkages between elected officials and those they represent, by reorganizing electoral districts and introducing changes in the system of voter lists. Additional reforms are also needed to (1) introduce plurality in the integration/composition of local governments; (2) allow for absentee voting by Salvadorans living abroad; (3) enact a political parties' law to regulate public and private party financing as well as aspects of internal party practice (e.g., the establishment of quotas to promote gender equality); (4) regulate electoral propaganda; and (5) introduce both residential voting, to allow citizens to vote closer to the places where they live, and provisions for referenda.[60]

Revitalizing the Dialogue between Leading Political Forces

One of El Salvador's greatest political problems has been the progressive deepening of polarization between the two major parties, coupled with their dwindling ability to carry out meaningful dialogue and reach agreement on key issues. Improving governance in the future will require that the principal political and social actors be able to reach minimum levels of consensus with regard to the most critical issues facing the country.

This revival and revitalization of dialogue between political and social actors is an indispensable condition if El Salvador is to successfully overcome the many challenges it faces and take advantage of opportunities that present themselves in the years to come. The 2009 electoral results and the establishment of El Salvador's first leftist government provide an opportunity to transform traditional forms of dialogue and political behavior and open spaces for negotiation that should be less subject to partisan conflicts. Whether this potential will be realized remains to be seen.

Conclusion

Close to two decades after the signing of the peace accords, the process of democratization in El Salvador has seen important progress. This is reflected most prominently in the FMLN's victory in the 2009 presidential elections, which demonstrated not only the transformation of the former guerrillas into a political party capable of competing in and winning national elections, but also the acceptance of the outcome by ARENA, the political party that had dominated politics for twenty years.

This chapter has analyzed the five main contributions the peace process made to the construction of democracy, contributions that made such a peaceful alternation in power possible. Not all the transformations laid out in the accords were realized with the same depth, nor did they all face the same obstacles. Nonetheless, the advances and shortcomings in the democratic system are more the product of institutional weaknesses and the behavior of key political actors than they are of the content of the peace accords themselves. The accords laid out a road map for essential reforms that would establish a more democratic and inclusive political system. By the end of the first decade of the 2000s, it was possible to affirm that, despite difficulties, the core provisions that were agreed upon had been executed and thereby new possibilities for democratization have unfolded.

The challenges for democratic governance outlined in this chapter are directly associated with strengthening new institutions, to endow them with greater efficiency and effectiveness, and with the need to improve the performance of political actors. Equally important is overcoming the polarization that has been a defining element in Salvadoran politics both during the conflict and throughout the postwar period. Overcoming El Salvador's numerous and significant challenges of governance requires establishing some basic agreements among political parties. But since Funes's election, both ARENA and the FMLN have shown signs of internal division and strain—ARENA over how and why it lost the election and who will take the party into the future; and the FMLN over the pace of change and reform, particularly in the socioeconomic arena. Personalities certainly play a role, and clashes among individuals get played out over questions of political substance. How and whether the right and left can find common ground in a national project to meet El Salvador's political, economic, and social challenges will be the defining issue of the Funes presidency.

Notes

1. For an overview of the historical background of the Salvadoran conflict, see Enrique Baloyra. *El Salvador in Transition* (Chapel Hill: University of North Carolina Press, 1983); Tommie Sue Montgomery, *Revolution in El Salvador,* 2nd ed. (Boulder, Colo.: Westview Press, 1995); Rafael Menjívar, *El Salvador: El eslabón más pequeño* (San José: EDUCA, 1980); Carlos Rafael Cabarrus, *Génesis de una revolución: Análisis del surgimiento y desarrollo de la organización campesina en El Salvador* (Mexico

City: Centro de Investigaciones y Estudios Superiores de Antropología Social, 1983); Elisabeth Jean Wood. *Insurgent Collective Action and Civil War in El Salvador* (New York: Cambridge University Press, 2003); James Dunkerley, *The Long War. Dictatorship & Revolution in El Salvador* (London: Verso, 1982); James Dunkerley. *Power in the Isthmus: A Political History of Modern Central America* (London: Verso, 1989); and Charles D. Brockett, *Political Movements and Violence in Central America* (New York: Cambridge University Press, 2005).

2. Explanatory factors for the civil war in El Salvador include (1) the inflexible and exclusionary character of the political regime, its intolerance and resistance to allowing participation of the political opposition; (2) the successful electoral frauds, which constituted the most open expression of the excluding character of the political regime; (3) the prolonged military predominance, and the use of high doses of repression; and (4) the untrustworthy justice system. Meanwhile, the formation of citizen consciousness regarding injustice and exclusion had grown. As for economic factors, these include (1) the condition of poverty in which important sectors of the population lived; (2) the growing social inequality in the distribution of income and wealth; (3) the concentration of land ownership, and the surge in the number of landless families; and (4) a deterioration in the real minimum wage. Also worth consideration are aspects linked to the international environment: the defeat of the Somoza dictatorship and the 1979 triumph of the Sandinista revolution in Nicaragua, and the placement of the Central American conflict in the framework of the East/West confrontation. See Ricardo Córdova Macías, William Pleitéz, and Carlos Guillermo Ramos, *Reforma Política y Reforma Económica: Los retos de la gobernabilidad democrática,* Documentos de Trabajo, Serie Análisis de la Realidad Nacional 98-1 (San Salvador: Fundación Dr. Guillermo Manuel Ungo, 1998), 1–12.

3. Mitchell A. Seligson and Vincent McElhinny, "Low-Intensity Warfare, High-Intensity Death: The Demographic Impact of the Wars in El Salvador and Nicaragua," *Canadian Journal of Latin American and Caribbean Studies* 21, no. 42 (1996).

4. Regarding transformations of Salvadoran society in the last two decades of the twentieth century, see Carlos G. Ramos, "El Salvador: Transformación y conflicto social a fin de siglo," in *Más allá de las elecciones: Diez años después de los Acuerdos de Paz,* edited by Héctor Dada Hirezi (San Salvador: Facultad Latinoamericana de Ciencias Sociales–Programa El Salvador, 2002); Carlos Umaña, *Un nuevo mapa para El Salvador* (San Salvador: Ediciones Tendencias, 1996); and Carlos Briones et al., "El cambio histórico en El Salvador," Nación MMXXI National Analysis and Proposals Group, San Salvador, 1995.

5. Gobierno de El Salvador, *Informe sobre el cumplimiento de los acuerdos de paz al 31 de Octubre 1995.*

6. Rep. Jim Leach, Rep. George Miller, and Sen. Mark Hatfield, *U.S. Aid to El Salvador: An Evaluation of the Past, a Proposal for the Future,* Report to the Arms Control and Foreign Policy Caucus (Washington, D.C.: U.S. Congress, 1985).

7. Benajmin C. Schwarz, *American Counterinsurgency Doctrine and El Salvador: The Frustrations of Reform and the Illusions of Nation Building* (Santa Monica, Calif.: RAND Corporation, 1991), v.

8. For an overview of the Salvadoran peace negotiation process, see Ricardo Córdova Macías, *El Salvador: Las negociaciones de paz y los retos de la posguerra* (San Salvador: IDELA, 1993); and Salvador Samayoa. *El Salvador: La reforma pactada* (San Salvador: UCA Editores, 2002).

9. See Edelberto Torres-Rivas, "Los caminos hacia la democracia política en América Central," in *Un desafío a la democracia. Los partidos políticos en Centroamérica, Panamá y República Dominicana* (San José: BID, IDEA, OEA, and PNUD, 2004); and Rubén Zamora, "Participación y democracia en El Salvador," in *Pasos hacia una nueva convivencia: Democracia y participación en Centroamérica,* edited by Ricardo Córdova Macías, Günther Maihold, and Sabine Kurtenbach (San Salvador: Fundación Dr. Guillermo Manuel Ungo, Institute of Iberoamerican Studies Hamburg, and Iberoamerican Institute of Berlin, 2001).

10. Antonio Cañas and Héctor Dada, "Political Transition and Institutionalization in El Salvador," in *Comparative Peace Processes in Latin America,* edited by Cynthia J. Arnson (Washington, D.C., and Stanford, Calif.: Woodrow Wilson Center Press and Stanford University Press, 1999).

11. Wood has characterized the South African and Salvadoran cases as the "insurgent path to democracy," in which mobilization "from below" drives the democratic transition. See Elisabeth Jean Wood, "Un camino insurgente a la democracia: La movilización popular, los intereses económicos y las transiciones de los regímenes en El Salvador y Sudáfrica," *Estudios Centroamericanos,* nos. 641–42 (March–April 2001).

12. From the many works published on the Salvadoran peace process, see Ricardo Córdova Macías, Carlos Guillermo Ramos, and Nayelly Loya, "La contribución del proceso de paz a la construcción de la democracia en El Salvador (1992–2004)," in *Construyendo la democracia en sociedades posconflicto: Un enfoque comparado entre Guatemala y El Salvador,* edited by Dinorah Azpuru et. al (Guatemala City and Ottawa: F&G Editores and IDRC Publishers, 2007); Elisabeth Jean Wood, "Challenges to Political Democracy in El Salvador," in *The Third Wave of Democratization in Latin America: Advances and Setbacks,* edited by Frances Hagopian and Scott P. Mainwaring (New York: Cambridge University Press, 2005); Cynthia J. Arnson, ed., *El Salvador´s Democratic Transition Ten Years after the Peace Accords* (Washington, D.C.: Woodrow Wilson International Center for Scholars, 2003); Cynthia J. Arnson and Dinorah Azpuru, "From Peace to Democratization: Lessons from Central America," in *Contemporary Peace Making: Conflict, Violence, and Peace Processes,* edited by John Darby (New York: Palgrave Macmillan, 2003); Charles T. Call, "Assessing El Salvador's Transition from Civil War to Peace," in *Ending Civil Wars: The Implementation of Peace Accords,* edited by Stephen John Stedman, Donald Rotchild, and Elizabeth M. Cousens (Boulder, Colo.: Lynne Rienner, 2002); Antonio Cañas and Héctor Dada, "Political Transition"; and Ricardo Córdova Macías, "El Salvador: Transition from Civil War," in *Constructing Democratic Governance: Mexico, Central America, and the Caribbean in the 1990s,* edited by Jorge I. Domínguez and Abraham F. Lowenthal (Baltimore: Johns Hopkins University Press, 1996).

13. For an extensive discussion of the Jesuit murders and their impact on U.S. policy, see Teresa Whitfield, *Paying the Price: Ignacio Ellacuría and the Murdered Jesuits in El Salvador* (Philadelphia: Temple University Press, 1995).

14. William M. LeoGrande, *Our Own Backyard: The United States in Central America, 1977–1992* (Chapel Hill: University of North Carolina Press, 1998), 571.

15. Although opinions regarding the starting point of the democratic transition vary, the most widely accepted notion places it at the signing of the peace accords and the process of implementing the political agreements of 1992. See Carlos Briones and Carlos G. Ramos, *Gobernabilidad en Centroamérica: Gobernabilidad, economía y democracia en El Salvador* (San Salvador: Facultad Latinoamericana de Ciencias Sociales–Programa El Salvador, 1995).

16. See Wood, "Camino insurgente," 191.

17. As noted by the Salvadoran politician and social scientist Rubén Zamora, "there was no possibility [in the peace agreement] of addressing the second cause of conflict, economic exclusion. This point is very important. Many people fault both the peace agreements and the FMLN, especially on the left, for failing to address the economic transformation that El Salvador needed. I do not believe that such criticism makes sense. . . . What happened with the peace agreements was that there was no consensus at all between both the parties over what constituted the problems of economic exclusion." Rubén Zamora, in *El Salvador's Democratic Transition,* ed. Arnson.

18. Álvaro Artiga-González, "La difícil democratización del régimen político salvadoreño," in *Más allá de las elecciones: Diez años después de los Acuerdos de Paz,* edited by Héctor Dada Hirezi (San Salvador: Facultad Latinoamericana de Ciencias Sociales–Programa El Salvador, 2002), 27.

19. See Carlos G. Ramos, *El Salvador: En el incierto camino de la gobernabilidad democrática,* Cuaderno de trabajo 11 (San Salvador: Facultad Latinoamericana de Ciencias Sociales–Programa El Salvador, 1996), 10–11.

20. For more on economic reform, see Alexander Segovia, *Transformación estructural y reforma económica en El Salvador* (Guatemala: F&G y Democracia y Desarrollo Consultores, 2002).

21. On economic and political reform processes, see Córdova, Pleitéz, and Ramos, *Reforma Política y Reforma Económica.*

22. Álvaro de Soto and Graciana del Castillo, "Obstacles to Peacebuilding," *Foreign Policy,* Spring 1994, 70–72. For a more far-reaching and comprehensive reflection on the challenges of postconflict economic reconstruction, see Graciana del Castillo, *Rebuilding War-Torn States: The Challenge of Post-Conflict Economic Reconstruction* (New York: Oxford University Press, 2008).

23. James K. Boyce, "El Salvador's Adjustment toward Peace: An Introduction," in *Economic Policy for Building Peace. The Lessons of El Salvador,* edited by James K. Boyce (Boulder, Colo.: Lynne Rienner, 1996), 1–2.

24. For a more in-depth view of military reform in the peace process, see Ricardo Córdova Macías, *El Salvador: Reforma Militar y Relaciones Cívico-Militares* (San Salvador: Fundación Dr. Guillermo Manuel Ungo, 1999); Ricardo Córdova Macías, "Las relaciones cívico-militares en Centroamérica a fin de siglo," in *Pasos hacia una nueva convivencia,* ed. Macías, Maihold, and Kurtenbach; and Philip J. Williams and Knut Walter, *Militarization and Demilitarization in El Salvador's Transition to Democracy* (Pittsburgh: University of Pittsburgh Press, 1997).

25. Córdova, "Relaciones cívico-militares," 335.

26. See Armed Forces of El Salvador, *Doctrina militar y las relaciones ejército/sociedad* (San Salvador: Armed Forces of El Salvador–ONUSAL, 1994).

27. E.g., in his analysis of civil-military relations in Central America, J. Mark Ruhl states that "in spite of these significant advances, the democratization of civil-military relations in Central America remains incomplete in several important aspects." He refers to the institutional autonomy of the armed forces, stating that they "are subject to little effective oversight by civilian defense ministries or legislative committees," and that "military establishments still play an unduly large internal-security role." See J. Mark Ruhl, "Curbing Central America's Militaries," *Journal of Democracy* 15, no 3 (July 2004). See also Wood, "Challenges"; Call, "Assessing El Salvador's Transition"; and Williams and Walter, *Militarization.*

28. Córdova, "Relaciones cívico-militares."

29. Córdova, Ramos, and Loya, "Contribución del proceso de paz." For a more in-depth view on the subject of public security in the postconflict period, see Gino Costa, *La Policía Nacional Civil de El Salvador (1990–1997)* (San Salvador: UCA Editores, 1999); and FESPAD, *Estado de la seguridad pública y la justicia penal en El Salvador julio 2002–diciembre 2003* (San Salvador: FESPAD, 2004).

30. FESPAD, *Estado actual de la seguridad pública y la justicia penal en El Salvador (June 1999–March 2001)* (San Salvador: FESPAD, 2001), 22.

31. FESPAD, *Estado de la seguridad pública y la justicia penal en El Salvador 2001* (San Salvador: FESPAD, 2002), 16.

32. Ibid.

33. Ricardo Córdova Macias and José Miguel Cruz, *La Cultura Política de la Democracia en El Salvador, 2008: El impacto de la gobernabilidad* (San Salvador: Fundación Dr. Guillermo Manuel Ungo, IUDOP, Vanderbilt University, and U.S. Agency for International Development, 2008).

34. IUDOP, *Boletín de Prensa* 25, no. 1 (2010).

35. United Nations Development Program, *¿Cuánto cuesta la violencia a El Salvador? Cuadernos sobre desarrollo humano No. 4* (El Salvador: United Nations Development Program, 2005), 60.

36. FESPAD, *Estado actual de la seguridad pública,* 32.

37. Roberto Turcios, "Los procesos electorales 1994 y 1997," in *Colección Aportes No. 5: De los acuerdos de Chapultepec a la construcción de la Democracia* (San Salvador: Facultad Latinoamericana de Ciencias Sociales–Programa El Salvador, 1998), 16.

38. Rubén Zamora, "Los partidos políticos: Transformaciones en el proceso de transición," in *Colección Aportes No. 5: De los acuerdos de Chapultepec a la construcción de la Democracia* (San Salvador: Facultad Latinoamericana de Ciencias Sociales–Programa El Salvador, 1998), 10.

39. Rubén Zamora, *El Salvador: Heridas que no cierran—Los partidos políticos en la post-guerra* (San Salvador: Facultad Latinoamericana de Ciencias Sociales–Programa El Salvador, 1998), 318.

40. The only measure considered, as mentioned above, was the legalization of the FMLN as a political party.

41. Karl defines democracy in the following terms: "a set of institutions that permits the entire adult population to act as citizens by choosing their leading decision makers in competitive, fair and regularly scheduled elections which are held in the context of the rule of law, guarantees for political freedom and limited military prerogatives." See Terry Lynn Karl, "Dilemmas of Democratization in Latin America," *Comparative Politics* 23, no. 1 (October 1990): 2.

42. See Córdova, Ramos, and Loya, "Contribución del proceso de paz."

43. Since the 2004 elections, voters have used the new Documento Unico de Identidad (Unique Identification Document, or DUI in Spanish).

44. However, the political parties PDC and PCN decided to publicly support the ARENA party candidate, whereas the CD party supported the FMLN candidate.

45. Those interested in the 2004 electoral process, see CIDAI, "Las elecciones presidenciales: Un triunfo del bloque hegemónico de derecha," *Estudios Centroamericanos,* nos. 665–66 (March–April 2004); and José Miguel Cruz, "Las elecciones presidenciales desde el comportamiento de la opinión pública," *Estudios Centroamericanos,* nos. 665–66 (March–April 2004).

46. These calculations are based on the difference in votes between the two parties with the most votes. See Álvaro Artiga-González, "Las elecciones 2006 en perspectiva," *Estudios Centroamericanos,* nos. 688–89 (February-March 2006), 240.

47. Córdova, Ramos, and Loya, "Contribución del proceso de paz"; and Álvaro Artiga-González, "Las elecciones 2006 en perspectiva," op. cit.

48. Córdova, Ramos, and Loya, "Contribución del proceso de paz."

49. "Elecciones sin alternabilidad," editorial, *Estudios Centroamericanos,* nos. 665–66 (March–April 2004): 210–14.

50. CIDAI, "Las elecciones presidenciales," 196.

51. Artiga, "Elecciones 2006," 238.

52. European Union Election Observation Mission for the El Salvador 2009 Presidential Elections, "Preliminary Report," San Salvador, March 17, 2009: "The Salvadoran people opt for alternation in a peaceful and organized election after a campaign that was marked by a competitive imbalance between contenders."

53. Córdova, Ramos, and Loya, "Contribución del proceso de paz."

54. Carlos G. Ramos, "Construcción democrática y violencia en el proceso político salvadoreño," paper presented at International University Symposium for Development and Peace; UCPR, Colombia, September 2010.

55. National Commission for Public Security and Social Peace, *Seguridad y Paz, un reto de país: Recomendaciones para una Política de Seguridad Ciudadana en El Salvador* (El Salvador: Comisión Nacional para la Seguridad Ciudadana y Paz Social, 2007).

56. Córdova and Cruz, *Cultura Política.*

57. United Nations Development Program, *El camino hacia un nuevo ciclo político: Escenarios de gobernabilidad 2009–2010* (San Salvador: United Nations Development Program, 2009).

58. For more on the effects of this distance between a reform process favoring concentration of wealth and another motivated by the opening of political participation, see Ramos, "El Salvador"; Rubén Zamora, "La encrucijada de la economía salvadoreña," in *Colección Aportes No. 11* (San Salvador: Facultad Latinoamericana de Ciencias Sociales–Programa El Salvador, 2001); and Carlos G. Ramos, "La evolución de los movimientos sociales," in *Colección Aportes No. 5: De los acuerdos de Chapultepec a la construcción de la democracia* (San Salvador: Facultad Latinoamericana de Ciencias Sociales–Programa El Salvador, 1998).

59. Ramos, "Evolución," 3.

60. Regarding the agenda for electoral reforms, see Fundación Dr. Guillermo Manuel Ungo, Fundación Nacional para el Desarrollo, and Facultad Latinoamericana de Ciencias Sociales, "Memoria del Foro Nacional sobre las Reformas Electorales: San Salvador," November 2009.

Chapter 4

The Limits of Peace and Democracy in Guatemala

Edelberto Torres-Rivas

In the period since the signing of the Acuerdo de Paz Firme y Duradera (Firm and Lasting Peace Accord), the effort to consolidate democracy in Guatemala has followed a tortuous path, strewn with obstacles. It is generally accepted that in Guatemala, as in El Salvador, peace accords have served to advance the democratic process, the initial stages of which have unfolded under the shadow of violent armed conflict. Guatemala has had almost twenty-five years of experience with formal democracy; and in the decade and a half since the signing of the peace accords, democracy has made further progress. At the same time, it faces serious institutional limitations, not only in terms of what constitutes political democracy in an ideal sense but also in terms of what has actually been accomplished.

Democratic political consolidation requires two mutually reinforcing elements: on the one hand, the strengthening of democratic institutions; and on the other, a broadening of citizenship to include all sectors of society, particularly the indigenous majority in the case of Guatemala. Political institutions are strengthened by citizen participation, and participation itself acquires greater meaning to the extent that it is carried out through democratic political institutions. But Guatemalan democracy is deficient. The political regime goes through the motions of elections, but with scant citizen participation and weak political parties that lack permanent organic structures. All this is played out against a backdrop of deep poverty and inequality along with spiraling levels of violence, stoked by marginalization and the growing activities of organized crime.

Attempts to assess the advances and difficulties of political development in Guatemala since the signing of the 1996 peace accords must take into account what went before. First, the accords ended a long and painful period of internal war generally considered to have lasted thirty-six years (the date of origin is open to debate). But the very term "internal armed conflict" is an official characterization that glosses over a basic reality: What took place in Guatemala was not a civil war so much as the actions of a brutally counterinsurgent state. One must not underestimate how heavily the experience of unrestrained violence by the state weighs on Guatemalan society. The imprint of this violence, which began in 1962, constitutes the most negative legacy of the period of conflict and military rule.

Second, the period of democratization ushered in by the accords was not entirely new but represented a continuation of a process inaugurated a decade before. Most analysts date the beginning of Guatemala's democratic transition to March 1986, when a general who had come to power through a military coup relinquished the presidency to a democratically elected civilian. It is more difficult to determine when the various social processes involved in democratization were born, but there is general agreement that the 1986 elections—the first free elections in a half century—initiated the democratic transition, ending a period of more than three decades of military dictatorship.[1]

Paradoxes of History

In Guatemala, repressive force was a modality of the state that preceded the rise of guerrilla movements. Military power was focused on preventing eruptions of any kind, not in the name of defending democracy but in defense of so-called national security. Military power was directed not only against guerrilla subversion but also against the civilian opposition that used peaceful means in its struggle for democracy. Prolonged, senseless ethnic slaughter took place. Unarmed men, women, and children were murdered or disappeared.[2]

Guatemala's authoritarian form of government, like those in other countries—including those without internal armed conflict—was the child of anticommunist ideology, the Cold War, and the U.S. doctrine of national security.[3]

In societies with a long history of military dictatorship, the principal obstacle to establishing democratic regimes is the inevitable legacy of authoritarian political culture. That culture determines the daily behavior of both those who rule and those who obey. In the twentieth century, Guatemala experienced seventy-five years of dictatorial rule. There is not yet enough research detailing the ways that authoritarian culture permeates the most intimate aspects of Guatemala's social structure and how it manifests itself in daily life—how it is implicit not only in political relationships but also in the whole range of interpersonal relationships: at work, at home, in school, in economic life, and also in the ways free time is enjoyed. This cultural condition, the product of the pre-1986 period of state terrorism, is the biggest implicit obstacle to the practice of democracy.

The nature of the war gave rise to certain paradoxes that shaped the nature of Guatemala's peace process. First, the peace accords were signed after the armed conflict had already virtually ended. The strategic defeat of the guerrilla insurgency was achieved through a scorched earth policy that included severe repression of unarmed indigenous groups, only some of whom were guerrilla sympathizers. By 1983, the military had dealt a blow to the guerrilla forces from which they never recovered. It is difficult to clearly establish why the armed forces were unable to transform their military victory into a political victory as well.[4]

By the end of the 1980s, peace initiatives had evolved independently of the status of the guerrilla conflict. Dialogue, both before and after the opening of formal peace negotiations between the government and the guerrillas, took place in a setting in which the political aspects gained autonomy; what was negotiated was a conflict that was for all intents and purposes over. The government and the guerrillas signed a cease-fire in March 1996, several months before the conclusion of the accords, so the war itself—defined as a deadly conflict between enemies—was not one of the subjects of negotiation. A cease-fire is usually the result of arduous negotiations, but strictly speaking, the end of the armed conflict in Guatemala was not a negotiation. Rather, it was a series of proposals put forward for political-institutional and socioeconomic changes that were said to have been central to the origins of the insurgency. The government and the army were on one side of the negotiating table and the guerrillas were on the other, even though the guerrillas had been virtually wiped out in 1981–83 and had no military importance after that point. The agreements signed constituted a cultural and political victory for the guerrillas irrespective of their actual military strength, as well as for certain sectors of civil society.

A second paradox of Guatemala's transition was that democratization began before the end of the war, heightening the difficulties of strengthening democratic coexistence. In peace settlements in other parts of the world, warring parties decide first to stop fighting and only then agree to the dates and conditions for elections. In Guatemala, as in El Salvador, things happened the other way around. In addition, democracy did not come about as the result of active grassroots mobilization or of demands and pressures coming "bottom-up" from democratic forces in society. Remarkably, the call for elections in the mid-1980s came from sectors of the oligarchy that did not believe in democratic methods and had never practiced them. In addition, as was also the case in several other Latin American countries, the process of convening the elections was undertaken by the military itself; these were the very same forces prosecuting the war and responsible for massive human rights violations.

A final contradiction concerns the imbalance between the parties to the negotiations, whether measured in terms of political weight or capacity to fulfill commitments. The peace accords included matters of substance and different commitments for each side to fulfill, but the ability to sign the accords was not equivalent to the capacity to carry them out. No social movement arose to demand that the state fulfill its commitments; and the other party to the negotiations, the guerrillas, did not have the political strength to exert pressure. These contradictions have limited both peace and democracy in Guatemala.

A Cursed Legacy: The Terrorist State

A militarized state is part of the Guatemalan political tradition, but until 1963 it was expressed through the power of a personalistic caudillo, not through institutionalized military control. All this changed when the 1944 October Revolution initiated by President Juan José Arévalo ended with the overthrow of President Jacobo Arbenz in 1954. Faced with the likely electoral victory and return of former president Arévalo in 1963, military power became more formal and institutionalized. On March 30, 1963, a group of senior officers carried out a coup d'état to remove General Manuel

Ydígoras Fuentes and replaced him with Colonel Enrique Peralta Azurdia.[5] This institutional response by the armed forces represented the first coup carried out in Latin America that was not in response to the threat of guerrilla insurgency but rather out of fear of potentially losing a free and competitive election.

From 1963 on, the Guatemalan state could be characterized as counterinsurgent in function and terrorist in nature. In the authoritarian national tradition, this development continued a historic trend of relying on structures of violence to maintain social order. Authoritarian rule began during the Spanish colonial period, continued after the declaration of independence in 1821, was strengthened by the Liberal Revolution of 1871, and continued throughout the twentieth century. Beginning in 1963, the military as an institution was at the core of the state and exercised almost total power. It was able to rely on material resources, technical assistance, and political support from the United States—all of which made possible the modernization of methods of violence and terror. The state's practice of terror was widespread, manifest in an excess of cruelty in killing the enemy and in the mass murder of innocent civilians not involved in the conflict.

The logic of counterinsurgency had several components. The enemy was seen as having infiltrated all levels of society, thereby creating a "vertical" danger from top to bottom. The enemy was located in three concentric circles: in the first circle were active militants, called "subversives"; in the second circle were those suspected of involvement; and in the much larger, outside circle were "innocent" civilians, those who, by not actively supporting the army, were considered to be against it. Terror was created by killing people in all three of these circles. As one North American analyst put it: "If a bridge is destroyed [by the guerrillas], all of the people from the surrounding villages must be rounded up and some of them must be executed."[6] This broad definition of the enemy was a primary trait of state terrorism. In later years, General Héctor Gramajo, defense minister from 1987 to 1990, proposed that a "30/70 formula" be used—a strategy of killing 30 percent of the people in order to "save" 70 percent.

The initial appearance of the guerrillas in the years 1964–66 and their resurgence in 1980–83 served as rationale and justification for the counterinsurgent state, helped to perfect the instrumentality of state terrorism, and contributed to the marginalization of the judicial system. The ubiquity of force was even more acute given that Guatemala was a society characterized by high degrees of ethnic, class, and gender inequality. The existing levels of exclusion and inequality were exploited by the military, explaining not only how state terror was possible, but also how it could last as long as it did. State terror reached its peak between 1980 and 1983 and had a strong anti-ethnic tenor; 600 indigenous villages were destroyed and about 60,000 indigenous Guatemalans were murdered (81 percent of the total deaths during that period).[7]

The construction of the terrorist state was made possible in part by the United States, which channeled administrative, political, financial, and human resources toward helping the Guatemalan armed forces develop the ability to carry out a dirty war. It was also made possible through the collaboration of major political and civilian groups, such as the far-right Movimiento de Liberación Nacional (National Liberation Movement) and the Partido Institucional Democrático (Institutional Democratic Party), in addition to businessmen, journalists, and anticommunist intellectuals. The state apparatus had a threefold purpose: to wipe out the guerrillas, to end political and civil society opposition, and to destroy the social base of the insurgency. The practice of state terrorism actively undermined the administration of justice. This undermining did not mean substituting military for civilian jurisdiction, but rather the refusal of the military to consider as crimes the kinds of actions carried out by agents of the state in the course of counterinsurgency. Indeed, state agents could act with impunity, and the illegal acts they committed usually remained unpunished. It is no coincidence that in all the years of the counterinsurgency war, there were no political prisoners, because anyone considered a suspect was killed rather than imprisoned. Nor was there a system of habeas corpus or any other form of protection. During the war, no member of the military was ever criminally prosecuted for a human rights crime, either by a civilian or military court.

This impunity was justified by the nature of the enemy that the state defined in ideological terms. To confront the forces of evil, any action was acceptable—these would not be considered crimes, but rather punishments. This view had a dual psychological effect on the agents of repression. Soldiers believed that their acts of cruelty furthered a heroic mission and were thus morally acceptable. Their violent acts were a duty to protect their country, while, pari passu, the enemy became a dehumanized abomination—something to be destroyed at all costs.[8] The dynamics of terror struck society at all levels. The counterinsurgent state was based on the "trivialization of terror," whereby citizens became insensitive to the pain of others or achieved the capacity to accept the worst crimes without protest. The state was thus guaranteed society's immobility, complicity, and silence. Three military rulers during the 1970s–Carlos Arana, Kjell Laugerud, and Romeo

Lucas—implemented this counterinsurgent strategy, and Lucas took it to an extreme bordering on genocide. One cannot overstate the extent to which state terrorism has had long-lasting effects on society as a whole. The damage it caused lives on for tens of thousands of individuals harmed by the violence.

The Two Stages of the Democratic Transition

In the years 1981–83, a crisis arose within the military leadership. This was due to tactical disagreements over the direction of the war, power struggles, a reaction to corruption among high-ranking officers who were linked to organized crime, and the discrediting and international isolation of the government of General Romeo Lucas. The crisis was manifest in successive coups d'état that finally brought General Efraín Ríos Montt to power on March 24, 1982, followed by General Oscar Mejía Víctores on August 9, 1983. The latter attempted to institutionalize the counterinsurgency effort by implementing the National Security and Development Plan in 1984 and drafting preliminary plans for a National System of Inter-Institutional Coordination for Reconstruction and Development.[9]

The military elite was in crisis, but it was still alert to conditions that would work against its future hold on power. The military leadership decided to turn the government over to civilians while retaining control over military issues. In Guatemala, "democratic transition" is a term used to describe a political space and a moment in which institutions were established that allowed for the holding of democratic elections. Those institutions, in turn, made possible a cautious exercise of political and some civil rights—freedom of expression and organization, free and autonomous political participation, access to justice—with a modicum of security and respect for the right to life. This first stage of the transition has also been described as the "authoritarian transition to democracy"; this term captures the complex interplay between a simultaneous state of armed conflict and the holding of elections without fraud. The terrorist power of the state was still present, even when formal power was in the hands of civilian regimes, leading to the coining of the phrase the "dead of the transition."[10]

The road to the transition began with a call for the appointment of a Constituent Assembly, initiated in 1984 by the Mejía Victores administration, and followed in 1985 by presidential elections. Vinicio Cerezo of the Christian Democratic Party was elected and served from January 1986 to

January 1991. Cerezo was followed by President Jorge Serrano, who held office from January 1991 to May 1993. Serrano instigated an *autogolpe*, or self-coup, in May 1993, nearly causing a breakdown of the constitutional order. This crisis was solved peacefully when the National Congress chose Ramiro de León, then the country's human rights ombudsman, to finish out Serrano's term in office. De León served from May 1993 until January 1996, and was followed by Alvaro Arzú, who took office in January 1996.

The elections during this period were free of fraud, and the decade they spanned witnessed both electoral democracy and ongoing armed conflict. It was during this decade that peace negotiations between the Guatemalan government and the guerrillas began, even as the economy stagnated and poverty increased. This period of electoral democracy coupled with worsening socioeconomic conditions gave rise to incipient popular organizations, especially among indigenous Guatemalans.

The signing of the peace accords at the end of 1996, during the Arzú administration, marked the beginning of the democratic transition's second phase. This period was marked not only by the absence of armed conflict but also by four peaceful transfers of power in the executive branch from one democratically elected leader to another; first with the inauguration of Alfonso Portillo in January 2000, followed by that of Oscar Berger in January 2004, Álvaro Colom in January 2008, and Otto Pérez Molina in 2012. During this second stage of the transition, the rules of the democratic game laid out in the Constitution of 1985 and other legislation have been followed, and those who have failed to respect the rules have been ejected from the game. But this observation should be tempered with the caveat that political parties may have only respected the rules of play because of historic problems of institutional weakness. Electoral democracy during this period has not been built upon a solid and permanent system of political parties. The weakness of parties has been especially visible on the left; but those on the right have also been unable to build a national party structure.[11]

There are many differences between the first and second stages of the transition to democracy, but two should be highlighted. In the second phase and to the benefit of civilian power, the military lost its ability to autonomously carry out illegitimate violence, and various aspects of the terrorist state were slowly dismantled. As the democratic transitions scholar Juan Linz has indicated, a monopoly on the use of force without civilian control detracts from the legitimacy of the democratic process; the decision to use violence cannot be made without consultation with or authorization from the civilian political authorities.[12] And this much was achieved in Guatemala. Another key difference in the second stage has been the increased respect for human rights, along with greater indigenous participation in politics. Political development is not achieved solely by holding elections, but rather by broadening the public sphere to include a more pluralistic group of actors. Elections have drawn more groups in, with the natural result of shifting alliances and competition among political parties and other political players.

During the second phase of the transition, the electoral process has become the primary mechanism of identification for social actors and interests. But democracy has also begun to experience problems related to its authoritarian heritage, the armed conflict, and the persistence of an unjust socioeconomic structure. The new climate of freedoms has benefited primarily upper-class groups and, to a certain extent, those of the middle class. Paradoxically, the popular movements that were very active in the first stage have not been able to regroup during this period. The labor movement has practically disappeared; and university students have become depoliticized. The newly created Movimiento Sindical Indigena y Campesino (Indigenous and Peasant Farmer Labor Movement) had sixteen of its leaders murdered in 2009 alone.[13] In the 1990s, a self-described Mayan indigenous movement emerged, but it then divided and ceased functioning. Nongovernmental organizations (NGOs) have also been formed to defend social, ethnic, and gender rights. They have been very active, but their offices and members have been hard-hit by anonymous and clandestine criminal groups.

Despite some of these advances, institutional features and behaviors from the counterinsurgency period have persisted. Just as counterinsurgent power arose before the insurgency, it survived the insurgency's end. It was so deeply rooted in society and in the structure of the state that its exercise has not disappeared entirely, even twenty-five years after the beginning of democratic rule and more than fifteen years after the signing of the peace accords. Examples of this persistence are the fact that the intelligence services are still in the hands of the military,[14] and the dozens of anonymous nighttime break-ins into the offices of popular organizations and human rights groups.

This assessment of the second stage of democratization would not complete without a discussion of municipal governments, which have become increasingly important in defining national politics. Local and regional power has gradually gained independence from the political center in Guatemala City, and the organization that has occurred in about 100

municipalities (of a total of 324) has determined the outcome in a significant number of district congressional elections. This kind of regional power
was decisive in the election of President Álvaro Colom in 2007. The second
phase of democratization has also demonstrated the weakness of the Guatemalan state in controlling surging rates of common crime, particularly in
urban areas, and in preventing the expansion of organized crime in different
parts of the national territory.

Challenges in Postwar Guatemala

This section analyzes the first fifteen years of the postwar period, which
saw the peaceful transfer of power in three general elections.[15] This review
of these years of peace focuses in particular on the success of two elements:
the quality of power exercised by the governments, and the growth in citizen participation. It is these filters that allow us to qualify the nature of
democratic governance in Guatemala. How well has the Guatemalan state
complied with the peace accords, including the dismantling of the counterinsurgent state? And how much has the strengthening of the state been supported by an expansion of citizenship or the construction of a social base, a
polis, that gives democracy its meaning?

Elections

Elections have been a consistent bright spot in any analysis of the Guatemalan transition to democracy. The first three elections, beginning in
1985, took place as part of the counterinsurgency strategy, but the subsequent three took place in the context of ideological pluralism and included
a political party linked to the former guerrilla organization, the Guatemalan National Revolutionary Unity (Unidad Revolucionaria Nacional
Guatemalteca, URNG). The first three elections, for the most part, were
exercises in rather limited democracy. They were held in a highly charged
atmosphere, where the major players defined themselves along very narrow
political and ideological lines with little to no serious debate. Presidential
elections follow a system where the winner must gain an absolute majority of 50 percent or more of the vote. A second round is held when the
necessary majority is not reached. For the unicameral National Congress,
however, there are two different systems. Twenty percent of the representatives are chosen at a national level, elected by a simple majority, but the

remaining representatives are elected in local districts following the system of proportional representation laid out in the D'Hondt method, which uses a mathematical formula to allocate seats on the basis of party, not individual vote totals.

The first postauthoritarian elections in 1985 and the subsequent elections in 1990, 1995, and 1999 served as an opportunity to establish political-ideological identities; their purpose was to begin to establish sufficient guarantees for democratic competition and consolidation. These initial elections were certainly decisive; they had a stabilizing effect in that they favored the extension of citizenship, but they were limited by the lack of a full range of ideological options for voters. By contrast, by 2003 and 2007 things had changed; the presidential candidates came into the election with defined ideological profiles, and the rules of the electoral game were widely acknowledged and accepted. Elections in Guatemala have become increasingly competitive, free, and inclusive. Over time, there have been greater numbers of political actors pursuing their political interests. They seem convinced of the benefits of electoral competition and of accepting losses in the electoral sphere. There is tacit acceptance of a key tenet of democracy—that the only path to governing the country is to win an election.

Nevertheless, despite the involvement of a large number of different parties, elections have not brought a pluralism that serves to outline ideological or programmatic differences. The contests have been to some extent boring, with few real choices and undifferentiated marketing. Candidates are distinguished by their personal histories, and known for their personalities and media appeal rather than their politics. Most of the rivalries are among right-wing parties and conservative interests. Various leaders of the right have demonstrated little capacity to steer the country in a good direction and have demonstrated a lackluster performance in office. Indeed, some of their best moments have been reflected in simple matters of administration.

At the other end of the ideological spectrum there has also been division since the outset of the democratic transition, which has continued during the postconflict period. The leftist New Guatemala Democratic Front (Frentre Democrático Nueva Guatemala, FDNG), formed in 1995 before the signing of the peace accords, disappeared from the electoral scenario and has been replaced over the years by other parties formed by former members of the FDNG, namely, the New Nation Alliance (Alianza Nueva Nación, which ceased to exist in 2008),[16] and the Encounter for Guatemala (Encuentro por Guatemala), led by Nineth Montenegro. The former guerrilla party, the URNG, has also suffered divisions, the most important of which took place in 1999 when the Rebel Armed Forces (Fuerzas Armadas Rebeldes, FAR) split off from the URNG. The political left should have been strengthened by the evolution of the URNG into a political party, which presented a program inspired by prudence but which had very little popular support. For now, it appears that a triumph of leftist forces is impossible, even when united.[17] Thus far, Guatemalan democracy has not seen a true test of its pluralist capacity, except for the victory of the center-left in 2007. In these latter elections, Álvaro Colom of National Unity for Hope (Unidad Nacional de la Esperanza) was elected. Colom described himself as a social democrat, although it was not clear if everyone in his party shared this ideology.

At some point in the future, the process of democratization may need to be tested in the face of confrontation, for example, the case of electoral victory of more radical leftist parties and the reaction to such a victory from the more dominant and conservative groups.

Another element that diminished the legitimacy of the democratically elected governments in the postwar period is the low level of voter turnout in elections. In Guatemala, voting used to be mandatory, although no one was ever punished for not voting. The 1985 Constitution changed voting to a civic right for all potential voters. In Guatemala, participation is usually measured by the ratio between the total number of citizens who actually vote and the number entered in the Electoral Registry; this is known as secondary participation and reflects a larger percentage of voters. But primary participation takes into account the total number of citizens eligible to vote, consisting of all men and women over eighteen years of age. Measured in terms of primary participation, no more than half of eligible Guatemalan citizens have ever voted in any given election. This highlights a key issue: the total population that has the right to vote is greater than the total numbers enrolled in the Electoral Registry. Once a person has registered, their tendency to vote is higher.

Secondary participation (i.e., those registered to vote) in the first democratic election in 1985 was 69.3 percent, followed by 56.4 percent in 1990. In 1995, the total fell to 46.8 percent, but rose to 53.8 percent in 1999, 58.3 percent in 2003, and 60.4 percent in the 2007 elections. Explanations for the relatively low rates of primary participation include a history of electoral fraud, pervasive fear throughout the interior of the country, and extreme poverty, all of which work against greater interest in public affairs. Finally, one should stress that electoral participation is lower among women and younger voters, whereas those in urban areas vote in greater numbers than those in rural parts of the country.[18] However, reforms to the Electoral Law that decentralized voting stations helped achieve more participation in rural areas in 2007.

Understanding electoral democracy in Guatemala requires considering the indigenous population, whose political and social presence has grown despite their underprivileged living conditions. Poverty and low levels of income signify low levels of education, high rates of disease, the lack of personal protection, and abysmal housing conditions—that is to say, an existence devoid of dignity or future. In several of the recent national elections, indigenous voter turnout has been equivalent to that of nonindigenous citizens. At one point fully one-third of the mayors elected in the country were Mayan, and the few social movements that have arisen in recent years are ethnic in orientation. For many, the issue of citizenship for the indigenous population is based on dual identities—ethnic and national—which are presumed to be compatible. The idea is to construct a racial democracy in which indigenous and mestizo citizens have equal rights to political participation as well as equal rights to be elected to public office.

There have been several attempts to create indigenous political parties, but none has been successful. The last effort occurred in the 2007 elections, when the Nobel laureate Rigoberta Menchú ran for the presidency with the support of her political group, Winaq, in alliance with the leftist party, Encounter for Guatemala (Encuentro por Guatemala). Menchú won 3.5 percent of the total votes.

In Guatemala political parties, one of the most important institutions of an electoral democracy, have failed to become institutions for representing, mediating, and structuring citizens' interests. Party formation was weak to begin with, and parties are built around cults of personality that lead to caudillo-style politics. In addition, electioneering as an end in itself rather than as a means to an end has led to rank opportunism and a blurring of lines between the public and private spheres. Many parties are managed as if they were private property, feeding clientelistic tendencies. For these reasons and others, politicians and parties in general are discredited, a state of affairs not uncommon in many countries of Latin America. Nonetheless, confidence in political parties in Guatemala is far below the average in the region.[19]

The weakness of the political party system is demonstrated by the excessive number of parties rather than by their absence. Given that democracy itself in Guatemala is focused almost exclusively on elections rather than governance, political parties are built to be vote-gathering machines and nothing more. They come to life every four years when there is an election.

Thus far, parties have failed to live up to expectations once a candidate reaches office. They are limited in efficacy, and in many cases serve as a cover for corrupt officials. This leads to the discrediting of parties and impedes the possibility that certain public policies, particularly social policies that can only succeed over the medium term, can continue. In other words, the party that occupies the government leaves office with its electoral strength greatly diminished.

The problems of governance appear in the legislature as well as in the executive branch. Parties in Guatemala do not have strong political-ideological identities or a national presence. A harmful effect of this is great partisan fragmentation. In the 2003–6 Congress, for example, 43 representatives out of a total 154 had switched parties, and many of them more than once. The lack of party loyalty is even greater at the municipal level, where mayors hop from one party to another to ensure their own reelection.[20]

In light of these factors, it is important to note the work of the Permanent Forum of Political Parties. Since 2002, it has developed programs to strengthen the party system, endow the electoral process with ethics rules, repair the reputation of politics itself, and create a public space for political dialogue. In October 2003, twenty-one political parties unanimously approved the Shared National Agenda, which represented a multiparty effort to construct a Guatemala for the twenty-first century. Its many recommendations included support for the peace accords, reform of the electoral and party systems, completing the demobilization of the Presidential General Staff (Estado Mayor Presidencial),[21] reactivating the Fiscal Pact, and meeting other goals related to the indigenous population. The success of this group and its proposals, however, has been limited given that the representatives of the political parties in this Permanent Forum have little impact on the actual decisions of the parties.

Political Institutions

In general, the democratic institutions created under the political Constitution of 1985 have functioned with varying degrees of quality and relevance. For example, the Supreme Electoral Tribunal and the Human Rights Ombudsman enjoy great prestige, while the Constitutional Court and the Attorney General's Office were not as well regarded, in part because their creation and functioning were highly politicized. An analysis of institutional development would not be complete without reference to the legislative and judicial branches. Have their actions contributed to the consolidation of the democracy? In the postwar period, the performance of the legislative branch has been largely uneven. The national legislature has essentially three functions: to enact laws, to elect judges to the upper levels of the judicial system, and to supervise and control the executive branch and decentralized institutions. The record in fulfilling these objectives is mixed; and the legislative branch is, in fact, an accurate reflection of the dysfunctional nature of the political parties. The legislature produces few laws, suffers from an excess of politicking when electing judges, and has a strained relationship with the executive branch. This was particularly evident during the Portillo and Berger administrations, which did not enjoy a majority in Congress. The fractionalization of Congress makes for a political situation characterized as "ungovernability from above."[22] There are some signs of a learning process leading toward greater institutionalization. However, the behavior of opposition parties shows that the democratic system is still weak. These parties systematically oppose the government even on issues of vital national interest. Examples include the approval of the government budget in 2009 and proposals in 2010 to extend loans to help victims of national disasters.

The judicial branch was the most adversely affected by the era of the terrorist state. Indeed, it lost its independence vis-à-vis military power and did not carry out its functions with respect to criminal jurisdiction. The judiciary as a whole has been a focus of attention for the international community; buildings have been built, and judges and other officials have been certified or trained. The Attorney General's Office has been modernized in technical terms, and the National Civilian Police force has been created.[23] Today there are justices of the peace in all the departmental capitals. However, the judicial system as a whole appears to suffer from a structural incapacity to absorb the various efforts at modernization, such that it is incapable of imparting prompt, free, and effective justice.

Although all of Guatemalan society suffered the negative effects of the counterinsurgency state, one state institution that was in fact under military control was the judiciary.[24] That has resulted in a double deficit. There is a lack of independence among judges from this period who were placed on the bench for clearly political reasons; and there is rampant mediocrity and professional incompetence. Even worse, during the current crime wave, the judiciary has been complicit with organized crime groups, and the sizable resources from the illegal narcotics trade has been used to corrupt the courts. As noted in chapter 12, one of the principal tasks of the United Nations International Commission Against Impunity in Guatemala (Comisión

Internacional Contra la Impunidad en Guatemala, CICIG) has been to lend assistance to the judiciary to confront the problem of parallel structures within the government linked to organized crime. With the advent of electoral democracy, the intractability of a "syndrome of backwardness" poses an ongoing obstacle to the modernization of the judicial system.[25] The naming of respected criminal law specialist Claudia Paz y Paz as attorney general in December 2010 represented an important step forward in this regard.

Civil Society

"Civil society" is defined here as a place of association, independent of the state, where people come together to make demands of and influence public life. Civil society in Guatemala has not grown at the same pace as democracy. Popular social organizations lost importance in the aftermath of the peace accords as compared with the period that preceded their signing. They have been replaced in part by NGOs, which have grown in number, activities, and influence. It seems counterintuitive, but during the first two civilian administrations, when repression was still very much present, groups such as the Mutual Support Group (Grupo de Apoyo Mutuo), the National Coordination of Guatemalan Widows (Coordinadora Nacional de Viudas de Guatemala), and social movements with growing ethnic awareness were created.[26] In those years, active organizations included the Mayan Defender's Office (Defensoría Maya), the Office of the National Indigenous and Peasant Coordinator (Coordinadora Nacional Indígena Campesina, CONIC), and the Runujel Junam Council of Ethnic Communities. In the years before the signing of a peace treaty, these organizations suffered under the legacy of state terrorism, tenuous guarantees for human rights, and the fragility of the rule of law.

The years of the peace negotiations witnessed the creation of the Civil Society Assembly (Asamblea de la Sociedad Civil, ASC), based on one of the recommendations of the original Framework Agreement of January 1994. The ASC was made up of representatives of the academic and popular sectors, and excluded the private sector and the political parties. The ASC worked closely with the peace negotiators and made concrete proposals for the accords, including, for example, the draft agreements relating to the identity and rights of indigenous peoples. However, for all its actions, the ASC suffered from internal conflicts and ceased functioning in 1996.

In subsequent years, other organizations survived yet with diminished strength, but others have emerged. Some social movements function in the electoral scenario. But they lack the organic connections to a base and the convening power demanded both by the dramatic levels of poverty present in the country and by employer-led assaults against worker's rights— assaults condoned by Guatemala's conservative democracy. Important actions advocating better wages or control of land have been undertaken by the Social Organizations Collective (Colectivo de Organizaciones Sociales); the Popular Labor, Peasant, and Indigenous Movement (Movimiento Indígena, Campesino, Sindical y Popular); the teachers' front; and the campesino mobilizations led by CONIC. The claim for land ownership is the greatest source of social unrest. It is deplorable that more than half a century after President Arbenz began his agrarian reform project in 1954, issues of ownership and access to land remain unresolved.

Beyond popular social movements per se, what have emerged in recent years are umbrella organizations that have gathered a variety of social groups of different nature and ideology, including NGOs, think tanks, Mayan organizations, private-sector organizations, religious organizations, universities, and human rights groups. One of the most relevant ones is the so-called Citizen Convocation (Convocatoria Ciudadana), which gathers fifty organizations. This group has made its mark in pressuring for transparency in the selection of public officials, particularly those linked to the judicial sector (e.g., Supreme Court magistrates and the attorney general). There are other similar organizations such as Foro Guatemala and Pro Justicia. The emergence of these groups stems from a concern with the high levels of violence and the corruption in the judicial system.[27]

The State and the Rule of Law

To understand democracy in a broader perspective, one must bear in mind not just the act of voting but also what takes place between elections. Indeed, it is during the period between elections that democratic life is put to the test. Opportunities arise to put into practice the exercise of civic, social, and economic rights; to organize into interest groups; to make demands; and to interact (sometimes in conflict). Yet Guatemala has experienced a growing wave of criminal violence, which has made a mockery of the basic civic right to security. Respect for the values of liberty, tolerance, and social participation is diminished by the widespread fear of crime among Guatemalans, particularly in urban areas. Human rights violations persist, although they are not as severe as in the past. For the most part, they are ascribed to the poor performance of the National Civilian Police or attributed to the actions of individuals.[28]

Freedom of the press and expression does exist, although it has not been institutionalized as an integral element of public debate. However, neither the political parties nor civil society organizations enrich public opinion. Rather, the political agenda is set by the communications media, and print media in particular. The Guatemalan press is not at all pluralistic in its views, and the print media is owned by and advances the interests of big business. During the years of military dictatorships, it practiced self-censorship, and it has now become prone to sensationalism. What does this mean? The press does not impartially report political news, but it describes and passes judgment on issues in highly politicized ways.

Despite this gloomy outlook, freedom of belief and opinion does exist. The country has witnessed a significant growth in the number and quality of publications reflecting a greater diversity of views. In 2004, for example, it was estimated that the country published more than one book per day.[29] There are more journals and magazines as well as an intense level of political-intellectual activity, which is reflected in seminars, lectures, and other cultural gatherings that have seen a large public turnout. Even in the print media, opinion editorials represent a wide range of ideologies.

A democratic state is expected to be able to carry out two basic functions: the maintenance of order to assure citizens' security; and the guarantee of a minimum of social justice. It is precisely in these areas that the Guatemalan state has been the weakest in the postwar period. The state has been impotent in the face of a wave of crime and violence, and more people are victims of crime now than during most years of the war. In 1996, the year the peace accords were signed, the homicide rate in Guatemala was 40 per 100,000 persons; by 2009, that figure had jumped to 49 per 100,000, double the annual average during the years of the armed conflict and almost double the rate in the rest of Latin America. The number of stolen vehicles rose from 5,411 per year in 1996, to 8,764 in 2008, and reported crimes of all kinds (*delitos*) soared from 20,314 in 1996 to 30,857 in 2006, a jump of 51.9 percent in only a decade. As noted by the United Nations Development Program in its *National Human Development Report* for 2010, Guatemala is wracked by a new kind of conflict, against "criminal mafias in open defiance of the state."[30]

In addition, the government has shown both a lack of political will and a technical inability to implement programs to reduce the poverty and inequality that serve to foster criminal activity. It is true that inequalities are inherent in the current system, and it is impossible to entirely vanquish poverty, but the limited will to bring about actual change is signaled by the stagnation of spending on programs to support social or childhood services, although the Colom administration increased these programs significantly. The 2010 *National Human Development Report* summarized the situation well:

> Almost 25 years after the return to democracy—after the transition from a developmental state to a subsidiary state, after the signature of the Peace Accords that opened opportunities for the development of a state that would promote equality in a largely unequal society in which indigenous people had been historically excluded—the incidence of poverty has been reduced only slightly and inequalities have not diminished enough.[31]

Various social indicators illustrate the continuing disparities that exist in Guatemala, in spite of the advances in recent years. Overall, Guatemala's Human Development Index (HDI) has improved, rising from 0.451 in 1990 to 0.514 in 2000 and to 0.560 in 2010.[32] The *National Human Development Report* breaks down the index, showing that over the years the improvement has occurred across the board, among both high and low socioeconomic strata, in urban and in rural areas, and among nonindigenous and indigenous Guatemalans. However, the gap is still very large between urban and rural areas, between nonindigenous and indigenous people, and, particularly, between high socioeconomic strata and low socioeconomic strata. For instance, in 2010 there was a 12-point gap between the nonindigenous and the indigenous populations. In addition, the HDI for the high-income stratum was 0.90, well above the average for Latin America and close to that of developed countries, whereas the HDI for the lower income stratum was 0.52, comparable to that of Sub-Saharan Africa.[33]

With regard to poverty, various indicators demonstrate that the change was scant between 1989 and 2006. Again using data from the *National Human Development Report,* if one measures poverty as family consumption per capita, there was a reduction of 8 percentage points in overall poverty in that period. In relative terms, 62.8 percent of Guatemalans lived in poverty in 1989, a number that diminished to 50.9 percent by 2006. But in absolute terms, the number of poor people increased from 5.4 million in 1989 to 6.6 million in 2006. Extreme poverty, in addition, only diminished from 18.1 percent to 15.2 percent in the same period.[34]

National Reconciliation on Hold

Progress on what has generically been called national reconciliation has not been sufficient. Two important landmarks were the publication by the Catholic Church of the four volumes of *Guatemala: Nunca Más* (Guatemala: Never Again) in 1998; and the publication of the fourteen volumes of *Guatemala: Memoria del Silencio* (Guatemala: Memories of Silence) by the United Nations Historical Clarification Commission in 1999, as mandated by the peace accords. Both of these documents brought to light the tens of thousands of crimes committed against indigenous people and almost entirely by the army, and they have provided an opportunity for individual claims to seek redress. The National Reconciliation and Reparations Commission (Comisión Nacional de Reconciliación y Resarcimiento) was finally able to obtain funding and since 2003 has provided assistance to victims and their family members. The Forensic Anthropology Foundation, which began its work in 1992, has also made an extraordinary contribution to uncovering the truth about massacres committed during the war. As described in chapter 12, forensic teams have participated in more than 400 exhumations, which have permitted families to identify and rebury victims.

To date, few people have dared to make formal accusations due to the lack of will to bring those responsible for the atrocities to justice. A state that fails to punish criminals from previous regimes becomes indirectly complicit in those crimes. Criminals from within the military are rarely charged with a crime, and when they are, they are usually soldiers from the lower ranks. In the case of the murder of the anthropologist Myrna Mack, Noel de Jesús Beteta (no military rank) is under arrest, Captain Juan Valencia Osorio has been sentenced but is a fugitive from justice, and Colonel Guillermo Oliva and General Edgar Godoy were acquitted. And one cannot forget the case of the murder of Monsignor Juan Gerardi, director of the Catholic Church's research project on crimes committed during the civil war. His death on April 18, 1998, occurred forty-eight hours after the four volumes of the report *Guatemala: Nunca Más* were published. The intellectual and material authors of the crime have not been identified, but several accomplices were prosecuted; one of those detained was killed during a prison riot. Though the coconspirators remain at large, four men were convicted of the crime: Colonel Byron Lima; his father, Captain Byron Lima; Obdulio Villanueva, who was killed in prison; and Mario Orantes. Finally, in the case of the 1982 Dos Erres massacre, sixteen military officers were charged, including the generals Humberto Mejía Víctores, Efraín Ríos Montt, and Benedicto Lucas, along with Colonel Arévalo Lacs, commander of the Kaibiles School. In August 2011, four soldiers of the Kaibiles special forces unit, including a lieutenant, were convicted and sentenced to life in prison for their roles in the massacre, which the court deemed a crime against humanity.

In the opinion of an expert from the United Nations Verification Mission in Guatemala (known as MINUGUA), the main deficit of the justice system is a lack of human resources.[35] Numerous reform projects were designed, but for the most part they have produced only minor results. Despite the importance of some of these changes, the public does not believe that the administration of justice in the country has improved.[36] The justice system is the Achilles' heel of Guatemalan democracy.

The Peace Accords in Retrospect

With respect to the peace accords, the subjective dimension of politics, the trust in the accords themselves, and the satisfaction with their outcome have been assessed at length. However, the objective dimension—the extent to which the accords led to the reconstruction of the institutions of a democratic state and the dismantling of the military's structures of repression and terror—has been given less consideration. These are two aspects of a new reality that must be analyzed in reviewing what has been achieved in the years since the end of the internal armed conflict. Many make the mistake of thinking that the process of institutional change began and ended with the signing of the peace accords. Although the accords undoubtedly marked a turning point, it is still too early to understand their full significance for the process of institutional reform.

The material, cultural, and ideological influence of international forces in favor of democratic consolidation around the world has been visible in Guatemala throughout the postconflict period. The UN verification mission known as MINUGUA was a powerful actor in supervising and monitoring compliance with the peace accords. It marshaled the power and backing of the United Nations mostly to prevent backsliding rather than to promote advances. Another face of the international community was the Consultative Group, made up of representatives from donor countries that took into consideration reports by the Guatemalan government and tied continued aid to advances in democratization.[37]

By dint of repetition in certain political and social circles, the notion that there was a causal and reciprocal relationship between compliance with the peace accords and democratic consolidation has been accepted as gospel. Thus, there is a belief that when there is a violation of the peace accords, democratization collapses and progress stops. However, just as respect for the right to life is not dependent on the penal code, the fate of democracy is not necessarily wedded to the accords. The accords form a diverse group of proposals, objectives, and measures at various levels of implementation that without a doubt provide programmatic support for the construction of democracy. Unfortunately, the accords were never widely known or understood by the population; they have not become a part of popular culture, nor did social forces adopt them as their own. In other words—and taking this reasoning to its extreme—the democratization efforts could continue even if the accords did not exist. The efforts at social transformation were not dependent on the peace accords, which failed to generate sufficient political or social tension. Although peace negotiations allowed the parties to define certain aspects of democratization in Guatemala, democratic development in this era of globalization is part of a worldwide movement. Many countries in Latin America do not have peace agreements yet are undergoing processes of democratization. The so-called geography of democracy is expanding around the globe.

The accords have been mythologized by those who build legends out of reality. That said, they form part of a political discourse and rhetoric that is useful in certain settings. At some point, the effort to construct democracy will have to weather certain kinds of confrontation—for example, the kind that would be generated by an electoral victory of forces of the left. This would be a test for the dominant forces in society.

The accords contained three types of recommendations or policies:

- *Operative recommendations:* These recommendations were aimed at making the more substantive elements of the accords viable; some of them were implemented immediately and with greater ease. In this category are the cease-fire; the demobilization and reincorporation of the URNG into civilian life; the demobilization of military as well as paramilitary forces; the official time line for accord implementation; and, especially, reform of the Constitution in twelve areas related to indigenous rights, the role of the army, and the judicial and electoral systems.
- *Technical recommendations:* These recommendations were more complex, and thus needed to be carried out over a longer period of time,

and for which implementation depended on the political will of the government, the political parties, and other relevant actors. These measures included the creation of the Historical Clarification Commission (Comisión de Esclarecimiento Histórico), the creation of the National Civilian Police, the dissolution of the Presidential General Staff, fiscal reform, and changes in the budgetary structure to boost social spending.

- *Proposals to change the nature of power:* This third group consisted less of recommendations, but, rather, proposals to change the fundamental nature of power relations in Guatemala. Examples of these accords are the Agreement on the Strengthening of Civilian Power and the Role of the Armed Forces in a Democratic Society and the Agreement on Identity and Rights of Indigenous Peoples, as well as certain provisions of the Agreement on Socio-Economic Aspects and the Agrarian Situation. The idea that these agreements could be implemented via long-term policies is an illusion. Successful implementation is not a question of time but, rather, of politics—of building powerful political support, multiparty alliances, and social forces strong enough to change the correlation of forces within the state and overcome the crises that this change could provoke. In other words, only a democratic state led and supported by popular forces can successfully implement the accords. The governments led by conservatives and even the center-left Colom administration were unable and unwilling to carry forth the peace accords' implementation. Ignoring this knot of contradictions precludes us from viewing history as a process of struggle, advances, and reversals; those who signed the accords are not the same forces that can carry forth their implementation. At the subjective level, one can recommend the building of a democratic system. At an objective level, however, the construction of democracy requires the effort of an entire generation.

A complete analysis of implementation in all three of the areas mentioned above is beyond the scope of this chapter, but a brief synopsis of the progress in key areas is important. With the exception of constitutional reform, most of the operative recommendations have been implemented successfully. The constitutional reform was supposed to take place within sixty days of the signing of the peace accords. But the referendum (*consulta popular*) to approve the reforms (along with others tacked on by political parties in Congress) was not carried out for almost two and a half years after the accords were signed. The reforms were rejected at the polls. The failure to pass the constitutional reforms was a major defeat of the accords' progressive intent and of the process of democratization under way.[38] Provisions had included electoral reforms to make voting in rural areas easier, the tightening of civilian control over the military, and the recognition of the multiethnic character of the nation and of customary law, among others. The defeat of the reforms constituted a victory for racism and for the oligarchic sectors of the country.

The implementation of provisions related to the demobilization of combatant forces, the return of refugees to their places of origin, the resettlement of the internally displaced population, and the incorporation of the URNG into the political life of the country has gone well. New bodies were created, including the Peace Secretariat (Secretaría de la Paz) and the Accompaniment Commission (Comisión de Acompañamiento), to help with specific peace-related tasks. Parity Commissions (Comisiones Paritarias) were established and included indigenous delegates, the first time the state institutionally recognized the existence of indigenous peoples and not just communities. Offices of indigenous affairs were established in a number of government ministries and entities, including the Supreme Court of Justice. A National Commission for the Peace Accords was formed, and laws were enacted covering such issues as decentralization, municipal codes, social development, indigenous languages, an end to ethnic discrimination, the civil service, the labor code, fiscal reform, and the creation of development councils. The most important of these laws was the August 12, 2005, Framework Law, which transformed the various aspects of the peace accords into commitments of the state.

New governmental institutions were established, including the Advisory Council on Security, the Secretariat for Strategic Analysis, the Presidential Secretariat for Administrative Affairs and Security, the Presidential Secretariat for Women, and the Presidential Commission against Discrimination and Racism. The government also launched a national program of compensation to assist victims of the conflict and, as noted above, established the Historical Clarification Commission, which published the extraordinary four-volume report *Guatemala: Memoria del Silencio.*

Some of the greatest setbacks concern the effort since 1996 to create a new National Civilian Police force. The force is poorly trained and inexperienced and compromised by military interference along with the infiltration of organized crime and drug traffickers.[39] Over time, the corruption of the National Civilian Police reached unimagined proportions. Between January and May 2010, for example, two chiefs of police were jailed, along with seven assistants, who were accused of robbing cocaine shipments and of participation in several murders. More than 100 police officers were named as accomplices. In February 2010, the minister of the interior was also accused and went into hiding.

As for the dismantling of the apparatus of state terrorism, it is important to emphasize that the state's repressive functions lost all justification with the signing of the peace accords and therefore diminished for political reasons. The army was reduced from 60,000 to 31,000 troops initially, and then to 16,500 in 2005; more than 100 officers went into retirement. At the end of 2003, civilians took over the Presidential General Staff, and the intelligence services were replaced and put under the control of the Ministry of the Interior (although a military unit continues to function there). The military budget has declined in relative terms. It was 1.5 percent of gross domestic product in 1990 and only 0.4 percent in 2004.[40] Because the army did not lose the war but committed massacres and acts of repression, it remains a fairly discredited institution, although public opinion polls demonstrate that it retains support among some segments of the population.

Overall, the army has lost political relevance; it is no longer a powerful actor in the decisionmaking process and its alliances are of little interest. That said, there are members of the military involved in organized crime alongside civilian mafias. There is talk of de facto along with "parallel," clandestine powers that have been linked to acts of violence against scores of human rights organizations and also to numerous murders of civil society activists. These acts remain in the shadows but raise suspicions about the persistence of counterinsurgency structures and practices. To fight crime, the administrations of Oscar Berger and Álvaro Colom used the army to combat crime, an internal security function in violation of the peace accords. Between 2005 and 2006, for example, some 8,000 former soldiers were added to the ranks of the National Civilian Police. The Ministry of Defense announced plans for further increases.[41]

Conclusion

Twenty-five years after the beginning of the transition from authoritarianism to democracy and more than fifteen years after the transition from war to peace, the future of Guatemala remains uncertain. Whereas democracy and peace have both stood the test of time, new and complex challenges make it difficult to predict the direction of the country in the years to come. The title of a scholarly article on Guatemala depicts the situation well:

"Guatemala on the Brink."[42] The hope that emerged in the aftermath of the signing of the peace accords in 1996 has largely dissipated and has been supplanted by fear, insecurity, and uncertainty. To be sure, there have been tangible advances and improvement vis-à-vis the Guatemala of the past; but new problems unforeseen at the end of the war have emerged in recent years, and these threaten to eclipse those positive developments.

It is not easy to summarize this interplay of light and shadow. On the positive side, important changes have taken place in society; 65 percent of Guatemalans have lived their lives under a democratic regime, and more than 40 percent have lived their lives without an internal armed conflict. There are both uses and abuses of the freedom to organize, freedom of expression, and freedom of religion. Learning how to live in a democracy is a slow process, and in Guatemala these lessons are lived above all at the local level, where both the good and the perverse features of democracy flourish. A strengthened civil society now has the political means to press the democratic state for needed improvements in the standard of living. A culture of dialogue exists. Recognition of the nation's multiethnic nature is a major step forward. Indigenous organizations, bilingual education, and the struggle against racism have gained legitimacy. And though impunity continues to be the norm, it is significant that a former president, three ministers of the interior, two police chiefs, dozens of midlevel officials, and at least 15,000 gang members have been jailed for their involvement in criminal acts. Moreover, in January 2012, a Guatemalan judge ordered Efraín Ríos Montt to stand trial on charges of genocide and crimes against humanity for the mass killings carried out during his rule in the early 1980s.

All in all, apart from the 1993 "self-coup" attempted by President Jorge Serrano and some short-lived attempts at destabilization, the democratic transition in Guatemala has not experienced any major setbacks; nor has the armed conflict resumed. But behind these apparent successes lie a myriad of unresolved, long-standing problems along with unforeseen new difficulties. On the economic side, the country has recovered from the global economic crisis of 2008–9 and the economy grew by almost 4 percent in 2010. Export agriculture in particular has shown great dynamism. However, prosperity has not been evenly distributed, something that is especially evident in rural Guatemala. On the political side, staggering levels of crime and violence have become the predominant concern for urban Guatemalans, even more so than during the armed conflict.

The limited success in bringing about widespread prosperity, the clear failure to curtail violence, and the expansion and penetration of state institutions by organized crime have several underlying sources, some of which are international and thus beyond the control of domestic actors.[43] Nonetheless, many analysts concur that the weakness of the Guatemalan state and its institutions is a major source of the problem.[44] Indeed, state weakness is the dominant characteristic of political life in Guatemala in the postwar period.

Any state should and must fulfill several basic functions; and at this point in history, the Guatemalan state is having trouble carrying out these functions.[45] Three of the most important functions are the maintenance of public order, the provision of means for cohesion and social integration, and the collection of fiscal revenues.[46] Among these functions, one stands out as a sine qua non: the maintenance of public order, which in a democratic state should be based on the rule of law. Maintaining public order involves not only providing for public security in the physical sense but also providing equal justice before the law.

In Guatemala, the incompetence of key state institutions has created gaps that are opportunistically filled by corrupt or criminal players, creating a broad sense of uncertainty and anxiety. The state's role in providing for social cohesion and integration has been impaired by numerous forms of structural inequality. In spite of meager improvements in social conditions, huge gaps persist in the standard of living, affecting in particular the indigenous population, women, and those who live in rural areas. Behind the state's incapacity to reduce these gaps is its weak capacity to collect taxes. In the postwar period, there have been several attempts—supported by the international community—to achieve a consensus on an increase in taxes. But different democratic administrations have been unable to forge agreement on the issue with the private sector, labor, and nongovernmental organizations. As a result, Scandinavian countries that provided generous assistance in the postwar period have suspended aid, and they may withdraw altogether unless there is progress in this area.

State weakness became especially manifest toward the end of the first decade of the twenty-first century, with devastating effects on democratic life. Some talk of a "failed state," and though it has not yet become that, its weakness has been augmented by many factors—neoliberal economic policies, which have transformed the state into a subsidiary power; the international economic crisis of 2008–9, which dealt a heavy blow to agricultural exports; the partial relocation of mafias and illegal drug businesses from Mexico to Guatemala; the immense social damage caused by three natural catastrophes, Hurricane Mitch in 1998, the drought of 2008, and Tropical Storm Agatha in 2010; and the growing threat of gangs, as hundreds of young deportees with criminal records become involved in drug trafficking.

Narco-trafficking linked to powerful foreign interests has corrupted state institutions, political parties, politicians, and members of the military and private sector, constituting a parallel structure of criminal power. The state has lost its monopoly on force, and public opinion polls carried out during the past five years have revealed the degree to which crime is perceived by the citizenry to constitute the greatest threat. Democracy is now threatened by new enemies. The road ahead is uncertain, and it is unclear how the current challenges can be overcome. Hopefully, Guatemalans will reject solutions that would take the country back to its authoritarian past, and instead will look for solutions that strengthen rather than undermine democracy.[47]

Notes

1. Between 1966 and 1970, there was a civilian president, Mario Méndez Montenegro. He was elected against the wishes of the army, which made him sign a pact surrendering part of his power to the armed forces. His Pyrrhic victory made his administration a continuation of the praetorian structure and was in fact a military government.

2. As background information to illustrate the anti-ethnic nature of the slaughter, Patrick Ball and his colleagues describe the ways that mass terror in western Guatemala was related to the class and ethnic position of the victims, including women and children. See Patrick Ball, Paul Kobrak, and Herbert F. Spirer, *Violencia institucional en Guatemala, 1960–1996: Una reflexión cuantitativa* (Washington, D.C.: American Association for the Advancement of Science and Centro Internacional para Investigaciones en Derechos Humanos, 1999), 102.

3. The subject of the counterinsurgent state and its "compatibility" with democratic processes has been discussed in various papers, e.g., by Edelberto Torres-Rivas and Gabriel Aguilera, *Del Autoritarismo a la Paz* (Guatemala City: Facultad Latinoamericana de Ciencias Sociales–Programa Guatemala, 1998), chap. 3.

4. The political scientist Dinorah Azpuru argues that the URNG's political strategy to garner international support and the dreadful international image of the Guatemalan military, together with the waning of the Cold War and the spread of the third wave of democratization, contributed to the political defeat of the Guatemalan government, in spite of its military victory. Dinorah Azpuru, "Peace and Democratization in Guatemala: Two Parallel Processes," in *Comparative Peace Processes in Latin America,* edited by Cynthia J. Arnson (Washington, D.C., and Stanford, Calif.: Woodrow Wilson Center Press and Stanford University Press, 1999), 97–125.

5. The military coup was not anti-Ydígoras but anti-Arévalo; it was actually part of the counterinsurgency, because it marked the beginning of the military governments in 1963.

6. Michael Calvert, "El patrón de la guerra de guerrillas," *Revista Militar de Guatemala,* October 1966, 45.

7. Comisión de Esclarecimiento Histórico, *Guatemala: Memoria del Silencio,* vols.1–12 (Guatemala City: Comisión de Esclarecimiento Histórico, 1999), table III, "Las violaciones de los Derechos Humanos y los hechos de violencia."

8. The repressive community has no capacity for self-censure, favors total obedience, and argues that discipline is a superior value. An extreme example is given by Hannah Arendt, *Eichmann en Jerusalem: Un estudio sobre la banalidad del mal* (Barcelona: Lumen, 2001). In Guatemala, I have been unable to document a single statement by a member of the military admitting guilt for the excesses committed.

9. The army developed a medium-term plan conceived to uphold its presence and influence in the democratic period; the Campaign Plan for Institutional Reencounter 1984 to guarantee the election time of the Constituent Assembly (July 1, 1984), followed by the National Stability Plan '85 and Consolidation '86 (also known as the National Stability Thesis).

10. Hundreds of political murders were carried out during the administration of Vinicio Cerezo (1986–91), the first president elected at this first stage of the transition. Ball, Kobrak, and Spirer, *Violencia institucional,* 87.

11. Despite being split, those conservative sectors won several elections. In turn, they implemented neoliberal policies.

12. Juan Linz, *La quiebra de las democracias* (Madrid: Alianza Editorial, 1993), 107.

13. International Labor Organization, *Report from the 97th International Conference* (Geneva: International Labor Organization, 2009).

14. The Secretaria de Inteligencia Estratégica was created in the postwar period. It depends on the presidency and the Ministry of the Interior through the General Direction of Civil Intelligence. However, it lacks institutional strength and capacity. In practice, the executive continues to use military intelligence as part of the Ministry of Defense.

15. Álvaro Arzú governed from January 1996 to January 2000, Alfonso Portillo governed from January 2000 to January 2004, Oscar Berger governed from January 2004 to January 2008, and Álvaro Colom took office in January 2008 and served until January 2012.

16. Asociación de Investigación y Estudios Sociales (ASIES), *Monografía de los Partidos Políticos 2004–2008* (Guatemala City: ASIES, 2008), 175.

17. In the first elections in which they took part, the united left got 14 percent of the vote; in the following ones the left split into several parties and failed to reach 5 percent, see Instituto Interuniversitario de Iberoamérica, *Perfil de Gobernabilidad de Guatemala* (Salamanca: BID y Agencia Española de Cooperación Internacional, 2005), 65–66. In the 2007 elections, once again the left was split into several groups and garnered less than 7 percent of the vote. One of the parties, Encuentro por Guatemala, had the Nobel Peace Prize winner Rigoberta Menchú as its presidential candidate.

18. See Dinorah Azpuru, *Cultura política de la democracia en Guatemala, 2008: El impacto de la gobernabilidad,* VIII Estudio de cultura democrática de los guatemaltecos (Nashville and Guatemala City: Vanderbilt University Press, U.S. Agency for International Development, and ASIES, 2008), 142–44.

19. The average confidence in political parties in the Americas in 2010 was 35.9 on a 100-point scale, but only 29.1 in Guatemala. See Dinorah Azpuru, *Consolidación democrática en las Américas en tiempos difíciles: Guatemala 2010,* IX Estudio de cultura democrática de los guatemaltecos (Nashville and Guatemala City: Vanderbilt University Press, U.S. Agency for International Development, and ASIES, 2010).

20. Luis Fernando Mack, *20 años de procesos electorales en Guatemala* (Guatemala City: Facultad Latinoamericana de Ciencias Sociales–Programa Guatemala, 2006).

21. The Presidential General Staff is an old military institution that was supposed to protect, but in fact enveloped, presidential functions; its modus operandi was always

linked to the repression of citizens opposing the government. It was finally dismantled in November 2003. United Nations Development Program and Dutch Institute of
Democratic Politics, *La Agenda Nacional Compartida* (Guatemala City: Magna Terra,
2003), 102–6.

22. See, e.g., Teresa Osio Bustillos, "Movimientos sociales y nuevas protestas:
Bolivia," in *Una nueva agenda de reformas políticas en América Latina,* edited by
Ludolfo Paramio and Marisa Revilla (Madrid: Fundación Carolina y Siglo XXI de
España Editores, 2006), 156.

23. During the decade 1997–2007, international assistance for the Guatemalan Judicial system totaled $188.8 million. United Nations Development Program, cited by
Instituto Interuniversitario de Iberoamérica, *Perfil de Gobernabilidad,* 132.

24. Jack Spence, *La guerra y la paz en América Central: Una comparación de las
transiciones en Guatemala, El Salvador y Nicaragua.* (Cambridge, Mass.: Hemisphere
Initiatives, 2004), 75.

25. Luis Pásara, *Paz, ilusión y cambio en Guatemala: El proceso de paz, sus actores, logros y límites* (Guatemala City: IIJ–Rafael Landivar, 2003), 193 ff.; Anita Isaacs,
"Guatemala on the Brink," *Journal of Democracy* 21, no. 2 (April 2010): 108–22.

26. Rody Brett, *Movimiento social, etnicidad y democratización en Guatemala,
1985–1996* (Guatemala City: F&G Editores), 7.

27. "La participación lenta pero segura," editorial, *Prensa Libre,* February 22, 2010.

28. In 2006, there were 24,020 complaints of human rights violations, which resulted
in 3,066 investigation proceedings and 20,954 specific actions. One of the principal
obstacles for the full observance of human rights is manifest in the area of public safety,
as the country is going through a period of violence and criminality. *Prensa Libre,* January 28, 2007.

29. This is according to information from the Office of the Publishers' Association,
which supervises assigning ISBNs for books, and was confirmed by its president, Raúl
Figueroa Sarti, Guatemala City, November 12, 2006.

30. United Nations Development Program, *Informe Nacional de Desarrollo Humano*
(National Human Development Report) (Guatemala City: United Nations Development
Program, 2010), xiv, 194.

31. Ibid., xiv.

32. International Human Development Indicators, "Country Profiles, Guatemala,"
http://hdrstats.undp.org/en/countries/profiles/GTM.html.

33. United Nations Development Program, *Informe Nacional de Desarrollo
Humano,* 47–48.

34. Ibid., 257.

35. Luis Pásara, *Las decisiones judiciales en Guatemala: Un análisis de sentencias*
(Guatemala City: MINUGUA, 2000).

36. In a survey conducted in 2002, the Judiciary received a 29 percent rate of general
approval; the Supreme Court of Justice, 28 percent; and the Police, 33 percent. ASIES, *La
Cultura democrática de los guatemaltecos en el nuevo siglo* (Guatemala: ASIES, 2002).

37. The Grupo Consultivo met several times abroad and in Guatemala during the
Arzú administration; its last meeting took place in the second year of the Portillo administration. The Berger government decided not to call it again in view of the country's
growing external debt.

38. See Edelberto Torres-Rivas, "Peace and Democracy: An Unpredictable Future,"
in *The Popular Referendum (Consulta Popular) and the Future of the Peace Process in*

Guatemala, Working Paper 241, edited by Cynthia J. Arnson (Washington, D.C.: Latin American Program, Woodrow Wilson International Center for Scholars, 1999), 51–55.

39. E.g., between 2003 and 2006, more than 98 police officers and chiefs were charged with common crimes, according to *El Periódico* in its year-end report, December 9 and 12, 2006.

40. United Nations Development Program, *Informe Sobre Desarrollo Humano 2006* (New York: United Nations Development Program, 2006), 342, 350. According to the Guatemala National Report for 2005, defense spending sank from 9.9 percent of total public expenditures in 1995 to 3.0 percent in 2004, but spending on security increased from 4.3 to 5.5 percent during the same period.

41. *El Periódico,* April 7, 2006, different pages report that the Army has 15,000 soldiers and that there are 19,200 private security agents—companies directed by ex-military officers. Also, to place criminal violence in numerical terms, it is assumed that there are 30,000 youth gang members, more or less well armed, and 20,000 policemen.

42. See Isaacs, "Guatemala," 108–22.

43. The increase in violence and the expansion and penetration of Mexican drug cartels in Guatemala have been attributed to the U.S.-supported crackdowns in Mexico and Colombia, which have pushed traffickers into the Central American region. See, e.g., Associated Press, "Mexican Drug Cartels Move into Central America," El Salvador, March 13, 2011, http://news.yahoo.com/s/ap/lt_salvador_obama_visit.

44. See, e.g., Mitchell A. Seligson, "Democracy on Ice: The Multiple Challenges of Guatemala's Peace Process," in *The Third Wave of Democratization in Latin America: Advances and Setbacks,* edited by Francis Hagopian and Scott Mainwaring (Cambridge: Cambridge University Press, 2005), 202–31.

45. See Edelberto Torres-Rivas, "Un Estado para el desarrollo humano: una utopia con los pies en la tierra," in *Guatemala: Un Estado para el desarrollo humano—Informe Nacional de Desarrollo Humano 2009–2010,* edited by United Nations Development Program (Guatemala City: United Nations Development Program, 2010).

46. Ibid. Additional and critical state functions are the establishment of a legal order, the promotion of development and equity, and representation in the international arena.

47. The period before the September 2011 presidential elections was marked by high levels of polarization between rural and urban areas and by the efforts of several candidates to evade constitutional restrictions prohibiting them from running for office. These elections were the seventh consecutive presidential election since the beginning of the democratic transition. In March 2011, first lady Sandra Torres de Colom announced that she was filing for divorce in order to sidestep the constitutional ban on family members of presidents running for office. She was ultimately prevented from running. Other efforts to evade constitutional prohibitions were made by Zury Ríos, the daughter of former dictator Efraín Ríos Montt, and former president Álvaro Arzú (who was prohibited by the Constitution from seeking a second term). See "Guatemala camina hacia una peligrosa polarización política," Infolatam, March 16, 2011, http://www.infolatam. com/2011/03/16/guatemala-camina-hacia-una-peligrosa-polarizacion-politica/.

Chapter 5

Nicaragua's Pacted Democracy

Shelley A. McConnell

Nicaraguan politics has been shaped by the country's revolutionary inheritance and the linked peace process and transition to democracy that brought the socialist experiment of the 1980s to an end. The insurrection that ousted the Somoza dynasty and ushered in a Marxist revolutionary regime, and the subsequent counterrevolution sponsored by the United States, polarized politics along lines that have endured through four changes in government. The twinning of the peace process with democratization meant that Nicaragua's ideologically driven conflict was institutionalized in two senses— conflict was no longer violent, but it also was made enduring, etched into the institutional framework of the emerging democracy through which peace was made. Nicaragua reversed Clausewitz's famous maxim—politics became war by other means.

In the first volume on postconflict transitions published by the Woodrow Wilson Center Press, *Comparative Peace Processes in Latin America,* the political scientist Rose J. Spalding examined the slow process by which the country was pacified following the 1990 elections in which the Sandinista

National Liberation Front (Frente Sandinista de Liberación Nacional, FSLN) lost power to the counterrevolutionary National Opposition Union (Unión Nacional Opositora, UNO) coalition.[1] The period under examination here—roughly 1995 to 2009—is one that placed politics at center stage as political parties struggled to control state institutions.

Politics makes for strange bedfellows, and nowhere more so than in Nicaragua. Thus, though they were historic enemies, the Sandinistas and Liberals cooperated via a political pact to exclude other parties from power and thereby clear the field so they could compete with one another. This chapter recounts how state institutions were shaped by this pact and the ensuing conflicts between the branches of the state, leading to constitutional reforms that refined each institution's scope of authority. The fact that the 1990 elections served as a vehicle for conflicting parties to exit the war gave construction of the electoral system special salience. The chapter describes the development of the party system and electoral system that prefaced Liberal victories in the 1996 and 2001 general elections, and explains how the pact altered the electoral system to favor the two leading parties. It also examines Nicaragua's progress toward resolving second-generation issues of democratic development, such as poverty, corruption, and crime.

The chapter concludes by reflecting on three questions posed by the reelection of the Sandinista leader Daniel Ortega to the presidency in 2006 and his administration through 2009. The first is whether and how Ortega's reelection shaped the postconflict state and its capacity for governance given the depth of Nicaraguan underdevelopment. The second is whether the electoral alternation in power signaled consolidation of a liberal democratic system or a hybrid regime that combined elements of authoritarianism with democracy. Finally, with an eye to the Latin American context mixing leftist and neopopulist presidents, the chapter considers whether Ortega reentered the presidency as a reformed leftist leader of an established party with Marxist roots or instead as a neopopulist who had abandoned ideology and relied on elections as a device for mass mobilization while his party was diminished to a personal vehicle.

Nicaragua's Political Legacy

"Postwar societies face the task of *constructing,* not reconstructing, democratic institutions," wrote Cynthia Arnson in her introduction to *Comparative Peace Processes.*[2] This was certainly the case in Nicaragua, which had never before been democratic and thus had no preexisting democratic institutions waiting to be revitalized. The country had been ruled by a dynastic dictatorship from 1934 until the 1979 Sandinista revolution. The dictator Anastasio Somoza García and his sons Luis and Anastasio Somoza Debayle were sustained in power by Nicaragua's National Guard and the support of the United States. The Somozas' sultanistic authoritarian regime was patrimonial and weakly institutionalized. Power was centralized in the person of the president, and by extension his family and close associates. Somoza's National Liberal Party held a majority in the rubber-stamp legislature, and the judiciary was not independent. The rule of law was absent, and human rights were not respected in what was a weak predatory state. The political culture reflected a Spanish colonial inheritance of clientelism and *caudillismo* (strongman rule).[3]

During those years, the Somoza regime held regular but fraudulent elections designed to provide a gloss of legitimacy to the government. Few parties were recognized, and the main opposition Conservative Party colluded with the governing National Liberal Party via a series of pacts designed to exclude rivals and guarantee each party a set percentage of the seats in the legislature. Nicaragua's electoral inheritance of an exclusionary two-party system, pacting, and U.S. intervention was a poor basis for democracy and foreshadowed some of the difficulties the country would later face in consolidating democratic governance.

The 1979 revolution empowered the FSLN, which was then a political-military organization that subscribed to an ideology mixing Marxism, nationalism, and a dose of Liberation Theology. The Sandinistas' tactical alliance with disgruntled businessmen introduced some liberal thinking as well. After coming to power, the FSLN set about transforming itself from a political-military group into a political party, but the metamorphosis was incomplete. It emerged with a vertical structure privileging a small group of party militants over the mass base, and it did not separate the armed forces from the party. Demilitarization was hindered by the Reagan administration's decision to fund a covert operation—the infamous "contras"—to topple the Sandinista regime that soon descended into a counterrevolutionary war.

The Sandinistas put in place a set of temporary institutions that were not democratic, and promised to hold elections within five years. They installed a five-person junta that included representatives from outside the FSLN, but this soon devolved into a Sandinista instrument. The junta created a legislature based on functional rather than territorial representation, but it was packed with organizations that were either linked directly to the FSLN or sympathetic to the revolutionary project. Popular tribunals were formed to charge, try, and sentence defendants who were alleged to have participated in abuses under the Somoza government, notably former National Guard members, but these courts were often staffed by untrained judges and did not always provide due process. In short, fundamental democratic features—such as the independence and interdependence of branches of the state, interparty competition, accountability, and the rule of law—were unfamiliar and largely missing from the institutions initially created after the Somoza dictatorship was overthrown.

When the revolutionary government set out in 1983 to create the laws needed to hold promised elections, the institutional framework changed in a democratic direction.[4] The law governing political parties defined them as organizations competing for state power and did not privilege the FSLN. Representation in the envisioned legislature would be restricted to political parties. The executive branch would be headed by an individual president rather than the collective leadership common to the FSLN party and the governing junta. The Constitution that would be approved in 1987 would feature both revolutionary and liberal democratic elements, including some civil liberties that could not be suspended during a state of emergency. The drafting committees for these laws consulted Nicaragua's history, but of necessity also looked abroad to gather information on democratic systems. The resulting institutional framework proved sufficiently democratic for competitive elections to be held in 1990 that would bring a conservative opposition coalition to power and end both the counterrevolutionary war and the proposed transition to socialism. Instead, Nicaragua would undertake a transition to democracy whose roots lay in the revolutionary institutional framework and whose future was at best uncertain.

Evolution of the Party System and the 1995 Constitutional Reform

Between the 1990 founding elections and the 2006 reelection of Daniel Ortega, power relations between the executive, legislative, judicial, and electoral branches of the state would be defined through practice, interbranch conflicts, and constitutional reforms in 1995, 2000, and 2004.[5] These, in turn, would alter the state's effectiveness and public perceptions of the utility of democracy in resolving pressing problems of governance. Nicaragua continued to hold legislative and presidential elections that met international standards, and it provided better protection of human rights and civil liberties than during the revolution and counterrevolutionary war.[6] However, Nicaragua's political institutions would struggle to provide human security and access to justice.

The 1987 Constitution, approved during the years of Sandinista rule, outlined the basic structure of the state but did not embody an underlying social compact. It had been preceded by the 1983 law that recognized parties as organizations competing for state power and made party formation relatively easy. A wide array of parties formed, but at the urging of the United States, the most important right-wing groups boycotted the 1984 elections and thus held no seats in the National Assembly that also would serve as a constituent assembly. The parties outside the legislature rebuffed the government's offer to consult them via ad hoc meetings. They rejected the resulting Constitution as "unilateral"—despite the fact that the six opposition parties that had participated in the 1984 elections held one-third of the legislative seats and played an active role in the constitution-making process.

Not surprisingly, in the postrevolutionary period the Constitution became an early target for reform. The primary proponent of reform was the UNO, which had won the 1990 election as a predominantly center-right fourteen-party coalition. The UNO had rejected its own victorious candidate, President Violeta Chamorro, after she authorized Daniel Ortega's brother Humberto to remain chief of the army, viewing him as the only one with sufficient authority to accomplish a rapid force reduction from roughly 100,000 to 15,000 troops. Chamorro came to rely on the FSLN and its legislative votes for support. The UNO coalition soon dissolved, resulting in clusters of Liberal, Conservative, and radical microparties, but in late 1994 UNO legislators united around an agenda of constitutional reform to trim the powers of the presidency.[7]

Those who had encouraged a military ouster of the Sandinista government via the contra war did so in the hope that the FSLN would be forever eliminated from politics. Instead, a peaceful transition to democracy had left the FSLN as the largest and most disciplined party in the legislature. However, a split that emerged in the FSLN in 1993 ended in the ouster of former Vice President Sergio Ramírez who would in 1995 gather Sandinista dissidents into a political party called the Sandinista Renewal Movement (Movimiento de Renovación Sandinista, MRS). These dissident Sandinistas had a power base in the legislature, and thus came to favor constitutional reforms boosting the power of the National Assembly vis-à-vis the presidency as a means of wresting power from both President Chamorro and the FSLN. Together, the UNO and Sandinista dissidents had the necessary legislative strength to enact reform.

The 1995 constitutional reform served as a useful correction of the hyperpresidentialist system that had developed in the 1980s amid the centralizing pressures of war and an attempted transition to socialism.[8] The reform prohibited presidents from holding consecutive terms, requiring that they wait out a term before running again, and limited them to two terms of office. The presidential term was shortened from six to five years. Relatives of the president were prohibited from seeking the presidency, and any official wishing to be a candidate was required to resign his or her government post a year in advance of the elections. Presidential candidates were required to obtain 45 percent of the valid votes cast or else go to a runoff, a proviso added in light of the burgeoning number of microparties that had sprung up as political space opened.

The reform also stripped the president of the power of decree in fiscal matters, meaning the ability to levy taxes and impose tariffs without legislative approval. It required legislative review of the budget, which had been the custom since 1989 but now became a legal requisite. It also required the president to receive legislative approval to declare a state of emergency or use military troops outside the country. The National Assembly was empowered to strip state officials of their immunity in order to permit their prosecution for alleged crimes. Together, these changes brought a substantial loss of presidential prerogatives. On its index of formal presidential powers, in 2002 the United Nations Development Program (UNDP) ranked Nicaragua as "medium low" in comparison with other countries in the region.[9] The reform also helped consolidate the shift begun in the mid-1980s from a revolutionary state whose function was to transform society into a liberal state whose function was to guarantee contracts and citizen rights.

When the legislature approved the reforms in January 1995, President Chamorro refused to acknowledge them, so they were published instead by the president of the National Assembly.[10] For five months, the two branches recognized different versions of the Constitution, at a time when the Supreme Court of Justice (Corte Suprema de Justicia, CSJ) had three vacancies that prevented it from reaching a quorum in order to adjudicate the issue. The crisis lingered on into June, when the term of office for members of the Supreme Electoral Council expired, leaving the fourth branch of government with no one at the helm as the 1996 elections loomed. It was not until Nicaragua's bilateral creditors placed pressure on the government that the two branches reached a settlement with the facilitation of Miguel Cardinal Obando y Bravo.

Via the accord, President Chamorro accepted the reforms in exchange for the National Assembly modifying their implementation through a Framework Law. The empty seats on the CSJ would be filled by legislative election without executive interference, but future magistrates would be chosen via legislative-executive accord. The two branches agreed to appoint a comptroller general by common accord, and slated other laws to be reformed by similar compromises, including the Electoral Law. Although the constitutional reform had given the legislature a strong role in developing the national budget, the Framework Law assured that tax laws would be jointly formulated with the executive branch and prohibited the legislature from raising the budget ceiling proposed by the president.[11]

Rise of the Liberals and the 2000 Pact

In the mid-1990s, an obscure Managua city councilman who became mayor in an indirect election set about unifying anti-Sandinista elements under the umbrella of a Liberal Alliance centered on the Liberal Constitutionalist Party (Partido Liberal Constitucionalista, PLC). This was not the National Liberal Party that had been abolished after the revolution as a corrupt vehicle of the old regime, but it included some of the same hard-line anti-Sandinista elements and established a peasant support base in the rural areas where the contras had operated. Mayor Arnoldo Alemán forged a coherent electoral vehicle with the slogan "Proudly Liberal," seeking to erase any stigma remaining from the dictatorship and reclaim the Liberal tradition.[12]

In the wake of the revolution and counterrevolution, both ideologically driven, the Sandinistas and Liberals were bitter antagonists. With democratic rules in place, their conflict was manifested in electoral competition. In the 1996 presidential race, Alemán would carry the Liberals to victory, beating the FSLN candidate, former president Daniel Ortega. The campaign polarized the country. Although twenty-three parties ran presidential candidates, the FSLN and Liberal Alliance were by far the largest of them, garnering 88 percent of the presidential vote. In the transition elections of 1990, Nicaraguan voters had been either with the Sandinistas or against them; six years later, with the countryside only recently pacified, the election still boiled down to "which side are you on?"

It therefore came as a surprise to many when, at the end of the decade, President Alemán formed a secret agreement with his erstwhile opponent Ortega to displace the small parties and share power between the Liberals and Sandinistas.[13] The two parties would continue to compete against one another in elections, but the consequences of losing were blunted by laws and constitutional provisions that awarded power to both the Sandinistas and Liberals at the expense of other parties. This agreement—called by its authors a "governability accord" designed to reduce the influence of microparties—became popularly known as "the pact," and in 2000 it was implemented through a series of constitutional and legislative reforms.

The pact gave the FSLN and PLC control over leadership selection in the main state institutions. The parties proceeded to pack the CSJ, raising the total number of magistrates from a dozen to sixteen. The Liberals and Sandinistas would each name half the CSJ magistrates. Other parties were shut out entirely. The pacting parties similarly increased the number of magistrates on the Supreme Electoral Council (Consejo Supremo Electoral, CSE) from five to seven, with each of the two parties naming loyalists to three of those seats. The presidency of the CSE was to be a purportedly neutral figure who in practice cast his votes on electoral matters consistently with the Liberals (in the 2001 election) and the Sandinistas (in the 2006 election). Here again, smaller parties were given no representation whatsoever. Finally, the Office of the Comptroller General was made into a collective body with five members, three of whom were nominated by the Liberals as the governing party and two by the Sandinistas as the so-called second political force. With the Liberals winning control of the executive branch in 1996 and 2001, and the FSLN cooperating with them to manage the legislature, the two parties enjoyed a virtual duopoly on the institutions of the state.

An Exclusionary Electoral System

A second and equally important aspect of the pact was a reform of Nicaragua's electoral system. Nicaragua succeeded in establishing a stable electoral system during the postwar period, and one that repeatedly delivered presidential and legislative elections with only minor irregularities. Nicaragua held general elections in 1996, 2001, and 2006 on schedule and without violence. Participation levels were generally high, with registration estimated at 95 percent and roughly three-quarters of the registered voters casting a ballot.[14] Nicaragua's elections were also widely observed by the international community and national observer organizations.[15]

Although establishing electoral rules and procedures is undoubtedly crucial to democratic consolidation, the Nicaraguan case illustrates that the specific terms of that electoral regime matter greatly, and in Nicaragua's case pose the question "transition to what?" As part of the 2000 pact, the Liberals and Sandinistas reformed the Electoral Law to create an electoral system that was the most exclusionary in Latin America. To register a new party, the applicant group had to form a board of officers in every munici-pality, some of which were extremely isolated. The CSE interpreted the law to require the presence of one of the seven CSE magistrates to witness the formation of these local party boards, meaning that protoparties had to obtain the cooperation of officials named by their established competitors. Failing to form even one board could be sufficient for denial of legality to the applicant protoparty, making this a long, drawn-out process that was easily sabotaged by the FSLN and PLC through their CSE magistrates. The two protoparties that tried to form—one a breakaway Sandinista group whose presidential aspirant, Joaquín Cuadra, was the former leader of the armed forces; and the second a breakaway Liberal group whose presi-dential hopeful, José Antonio Alvarado, had been a Cabinet minister and Alemán's protégé—were blocked when they could not register boards in all municipalities by the deadline.

Party formation also required collecting signatures of support from 3 percent of the registered electors, meaning that in a politically polarized postwar setting, citizens were asked to sign a piece of paper stating their party preference and listing their national identity card number, a dubious prospect for all but the most militant supporters. To prevent fraud, each signature was then scrutinized and matched to the one on file from issu-ance of the identity card, and was disqualified if it differed in the eyes of the untrained personnel comparing signatures. This complicated process required that parties collect a substantial overage of signatures in order to meet the minimum. Once someone had signed for one political party, he or she could not sign again for another, meaning that there was an ever-shrinking pool of eligible signers. The PLC was exempted from the need to obtain signatures. For its part, the FSLN employed its mobilizational capacity to collect far more than the needed number of signatures, effec-tively crowding out other parties. Although the signature collection process was later dropped after a ruling by the CSJ, the UNDP ranked Nicaragua's party system in 2002 as "very restrictive."[16]

A party that achieved legal recognition had to work hard to keep it. To retain its *personeria jurídica* (legal status), the party was required to name candidates for every race, and to win at least 4 percent of the vote in the general election for the presidency. Moreover, a party would not receive reimbursement for any campaign expenses unless it won a seat in the legislature. No state funds would be given in advance of the election, placing new parties at a disadvantage. These provisions were meant to discourage the formation of nuisance parties whose sole purpose was to obtain state finance, but it also affected legitimate aspirants. In comparison with other Latin American countries, the UNDP considered Nicaragua's threshold for public funding "high."[17]

Under the new law, parties that did form were discouraged from joining alliances that might have challenged the FSLN or PLC in size. Any alliances were required to adhere to a single party's banner, and political finance was channeled through that party such that the alliance would only receive funding as if it were a single party. Nonetheless, to retain its legal status, the alliance had to win 4 percent of the vote for each party in the alliance. The law also eliminated the possibility of independent candidates not affiliated with a national party. As a consequence of these provisions, in the 2001 elections the number of parties winning seats in the legislature was reduced to three—the FSLN, the PLC, and the Conservative Party, which won a single seat.

The magnitude of the changes was stunning, and the effect was worsened by subjective administration of the law. The CSE magistrates made no efforts to set aside party attachments and become neutral "notables," arguing that it was appropriate for large parties with a greater investment in the electoral system to administer the process. There was substantial room for the sort of discretionary decisionmaking that goes hand in hand with corruption. Candidates were sometimes disqualified on dubious grounds.[18] The regulations on political finance were weak, requiring little disclosure and inviting abuse. Anonymous donations to parties were banned, but no limits were placed on donations by state contractors and reporting requirements were rudimentary.[19]

Another change that would have important consequences for the 2006 election was that a presidential candidate could now win either by obtaining at least 40 percent of the vote and being the leading candidate, or by obtaining 35 percent of the vote and having a 5 percent lead over any other candidate. This reform gave Ortega a better chance of victory because the FSLN machine had shown it could consistently deliver about 40 percent of the vote. Liberals remained confident that they could win a majority out-right, as indeed they had in 1996 and would do again in 2001.

The pacted Electoral Law also determined that outgoing presidents would get a seat in the National Assembly, and thus diplomatic immunity. Given President Alemán's rapacious corruption, this unelected seat provision was no doubt welcomed, and indeed his later loss of that immunity would result in his conviction for money laundering and fraud. The law already gave a consolation prize seat to the runner-up in the presidential race, which protected Ortega from prosecution related to the 1990 "Piñata" appropriation of state properties (not to mention his stepdaughter's public accusation that he had sexually abused her over a period of many years). Now whenever Ortega and Alemán went head to head in electoral competition, neither needed to fear being left out of the political arena.

The reforms to the electoral system were a reaction to the permissive and participatory provisions of the 1983 Political Parties Law and an attempt to balance participation and governability. They suggested a certain comfort level with the Electoral Law as a mechanism for shaping the architecture of politics. Nonetheless, the reforms did not create conditions for democratic deepening. Instead, they introduced opportunities for discretionary decisionmaking by partisan actors and exclusionary provisions that impaired competition.

The Bolaños Presidency and the Deepening of the Pact

The pacted changes in the Electoral Law demanded substantial cooperation between the FSLN and PLC, but there was one item on which the Sandinistas would not collude. The FSLN rejected the PLC's desire to permit immediate reelection to the presidency, retaining the requirement that the president sit out for a term before seeking reelection. Alemán's immediate concern was therefore to find a loyal stand-in to hold the presidency for him, and for this he chose his vice president, Enrique Bolaños—a decision he would deeply regret.

Bolaños was not Alemán's first preference for the presidential nomination in 2001, but the PLC's main donors liked him better than alternative contenders, and Alemán reluctantly gave him the nomination. With Liberal Party backing, Bolaños handily won the 2001 presidential election with 56 percent of the vote, beating the perennial Sandinista contender Ortega by a 14-point margin in elections deemed satisfactory by international observers. Ortega retained the loyalty of Sandinista voters, winning 42 percent of the vote despite a smear campaign by his opponents in the wake of the September 11, 2001, terrorist attacks recalling Ortega's cordial relationship with Saddam Hussein. The intent had been to suggest that an Ortega victory would once again bring the wrath of the United States down upon Nicaragua. By evoking painful memories of the counterrevolution, both parties reinforced the loyalty of their core adherents.

As the runner-up, Ortega was assured a seat in the National Assembly. Alemán was given a seat as outgoing president. Among the ninety competed seats in the National Assembly, the Liberals obtained fifty-two to the Sandinistas' thirty-seven, and the Conservatives won a lone seat. Although the election was essentially unrestricted, the UNDP ranked it slightly lower than the 1990 and 1996 elections with respect to the presentation of candidates and party formation, due in large part to the exclusionary provisions of the pacted Electoral Law and radically reduced number of parties gaining legislative seats.[20]

After taking office in January 2002, President Bolaños surprised everyone by promptly seeking to prosecute former president Alemán for corruption. A handful of legislators loyal to Bolaños combined forces with the FSLN deputies to strip Alemán of the immunity he derived from holding a seat in the National Assembly, and Alemán was then prosecuted and found guilty of fraud and money laundering. He was briefly jailed, then confined to his house in lieu of jail. Despite the privileged conditions of Alemán's incarceration, this reversal of fortune made the PLC the junior partner in the pact. Using his amassed fortune and force of character, Alemán remained the PLC's leader, and his control of the party's nomination process, including the formation of the legislative list, allowed him to retain the loyalty of most PLC legislators. The PLC's goal was to obtain a pardon so that Alemán could be free to reenter politics, and to this end the party would make a stream of political concessions to the FSLN.[21]

Meanwhile, President Bolaños governed with the legislative votes of the Sandinista Front and a half-dozen PLC deputies. This was reminiscent of the Chamorro years and all the more remarkable given Bolaños's personal antipathy toward the FSLN, born of his opposition to the attempted transition to socialism when he was leader of Nicaragua's High Council on Private Enterprise (known by the abbreviation of its Spanish name, COSEP). He had sharply protested the revolutionary government's nationalization of properties, including his own. Cooperation between President Bolaños and the FSLN was in any case short-lived. When U.S. secretary of state Colin

Powell visited Nicaragua in 2003, he insisted that Bolaños break off his tactical alliance with the FSLN. Bolaños complied, and thereafter lacked the votes necessary to pass legislation and carry out his political program. The FSLN cast Bolaños' reversal under U.S. pressure as a betrayal. Soon the president became politically isolated, having been rejected by PLC and FSLN deputies alike.

As in 1995, the ensuing interbranch conflict threatened to unseat Nicaragua's fragile democracy. In September 2004, the Office of the Comptroller General, one of the government agencies whose leadership was determined by the pact, called for the president's impeachment on the grounds that he had failed to cooperate in an investigation of his campaign finances. The absence of clear constitutional procedures for impeachment, combined with quick action by the international community under the Inter-American Democratic Charter, scuttled that proposal.[22]

Shifting tactics, in November 2004 the FSLN and PLC set out to curb President Bolaños's power via new constitutional reforms and changes in ordinary legislation that were collectively understood as a deepening of the political pact. The reform created a "superintendency" to be led by someone named by the legislature that would regulate water, electricity, and telephones. In addition, the National Assembly would name the head of a property institute that would deal with properties still in contention since the land reform of the revolutionary era. The constitutional reform also gave the legislature the right to fire Cabinet ministers, and required all Cabinet nominees to be ratified with a 60 percent vote in the legislature.[23]

Bolaños refused to publish the constitutional reforms, arguing that they so deeply shifted the nature of the relationship between the legislature and the executive branch that in effect they were a replacement of the Constitution and not merely a reform, and thus ought to have popular ratification. As in 1995, this meant that the two branches of the state operated under different versions of the Constitution, an untenable situation that nonetheless dragged on for ten months. The president's argument was echoed by the Central American Court of Justice, but that ruling was greeted with derision by the CSJ, which countermanded the finding and ruled that the reforms were proper.

Bolaños then invoked the Inter-American Democratic Charter and called on the Organization of American States (OAS) to intervene. Months passed without progress in the OAS dialogue, and the threat of impeachment was renewed. Indictments against a half-dozen Cabinet ministers were viewed as a dress rehearsal for presidential impeachment. However, popular protests critical of leaders on both sides of the conflict suggested there was a political cost to these maneuvers. Although national elections were still a year away, new parties and their leaders gained ground in the preelection polls, providing an incentive for the FSLN and PLC to end their standoff with the president. In October 2005, an OAS negotiating team ultimately fostered an accord between Bolaños and Ortega to delay implementation of the reform. Modeling on the resolution of the 1995 constitutional crisis, this agreement was codified in a Framework Law that cleared the decks for political differences to be settled on the electoral battlefield the following year.[24] For all its faults, and however skewed the rules might be, democracy remained the only game in town.

The 2006 Elections

As Nicaraguans entered a new electoral cycle in 2006, the most salient feature of Nicaraguan politics was the continued dominance of the Liberal and Sandinista parties. As the campaign evolved, however, five political parties would emerge. The disqualification of candidates that marred the 2001 elections did not occur, and there was a heightened sense of free competition, including a fierce fight for Liberal votes between the PLC and a new Nicaraguan Liberal Alliance–Conservative Party (Alianza Liberal Nicaragüense–Partido Conservador, ALN-PC), whose presidential candidate, Eduardo Montealegre, would finish second. The election results contributed to the impression that the pact had lost its stranglehold on politics. The legislative seats were split, with the FSLN receiving thirty-eight of the ninety competed seats; the PLC, twenty-five seats; the ALN-PC, twenty-two seats; and the MRS, five seats. Nonetheless, the derivative nature of the new parties cast doubt on the proposition of an emergent multiparty system. The ALN was fundamentally a Liberal offshoot and the MRS was a Sandinista splinter group, whereas the fifth party was a personal vehicle for Eden Pastora, who had been a revolutionary hero and later had taken up arms against the revolutionary government. In short, the Sandinista-Liberal polarization had moderated in comparison with the 1996 and 2001 campaigns, but these two ideological tendencies that had informed the revolution and counterrevolution continued to describe politics.

In 2006, Nicaragua stood at the crossroads of tradition and modernity, combining old-fashioned *caudillismo* and clientelism with new democratic procedures and citizen demands for inclusion and accountability. Nowhere was this more evident than within the Liberal camp, which was divided between its shrinking peasant base represented by the PLC and a growing urban base that largely supported the ALN-PC. But what made the 2006 elections historically significant was that, on his fourth attempt, Ortega regained the presidency. Debate centered on whether this meant a return to the socialist revolutionary politics of the past or else a new market-oriented progressive government, but no one argued that the Sandinista victory would bring more of the same. Although Nicaraguans sometimes dismissed disputes between political leaders as "*a la cúpula,*" and of little relevance for the poor, continued high election turnouts belied the idea that ideology was dead and one leader was as bad as the next. The working relationship between Nicaragua's caudillo leaders did not imply that they favored the same policies or empowered the same people. Continued U.S. meddling in a fruitless effort to shift PLC supporters to Montealegre and thereby prevent a Sandinista victory, and the new phenomenon of Venezuelan support for the FSLN, suggested that foreigners also thought that party platforms and underlying ideologies mattered.

Three sets of questions arose from Ortega's reelection. The first concerned how it might shape the postconflict state. Would the Ortega administration seek to repoliticize the security forces and recentralize power in the presidency? Given Nicaragua's underdevelopment and structured insertion into the international economy, could the Ortega administration increase the state's capacity to deliver goods and services, helping to remedy unemployment, poverty, inequality, and crime? In a consolidated democracy, an election would not normally change state institutions, but in Nicaragua, elections and pacted electoral reforms had done so repeatedly.

A second set of questions surrounded the nature of Nicaragua's regime. Did the alternation in power, returning government to the Sandinistas, portend democratic consolidation or merely the perpetuation of a hybrid regime mixing electoral procedures with reserve domains of authoritarianism? The answer would depend in part on whether a *partidocracia* designed to artificially maintain two parties in power could effectively aggregate and articulate citizens' interests. The strength of democratic institutions would help determine whether conflict could be adjudicated peacefully. When there were diverse views, would state institutions mediate conflict, or would they respond only to the pacting parties and their caudillo leaders?

Third, the international context of the "Pink Tide"—in which social democratic and left-wing neopopulist presidents were elected in ten Latin American countries—posed the question of whether Ortega was a populist, and if so whether he would implement a radical leftist agenda. Did the 2000 pact signal Ortega's abandonment of his ideological roots in favor of an opportunistic bid for power? Did he conceive of economic and social policy in populist terms as mere instruments for manipulating support in order to attain power, or conversely was political office the instrument for enacting a long-standing leftist agenda focused on social justice? Was the FSLN essentially a vehicle for promoting Ortega's personal ambitions, or did the party play an important role in setting policy and operating government?

The answers to these questions would depend in part on the extent to which politics was frozen in past patterns. Some of these patterns predated the revolution and counterrevolution—political pacting and caudillo rule were an old inheritance—but the decades of conflict has given them new meaning, infusing power contests with ideological content as well as introducing new state institutions with which to tackle the problems of governance.

Poverty and Inequality

A particularly important question was whether Nicaragua's pacted democracy could deliver equitable development. In 2009, with a population of 5.7 million, Nicaragua ranked 124th out of 182 countries on the UN's Human Development Index.[25] Its gross domestic product (GDP) had risen from $2.8 billion in 1988 to $5.7 billion in 1998 and $6.6 billion in 2008 as the economy had recovered from the war, obtained debt forgiveness, and began to grow.[26] However, Nicaragua remained a dependent country, and its economy contracted in 2009 due to the world economic crisis. The International Monetary Fund expressed satisfaction with the Ortega administration's prudent management and expected growth to be restored in 2010.[27] Nonetheless, whether measured in crude terms or at purchasing power parity, Nicaragua had the second-lowest per capita income in the Western Hemisphere. Only Haiti fared worse.[28]

Nicaragua's income distribution was highly uneven. The UN noted that in the postwar period, from 1992 to 2007 the richest 10 percent of the population received 41.8 percent of the income, and the poorest 10 percent just 1.4 percent.[29] In 2005, an estimated 48 percent of Nicaraguans lived below the poverty line.[30] Between 2000 and 2006, 31.8 percent of the population lived on less than $2 per day, and 15.8 percent on less than $1 per day.[31] Inequality in Nicaragua was not worse than in other postconflict countries, and it predated the conflict, but the revolution's socialist egalitarian principles had politicized the problem, framing it in terms of class struggle.

Some of Nicaragua's poverty could be traced back to the "lost decade" of the 1980s, when the counterrevolutionary war and the U.S. embargo on trade and capital left the economy a shambles. Nicaragua was slow to recover; its per capita GDP in 2005 did not yet match the 1977 level.[32] The conflict also helped pattern Nicaraguan poverty. Nicaragua's Human Development Index score rose from 0.565 in 1980 to 0.699 in 2009, but progress had been nearly flat during the war, then rose gradually in 1990 and picked up sharply in 1995 once the country was fully pacified.[33] The conflict exacerbated migration, especially because the United States often accepted those fleeing Communism as political refugees. In 2007, Nicaragua received $740 million in remittances, constituting 12.1 percent of GDP, two-thirds of which came from North America. It was telling that fifteen years after the end of the war, poverty was still markedly worse on the Atlantic Coast and in the mountainous central part of the country where much of the counterrevolution had been fought.

Peace brought tangible improvements, but it was still a precarious existence for the poor. The infant mortality rate fell dramatically, from 51 per 1,000 live births in 1990 to 23 in 2008. Income inequality improved slightly, with the poorest quintile receiving 3 percent of national income in 1995 and 4 percent in 2000. Yet in 2001, among the poorest 20 percent of the population, only 78 percent of births were attended by a skilled health practitioner, whereas the figure for the richest quintile was 99 percent. From 2002 to 2004, 27 percent of the population was undernourished.[34]

The adult literacy rate for the decade 1995–2005 was just 76.7 percent, far lower than the regional average for Latin America and the Caribbean (90.3 percent) and a disappointment after the revolutionary government's literacy campaign in the 1980s.[35] But peace improved primary school completion, perhaps because schools had been targets of contra attacks. In 1990, at war's end, only 39 percent of children in the primary school age range completed their primary education. Within five years, nearly half did so; and by 2008, three-quarters completed primary school.[36] However, in 2007 an estimated 35 percent of children were not listed in the national register, and were thus excluded from the benefits of citizenship.[37]

Fertility rates for 2000–2005 were less than half of what they had been before the revolution, with women averaging 3 births rather than 6.8 births. Nonetheless, in 2005 a full 37.9 percent of the population was under the age of fifteen, placing tremendous pressure on the government to generate jobs.[38] The World Bank reported a ratio of employment to population of 58 percent among those over the age of fifteen in 2008, a figure virtually unchanged since 1990, and 45 percent of jobs were considered vulnerable.[39] In the 2005 Latinobarómetro survey, 65 percent of households reported having at least one unemployed adult. Job security was low, and 68 percent expressed concern about whether they would be unemployed sometime in the next twelve months.[40] The United Nations found in 2006 that 15 percent of households reported that at least one member had emigrated in search of work to Costa Rica (52.9 percent), the United States (34.5 percent), or Canada or Europe (12 percent), thus eroding the family structure.[41]

Despite improvements in the macroeconomic picture, the resources that Nicaragua could bring to bear on these problems were meager. In 2010, the government's annual budget was a paltry $1.5 billion.[42] Under the Bolaños government, the country substantially reduced its external obligations through debt forgiveness programs. In 1988, total debt as a proportion of GDP was 330.4 percent, and this fell to 177 percent in 1998 and to 54 percent in 2008.[43] However, the budget was burdened by internal debt accumulated from managing the collapse of major banks and issuing bonds to reimburse owners for properties nationalized during the revolution. In 2005, social spending was the lowest in Latin America, at just $68 per person.[44]

Grim as these figures might be, they were a marked improvement over the past quarter century. In particular, the restoration of economic growth held promise for greater social investment that could enable Nicaragua to reach at least some of its UN Millennium Development Goals.[45] However, as in other Latin American countries, neoliberal reforms had a limited payoff, and although 69 percent of Nicaraguans thought a market economy was necessary for development, the lack of a social safety net was keenly felt.[46] The Ortega government would benefit from a substantial infusion of funds from Venezuela. The exact value varied with the price of oil, but in 2009 may have reached as much as $450 million, an amount that dwarfed other donor country contributions and displaced their political leverage. The Venezuelan funds were administered off-budget and specifically dedicated to development, giving Ortega substantial running room in deciding how to resolve his country's problems, particularly in contrast to the heavy constraints imposed by the U.S. embargo during his first administration.[47]

Crime, Drug Trafficking, and Personal Security

After poverty and unemployment, crime was the most important problem affecting Nicaraguans in the postwar period, raising the question of whether the country's pacted democracy could deal effectively with human security. In the immediate postrevolutionary period, crime and personal security problems could be traced directly to the counterrevolutionary war. Once the United States made clear that its sponsorship of the contras was at an end, and once elections had been accepted as the process for legitimate access to power, the counterrevolutionary forces lacked the resources and the justification to continue their fight. They were in a weak bargaining position, and thus within three months they agreed to disarmament and resettlement by the UN and OAS in return for promises of land and jobs from the Chamorro government. More lengthy peace negotiations such as those in El Salvador and Guatemala would have treated socioeconomic as well as political grievances, helping make the peace sustainable. In Nicaragua, despite ongoing OAS verification efforts, the Chamorro government was unable to deliver the promised land and jobs, in part because the United States limited its aid to her government in an effort to force resolution of property disputes involving U.S. citizens. The low education and skill levels of many contras and cashiered regular army soldiers meant that some former combatants turned to criminal activity as a means of survival.[48]

Even a decade after the last remnants of irregular forces were disbanded, the areas suffering from the highest levels of common criminal activity were those where the counterrevolutionary war was fought, and where the contras settled afterward. Poverty and unemployment cultivated delinquency. The problematic legal regime governing property also continued to generate conflict. At the same time, globalization and regional integration increased the flow of goods and people across borders, including illicit goods and persons linked to criminal activity.[49]

According to Nicaraguan police data, the total number of cases filed in 2006 was 2,343 per 100,000 inhabitants, up from 1,732 in 2001, which suggests that crime had worsened under the Bolaños administration and during the period of the pact. Between 1994 and 2005, the number of robberies that involved force, violence, or intimidation rose from 302 to 390 per 100,000 inhabitants. After pacification was achieved, the country's homicide rates dropped rapidly, from 22 to 9 per 100,000 inhabitants but crept up again to 14 per 100,000 inhabitants in 2006.[50] The 8,423 officers in the National Police lacked the capacity to address crime outside the major cities, and the armed forces therefore broadened their mission to include policing in the countryside and on the Atlantic Coast.[51]

The increase in crime and murder rates could not be ascribed to gang activity. In comparison with other postwar countries in Central America,

Nicaragua had fewer young people involved in gangs, a fact the military loosely attributed to the strength of family structures and the country's social fabric. In 1999 some 8,500 gang members operated in 110 bands, but by 2005 those numbers had fallen to 2,201 members in 108 gangs. Crimes committed by youth gangs accounted for just 0.57 percent of all criminal activity. Police data showed that just 0.11 percent of Nicaraguans between the ages of thirteen and twenty-nine years were active in gangs.[52] In 2006, among the prison population, data showed 1.2 percent were under eighteen.[53]

A more likely explanation for rising violent crime rates and an increased number of cases was the expansion of drug trafficking and efforts to curtail it. In 2006, a total of 1,839 people were arrested for alleged involvement in drug-related crimes. Trafficked drugs included cocaine, crack, marijuana, and heroin. Nicaragua was primarily a transshipment point rather than a final destination for illicit drugs.[54]

Although the increased crime rates were regrettable, in comparative perspective Nicaragua suffered less crime than other postconflict countries in Central America. In 2006, only 7 percent of respondents ranked crime as Nicaragua's top problem, the lowest proportion among all postconflict cases. The Nicaraguan National Police were praised as a model force in the region. Perhaps not surprisingly in such a poor country, economic and social problems were of most concern for 45 percent and 30 percent, respectively.[55]

Transparency, Accountability, and Access to Justice

Nicaragua achieved a measure of vertical accountability through largely clean elections, a free press, and the opening of political space in which civil society groups tried to play a watchdog role. By contrast, horizontal accountability across government agencies had been weak to begin with and was all but eliminated by the pact. Government institutions were accountable to the parties that appointed their leadership, not the public. In 2010, Freedom House gave Nicaragua a low score of 3.31 on accountability and public voice.[56]

There was little transparency in government. One result was an apparent increase in corruption. The Sandinistas had gained a reputation for corruption after the 1990 elections when they engaged in the "Piñata," distributing land titles to party supporters and pilfering state-owned goods before turning over government offices. However, it was during the term of President Arnoldo Alemán that corruption became systemic.

Large-scale corruption was due in part to weak oversight capacity. The UNDP categorized Nicaragua's Office of the Comptroller General as "moderate" in terms of its authority, meaning that its decisions were in principle binding but lacked the legal weight to ensure their implementation. Elsewhere in the region plebiscites, referenda and revocation of mandates became new tools for political accountability, but not so in Nicaragua.[57]

Petty corruption was less tracked but ever present. Practices reportedly included offering small bribes to civil servants to speed up their issuance of licenses, tax evasion, and bribery of traffic police to avoid tickets and associated fines. Nicaragua scored a 2.5 on the Transparency International 2009 Corruption Perception Index, ranking 130th among the 180 measured countries, with the 5th-worst score in the Western Hemisphere.[58] The international reaction was adverse. The United States stripped more than a dozen political leaders of their visas on the grounds of corruption, including two CSJ magistrates and a member of the CSE. Alemán's bank accounts in Panama were frozen pending the outcome of a judicial proceeding against him there for money laundering.[59]

The rule of law remained weak in Nicaragua, scoring 3.43 out of 7 on the Freedom House index in 2010.[60] The UNDP found that 35.2 percent of Nicaraguans surveyed said they knew of at least one case where someone received privileged treatment.[61] As was true elsewhere in Latin America, women, poor people, and indigenous persons were less likely than others to have their rights respected. The United Nations reported in 2005 that just 60.3 percent of women, 23.5 percent of indigenous people, and 17.7 percent of poor people said their rights were always or almost always respected. Access to justice was further limited for poor people because Nicaragua had the lowest number of public defenders relative to its population of any Latin American country.[62] Conversely, wealth and connections could buy special treatment. Thus, although he was sentenced to twenty years in prison, former president Alemán was allowed to serve his term in the comfort of his ranch estate and at times had the freedom to travel in Managua.

Criminal processing was hampered by an inefficient judicial system.[63] In 2006, Nicaragua reported a total prison population of 6,139, including pretrial detainees and remand prisoners. Prisoners who had not yet gone to trial constituted 21.4 percent of the prison population, a testament to the slowness of the judicial process.[64] The problem could not be dismissed as a result of low resources alone. Nicaragua had 6 judges per 100,000 inhabitants compared with a regional average of 4.9, and dedicated 2.9 percent of its annual budget to the judiciary compared with a regional average of 2.5 percent.[65]

Some progress could be noted through the 2002 modernization of the penal code and a probity law for civil servants regulating conflicts of interest and requiring declaration of assets. In 2007, Nicaragua's National Assembly would approve a law on access to information that held promise for increasing transparency in government. However, the protected position of political parties that had a record of corruption and controlled the judiciary, the Public Ministry, and Comptroller's Office suggested that Nicaragua's pacted democracy would continue to function poorly with respect to transparency, accountability, and access to justice.[66]

Hybrid Regime, Weak State

Thirty years after the 1979 revolution, the rule of law remained weak and the peace was marred by insecurity due to poverty, crime, corruption, drug trafficking, and uncertain access to justice. Eighteen percent of Nicaraguans listed bad government as their country's most serious problem, and only 46 percent were satisfied with the performance of democracy.[67] Nonetheless, Nicaragua had made substantial progress in democratic political development. Perhaps the most impressive gain was made in civil-military relations. Nicaragua not only obtained civilian control over the military, but the armed forces also became nonpartisan and indeed a bulwark of democracy. Obedience to civilian authority was perhaps made easier by the fact that the military was born of revolution. Military officers were accustomed to taking orders from the leaders of a political party. Moreover, their leftist revolutionary origins meant that, unlike in neighboring El Salvador and Guatemala, these officers had never been allied with the landed oligarchy to repress the populace. They had committed few human rights violations during the insurrection and counterrevolution, so the amnesty in Nicaragua's 1990 Transition Protocol withstood the test of time and there was no popular pressure for a truth commission.

As part of the transition in 1990, the police had been transferred out of the military structure and given a mission more coherent with democratic governance, but ironically their independence from partisan influence was thus made less certain. Whereas the military pact had guaranteed the armed forces control over their own promotions, the chief of police was a presidential appointee. The lack of police action to protect opposition legislators during political clashes in the streets in April 2010 was attributed to government pressure, though the police chief argued that police intervention would have exacerbated conflict and potentially increased violence.

The nonpartisan, professional, yet subordinate nature of the military had important implications for state building. In 2010, Nicaragua was not yet a strong state, but it did provide essential government services to many citizens, and upheld an internal legal order, even if the quality of the services and justice left much to be desired. Portions of the Atlantic Coast and Rio San Juan remained remote and functionally ungoverned, with few municipal offices and schools, and some citizens living out their lives without a documented identity or much interaction with state authorities. These areas were sparsely populated, however, and if citizens were too poor to pay taxes and too distant for military recruitment, neither did they contest the state's authority or monopoly on the use of force. The state's legitimacy was not at issue. Although Miskito Indians had formed counterrevolutionary paramilitary groups in the 1980s, now the weak presence of the state on the Atlantic Coast did not spawn armed conflict and only marginally increased crime. Although drug cartels would penetrate some of these distant communities for transshipment of illegal narcotics, the armed forces visibly opposed drug trafficking, and unlike in Mexico there was little evidence of drug money penetrating state institutions and co-opting politicians or military officers.

The transformation of the military into a nonpartisan and largely apolitical institution precluded traditional forms of authoritarianism, and was important in classifying Nicaragua as an illiberal democracy rather than a competitive authoritarian regime. Other distinguishing elements were the low level of human rights abuses, a relatively free press, and general respect for civil liberties. These worsened under the Ortega administration, causing Freedom House to lower its civil liberties rating from a 3 to a 4, with particular concern expressed about the repeated use of violent intimidation and politicized courts.[68] Nonetheless, the military remained neutral in these political clashes and was thought by some to be a constraint on President Ortega's political ambitions.

With respect to procedures for processing conflict without violence, Nicaragua had established clean elections as the means to reach national office for many important posts, but these gains were eroded in 2008 when widespread fraud in municipal elections discredited the electoral system. The following year, Sandinista members of the CSJ's Constitutional

Chamber ruled that the 1995 constitutional prohibition on immediate reelection and the two-term limit did not apply to Ortega or 103 Sandinista mayors, who had filed an *amparo* appeal saying the limits violated their right to political participation. This partisan manipulation of the CSJ capped years of politicization of the judiciary and dramatically raised the stakes of the 2011 election, in which Ortega was expected to run for a third term. The 1979 revolution had put an end to the Somoza family's use of electoral fraud to sustain itself in power, but the 2009 ruling raised the specter of *continuismo.*

The Decline of Party Politics?

If the Ortega government seemed intent on eroding procedural limits on power, it revitalized efforts at participatory governance, an odd tactic in a polity governed through a party pact and where democracy was centered on (some would say reduced to) electoral competition. Citizen power councils (CPCs) were formed in each municipality and given a social audit function. These groups of local citizens, largely Sandinistas, gave input to and monitored implementation of the development plans in their municipalities. In some cases, government transfers were channeled through the CPC rather than through the municipality, but this did not necessarily imply a tense relationship between the CPC and the city council. Like the Zapatistas, the Sandinistas had been successful in local politics, winning many more mayoral races than the Liberals in 2004, and those mayors and the CPCs tended to be on the same political page.

The CPCs were an example of the innovation that the regional shift to the left had wrought, but it remained to be seen whether they would deepen democracy. Unlike the social audit nongovernmental organizations that had arisen spontaneously to combat local corruption under neoliberalism, the CPCs were organized directly by the presidency and closely managed by first lady Rosario Murillo. Opponents sometimes compared the CPCs to the neighborhood defense committees established by the FSLN in the 1980s, which were criticized for abusing their authority, but the CPCs were an arm of the presidency, not the party.

Civil society remained weak and largely quiescent. To the extent that popular mobilization took place, it was through the FSLN instead of independent nongovernmental organizations, another pattern with roots in the revolution. Party militants on occasion used rough methods, harassing a peaceful opposition march in August 2008 and injuring opposition law-makers in April 2010 after blocking their access to the National Assembly building. These were exceptions, however, and not indicative of a return to violence as a typical means of settling disputes. Rather, they hinted at an intermittent politics of intimidation where the instruments were more likely to be tax audits than arbitrary arrest or violence. Co-optation rather than confrontation remained the government's preferred mode, especially in dealing with the more powerful members of the business community.

Ideology and Social Democracy

The pact concerned sharing power in the institutions of the state and limit-ing electoral competition, which is to say procedural democracy, but did not address a comprehensive vision of democracy that would include social equality and economic welfare. Indeed, deep disagreements characterized the Liberal and Sandinista approaches to poverty, inequality, and social inclusion, and more broadly the substance of policy and methods whereby public goods and services should be distributed. The Sandinistas continued to proffer government intervention to redistribute on behalf of the poor, and the Liberals continued to advocate limited government, market-based strategies, and growth as a "rising tide that lifts all boats."

Although the political pact between Ortega and Aleman was opportunis-tic, and fostered a patron-client model with them as modern-day national caudillos, the patterns in that clientelism were informed by ideology. Who benefited, via which institutional channels? Echoing the socialist goals of the revolution, the Ortega government eliminated school fees and charges for public health clinic visits, distributed pigs and chickens in an effort to end hunger, and channeled resources through the CPCs. In the foreign pol-icy arena, Ortega made common cause with Hugo Chávez, whose "twenty-first-century socialism" had already found receptive audiences in Bolivia and Ecuador. Reflecting the market basis of Latin America's new leftist current, the Ortega administration did not nationalize property or oppose business as it had in the 1980s, for indeed many Sandinistas were by now themselves business owners. However, the Albanisa enterprise formed with Venezuela's Bolivarian Alliance for the Americas (ALBA) became a signif-icant investor in infrastructure development. It helped bolster Nicaragua's ability to generate electricity and build roads but also crowded out competi-tors in some industries. Venezuela had reached an oil agreement with the

Ortega administration that generated funds for Nicaraguan development that in some years rose to one-quarter of the national budget, and which, as noted above, were handled off-budget, allowing President Ortega discretion in directing their use. European donors could not compete with this Venezuelan largesse, and found themselves unable to use conditionality to encourage good governance by the Ortega administration.

Critics rightly noted that redistributive policies are not themselves development, and strategies contingent on Chávez's wealth were not sustainable. Their impact was not easily measured in national statistics, but they had limited reach. Although opponents suggested that the redistributive approach was intended to buy support for the government, it was by no means certain that patronage would translate into additional votes for Ortega at the polls in 2011. Nonetheless, the government made progress on its campaign promises of free education and health care, and it won credit for alleviating the plight of the poor, at least temporarily.

Ortega's growing opposition was similar to the antirevolution coalition of the 1980s, composed of owners of small and medium-sized businesses, liberal and conservative parties, and the Catholic Church. Of particular importance, however, these opposition actors had never taken up arms during the war and would not do so now. Despite U.S. protestations to the contrary, Violeta Chamorro's election in 1990 was a victory for the unarmed opposition, not the contras, who had boycotted the election. Afterward, the Sandinistas' old armed opponents had integrated into politics much the same way they had fought the war, as separate and ill-organized groups, and they no longer posed a threat. Moreover, the end of the Cold War meant that the second Ortega administration's progressive policies did not trigger a reflexive anticommunist U.S. reaction. The Obama administration was preoccupied with wars in Iraq and Afghanistan, along with economic woes, making it difficult for Nicaraguans to draw either negative or positive attention from the United States.

Neopopulism, Opportunism, and Ideology

The very existence of the 2000 pact seemed to sound the death knell of ideology and constitute proof positive that neopopulism would be a more important determinant of the Ortega government's policies than leftist ideology. Populism is understood here in political terms, as a way of competing for and exercising political power, rather than being defined by the class composition of a movement's main constituency or its distributive agenda. Populism's telltale features are mass movements centered on personalist and sometimes charismatic leaders who make direct appeals to the people. Whereas classical populists like Juan Perón and Getúlio Vargas had created populist parties, neopopulists often sidestepped party structures and mobilized the masses through media outreach, elections, and referenda.[69]

Ortega's repeated purging of his rivals within the FSLN and insistence on remaining its candidate after failing three times to gain the presidency suggested that the party had to an important degree become his personal vehicle that served more than constrained him. His willingness to form a pact with a right-wing ideological adversary to gain power was consistent with neopopulist opportunism. Neopopulism can also be demobilizing, confining participation to the electoral realm; and by insulating the government from citizen demands, the pact may have functioned in this way.

In practice, however, the reality was more complex and the case for neopopulism was less compelling. At the outset, it must be recalled that Ortega had faithfully played by the electoral rules before manipulating them via the pact, and thus he had accepted defeat in 1990 and 1996. Moreover, his successful 2006 presidential campaign was markedly low key. In contrast to past campaigns, he held no major rallies to appeal to the masses, and instead held small "reconciliation meetings" to woo back party members who had strayed and engage former contras and voters who were too young to remember the revolution. He relied on the party to organize those meetings and also mobilize votes for the legislative slate, a vital task now that constitutional reforms had increased the importance of the legislature relative to the executive branch. This was no populist campaign. In the end, he won with a plurality, not a majority, and indeed with a lower percentage of the vote than he had received in the past. His election had less to do with mass mobilization of "el pueblo" than with carefully contrived electoral rules, a split in the opposition, the FSLN party organization, and the long shadow of the revolution that kept the party base loyal.

The establishment of the CPCs opened the door to a more populist mode of governance. Though often read through the narrative of the 1980s, these were misunderstood as the expansion of the FSLN, but in fact constituted an end run around the revolutionary party. They allowed the presidency to keep tabs on Sandinista mayors as much as Liberal ones, and to communicate directly with the people to discipline the party at the local level. This cast doubt on the contention that the FSLN was merely a personal vehicle for Ortega; if that were the case, there would have been no need to circumvent party channels and invent a rival structure connecting the president to his political base. Yet to the extent that the CPCs prevented Ortega from needing to rely on the FSLN to mobilize support for his administration and future candidacy, they paved the way for a more populist approach to politics in future elections.

Whether Ortega would ever choose a neopopulist antipolitics was in doubt. He needed the FSLN with its party discipline to manage the legislature, which the pact had made more powerful through constitutional reforms. By structuring national-level politics around two dominant parties and empowering them to populate all the top political offices, the pact bound Ortega to the FSLN party apparatus and its leftist revolutionary origins in powerful symbolic and practical ways. Elsewhere in Latin America, radical populist leaders like Hugo Chávez might toy with the idea that representative democracy based on political parties should be set aside in favor of direct democracy without parties, but in Nicaragua any such scheme would imply breaking the pact and was therefore not undertaken lightly.

Pacted Democracy in Comparative Perspective

The pacted nature of Nicaraguan democracy was familiar to Latin America scholars. The Pacto de Punto Fijo signed in Venezuela on January 23, 1958, established a two-party system by excluding others (notably the Communists) and providing political protection, behind which the leading parties grew increasingly corrupt. The Venezuelan majority remained poor despite that country's oil wealth. In Colombia, which lays claim to being Latin America's oldest democracy, two parties traded power back and forth for decades, and the exclusion of other parties took violent forms. These were not hopeful precedents.

Those who lamented the weakness of party systems in Latin America may have found Nicaragua's pacted democracy appealing.[70] The sheer presence of Nicaragua's political parties stood in stark contrast to the collapsed party system in Peru, for example. But although Nicaragua's parties appeared strong based on their vote-getting ability, they lacked democratic internal structures. They were more than just electoral vehicles for their respective caudillos, playing important roles between elections, but were no better than Guatemala's electoral parties when it came to articulating citizen interests. Progress toward the consolidation of a two-party dominant system came at the expense of competition and accountability, threatening the independence of powers and increasing arbitrary governance and corruption. Nicaragua's high threshold for party formation and entry into the legislature was intended to increase governability, and it did help prevent the sort of fractured party system seen in Ecuador. Nonetheless, politics in Nicaragua fell victim to the same episodic executive-legislative gridlock that had repeatedly destabilized Ecuadoran governments. Indeed, interbranch conflicts brought threats of impeachment to both presidents Chamorro and Bolaños.

Early power struggles between the institutions of the state were normal processes whereby the scope of institutional authority was tested and refined. Beginning in 2000, however, the political pact between the Sandinista and Liberal parties institutionalized their competition for control of the state, assuring that it would remain nonviolent despite their opposed ideologies but also artificially preserving their rivalry in the political architecture of state institutions. Policy was brokered rather than debated, and key decisions were made by a handful of leaders in parties to which the public had little access. Pacted democracy did not indicate the development of trust between leaders, who constantly maneuvered to shift the power equation and gain advantage.

Pacting implied leaders knew how to collaborate as well as compete. For the Liberals and Sandinistas, it was no longer a zero-sum game, because the Electoral Law assured the losing presidential candidate of a seat in the legislature and gave the "second political force" ample power in naming top officials. However, this did not imply the development of a culture of tolerance. At election time, polarization reemerged and both sides invoked imagery of the war and demonized their adversaries. Other groups were sometimes excluded from competing for power in elections, and afterward were almost entirely shut out of the exercise of power.

These patterns suggested that the pact had institutionalized rather than eliminated the ideological conflict that had initially found expression through the revolution and counterrevolution. It temporally extended that conflict into the new century even as it confined the conflict mainly to the electoral arena and provided the FSLN and PLC with guarantees that electoral losses would not severely damage either party. The mutual suspicion and electoral competition between the two parties went on unabated, but the pact buffered each party against losses to one another by assuring the loser an important degree of power in all the main institutions of the state. In established democracies, this emerges as a voluntary and ongoing decision by the electoral victor not to employ all its potential for injuring the loser given the prospect of a future electoral reversal.[71] In Nicaragua's new democracy, the decision took the form of a backroom deal to guarantee not just the survival but also the preeminence of the pacting parties at the expense of others. In the process, it also institutionalized the fault lines of the revolution and counterrevolution, preserving the primacy of the Sandinista/anti-Sandinista ideological axis and the parties through which it was expressed.

After 1990, the broad framework of the regime was set, and was understood to include a market and competitive elections. Some institutions were customary, and some practices endured, but this did not mean there was a broad consensus on a set of democratic procedures. As the power ratio shifted from favoring the Liberals to favoring the Sandinistas, the pact was renegotiated and political procedures changed. In the process, democratic institutionality was undercut. Although the legal framework mattered a great deal, the 2009 manipulation of the Constitution by the CSJ to permit Ortega's candidacy suggested that even that most fundamental constraint was not absolute for someone willing to absorb the political costs associated with the raw exercise of power. Having been based on individuals, the pact increasingly made the law subject to leaders rather than the reverse, and thus impeded the generation of legitimacy for state institutions.

When polled in 2005, Nicaraguans defined democracy in terms of elections and civil liberties.[72] This was a narrow political standard. The Inter-American Democratic Charter also included in its definition of democracy "access to and the exercise of power in accordance with the rule of law, . . . the pluralistic system of political parties and organizations, and the separation of powers and independence of the branches of government," as well as transparency.[73] These elements of democracy remained weak and were specifically imperiled by the pacted nature of Nicaragua's political system.

Nicaragua's artificially maintained two-party dominant system did not produce a consolidated liberal democratic regime. Informal institutions, including political pacts, can enable governments to "muddle through" in the face of increased citizen demands for inclusion and policy performance despite weak state capacity.[74] In a postwar setting with deep polarization, pacting may have been viewed as a shortcut to a stable bipartisan system. In Nicaragua, however, the 2000 pact limited the use of elections as a tool for achieving vertical accountability by reducing opportunities for opposition and insulating key party leaders from electoral losses. The partisan duopoly on state institutions nullified the checks and balances that provide horizontal accountability in consolidated democracies. The pact had trapped Nicaraguan politics in the amber of past conflict, creating a stable but illiberal democracy.

Notes

1. See Rose J. Spalding, "From Low-Intensity War to Low-Intensity Peace: The Nicaraguan Peace Process," in *Comparative Peace Processes in Latin America,* edited by Cynthia J. Arnson (Washington, D.C., and Stanford, Calif.: Woodrow Wilson Center Press and Stanford University Press, 1999), 31–64.

2. Arnson, *Comparative Peace Processes,* 7.

3. For a general history of Nicaragua under the Somoza dictatorship and the early years of the revolution, see John A. Booth, *The End and the Beginning* (Boulder, Colo.: Westview Press, 1985).

4. The making of the 1983 Political Parties Law is discussed in more detail by David Close, *Nicaragua: Politics, Economics and Society* (London: Pinter, 1988).

5. The term "founding election" refers to the first competitive election in which all major parties participate leading to a transition from authoritarian rule. For comparisons of founding elections, see Samuel P. Huntington, *The Third Wave: Democratization in the Late Twentieth Century* (Norman: University of Oklahoma Press, 1991).

6. Nicaragua scored 4.20 on the 2006 Freedom House index for civil liberties and 4.49 for public voice and accountability. See Freedom House, *Countries at the Cross-roads 2004,* http://www.freedomhouse.org/template.cfm?page=140&edition=7&ccr page=31&ccrcountry=136.

7. The demilitarization process and 1995 constitutional reform are covered in more detail by David Close, *The Chamorro Years* (Boulder, Colo.: Lynn Rienner, 1999).

8. An alternative evaluation is given by Antonio Lacayo Oyanguren, *La difícil transición nicaragüense en el Gobierno de doña Violeta* (Bogotá: Colección Cultural de Centro América, 2005).

9. United Nations Development Program, *Democracy in Latin America: Towards a Citizens' Democracy* (Buenos Aires: Aguilar, Altea, Taurus, Alfaguara, 2005), 92.

10. For a more complete discussion of the 1995 reform process and resulting political crisis, see the entry by the present author in *Nicaragua without Illusions: Regime Transition and Structural Adjustment in the 1990s,* edited by Thomas Walker (Lanham, Md.: Rowman & Littlefield, 1997).

11. Asamblea Nacional de Nicaragua, "Ley No. 192, Ley Marco," as published in *El Nuevo Diario,* July 3, 1995.

12. The Liberals even contested the revolution's cultural spaces, claiming to be the authentic heirs to the nationalist legacy of Sandino, who was indeed a Liberal.

13. The politics leading to the pact are explored by David R. Dye, Jack Spence, and George Vickers, *Patchwork Democracy: Nicaraguan Politics Ten Years after the Fall* (Cambridge, Mass.: Hemisphere Initiatives, 2000). The early effects of the pact are explored by Katherine Hoyt's chapter in *Undoing Democracy: The Politics of Electoral Caudillismo,* edited by David Close and Kalowatie Deonandan (Lanham, Md.: Lexington Books, 2004).

14. United Nations Development Program, *Democracy,* 81–84.

15. In all three elections, the OAS, European Union, and Carter Center observed, as did Ethics and Transparency, a national observer organization that conducted a quick count. These groups documented myriad faults in the elections but found they were not serious enough to injure the legitimacy of the processes. See, e.g., the Carter Center's election reports, http://www.cartercenter.org/news/publications/election_reports.html.

16. United Nations Development Program, *Democracy,* 86.

17. Ibid., 88.

18. An example of a controversial CSE decision came in the municipal election in 2000 when a popular candidate for mayor of Managua was blocked from running when the CSE redrew the electoral districts so that his house fell outside the capital, making him ineligible under the new Electoral Law. However, the pacting parties did not invent the practice of prohibiting candidacies. Elements of the 1995 constitutional reform were explicitly designed to prevent president Chamorro's son-in-law, Antonio Lacayo, from seeking the presidency.

19. For a full discussion of Nicaragua's political finance laws, see Daniel Zovatto and Stephen Griner, eds., *Funding of Political Parties and Election Campaigns in Latin America* (San José: International IDEA, 2005).

20. United Nations Development Program, *Democracy,* 82.

21. For a thorough analysis of the symbiotic relationship between Daniel Ortega and Arnoldo Alemán, see David R. Dye, *Democracy Adrift* (Managua: Prodeni, 2004).

22. For a detailed discussion of the international response to the impeachment threat, see Shelley A. McConnell, "Can the Inter-American Democratic Charter Really Work? The 2004–05 Constitutional Crisis in Nicaragua," draft prepared for the Twenty-Seventh Congress of the Latin American Studies Association, Montreal, September 5–8, 2007.

23. Asamblea Nacional de Nicaragua, "Ley No. 520, Reforma Parcial a la Constitución Política de la República de Nicaragua," published in *La Gaceta,* February 18, 2005.

24. Asamblea Nacional de Nicaragua, "Ley No. 558, Ley Marco para la Estabilidad y Gobernabilidad del País," published in *La Gaceta,* October 20, 2005. Implementation of the reform was delayed until January 2008.

25. United Nations, *Human Development Report 2009,* http://hdr.undp.org/en/statistics/.

26. World Bank, http://devdata.worldbank.org/AAG/nic_aag.pdf.

27. "Statement by an IMF Mission to Nicaragua," March 2010, https://www.imf.org/external/np/sec/pr/2010/pr1084.htm.

28. International Monetary Fund, *World Economic Outlook Database.* April 2010, http://www.imf.org/external/pubs/ft/weo/2010/01/weodata/index.aspx.

29. United Nations, *Human Development Report 2009,* "Nicaragua," http://hdrstats.undp.org/en/countries/data_sheets/cty_ds_NIC.html.

30. Central Intelligence Agency, *The World Factbook,* "Nicaragua," https://www.cia.gov/library/publications/the-world-factbook/geos/nu.html.

31. United Nations, *Human Development Report 2009,* "Nicaragua," http://hdrstats.undp.org/en/countries/data_sheets/cty_ds_NIC.html.

32. United Nations, *Human Development Report 2008,* "Nicaragua," http://hdrstats.undp.org/countries/data_sheets/cty_ds_NIC.html.

33. United Nations, *Human Development Report 2009,* "Nicaragua: HDI Trends," http://hdr.undp.org/en/statistics/.

34. World Bank, "Millennium Development Goals: Nicaragua," http://ddp-ext.worldbank.org/ext/ddpreports/ViewSharedReport?&CF=1&REPORT_ID=1336&REQUEST_TYPE=VIEWADVANCED&HF=N/IDGProfile.asp.

35. United Nations, *Human Development Report 2008,* "Nicaragua."

36. World Bank, "Millennium Development Goals: Nicaragua."

37. United Nations Development Program, *Valoración Común de País: Nicaragua* (Managua: Sistema de las Naciones Unidas, 2007), 30. It is not clear whether, in

reporting primary enrollment figures, the government has adjusted its school age population figures to include estimated numbers of unregistered children.

38. United Nations, *Human Development Report 2008,* "Nicaragua."

39. World Bank, "Millennium Development Goals: Nicaragua." Note that the official open unemployment rate was just 5 percent, a figure that did not capture underemployment and the extent to which Nicaraguans worked in the informal sector without steady income or access to benefits.

40. Corporación Latinobarómetro, *Latin America 2005,* http://www.revistafuturos.info/documentos/docu_f13/LatBar2005.pdf, 71.

41. United Nations Development Program, *Valoración Común de País,* 17, 52.

42. Ministerio de Hacienda, Gobierno de Nicaragua, *Presupuesto General de la República 2010,* http://www.hacienda.gob.ni/documentos/presupuesto/presupuesto-gral.-de-la-republica/presupuesto-2010/anexo-i-anexos-del-presupuesto-genaral-de-la-republica/E_01_Balance_Presup.pdf/view. The figure is given in Nicaraguan cordobas at 32,335,408,000, which in June 2010 converted to $1,513,475,700.

43. World Bank, http://devdata.worldbank.org/AAG/nic_aag.pdf.

44. United Nations Development Program, *Valoración Común de País,* 21.

45. For an assessment of the substantial investment Nicaragua and its donors will need to make in order to meet the Millennium Development Goals, see Sistema de Naciones Unidas, "Escenario de inversión social para alcanzar los Objectivos de Desarrollo del Milenio y Metas Nacionales de Nicaragua," 2008.

46. Corporación Latinobarómetro, *Latin America 2005,* 78.

47. The value of Venezuelan assistance varied with the price of oil, but was estimated by the Central Bank in 2009 at $450 million. In accordance with a 2006 agreement, Venezuela sells Nicaragua 10,000 barrels a day at 50 percent of market value through the Albanisa Corporation, a joint enterprise of the two countries. Nicaragua pays 60 percent of the cost within ninety days, and the remainder in twenty-five years at a 1 percent rate of interest. The transaction involves Nicaragua paying full price to Albanisa, which then returns half the money for development projects connected to ALBA. The agreement was not reviewed by the Nicaraguan National Assembly, and the funds generated are handled through government accounts on which there is little oversight. See http://www.docstoc.com/docs/43982228/Country-Brief-NICARAGUA.

48. Rose J. Spalding argues that substituting elections for a full peace process had negative repercussions in Nicaragua; Spalding, "From Low-Intensity War to Low-Intensity Peace." Also see David R. Dye et al., *Contesting Everything, Winning Nothing: The Search for Consensus in Nicaragua 1990–1995* (Cambridge, Mass.: Hemisphere Initiatives, 1995), concur that holding elections before disarmament left many issues unsettled, which were then contested politically and via extended low-level violence.

49. The list of causal factors here comes from the Nicaraguan Armed Forces, "Apreciación de la Seguridad," briefing by Lieutenant Colonel Nicaragua to the Carter Center's election observation delegation, Managua, November 2, 2006.

50. Time series crime data through 2005 were reported in Policía Nacional, *Anuario Estadístico 2005* and data on 2006 are from Policía Nacional, *Anuario Estadístico 2006.*

51. U.S. Department of State, *2009 Human Rights Report, Nicaragua,* http://www.state.gov/g/drl/rls/hrrpt/2009/wha/136120.htm. The Nicaraguan National Police were reported to have 9,595 employees, including 8,423 police officers, 857 civilian personnel, and 315 volunteers filling staffing gaps. Officers were paid low salaries of roughly $100 per month.

52. U.S. Agency for International Development (USAID), "Central America and Mexico Gang Assessment Annex 5: Nicaragua Profile," April 2006. Note that the Nicaraguan Armed Forces report a substantially higher figure of 4,500 youth involved in gangs, but they echo the general sentiment of the USAID report that these are not linked to international criminal networks.

53. International Center for Prison Studies, "World Prison Brief: Nicaragua," http://www.kcl.ac.uk/depsta/law/research/icps/worldbrief/wpb_country.php?country=84, based on figures from the United Nations and Nicaragua's Ministerio de Gobernación.

54. Data on arrests from Policía Nacional, *Anuario Estadístico 2006.* General profile of the drug trade from U.S. Bureau of International Narcotics and Law Enforcement Affairs (INL), *International Narcotics Control Strategy Report* 2007, http://www.state.gov/p/inl/rls/nrcrpt/2007/vol1/html/80856.htm.

55. Data from Americas Barometer 2006, as cited in chapter 2 of the present volume.

56. Freedom House, *Countries at the Crossroads 2010,* http://www.freedomhouse.org/modules/publications/ccr/modPrintVersion.cfm?edition=9&ccrpage=43&ccrcountry=194.

57. United Nations Development Program, *Democracy in Latin America,* 99.

58. Transparency International, "Corruption Perception Index," 2009, http://www.transparency.org/policy_research/surveys_indices/cpi/2009/cpi_2009_table.

59. Transparency International, *Global Corruption Report,* 2006, 216, http://www.transparency.org/publications/gcr.

60. This placed Nicaragua well below the satisfactory performance level of 5.0, as noted in Freedom House, *Countries at the Crossroads 2010.*

61. United Nations Development Program, *Democracy,* 102.

62. Nicaragua has 0.3 public defenders per 100,000 inhabitants, compared with a regional average of 1.5, according to United Nations Development Program, *Democracy,* 110, 113.

63. A summary of internationally funded modernization of Nicaragua's judiciary and its loss of impartiality is given by Borja Días Rivillas, "Politización de justicia en Nicaragua: Del pacto político de 2000 al final de la cruzada contra la corrupción de Enrique Bolaños," unpublished paper presented at 2007 Meeting of Latin American Studies Association, Montreal, September 5–8, 2007.

64. International Center for Prison Studies, "World Prison Brief."

65. United Nations Development Program, *Democracy,* 113.

66. A detailed critical review of politicization of the Public Ministry, Comptroller General's Office, and judicial system is given by Dye, *Democracy Adrift,* 41–52.

67. Latin American Public Opinion Project surveys (LAPOP), 2006, available at www.lapopsurveys.org.

68. Freedom House, *Freedom in the World: Nicaragua,* 2010, http://www.freedomhouse.org/template.cfm?page=22&year=2010&country=7888.

69. For a discussion of the debate on definitions of populism, see Kurt Weyland, "Clarifying a Contested Concept: Populism in the Study of Latin American Politics," *Comparative Politics* 34, no. 1 (2001): 1–22.

70. On the weakness of party systems and evidence that regional leaders were deeply concerned, see United Nations Development Program, *Democracy,* 156. A useful scholarly analysis is given by Scott Mainwaring and Timothy Scully, *Building Democratic Institutions: Party Systems in Latin America* (Stanford, Calif.: Stanford University Press, 1995).

71. This concept, called contingent consent, is formulated in Philippe C. Schmitter and Terry Lynn Karl, "What Democracy Is . . . and Is Not," *Journal of Democracy* 2 (Summer 1991): 67–73.

72. See www.latinobarometro.org/.

73. Organization of American States, "Inter-American Democratic Charter," Articles 3 and 4, http://www.oas.org/OASpage/eng/Documents/Democractic_Charter.htm.

74. On informal institutions, see Gretchen Helmke and Steven Levitsky, eds., *Informal Institutions and Democracy: Lessons from Latin America* (Baltimore: Johns Hopkins University Press, 2006).

Chapter 6

A Historical Perspective on Counterinsurgency and the "War on Drugs" in Colombia

Marco Palacios

During World War II, it was broadly understood that coffee, Colombia's principal export, would serve as the basis for further Colombian industrialization. A half century later, the country began a process of premature deindustrialization when drug trafficking burst onto the scene. As it had during Colombia's coffee export booms, the United States played a vital role in the new cocaine-driven economy. The United States constitutes the largest illicit drug market in the world, and its laws criminalize the entire chain of drug-trafficking activities, from production to consumption to money laundering.

This chapter is a concise examination of the roots of internal armed conflict in Colombia, focusing on the role of the weakness of the Colombian

I am grateful for comments by Cindy Arnson and the participants in the original conference on "Comparative Peace Processes in Latin America," held at the Woodrow Wilson Center, as well as observations by Mónica Serrano and communications from Herbert Tico Braun, Fernando Cubides, and Aura María Puyana. I especially thank two anonymous reviewers for their comments on this chapter.

175

state in allowing multiple armed actors to emerge and flourish. This weakness is evident, inter alia, in the manner in which successive Colombian governments disregarded both the coca- and poppy-producing campesino (peasant) base of production and in the clientelistic-*latifundista* (large landowner) networks through which the illicit narcotics trade flourishes, particularly in the Caribbean regions. The chapter also explores how the illicit drug economy intersected with and transformed the conflict, contributing to the corruption of politics and spawning ever-newer and ongoing forms of violence.

In addition, I argue that the pacification policies of two Colombian administrations, that of Andrés Pastrana (1998–2002) and Álvaro Uribe (2002–10), are best understood in the context of the multi-billion-dollar U.S. aid package known as Plan Colombia, the emphasis of which shifted following the terrorist attacks of September 11, 2001. U.S. global security strategy served to merge Colombia's "wars" against drug trafficking and against armed insurgency into one. Over a period of almost a decade, Plan Colombia contributed to a strengthening of the state in the military arena but not in other areas that would fortify its democratic legitimacy. The reluctance to diagnose social realities and thereby to implement the appropriate policies was one of the greatest limitations of militaristic policies pursued from 1999 onward. President Juan Manuel Santos, who was inaugurated in August 2010, acknowledged some of the social realities underlying armed conflict in Colombia, and announced policies early in his administration to begin to address land tenure issues in rural areas that are at the core of the conflict. As of this writing, it is too early to tell whether these efforts will be successful.

Armed Conflict and Perceptions of Normalcy

The current armed conflict with guerrillas began in the mid-1980s, not forty or fifty years ago as is commonly claimed. The 1980s marked a change in the numbers of combatants, casualties, and destroyed properties; the territorial coverage of the conflict; and the financial resources and political and social support available to armed actors. In fact, from 1954 to 1985, homicide rates in Colombia were only slightly higher than those in Panama or Brazil. From a statistical standpoint, the political conflict had only a minimal impact. The blossoming drug trade sent those statistics soaring.[1] From the mid-1980s onward, narco-trafficking began to impel mafia-driven modernization,[2] further corrupt political practices, and accentuate the state's secular weakness.

Drug trafficking accelerated the expansion of the armed conflict; in the 1960s and 1970s, guerrilla organizations were limited and marginal, and their members could be counted in the dozens or hundreds, not in thousands. Of particular importance among these groups were the National Liberation Army (Ejército de Liberación Nacional, ELN), an organization founded in 1962 with roots in the universities that, with help from Cuba, set up its first guerrilla camp in 1964; and the Revolutionary Armed Forces of Colombia (Fuerzas Armadas Revolucionarias de Colombia, FARC), which evolved from armed campesino groups guided by the Colombian Communist Party during the period in Colombian history known as La Violencia (1946–64).[3] In the mid-1950s, the FARC morphed into local "peasant self-defense groups." Following Operación Marquetalia, a conventional military offensive launched in 1964, they again became mobile and offensive guerrilla groups and two years later adopted the name FARC, to which they later added "-EP" (Ejército del Pueblo), or People's Army.[4]

From their inception, these guerrilla organizations faced counterinsurgency tactics inspired by the U.S. national security doctrine. Frequently, when guerrillas established their power in a locality, local paramilitary forces would appear. These paramilitary groups enjoyed legal status between 1965 and 1989, as well as backing and encouragement from the Colombian army and established local elites. In the 1980s, paramilitary groups mimicked guerrilla tactics, strategies, and organizational structures, as noted by the Colombian sociologist Fernando Cubides.[5]

The cocaine economy of the past twenty-five years has been an important component of the country's gross domestic product and exports. In the 1970s, due to increased repression in Mexico, Colombia replaced Mexico as the United States' principal supplier of marijuana. By the late 1980s, Colombia was already the principal cocaine exporter, even though Peru and Bolivia surpassed it in terms of coca cultivation. As Colombia's cocaine economy consolidated, the cultivation of coca as well as poppies and marijuana increased, along with the processing of these drugs and their integration into international networks.[6] From 1997 onward, Colombia became the world's leading producer of coca leaf, a position apparently disputed by the resurgence of coca production in Peru in 2010. A considerable part of the enormous financial resources from the drug business were aimed at securing the control of territory, all the while fostering and broadening the armed conflict and the power of paramilitary and guerrilla groups.[7]

Along with the increased production of coca, cocaine, heroin, and other drugs, Colombia became more dynamic and successful in improving its participation in the world drug market. In spite of the fluid and distinct nature of relationships in particular localities, paramilitaries and guerrillas established an order and a system of justice in these areas that were more or less respected by local populations.[8] It was, however, in the big cities where financing was obtained; secure routes were established for sending merchandise to consumer countries; and commercial, banking, and investment strategies were designed for laundering illicit profits. All these activities required political protection. And, given their illegal nature, compliance with the contractual obligations incurred by different actors involved in the drug trade was enforced though private violence.[9]

The Colombian Malady: A Weak State

Both the illegal armed groups (guerrillas, paramilitaries, and now, new criminal bands) and the government responses to them underscore the historical failure on the part of the ruling classes to build a basic consensus regarding the nation's political organization and in forming a democratic state that guarantees equality before the law, the protection of civil, political and social rights, and the rule of law. The fragility of Colombian democracy points to the existence of a weak state that has tolerated and encouraged the political supremacy of a complex system based on *latifundism* and clientelism and its related ideological dogmas. Thus, the Colombian state has seemed incapable of ending both a prolonged armed conflict and the urban crime organized around drug trafficking.

We should make no mistake: Colombia has modernized in a very peculiar fashion, with economic growth, sociodemographic change, and chaotic urbanization; both constitutionalism and corruption; both social exclusion and social mobility; both legality and violence; and both electoral and clientelistic democracy.

By the beginning of the twenty-first century, cocaine-producing Colombia had consolidated a system of antidemocratic subversion in the form of small criminal republics under the control of the disarmed paramilitary right, which was most evident in the Caribbean region. This system unified the domination of the cattle barons, old-school electoral clientelism, and the nouveau riche whose wealth derives from drug-laundered money.[10]

Figure 6.1. Map of Colombia

Source: Cartography by Congressional Research Service, Library of Congress.

Four traditions rooted in the colonial period helped open the way: *latifundism,* clientelism, contraband, and colonization.

To better understand the role of these traditions in modern-day Colombia, one can divide the country into three interconnected entities (figure 6.1). First are the metropolitan areas and principal cities inhabited by two-thirds of the population, which can be called "islands of legitimacy"; paradoxically, it is in the "islands" that the drug trafficking mafias are capable of organizing their business, buying state protection, and laundering money. Second are the nine recently colonized territories or "territories of de facto power," inhabited by approximately 5 percent of the nation's total population.[11] And third is the remainder of the country—in municipalities throughout the departments of the Caribbean region, the Cauca, and the coffee-growing regions—that oscillates between the two extremes and can be called "the country in the middle," which constituted an enthusiastic support base for President Uribe's democratic security policy aimed at establishing a military and police presence throughout the nation's territory.[12]

The "territories of de facto power," those remote areas with only a tiny percentage of the country's population, are the geographic heart of the armed organizations. The FARC in particular claims to represent the interests of socially excluded campesinos who have been stripped of their rights as citizens. The poor and nomadic coca-growing population, persecuted and stigmatized, and the small village intermediaries personify the FARC's idea of injustice in rural Colombia.

Regardless of their initial origins, from the 1980s onward, paramilitary organizations became fused to the drug-trafficking chain, though not directly born of it. Guerrillas and paramilitaries both adopted a kind of populist discourse with regard to whom they considered the victim: The FARC "protected" the coca growers, while the paramilitaries "protected" the landowners who were blackmailed, kidnapped, and assassinated by the guerrillas. Each side did so under the guise that the state was incapable of guaranteeing the lives, honor, and property of its citizens.

In spite of contamination from drug trafficking and the generalized deterioration of political ideologies, guerrillas and paramilitaries represented contrasting interests and world views, even though their social origins and use of violence have been similar. Thanks to the political networks inherent to latifundism, paramilitaries maintained systematic ties to those in power in towns and urban areas, whom in the 2000s they have attempted to dominate more through organization than through arms. The so-called parapolitics scandal that erupted in 2008, in which as much as a third of elected members of the Colombian Congress were accused, and many convicted, of having illegal ties to paramilitary groups, was the unqualified expression of this relationship.

From Country to City and from City to Country

Regardless of what was written in Colombia's constitutions, the Colombian state was not able to centralize along lines characteristic of modern politics. In the 1960s, guerrillas did not believe that state power in Colombia had been consolidated in the capital, as it had been in France in 1789 or in Tsarist

Russia in 1917. Colombia was more similar to China during the first two decades of the twentieth century, plagued by "warlords." Moreover, the guerrillas inherited the leftist strategy of the 1920s: Organize class struggle on the political peripheries, in areas that in the Colombian case were nonetheless important productive centers—banana plantations, railroads, the transportation networks on the Magdalena River, oil camps, and coffee haciendas.

The period in Colombian history known as La Violencia (1946–64) intensified political fragmentation in the country. Marxist revolutionaries put forward the idea of armed struggle as a sequential fight that would begin by controlling the remote borders, precisely where enclaves of guerrillas from the Violencia era were located after refusing the amnesties proposed by the government of General Gustavo Rojas Pinilla in 1953 and later by the National Front in 1958. These enclaves were the guerrillas' embryonic "support bases." The notion of prolonged popular war was thereby "Colombianized," spreading "from the country to the city," or in other words, from the "territories of de facto power" to "the country in the middle," and finally to the cities, once the Leninist hour of insurrection arrived.

The United States aided in the centralization of the Colombian state through military assistance provided within the logic of the Cold War. The economic assistance programs carried out under the Alliance for Progress had a security component, spawning the creation of the Military Civic Action Brigades (1958), Operación Marquetalia (1964), and the legalization of paramilitary local self-defense groups in 1965.[13] Over the long run, one of the most efficient U.S. instruments for institution building was the School of the Americas, founded in 1946, an anticommunist breeding ground for a Latin American military elite specializing in counterinsurgency.[14]

It is important to note that the initial guerrilla organizations could not keep up with the unexpected demographic and social changes in the country or decipher the political and cultural significance of the globalized demand for drugs. The end of the Cold War and the implosion of the Soviet system debilitated the already weak Colombian Communist Party and opened the way for the FARC to emerge as a political actor. In the mid-1980s, the FARC decided to extricate itself from the Communist Party, becoming further militarized while its leaders embraced a mentality of border lords. The peace processes of this period, first under President Belisario Betancur (1982–86) and then under presidents Virgilio Barco (1986–90) and César Gaviria (1990–94), served as an ideal means to obtain influence in the urban world and "combine all forms of struggle." By the 1990s, FARC leaders believed that income from protection and extortion all along the drug trafficking chain would make up for the lack of "mass-based organizations" and give them power over their paramilitary competitors, who in this area had the advantage as far as experience and social and political networking were concerned. Because it was incapable of mobilizing the peasantry outside the active zones of colonization, the FARC became entrenched in the Leninist routines of "democratic centralism," pushing into the background the concepts of "criticism and self-criticism."[15]

This geographical pattern was replicated by the local paramilitary organizations. But drug trafficking also had a profound effect on them. Trafficking organizations and the Medellín cartel in particular found refuge in the rural areas of Puerto Boyacá. They moved into agriculture and cattle ranching, taking over large areas of land for military and commercial (including money-laundering) purposes. To a large extent, this process explains the dynamics of the armed conflict after 1985, with movement from the city to the countryside. Gradually, the paramilitary organizations moved from being the rear guard to being at the conflict's center of gravity. Paramilitaries combined to varying degrees the business of drug trafficking with the work of counterinsurgency; nonetheless, at particular times and in some places, they also formed alliances with the guerrillas for the purposes of moving drugs.

The rise, organization, and preservation of powerful drug-trafficking mafias became the principal source of corruption and intimidation of members of the political class, security forces, judges, and journalists. Colombia also experienced one of the highest homicide rates in the Western hemisphere and witnessed an astounding concentration of landownership[16] made possible by an outdated cadastral system.[17] As part of this process, Colombia became one of the countries with the world's highest levels of forcibly displaced people, of whom the overwhelming majority are poor campesinos.[18]

It is worth calling attention at this point to one of the more ignored aspects of Colombia's armed conflict. Deaths in combat are fewer than those in traffic accidents. From 2002 to 2008, an average of 4,844 people per year died in traffic accidents, while 2,793 people were killed in combat.[19] The latter number may actually be inflated because of the so-called false positives scandal, in which members of the armed forces murdered innocent civilians and presented them as guerrillas killed in combat, in order to receive promotions and other benefits.

Statistics also demonstrate that crimes against life, personal security, and property are concentrated in urban, not rural areas, including Bogotá, Medellín, Cali, Barranquilla, and the remaining twenty-eight departmental capitals. It is true, nonetheless, that urban crime rates have dropped rapidly since 1993 in Bogotá and since 1998 in Medellín and in Cali, although homicides related to organized bands significantly increased in 2009 and 2010 in Medellín, Bogotá, and other major cities.[20]

Moreover, contrary to what is commonly believed with respect to economic costs, the conflict affects no strategic sector of the national economy. In fact, during the last two decades of the twentieth century, average per capita economic growth rates have been higher in Colombia than in relatively peaceful countries such as Mexico.[21] It is therefore worth rethinking the centrality attributed to the problem of war and peace in Colombia as something that limits normalcy; this issue is subject to rhetorical manipulation by political leaders and opinion makers both in Colombia and abroad. This kind of manipulation makes the extremely high urban murder rates of the last decade of last century seem almost normal when compared with the destruction caused in rural zones by guerrilla warfare.

Decentralization to Strengthen the State

The illegitimacy of state institutions at the local level has often gone largely unnoticed. If, a century ago, oligarchs believed the Liberal and Conservative parties were a suitable means of transferring the benefits of civilized politics from the nation-state to the localities, now, by contrast, new local political bosses pragmatically use the electoral system to project their message nationally from the halls of congress. Clientelism historically has engaged the central government and the municipalities, but today the correlation of forces has changed. There are now local and provincial bigwigs who fish the turbulent, crisis-ridden waters of the traditional parties and exercise more real or potential armed power.

These bosses have taken advantage of the political and fiscal decentralization born of the extreme crisis of political legitimacy in the 1980s. As indicated in the commentary by Ana María Bejarano that follows this chapter, the popular election of mayors (mandated in 1986 and first put in practice in 1989) was an intelligent response to the loss of legitimacy arising from the tragic events connected with the M-19 guerrillas' attack on the Palace of Justice in 1985. Then, a commando group violently took over the Palace of Justice, taking those in the building hostage and demanding a "public trial" of the president of the Republic, whom they accused of "betraying the peace process." The response was a scorched-earth military operation to take back the building and free the hostages. In the twenty-seven hours that the operation lasted, most of the building was consumed in a horrific fire. Amid the flames, gases, and bullets, more than 100 Colombians died, including 11 of 24 Supreme Court judges. Of the 36 guerrillas who staged the attack, only 1 got out alive. A total of 11 captured by the army subsequently disappeared, probably after being tortured.[22]

The need to restore legitimacy was also a principal concern of those participating in the Constituent Assembly to draft a new Constitution in 1990 and 1991. Accordingly, the new Constitution consecrated the direct election (rather than appointment) of governors, indigenous representation in the Senate, financial security for municipalities, and the channeling of oil royalties to oil-producing departments and municipalities (which, in turn, were located in "territories of de facto power"). In short, new relationships were established between the national government and other entities throughout the national territory that ultimately served to diminish the coherence of public policies and the transparency of their implementation.

Even more important, regionalism and the dynamic of regional power in Colombia today owe less to the Constitution itself than they do to the ways, some violent, in which local agents engage in the disputes over control of the ballot box. These disputes take place not only in "territories of de facto power" but also throughout the Caribbean region, from Urabá to the Sierra Nevada of Santa Marta. In these areas, the fusion of new drug-trafficking groups, local politicians, and dirty war is palpable. This is one of the unintended consequences of the paramilitary demobilizations (discussed below) as a result of negotiations from 2003 to 2005 that began in the town of Santa Fe de Ralito, Córdoba.[23]

Thus, against the purpose and core of decentralization, Colombia moved from armed clientelism to a kind of surreptitious clientelism that intensified the territorial fragmentation of the state and brought to light both discontinuities in the chain of command of public administration and the continual interference of opportunistic factions.

The War on Drugs, Plan Colombia, and the Internationalization of the Colombian Conflict

The rise of Colombia as an issue of national security concern to the United States derives from its role in the global drug economy and especially from the way that, in the post–Cold War period, drugs replaced Communism as the principal enemy of the free world. But the passage from the era of the Alliance for Progress to the era of Plan Colombia also marked a profound change in the way development and peace processes were understood. From the first negotiations in 1982 under the government of President Belisario Betancur, the quest for a negotiated peace had been a domestic political issue in Colombia, in which socioeconomic conflicts were a central reference. It was the exclusive domain of the professional politicians who so deftly exploited it, within a framework that quite excluded the issue of drug trafficking.[24] This separation of the issues of peace with the guerrillas and drug trafficking can be seen in the reaction to the 1983 assassination of the minister of justice by hit men sent by Pablo Escobar, head of the Medellín cartel, the most powerful and violent drug-trafficking organization in Colombian history. The assassination occurred shortly after the discovery and destruction of extensive cocaine processing centers in the southeastern part of the country, in zones where the FARC was present. One of President Betancur's first reactions was to resume the extradition of drug traffickers to the United Sates. However, Betancur refused to embrace then-U.S. ambassador Lewis Tambs's assertion that a "narco-guerrilla" had begun to rule in Colombia. But Betancur went even further: Peace, including drugs, was a national issue, not a bilateral one in the U.S.-Colombian relationship.

As it evolved initially between 1998 and 2000, Plan Colombia represented a 180-degree shift in emphasis: U.S. global security policy would be projected through the strengthening of a reputedly weak ally. Within the United States, Plan Colombia's main source of legitimacy was the war on drugs, Washington's response to the consolidation of drug trafficking. This "war" was born of the demand for narcotics in its own territory and in the world's wealthier nations, and to drug trafficking's entry into the globalization of markets and organized crime, especially of illegal arms and drug profits. The "war on drugs," a bellicose metaphor coined during the Nixon administration, led to the creation of the Drug Enforcement Administration in 1973. This "war" has not ceased in Colombia since the fumigation of marijuana crops at the end of the 1970s, and since 1982 it has become more active and explicit than ever.

Plan Colombia sealed the Pastrana and Uribe administrations' unconditional adherence to Washington's security policies. Originally conceived by the Colombian government as an economic program for peace that would offer the peasant population viable alternatives to growing coca, Plan Colombia ended up as a war plan aimed at remedying the Colombian government's fiscal and military deficits.[25] In keeping with Plan Colombia's original concept, in December 1998 State Department official Philip Chicola met in San José, Costa Rica, with representatives of the FARC. This opening was harshly criticized in the United States, mainly by Republicans, and the attempt at dialogue was canceled following the assassination of three U.S. indigenous rights activists at the hands of the FARC in March 1999.[26]

After being presented in September 1999, Plan Colombia became law in the United States the following July. The events of September 11, 2001, reinforced a tendency about which critics of the plan had already warned: the unification of the "war on drugs" and the "war on terrorism."[27] The official U.S. discourse shifted from the fight against a Colombian "narco-democracy" to the war on "narco-terrorism." The former alluded to the relationship between drug cartels and politicians and government officials in Colombia, and reached its climax with Proceso 8000 (the investigation of allegations that President Ernesto Samper's presidential campaign had accepted money from the Cali drug trafficking cartel in 1994), the canceling of President Samper's U.S. visa in 1996, and the 1996 and 1997 "decertifications" of Colombia as a cooperative partner in the war on drugs.[28] The war on "narco-terrorism," meanwhile, was aimed at the FARC, which was deemed to embody the twin evils of drug trafficking and terrorism.

Originally, the Pastrana government and the administration of President Bill Clinton appeared to have reached an agreement in 1998 to separate the war on drugs from the fight against guerrilla insurgents, considered one of Colombia's oldest internal issues. In October 1998, for example, before his first presidential visit to Washington, Pastrana sought to "denarcotize," or downplay, drug policy in bilateral relations: "Colombia is suffering from two clearly differentiable wars—the drug-traffickers' war against this country and the world, and the confrontation with guerrillas over a model they consider unjust, corrupt, and promoting privileges."[29] A few days later in Washington, however, he changed his tune and backed "narcotization": "The only peace agreement acceptable to me and to the Colombian people would be one that strengthened our capacity to wipe out cocaine production in Colombia."[30] President Uribe subsequently introduced a new twist, adding terrorism as well as the internationalist dimension of drugs to the mix: "In Colombia, terrorism, drugs, violence, and insecurity are one and the same. . . . Our problem is an international threat. If Colombia fails to destroy drugs, then drugs will destroy the Amazon basin. If Colombia fails to stop terrorism, democracy in the region will be threatened."[31]

Since 2000, the basic documents concerning Colombia's peace policies have been mere rhetorical variations of Plan Colombia.[32] The limits thus

Figure 6.2. U.S. Military and Socioeconomic Aid to Colombia, 1996–2010 (millions of current dollars)

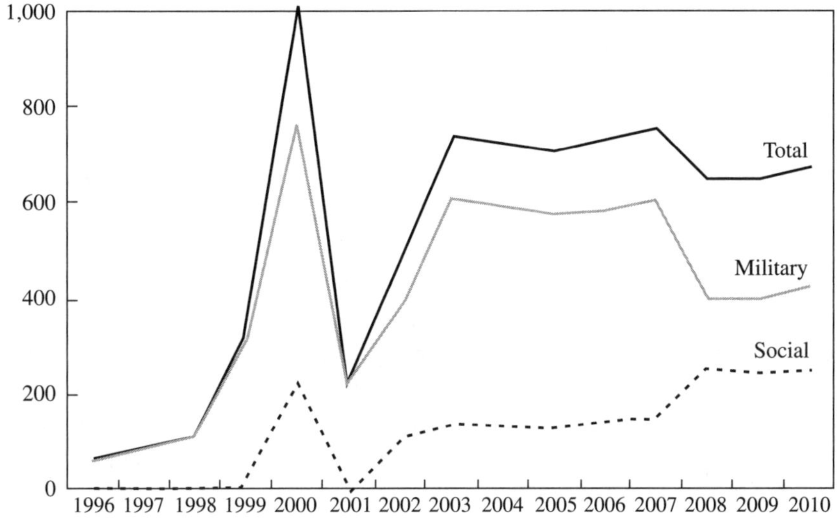

Source: Adapted from Adam Isacson, "Don't Call It a Model," http://wola.org/index.php?option=com_content&task=viewp&id=1134&Itemid=2.

placed on national sovereignty[33] were openly supported by the majority of Colombians and had the tacit consent of politicians, including the center-left coalition the Polo Democrático.[34] Even so, Colombian leaders managed to retain important, albeit risky, degrees of autonomy.

Plan Colombia can be understood as the set of legal provisions and budgetary disbursements from the U.S. government, executed by different agencies for the purpose of promoting Colombian national security, viewed as threatened by drugs, "terrorism," or a combination of both. Even though a goal of Plan Colombia was to reduce coca production by 50 percent, in 2008 Colombia remained the source of 90 percent of the cocaine entering the United States.[35] From 1996 to 2010, U.S. military and economic assistance reached $6.14 billion, of which $5.56 billion was transferred as part of Plan Colombia (2000–2010). Related economic, social, judicial, and human rights aid amounted to $1.8 billion from 1996 to 2010, of which $1.79 billion came during the years of Plan Colombia.[36] In a historical context of fiscal difficulties in Colombia, U.S. military aid was crucial to driving back the FARC (figure 6.2).

Plan Colombia and the Search for Peace

Volatile Legitimacy

During the past decade, Colombians have changed their minds about how the armed conflict should be ended. From mass demonstrations and the symbolic votes of 100 million Colombians in favor of negotiated peace during the departmental and municipal elections of 1997, a shift occurred in 2002 to majority support for President Uribe's hard-line approach, overwhelmingly ratified in the 2006 elections.

Since 1982, with a hiatus in 1994 to 1998, peace processes have been marked by a volatile legitimacy. Both in and outside the country, questions arose regarding just what should be legitimated: What should be the format of the process? Should the agenda for negotiations include substantial economic, social, and political reforms? Could negotiations proceed without a cease-fire? Who could negotiate for the authorities: the central government only, or the government and local governments, or the government and so-called civil society? As for the illegal armed actors, could the paramilitaries or narco-guerrillas be political players? What could be pardoned? How should reparations be made and to whom? Practically speaking, these questions are very difficult to resolve, and the application of specific measures would be even harder to verify. It is important to point out that, as far as the U.S. electorate is concerned, the war on drugs is what gives legitimacy to peace efforts in Colombia.

Presidential Peace

Although Plan Colombia introduced a sense of continuity and greater administrative coherence, the state has lacked a policy for peace. Colombian presidentialism implies temporary peace projects linked to the electoral cycle. The president maintains a monopoly on giving or repealing special status to an armed group. Only he holds the key to opening and closing a peace process. Initially, such special status was reserved for guerrilla groups, in keeping with concepts of political crimes spelled out in the penal code. Paramilitaries were instead to "submit to justice" (1992–97). But near the end of his term in office, President Ernesto Samper (1994–98) discreetly recognized the political nature of the paramilitaries through the Nudo de Paramillo Agreement, under which paramilitaries—supposedly unified and with a central command represented by the United Self-Defense

Forces of Colombia (Autodefensas Unidas de Colombia, AUC)—promised to adhere to the fundamental clauses of International Humanitarian Law.[37]

Meanwhile, the charismatic personality of the AUC's leader, Carlos Castaño, stoked the media's voracious appetite for interviews. In the resulting synergy, the paramilitaries appeared as a powerful, politicized, unified, armed counterguerrilla force. Their complex internal fragmentation was kept hidden, and their organic link with drug traffickers and large landowning interests was minimized. Colombians began to change their minds about the paramilitaries, comparing their illegal status and number of troops with those of the guerrillas. This comparison was reflected in President Uribe's Law 782 of 2002, which accorded special treatment to the paramilitaries in order to induce them to demobilize. In fact, during the 2001–2 presidential campaign, the paramilitaries openly expressed their preferences for Uribe.[38] This was no trivial matter. Eliminating their own discourse as an element of political identity, there was nothing left but to establish the rules for paramilitary demobilization and reinsertion. The contrast with the guerrillas was profound; not even during the moments of closest rapprochement with Pastrana did the FARC ever stop identifying the Colombian state as the enemy.

The history of peace policies in Colombia is replete with conflicts between the president and the Congress, although such differences never led to a total blocking of policy. Occasionally, court rulings also contradicted peace policies. The Uribe administration made an effort to overcome these problems by establishing firm presidential control of all aspects of the peace process, circumscribing civil society to a purely ceremonial role, as seen in conversations between Uribe's government and the ELN in Cuba.

A Band-Aid Peace

During the peace processes that were considered successful (1990–94 and 2003–6), the prevailing model was that of a "band-aid": no minimal social reforms, and even budgetary implications were minimal and with low political cost. Benefits to the demobilized accrued mainly to the leadership and to some midlevel commanders. Those from the ranks who were "reinserted" appeared to gain only the legalization of their status and a temporary and limited income; many became newly available to join black-market protection squads.[39]

Besides the problems of the entry-level "reinserted," this band-aid approach left territorial power vacuums, which themselves became the sources of renewed confrontations. For example, in 1991, following the demobilization of the People's Liberation Army (Ejército Popular de Liberación), the FARC and the paramilitaries responded by trying to fill the void, massacring or co-opting former combatants and sympathizers who had regrouped in the new and short-lived Esperanza, Paz y Libertad (Hope, Peace, and Liberty) Movement. In the area of Urabá, the offensives and counteroffensives between 1991 and 1995 left the civilian population in mourning. This alarming pattern appears to be repeating itself in certain regions abandoned by demobilized paramilitaries to which the FARC has returned, along with the possibility that certain paramilitary groups are reactivating.

Two Enemies and an Inconvenient Ally

The radical division of the field of illegal armed actors has played a role in the delegitimation of the peace process. Leftist guerrillas have been the enemies of the state, and the paramilitaries have been an awkward ally. This awkwardness was due not to their role as a counterguerrilla force but rather to their systematic participation in drug trafficking. Since their founding, the FARC and ELN have maintained a rivalry at times resolved through armed confrontation. Each organization jealously preserved its political identity and a communitarian narrative sprinkled with myths, dates of near-liturgical status, heroes, and graves. On the other side, from 1997 to 2005, the paramilitaries recovered a kind of legality first accorded in 1965 but effectively ended in 1989. In the context of peace processes, the government was thus trapped between two antagonistic guerrilla formations, both of which were sworn enemies of the paramilitary federation that has taken on greater autonomy. This triangulation has made negotiations difficult given the way all three groups systematically interfere with one another.

PASTRANA IN THE CAGUÁN

Pastrana's talks with the FARC serve as a good example of the Colombian government's ambiguous position regarding the counterdrug-versus-counterinsurgency problem, choosing to substitute the word "and" for the word "or" when using these words together. Pastrana's original design for the process foreshadowed its failure.[40] The government agreed to negotiations with the FARC based on three premises, each of which was highly problematic: (1) the establishment of a demilitarized zone (*zona de despeje,* or DMZ) in El Caguán, in place between October 1998 and February 2002 and extended by the president seven times, most of the time traumatically; (2) the carrying out of negotiations in the midst of war; and (3) an open agenda for the negotiations. The central issues of drug cultivation and trafficking entered only obliquely. As a result, the talks constantly broke down and the parties routinely engaged in a tug of war when it came time for the president to decree an extension of the DMZ.

Three encounters between President Pastrana and FARC commander Manuel Marulanda Vélez, all of them in FARC territory, summed up the theatrical nature and precarious legitimacy of the negotiations. First, Pastrana and Marulanda embraced in July 1998, before Pastrana had taken office; the two committed themselves to peace talks and announced that peace would be based on a "mini–Marshall Plan" for the development of rural Colombia. Second was the January 1999 episode of the "empty chair" during the inauguration of the peace process over which Marulanda and Pastrana were to preside; in a show of disdain, Marulanda did not show up, instead sending a message reiterating the friend/enemy polarities dating from 1964. The third encounter took place in February 2001, when the spark of old affection led to the signing of the Los Pozos Agreement, reviving from the ashes a process everyone thought dead.

Pastrana's peace policy can be summarized as four years of hopes and reversals. During this time, the apparent advantage remained with Marulanda and the FARC Secretariat. They hoisted the flag of dialogue in order to use the DMZ to strategically build up their military and logistical apparatus, using the negotiations to gain political legitimacy at the expense of the paramilitaries and in favor of their coca-growing campesino base. At the same time, the government, as part of the negotiations over Plan Colombia in Washington, agreed to the so-called unification of the counterinsurgency and counternarcotics wars, in which the paramilitaries would be recognized as potential counterinsurgency allies and the guerrillas and their social base would bear the brunt of the drug trafficking stigma.

Pastrana allowed the FARC Secretariat to take a leading role in the peace process and transferred the main stage to the DMZ. The ELN and the paramilitaries were relegated to the role of stage hands, lightening or darkening the stage and speaking from time to time. Pastrana granted political recognition to the ELN in direct talks held in Caracas in February 1999. At the end of May that same year, he revoked that status after the ELN carried out a mass kidnapping of Catholic worshippers at a Sunday mass in Cali. In June he reinstated their political status so that talks could continue. But, once again, the talks went nowhere and broke down for good in June 2002.

From the outset, dialogue with the FARC Secretariat was marked by an ambiguity that never faded over the years. Against this improvised process, and abetted by the FARC's excesses and arrogance born of its apparent sovereignty in the DMZ, the paramilitaries—with help from important media groups—projected themselves publicly, making better use the umbrella of the AUC that had served them so well since the Nudo de Paramillo Agreement. They focused on coming up with an alternative, attempting to wash away their drug-trafficking sins through a process of self-criticism that provoked a great deal of internal tension. The goal was to slow down the talks in the DMZ, which appeared more and more like some kind of theater of the absurd or cheap comedy, depending on the audience. The paramilitaries also blocked the ELN's proposed DMZ in southern Bolívar Department; it would have been a second Caguán. The government was incapable of overcoming the paramilitary's veto, backed as it was by popular mobilizations in the zone. The government thus lost the opportunity to reach an agreement with a militarily weak and politically disoriented ELN guerrilla force.

By the end of 2001, President Pastrana appeared to understand that the international environment after 9/11 had made the turbulent effort to "negotiate in the midst of war" impossible; in the DMZ, criminal drug-trafficking organizations could serve as platforms for world terrorism. To be sure, the "open agenda" had led to few advances. However, the model of negotiations also failed due to internal factors that were present from the start. First was the autarchic nature of the FARC with regard to its military resources (it bore the stigma of kidnapping and drug trafficking) and its growing isolation from urban political and social groups as soon as they severed ties with the Communist Party. Second was the connection between the peace processes and electoral cycles. The 1990–94 agreements with the guerrillas were an integral part of the political process surrounding the Constituent Assembly and the 1991 Constitution. The key to the results of four of the five of the most recent presidential elections—Ernesto Samper-Andrés Pastrana in 1994, Andrés Pastrana-Horacio Serpa in 1998, Álvaro Uribe-Horacio Serpa in 2002, and Álvaro Uribe-César Gaviria-Horacio Serpa in 2006—seemed to reside in the way candidates presented their respective plans for peace. Third was the rapid territorial expansion of the paramilitary organizations, ever more organized and coordinated (at least as far as propaganda was concerned) by Carlos Castaño, with increasing financial resources from drug trafficking and political resources coming from many of the factions in power who chose to channel their support to Castaño after rejecting the experiment represented by the DMZ.

It goes without saying that the paramilitaries never fulfilled the promises they made as part of the aforementioned Paramillo Accord with respect to humanizing the war; on the contrary, during these years they were the leading violators of human rights. Fourth was President Pastrana's inability to understand the strategic importance of human rights, not only as valuable in and of themselves but also as a source of broad legitimation of his original Plan Colombia, which might have attracted support from both the European Union and many nongovernmental organizations in the United States. Taken together, these factors explain why a trustworthy, neutral third party capable of pressuring the parties into a pact failed to emerge, in contrast to the role played by the United States and international nongovernmental organizations in El Salvador.

In contrast to initial expectations, Pastrana's four-year term ended with the discrediting of peace processes and the discrediting of the FARC as a negotiator in good faith. This crack in public confidence regarding the peace process later widened into a gaping hole during the political dialogues with paramilitaries under the Uribe government. Put simply, Pastrana neglected human rights and paid the internal costs of designing and implementing a militarized Plan Colombia. The most serious of these costs was the radicalization of distrust in the government—both within the FARC and with the paramilitaries and their political allies.

PAX URIBISTA

During the long presidential campaign that ultimately led to his election in 2002, Uribe declared that he was a staunch enemy of the increasingly unsustainable peace process in the Caguán and attached little importance to human rights. He proposed doubling the number of military troops, professionalizing them over the short term, creating groups of "campesino soldiers" and a national network of 1 million informants, and paying citizens for information. These proposals were quite popular given the international climate after 9/11, and appeared credible in light of the FARC's early attempts to not only discredit Uribe but also kill him.[41]

After taking office, Uribe begin to implement a strategy based on increasing the size of the armed forces, which in effect doubled in size during his eight years in office. At the same time, the plan to launch a network of informants never really took off. Before the first year of Uribe's term was over, 75 percent of Colombians expressed a belief that the state had recovered control of the national territory. The average citizen enjoyed a return to the much-longed-for freedom to move around the country. People celebrated the increase in internal tourism, which generated employment in the formal as well as informal sectors. During Uribe's first term, homicide rates dropped, except those directly attributable to the armed conflict. Collective kidnappings by the guerrillas (referred to as *pescas milagrosas,* or "miraculous fishing"), individual kidnappings, attacks on the civil population, and bombings of pipelines and electrical towers all declined.

The self-esteem and trust of millions of Colombians soared. Wealthy businessmen who had willingly paid a one-time tax of 1.2 percent of their total worth as well as rural landowners were immensely satisfied with the military's strikes against the FARC units that organized kidnappings and extortion throughout Cundinamarca and Tolima departments. In addition, the forces of law and order returned to some two hundred municipal capitals that had struggled alone in recent years.

The first year of Uribe's administration also witnessed the beginning of peace talks with the AUC, which declared a unilateral cease-fire in December 2002, less than six months after the new president had taken office. The cease-fire led to an agreement signed in the town of Santa Fe de Ralito, Córdoba, in July 2003, in which paramilitaries agreed to demobilize completely by December 2005. The key to this pact was that the involvement of paramilitaries in drug trafficking would be forgiven and forgotten and that they would not be extradited to the United States as long as they engaged in the peace process in good faith. The peace talks between 2003 and 2005 went through numerous crises and near-breakdowns, including one occasioned by the abduction and presumed murder of AUC leader Castaño in 2004, apparently at the hands of rival paramilitary leaders. Throughout this time, incentives to participate in electoral politics, including through threats, intimidation, and extortion, replaced incentives born of direct violent action. Manipulations of the electoral process—which would subsequently erupt as the "parapolitics" scandal in 2008—constituted a central pillar of the "Pax Uribista," contributing to the illusion that the state had recovered a "monopoly of legitimate violence."[42] Meanwhile, as talks with the paramilitaries went forward, the government in 2004 launched the military offensive known as Plan Patriota. Some 17,000 elite troops were sent to wipe out the FARC's General Staff–Eastern Bloc, its most powerful arm.[43]

This ability to reach agreements with the AUC and place military pressure on the FARC consolidated popular support among those who had voted for Uribe. As a consequence, the president launched a bid in Congress for his immediate reelection. This initiative required a constitutional reform, because the 1991 Constitution had limited presidents to one term. A heavy dose of presidential patronage assured the reform's passage.

But not everything came up roses. In urban areas, selective assassinations of union organizers and journalists did not let up. And in the countryside, the FARC reacted like any other guerrilla group in retreat (and as it had in Marquetalia in 1964): It ceded territory to buy time. It maintained its power by cutting back on operative capacity, launching selective attacks and attempting to take its brand of low-intensity, corrosive terrorism to the nation's capital.

Uribe remained very much in tune with the George W. Bush administration. As we have seen, he offered credible formulas to paramilitaries and achieved the demobilization of most of their fronts. And most important, he ran away with the reelection, winning the first consecutive term since President Rafael Nuñez in 1892. Within Colombia, he emerged unscathed by successive scandals: over impunity for paramilitaries; their infiltration of the Administrative Department of Security; the wiretapping of opposition political leaders, journalists, and even Supreme Court justices; and the investigation or jailing of scores of Uribe supporters in the legislature for their links to paramilitary groups.

Uribe understood much better than Pastrana that Plan Colombia was an updated version of counterinsurgency warfare. He began by proscribing from the official lexicon the term "armed conflict." The enemy was world terrorism, which in Colombia took the form of narco-terrorism, pure and simple. This presidential discourse was useful to the paramilitaries. The profound simplification of the conflict was a heaven-sent structure of opportunity. The paramilitaries quickly became the privileged interlocutors with the government, opening a path to negotiations that took place on their home turf, and all the while continuing to massacre the civilian population and swell the waves of displaced persons.[44]

Once the initial obstacles in the Santa Fe de Ralito negotiations had been overcome, Congress was asked to play its role in making the essential adjustments to the legal framework in which the negotiations unfolded. The Justice and Peace Law (Ley de Justicia y Paz, LJP) of July 2005, the first drafts of which had been presented by the government two years earlier, offered an ex post facto resolution of the legal issues. But in the two years between the government's first proposal of an "alternative penalties" law and the passage of the LJP, deep fissures emerged within the Uribe government and in the progovernment coalition in Congress over the degree of impunity that paramilitary leaders should expect. The final version of the

LJP, in fact, went against trends in the international human rights movement and the related discourse on justice. The globalization of human rights has seen the creation of an International Criminal Court (to which the Colombian government has adhered), the disappearance throughout the world of the notion of political crimes (a category allowing for amnesty of guerrillas and other insurgents), and the emergence of norms of transitional justice, whereby those who contributed to massive human rights violations during armed conflict or dictatorship are brought to justice.

As noted above, since 1998 the paramilitaries had carefully analyzed the ups and downs of Pastrana's peace process with the FARC, setting up the organizational facade of the AUC. This umbrella organization served to cover up their tactical position, to consolidate networks and resources at the level of local governments, and to gain national political recognition with an eye toward negotiating with optimal conditions of impunity. Seen in this light, the LJP constituted a great victory, as it granted impunity to nearly all paramilitary leaders for crimes against humanity, reduced sentences excessively, and upset the balance between peace and just reparations for victims. Only 7 percent of demobilized paramilitaries were to be tried under the LJP.[45] In May 2006, the Constitutional Court ruled to uphold the essence of the LJP even after declaring several of its articles unconstitutional and attempting to balance reparations made to victims by affecting the legally or illegally amassed property of those who broke the law. By adding together all sentences corresponding to crimes committed before July 25, 2005, judges were to grant substantial reductions so that, ultimately, sentences would range from five to eight years in prison.[46]

The struggles for accountability in countries such as Argentina and Chile have demonstrated the role of the international community in promoting justice for human rights crimes, as well as the ways that domestic possibilities for seeking justice change over time. In the Colombian case, it remains to be seen whether international entities such as the International Criminal Court will pass judgment on the crimes against humanity omitted by the LJP, including crimes attributed to the guerrillas and security forces and also the paramilitaries. An added stumbling block in the AUC process involved determining how to forgive and forget the paramilitary's obstinate participation in drug trafficking, especially given the fact that most of their leaders were wanted for extradition by the U.S. government.

When evidence of the demobilized paramilitary leaders' continued involvement in drug trafficking became too flagrant and overwhelming to ignore, and amid the burgeoning parapolitics scandal, President Uribe extradited thirteen top paramilitary leaders to the United States in May 2008 to stand trial on drug-trafficking charges. As much as extradition had been feared by the paramilitary leaders themselves, human rights groups and opposition politicians criticized the extraditions as effectively closing off the possibility of bringing paramilitary leaders to justice in Colombia for crimes against humanity.

Throughout the process of paramilitary negotiation demobilization, the FARC remained at the other extreme. From the beginning of Pastrana's peace process, the way that they were viewed politically seemed to depend on a verdict from the U.S. government: leftist guerrillas or drug traffickers? In 1997, the State Department had already placed the FARC and the ELN on the U.S. list of "foreign terrorist organizations"; the AUC was added to this list in 2001. In March 2006, the U.S. Department of Justice accused the FARC of being the world's largest drug-trafficking organization. According to the U.S. government, in ten years the FARC had exported some $25 billion worth of drugs to U.S. markets.[47]

With the advent of Plan Colombia, key decisions regarding war and peace in Colombia were made in Washington, where budget disbursements were justified by the war on drugs. Under the rubric of a "narcotized" bilateral relationship, the intellectual rationale appeared to be predicated, for the Uribe government, on the conversion of paramilitaries into political actors, and, for the United States, on reducing the FARC to a band of drug traffickers.[48]

Once the problem of the paramilitary fronts was taken care of, Uribe similarly guaranteed the guerrillas that they would not be extradited as long as they accepted the LJP. At the same time, he proposed a new war tax similar to the one passed in his first year in office.[49] By initially establishing as one of the foundations for peace a policy of no extradition, President Uribe seemed to be renouncing the centrality of drug policy in bilateral relations—a sine qua non for U.S. congressional support of Plan Colombia or its equivalents. Like several of his predecessors, Uribe appeared able to negotiate the thorny path laid out by different agencies in Washington. Indeed, it seemed that it was in the U.S. capital that the decision would be made regarding whether, in the interest of peace in Colombia, to extradite on drug-trafficking charges those who had or would in the future avail themselves of the provisions of Colombian law. At the same time, the negotiations of the ELN with the government in Havana collapsed, among other things because this rather marginal guerrilla group would not agree to discussions according to the formula of the LJP.

Thirty-thousand paramilitaries (most likely an inflated figure) ultimately demobilized and surrendered 16,000 arms,[50] but the price to Colombia was high, including the emergence of *nuevas bandas criminales* (new criminal bands). According to a report by the Administrative Department of Security at the end of 2009, there were six of these organizations in existence, with some 3,750 members active in 162 municipalities, mostly located in territories formerly occupied by the paramilitaries.[51] Even with the 2008 extradition of major AUC figures, the paramilitaries were left with enormous resources for reactivating or building local and regional strongholds capable of being extended throughout the country: landed estates, illegal businesses, electoral networks, bank accounts, and public services subject to clientelism, ineptitude, and corruption. And as if this were not enough, there were signs that gangs of demobilized paramilitaries were taking the conflict into the cities. The Colombian anthropologist and security expert Gustavo Duncan has described their maneuverings to control illegal and legal profits in three important areas of commerce in urban areas: drug trafficking, "Sanandresitos" (illegal but tolerated street markets that sell contraband merchandise in the country's principal cities), and wholesale food markets.[52]

During Uribe's second term, the state was able to dramatically reduce the FARC's military capacity, but not to the point of forcing it to negotiate its demobilization. Uribe resisted any type of negotiated "humanitarian accord" or exchange of civilian and military prisoners being held in FARC camps in the jungle for guerrillas who were serving time in the country's prisons. His policy was manifested in several successful military operations, including the killing of senior FARC leader Raúl Reyes in a guerrilla encampment inside Ecuadoran territory in 2008, and the spectacular rescue that same year of prominent FARC hostages, including the former presidential candidate Ingrid Betancourt, three U.S. military contractors, and eleven members of the Colombian military and police forces. Although dismantling the paramilitary structures proved more problematic, it is clear that the use of violence by these groups has substantially declined.

What conclusions will politicians and bureaucrats in Washington draw regarding Plan Colombia, given the fact that cocaine continues to flood U.S. markets via Mexico? By 2010, Plan Colombia had accomplished two of its goals. First, it had succeeded in reducing the cultivation of coca, from 160,000 hectares in 2000 to 68,000 in 2009. Part of the explanation for this decrease was the increase in manual eradication programs, which imply sensitive negotiations between the local authorities and the coca producers, primarily peasant farmers. Manual eradication programs began in 2000. In 2004, the area of manual eradication was less than 5 percent of the fumigated area, but it jumped to 30 percent in 2005 and to 60 percent in 2009.

Second, the strengthening of the armed forces, reflected in the killing or capture of senior members of the FARC Secretariat and the dramatic rescue of prominent hostages, has weakened the FARC to the point that some call a phase of *repligue profundo,* or "profound withdrawal."[53] The FARC also suffered considerable desertions and showed signs that its internal communications lines had been severely disrupted. Whereas in 2004 it was estimated that the FARC had 17,000 combatants, by 2010 that number had fallen to 8,000 or less. Though this size was still considerable, the generational changes in the FARC's directorate, its political isolation, the widespread repudiation of the "islands of legitimacy," and pressure from the military all contributed to the FARC's apparent loss of initiative in the political, military, and diplomatic realms.[54]

At the same time, however, the FARC has not been defeated militarily, and the flow of Colombian cocaine to the United States via Mexico and to Europe via South America and West Africa has continued. Parapolitical activity has increased, the number of internally displaced persons has risen (figures are being debated of anywhere between 3 million and 5 million displaced people), and the human rights situation, especially the number of extrajudicial killings, has deteriorated.

Furthermore, aerial fumigation of coca crops with the herbicide glyphosate showed diminishing returns; the relationship between hectares of coca sprayed and hectares destroyed went from 3:1 in 2002 to 9:1 in 2003 and 23:1 in 2004. The migration of peasant populations widened the borders of the coca map to include one-fourth of the nation's municipalities in twenty-three departments.[55] And so the vicious circle continues—fumigation makes large plantations unfeasible, and hence isolated coca plots grow in importance, and are in turn much more expensive to fumigate.[56] Resentment grows among both those peasants affected and authorities in the municipalities where spraying occurs. Fumigation has led to the dispersion of coca cultivation and the related multiplication of the number of municipalities that produce coca. At first, that development favored the growth of the FARC. But the weakening of its military structures has been such that the FARC has not been able to capitalize on the dispersion and remains in retreat.

Conclusion

Since the 1980s, the rate of growth in the concentration of landownership in rural Colombia has been among the fastest in the world. In the shadow of the armed conflict, paramilitary leaders have amassed fortunes and power by acquiring productive land through force of arms. Even more alarming, following the demobilization and in peacetime, these fortunes have not only remained intact but also have served as the basis for networks of political and electoral power built largely on the backs of the demobilized.

Although a new democratic Constitution was issued in 1991, it has proved incredibly "flexible" and easy to modify (e.g., in the case of no extradition for Colombian nationals or the consecutive reelection of a president). On many legal levels, the country is once again cultivating the age-old principle of negotiating everything, including the law and public order. There are few examples of a step-by-step, meticulous, and precise negotiation such as the one woven together by the paramilitaries and the government and that resulted in the Justice and Peace Law.

In these circumstances, it is useful for an understanding of U.S. military aid to place it in its long-term historical perspective. Plan Colombia narrowed the understanding of the conflict and channeled policies toward a military solution. Despite rhetoric to the contrary, social and political conceptions were disqualified, and the weight of the counterdrug and counterinsurgency battle was reduced to a matter of Blackhawk helicopters, professional battalions (comprising troops recruited from the lower-income classes), and heavy firepower as well as air cover and expanded mobility. The events of September 11, 2001, placed Plan Colombia completely within the context of U.S. national security policy, something that accentuated even more the militarization of the problem of drugs and insurgency.

Attention to the significant advance of (demobilized) paramilitaries in the legal political life of Colombia deflected attention from the long-standing traditions of latifundism-clientelism in a country that has never undergone a serious agrarian reform and whose political and legal institutions are still subject to the logic of armed and formerly armed clientelistic groups interwoven with professional right-wing politicians. These networks themselves were made possible only because of the eruption of drug trafficking and its social modalities.

The guerrillas, despite financial resources from the drug economy (as well as kidnappings and other kinds of organized crime) have not been able to integrate themselves into power circles that would upset the traditional balance between Colombian clientelism and latifundism. The FARC in particular, despite the armed clientelism that seems inherent in its agrarian trajectory, appears to be isolated from the central networks that connect the local to national and international clienteles. Their kind of armed clientelism is thus socially and politically anachronistic and more peripheral because it is accepted by most sources that the FARC shrank substantially during the eight years of Uribe's presidency.

Pax Uribista and the postconflict situation with respect to the paramilitaries did not succeed in strengthening the state, except in the military arena. At the end of Uribe's presidency—and despite military-led development efforts in former zones of FARC presence—the state continued to be weak, particularly vis-à-vis electoral democracy and social policies in internal frontier zones. The president himself may have been strong, but this is not a remedy for what is called the Colombian malady. Uribe's strength was a function of the moment and of his charisma. And his personal popularity came, in many instances, at the expense of institutions and democratic practices, leading to the intellectual impoverishment of politics. Nevertheless, the February 2010 decision by the Constitutional Court, which declared invalid a proposed referendum to allow Uribe to run for a third term, signaled the independence of the judiciary and injected a new dynamic into the political game. Uribe gave free rein to the notion that armed conflict does not really exist in Colombia, nor is it deeply rooted in the country's history and geography. In reality, the keys to the problem lie in the nation's agrarian history, in the history of the rural roots of drug trafficking, in the intersection between mobile and clientelistic politicians with even more mobile drug traffickers, and in the inextricable association of all these factors with the weakening of the two traditional political parties.

The election of President Juan Manuel Santos in June 2010, with historic levels of the popular vote, opened the possibility that Colombia's party system would be strengthened during his term. The rhythm of military operations against the FARC continued unabated, marked early in his administration by the killing of Jorge Briceño (alias Mono Jojoy), a member of the FARC Secretariat and the military leader of its Eastern Bloc. Santos distanced himself from the United States, focusing instead on improving relations with Colombia's neighbors, most notably Venezuela and Ecuador. And to the surprise of most observers, Santos made the issue of land—particularly the restitution of campesino properties confiscated by paramilitaries and drug traffickers—a central focus of his administration. These initiatives, if successful, could have far-reaching and unexpected implications, accompanying the military strengthening of the state with a strengthening of its social capacity and accompanying legitimacy, factors that have eluded it for so long.

Notes

1. Alejandro Gaviria, *Increasing Returns and the Evolution of Violent Crime: The Case of Colombia,* Discussion Paper 98-14 (San Diego: University of California, San Diego, 1998), http://econ.ucsd.edu/publications/files/ucsd9814.pdf.

2. Philippe Burin des Roziers, "Culturas mafiosas en Colombia: Entre arcaísmo y modernidad," in *Las dos Colombias,* edited by Jean-Michel Blanquer and Christian Gros (Bogotá: Grupo Editorial Norma, 2002), 279–87.

3. La Violencia, capitalized, refers to a series of provincial and local sociopolitical conflicts, within the traditional framework of liberal/conservative sectarianism. Its greatest destructive power was unleashed between 1948 and 1953. The varying statistical calculations ranging from 80,000 to 400,000 deaths reveal the sectarian nature of the phenomenon. The Cold War exacerbated the liberal/conservative polarization.

4. These organizations maintain up-to-date Web sites—www.farc-ep.org and www.eln-voces.com—although the FARC Website in 2008 was either blocked or hacked into in most of the world.

5. Fernando Cubides, *Burocracias armadas: El problema de la organización en el entramado de las violencias colombianas* (Bogotá: Grupo Editorial Norma, 2005), 67–83.

6. It is worth noting that the distribution of profits from the coca/cocaine chain follows a pattern similar to that of other raw materials of plant origin. In a 2010 study (based on statistics from 2008), the United Nations found that the thousands of coca growers in the Andean countries earned just 1.3 percent of the profits from the drug trade. Local dealers received 1 percent, Colombian traffickers who export to the United States received 13 percent, traffickers who take large quantities into the United States (an overwhelming majority of whom are Mexican) took in 15 percent, and middlemen dealers inside the United States made about 70 percent of total profits.

7. Alexandra Guáqueta, "Change and Continuity in U.S.-Colombian Relations and the War against Drugs," *Journal of Drug Issues* 35, no. 1 (2005): 27–56.

8. Marco Palacios, *Between Legitimacy and Violence: A History of Colombia, 1875–2002* (Durham, N.C.: Duke University Press, 2006), 221–22.

9. Ciro Krauthausen, *Padrinos y mercaderes: Crimen organizado en Italia y Colombia* (Bogotá: Editorial Espasa, 1998).

10. Alejandro Reyes Posada, "Paramilitares en Colombia: Contexto, aliados y consecuencias," *Análisis Político* 12 (1991): 35–41; Mauricio Romero, *Paramilitares y autodefensas, 1982–2003* (Bogotá: Editorial Planeta / IEPRI, 2003); Alfredo Rangel, ed., *El poder paramilitar* (Bogotá: Grupo Editorial Planeta / Fundación Seguridad y Democracia, 2005); The most complete press coverage of the paramilitaries in the past five years can be found in *Revista Semana.*

11. These territories are Urabá-Darién, Caribe–Since–San Jorge, Serranía del Perijá, Magdalena Medio, Pacific Territories (Nariño and Chocó), Saravena-Arauca, the Andean Piedmont in Orinoquia, Ariari-Meta, and Caquetá-Putumayo.

12. Palacios, *Between Legitimacy and Violence,* 260–68.

13. Luis Eduardo Fajardo, *From the Alliance for Progress to the Plan Colombia: A Retrospective Look at U.S. Aid to Colombia,* Working Paper 28 (London: Crisis States Program, London School of Economics and Political Science, 2003). For information regarding the early participation of the United States in counterinsurgency, see the monograph by Dennis M. Rempe, *The Past as Prologue? A History of U. S. Counterinsurgency Policy in Colombia, 1958–66* (Carlisle, Pa.: Strategic Studies Institute, 2002), https://www.strategicstudiesinstitute.army.mil/pubs/display.cfm?pubID=17.

14. Counterinsurgency strategy requires operating like the enemy: knowledge of local society, penetration of it, and waging war with mobile units. Las Brigadas, supervised by the army, offered health and literacy services to campesino populations that sympathized with the guerrillas, or were in danger of doing so. Paramilitary formations were the armed and "dirty" face of counterinsurgency and were characterized by their local roots and informal nature. They acquired legal status between 1965 and 1989. For information regarding more recent times, see Human Rights Watch, "La redes de asesinos de Colombia: La asociación militar-paramilitares y Estados Unidos," November 1996, http://www.hrw.org/spanish/informes/1996/colombia2.html#historia; "Paramilitaries as Proxies: Declassified Evidence on the Colombian Army Anti-Guerrilla 'Allies,'" National Security Archive Electronic Briefing Book no. 166, October 16, 2005, http://www.gwu.edu/~nsarchiv/NSAEBB/NSAEBB166/index.htm.

15. Marco Palacios, "Colombia: ni estado de guerra, ni estado de paz; estado en proceso de paz," *Foro Internacional* 40 (2000): 15–40.

16. According to the World Bank, the concentration of land in Colombia is the highest in the world and this combined with its underutilization causes a "vicious circle of low growth, violence and even greater inequality." World Bank, *Colombia: Land Policy in Transition* (Washington, D.C.: World Bank 2004), http://www-wds.worldbank.org/external/default/main?pagePK=64193027&piPK=64187937&theSitePK=523679&menuPK=64187510&searchMenuPK=64187511&theSitePK=523679&entityID=000160016_20040312102005&searchMenuPK=64187511&theSitePK=523679; Luis B. Flórez E. (vice comptroller general of the republic), "Extinción de dominio, reforma agraria, democracia y paz," paper presented at the symposium "La Extinción de la Propiedad Ilícita: ¿Una Vía para la Reforma Agraria?" Bogotá, June 9, 2005, http://www.contraloriagen.gov.co:8081/internet/cartelera/Archivos/1516/Foro%20Rural%20Junio%209%202005.doc. Paper by the executive comptroller for defense, justice and security, "La gestión de la reforma agraria y el proceso de incautación y extinción de bienes rurales," paper presented at the symposium "La Extinción de la Propiedad Ilícita: ¿Una Vía para la Reforma Agraria?" Bogotá, June 9, 2005, http://www.contraloriagen.gov.co:8081/internet/cartelera/Archivos/1516/Ponencia%20CDSD%20Bienes%20rurales%20foro.doc; and an editorial, "¿Hasta Cuando?" *El Tiempo,* June 12, 2005.

17. Geoffrey Demarest, "Cadastres and Global Security," http://www.is.esri.com/library/userconf/proc04/docs/pap2177.pdf.

18. For complete, up-to-date, and trustworthy information regarding internal displacement in Colombia, see two Web sites: that of the United Nations, http://www.acnur.org/index.php?id_pag=565; and that of the Internal Displacement Monitoring Centre, http://www.internal-displacement.org/.

19. Statistics on deaths in traffic accidents were taken from the bulletins of the National Institute of Legal Medicine and Forensic Sciences and can be found at www.medicinalegal.gov.co. Information on deaths related to the armed conflict is from the Ministry of Defense and can be found at www.mindefensa.gov.co.

20. María Victoria Llorente, "Los reinsertados de Medellín y la ¿donbernabilidad," *Semana,* June 17, 2009; María Victoria Llorente, "Medellín podrá terminar el año con 2000 homicidios," *Semana,* November 25, 2009.

21. Alicia Puyana and José Romero, "Growth without Increased Productivity or Better Jobs: Is Development Possible?" paper presented at the seminar "Human Capital, Training, and Labor Markets in Latin America," Institute for the Study of the Americas, London, February, 2005, graph 5.

22. Palacios, *Between Legitimacy and Violence,* 206–8.

23. Santa Fe de Ralito, a village in the Córdoba department located in an enclave dominated by paramilitaries, was the center for negotiations with Álvaro Uribe's government and a rallying point for their contingents during the demobilization and surrendering of arms processes.

24. Transitions to democracy, first in Europe—Spain, Greece, and Portugal—and later in Argentina, Brazil, Chile, and Uruguay, inspired President Betancur's peace talks (1982–86), which he included as part of the "democratic opening."

25. See the original version (in English) of Plan Colombia: President of Colombia, *Plan Colombia: Plan for Peace, Prosperity, and the Strengthening of the State* (Bogotá: Presidency of the Republic, 1999), http://www.usip.org/library/pa/colombia/adddoc/plan_colombia_101999.html; and also Adam Isacson, "Failing Grades: Evaluating the Results of Plan Colombia," *Yale Journal of International Affairs,* http://www.yale.edu/yjia/articles/Vol_1_Iss_1_Summer2005/IsacsonFinal.pdf, and Adam Isacson, "Las Fuerzas Armadas de Estados Unidos en la 'guerra contra las drogas'," in *Drogas y democracia en América Latina: El impacto de la política de Estados Unidos,* edited by Coletta A. Youngers and Eileen Rosin (Buenos Aires: Editorial Biblos and Washington Office on Latin America, 2005), 29–84.

26. Winifred Tate, "¿Sin lugar para la paz? La política de Estados Unidos hacia Colombia," *Accord,* 2004, http://www.c-r.org/accord/col/a14spnsh/noroomforpeace.shtml.

27. This was intended to gain supposed advantages from the "synergy" transforming two wars into one. See Angel Rabasa and Peter Chalk, *Colombian Labyrinth: The Synergy of Drugs and Insurgency and Its Implications for Regional Stability* (Santa Monica, Calif.: RAND Corporation, 2001), http://www.rand.org/pubs/monograph reports/MR1339/.

28. Juan Gabriel Tokatlian, "La polémica sobre la legalización de drogas en Colombia, el Presidente Samper y los Estados Unidos," *Latin American Research Review* 35, no. 1 (2000): 37–83; John C. Dugas, "Drugs, Lies and Audiotape: The Samper Crisis in Colombia," *Latin American Research Review* 36, no. 2 (2001): 157–74.

29. "Pastrana desnarcotiza la paz," *El Espectador,* October 23, 1998.

30. "Estados Unidos duplica su ayuda a la 'nueva' Colombia de Pastrana," *El País* (Madrid), October 29, 1998.

31. Speech by President Álvaro Uribe Vélez before the 58th General Assembly of the Organization of United Nations, September 30, 2003, http://www.presidencia.gov.co/discursos/discursos2003/septiembre/septiembre2003.htm.

32. Office of the High Commissioner for Peace, Presidency of the Republic, *Hechos de Paz V: Del Dialogo a la Negociación, Agosto 7 de 1998–Mayo 24 de 1999* (Bogotá: Presidency of the Republic, 1999), 441–66; Observatorio para la paz, *Plan Colombia: Juego de máscaras,* corrected electronic version (2001), http://www.mamacoca.org/junio2001/plancol_mascaras_es.htm; Bureau of Western Hemisphere Affairs,

U.S. Department of State, "Why Americans Should Care about Plan Colombia," Fact Sheet, February 21, 2001, http://www.state.gov/p/wha/rls/fs/2001/1040.htm; Ministry of National Defense, Presidency of the Republic, *Política de Defensa y Seguridad Democrática* (Bogotá: Presidency of the Republic, 2003), http://alpha.mindefensa.gov .co/dayTemplates/images/seguridad_democratica.pdf.

33. Juan Gabriel Tokatlian, *El Plan Colombia: Un modelo de intervención?* Working Paper 23 (Buenos Aires: Humanities Department, Universidad de San Andrés, 2001), 4–16.

34. During the 2005–6 electoral campaign, the Polo Democrático and its candidate, the former Constitutional Court magistrate and senator Carlos Gaviria, never mentioned Plan Colombia in their documents, although they repeated phrases dedicated to the defense of human rights in armed conflict and proposed a vague political solution to the conflict.

35. See David T. Johnson (U.S. assistant secretary for international narcotics and law enforcement affairs), "Release of the 2008 International Narcotics Control Strategy Report," Washington, February 29, 2008, cited by Mónica Serrano, "U.S.-Latin American Drug Relations: A Prognosis," unpublished paper kindly shared with the author.

36. Aid figures, by program and year, can be found at http://ciponline.org/colombia/ index.htm.

37. The "Nudo de Paramillo Agreement" was signed on July 26, 1998, by representatives from the National Peace Council, which aside from several state officials who made the government's influence manifest, included members of civil society and the AUC. See the complete text in www.ciponline.org/colombia/nudoagre.htm; Fernando Cubides was the first to underscore the political significance of the opening the media presented to paramilitaries following this agreement, as well as the paramilitaries' sense of internal organization tying together disperse groups, which in the end allowed them to negotiate as "political actors." Cubides, *Burocracias armadas,* 68–76.

38. Fundación Ideas para la Paz, "Negociaciones Gobierno Nacional Grupos ilegales armados de Autodefensas," May 26, 2002–April 25, 2004, http://www.ideaspaz.org/ new_site/secciones/publicaciones/download_documentos/cronologia_gobierno_auto defensas.pdf.

39. Alvaro Camacho Guizado, "Los usos del paramilitarismo," *El Espectador,* July 2, 2006.

40. Marco Palacios, "Agenda para la democracia y negociación con las guerrillas," in *Los laberintos de la guerra: Utopías e incertidumbres sobre la paz,* edited by Francisco Leal Buitrago (Bogotá: Facultad de Ciencias Sociales of Universidad de los Andes and Tercer Mundo, 1999), 59–107.

41. Uribe was well known because during his term as governor of Antioquia (1995– 97) he promoted the local private self-defense organizations known as the Convivir. Created by law in February of 1994, in 1997, the Constitutional Court ruled they could not distribute machine guns, assault rifles, and grenade launchers. Following scandals revealing how certain Convivir had participated in massacres and alliances with paramilitaries, the authorities decided to no longer authorize them once their licenses to operate expired. Report by the Inter-American Commission of Human Rights, http:// www.cidh.org/countryrep/Colom99en/chapter.4f.htm.

42. Mauricio Romero, *Parapolítica: La ruta de la expansión paramilitar y los acuerdos políticos* (Bogotá: Corporación Nuevo Arco Iris, 2007); Gustavo Duncan, *Los señores de la guerra: De paramilitares, mafiosos y autodefensas en Colombia* (Bogotá:

Planeta Colombia, 2006), 211–39; Daron Acemoglu, James.A. Robinson, and R. J. Santos, "The Monopoly of Violence: Evidence from Colombia," Harvard University, 2009, http://www.people.fas.harvard.edu/~jrobins/researchpapers/unpublishedpapers/jr_formationofstate.pdf.

43. See "Viaje al corazón del Patriota," *El Tiempo* (special edition), May 3, 2005; "Preguntas al Patriota," *El Tiempo,* May 4, 2005.

44. Francisco Leal Buitrago, "La seguridad durante el primer año de gobierno de Alvaro Uribe Vélez," *Análisis Político* 50 (2004): 40–54.

45. Rodrigo Uprimny Yepes, "Justicia transicional en Colombia: Algunas herramientas conceptuales para el análisis del caso colombiano," *Revista Foro* 53 (2005): 45–57; Rodrigo Uprimny Yepes and María Paula Saffon Sanín, "La Ley de 'Justicia y Paz': ¿Una garantía de justicia y paz y de no repetición de las atrocidades?" *Revista Foro* 55 (2005): 49–62; International Crisis Group, *Colombia: Towards Peace and Justice?* Latin American Report 16 (Brussels: International Crisis Group, 2006), http://www.crisis group.org/library/documents/latin_america/16_colombia_towards_peace_and_justice .pdf; Hernando Valencia Villa, "La ley de Justicia y Paz de Colombia a la luz del Derecho Internacional de los derechos humanos," Center for Peace Investigation, http://www.euro-colombia.org/descargas/actualizacionoctubre2005/documentovalencia.pdf.

46. Constitutional Court, Plenary Council, "Ruling No. C-370/2006," May 18, 2006.

47. "Pedidos de extradición contra jefes de las Farc se suspenderían si hay un acuerdo de paz," *El Tiempo,* March 23, 2006.

48. "Estados Unidos declara la guerra a las FARC," *El Tiempo,* March 23, 2006; "Estados Unidos halló 25 mil pruebas contra FARC," *El Tiempo,* March 26, 2006; "La guerrilla es ahora nuestro principal blanco: Anne Patterson," *El Tiempo,* March 26, 2006.

49. "Uribe anuncia más impuestos de guerra," *El Tiempo,* March 30, 2006.

50. "Gobierno les quitaría a 12 mil ex 'paras' sus mesadas," *El Tiempo,* July 7, 2006.

51. "Acciones del DAS contra las BACRIM," *Resultados y Operativos del DAS 2009,* December 30, 2009, available at http://www.das.gov.co/.

52. Gustavo Duncan, *Del campo a la ciudad en Colombia: La infiltración urbana de los señores de la guerra* (Bogotá, 2004), www.fescol.org.co/Doc%20PDF/EV-Gustavo-Duncan.pdf. The term "Sanandresitos" refers to the Colombian island of San Andrés, which has been a tax-free port since the early 1950s.

53. Fundación Seguridad y Democracia, "El repliegue de las FARC: Derrota o estrategia?" http://www.seguridadydemocracia.org/docs/pdf/ocasionales/Derrotao Estrategia.pdf.

54. See, e.g., Fundación Seguridad y Democracia, "Conflicto armado 2007: Informe especial," http://www.seguridadydemocracia.org/docs/pdf/especiales/informeEspecial 19-2.pdf.

55. See the Web site of the National Narcotics Office Drug Observatory, www.dne .gov.co; María Clemencia Ramírez, Kimberly Stanton, and John Walsh, "Colombia: Un círculo vicioso de drogas y guerra," in *Drogas y democracia en América Latina,* ed. Youngers and Rosin, 131–83; Francisco Thoumi, ed., "Drugs, Crime and Armed Conflict in Colombia," *Journal of Drug Issues* 35, no. 1 (2005): 1–227; and Zachary P. Mugge, "Plan Colombia: The Environmental Effects and Social Costs of the United States' Failing War on Drugs," *Colorado Journal of International Environmental Law and Policy* 15, no. 2 (2004): 309–40.

56. Laurel Sherret, "Futility in Action: Coca Fumigation in Colombia," *Journal of Drug Issues* 35, no. 1 (2005): 151–68.

Commentary: Two Decades of Negotiation in Colombia—Contrasting Results and Missed Opportunities

Ana María Bejarano

In the 1980s, it was said that Colombia was a laboratory of insurgent experiences. Since the 1990s, it also has become a laboratory of incorporation experiences. The Colombian case provides useful comparative lessons on the issue of political inclusion that may also be applicable to other cases.

The first section of this commentary addresses the Colombian experience regarding the incorporation of various guerrilla groups within the country. The second section discusses obstacles and continuing challenges to the political incorporation of those guerrilla groups that remain outside the country's legal political framework. In the past, many in Colombian society thought of negotiations with insurgent groups as possible and even necessary. Twenty years ago, guerrillas were part of an accepted popular myth that viewed them as fighting against the establishment in favor of the poor. Now, however, most Colombians believe that the government is winning the war against the guerrillas and it is not clear that the country would tolerate broad-ranging peace negotiations—especially with the principal guerrilla group, the Revolutionary Armed Forces of Colombia (Fuerzas

Armadas Revolucionarias de Colombia, FARC). Although weakened militarily, the FARC retains an ability to inflict damage. Even so, it is not clear what would be on a negotiating agenda or who in Colombian society would tolerate such an effort.[1]

Considering the past twenty to twenty-five years of peace negotiations in Colombia, there are many reasons for skepticism, along with some reason for a measure of optimism. First, the number of guerrilla groups has been reduced from seven to two; there are now fewer actors involved in the internal armed conflict. Some of the demobilization experiences have been successful, particularly that of the Quintin Lame Armed Movement. What one can see from a historical perspective is a gradual and painful expansion of the scope of control of the national territory by the state. In that sense, there is room for a more positive interpretation of what has occurred.

Since the 1990s, five different insurgent organizations have demobilized and become included in the Colombian political arena. The process has been staggered and uneven, but it has nonetheless shown noticeable advances. Of course different negotiations and demobilizations have led to different outcomes; thus, it is interesting to compare what factors made some successful and others failures. The continuum extends from the dramatic elimination of the Patriotic Union (Unión Patriótica, UP)—a leftist party born out of an early 1980s peace negotiation with the FARC—to the mixed experiences of the M-19 and the Popular Liberation Army (Ejército Popular de Liberación, EPL), and finally to the successful case of the Quintin Lame Armed Movement.

In differentiating among these experiences, one must consider first what some have called the political opportunity structure; in Colombia there has been a slow and painstaking democratization of the political regime. Colombia does not represent a typical transition from authoritarianism to democracy. Rather, it exemplifies what Laurence Whitehead has aptly labeled "democratization by stealth"[2]—*la democratización sigilosa del regimen político colombiano.* This process started in the mid-1980s, primarily with the decision to decentralize and submit the election of local authorities to a popular vote, something that admittedly has been a double-edged sword. On the one hand, decentralization exacerbated a struggle for local and regional power, which may partially explain the increased violence beginning in the middle to late 1980s and continuing into the 1990s. On the other hand, electoral reform 'opened opportunities for the participation and incorporation of some armed actors. Thus, decentralization in

Colombia illustrates the perils of democratization within a context of continued violence and state weakness.

Decentralizing reforms were followed by another substantial reform—the Constituent Assembly and the drafting of the 1991 Constitution—that represented an extraordinary opportunity in Colombian history. At the time of the assembly, there was a fortuitous coincidence, and a virtuous cycle emerged as the assembly became an incentive for the armed groups to speed up negotiations with the government. Ultimately, the government acted strategically to incorporate the armed actors into the assembly, which in turn made the assembly a more representative and inclusive space. The virtuous cycle that characterized this process will be difficult to repeat. At the time, a series of transitory measures allowed for the incorporation of two members of the EPL, one member of Quintin Lame, and one member of the Revolutionary Workers Party (Partido Revolucionario de los Trabajadores) within the assembly. The electoral system used to select the delegates to the assembly also opened up space for the remarkable participation of the M-19, which won nineteen seats in the 1990 elections. A lasting legacy of the assembly in terms of incorporation and inclusion is the electoral system that emerged after 1991, which has permitted the inclusion of several minority groups, including ex-guerrillas from the armed left, but also non-Catholic Christian groups, indigenous groups, and others.

The downside of this electoral reform process is that it created a centrifugal dynamic. It became an incentive for the fragmentation and atomization of political parties and the party system, which not only affected the traditional parties—the Liberals and Conservatives—but also the left and the minority parties and movements. With the electoral reform of 2003, however, there has been a move toward a more coherent party system. Recent elections have demonstrated that the 2003 reforms effectively led to a more coherent realignment of political forces. Initially, it seemed that the changes favored the right more so than the left, yet the left has also managed to carve out an important niche. In 2006, the left-wing Polo Democrático Alternativo (Alternative Democratic Pole) won eleven seats in the Chamber of Deputies and eight seats in the Senate (a number that declined in 2010 to five seats in the Chamber and eight in the Senate). Its presidential candidate in 2006, Carlos Gaviria Díaz, came in second with 22 percent of the vote, well above the Liberal Party. In the 2010 presidential elections, the Partido Verde (Green Party), an opposition group of leftists and independents, made a significant showing, garnering 21.5 percent of votes in the first round, which increased to 27.5 percent in the second round. Though still in the minority, the Colombian left has never before had such a strong presence in national politics.

In addition to political transformations at the national level, it is also important to consider political opportunities, or the lack thereof, and the dynamics of violence at the subnational level; these factors contribute in an important way to the various outcomes regarding political inclusion of ex-guerrilla forces. For example, much of the violence unleashed against the UP and the EPL in the 1980s and 1990s was related to increased competition between armed and unarmed actors in specific regions of the country and to the incapacity of the state to sufficiently control and protect these forces. Therefore, when discussing the state and the need to strengthen the state, not only should the discussion address the need to transform the armed forces and to build stronger judiciaries at the national level; it must also consider the subnational level and particularly those regions and localities where the state has been unable to provide a level playing field to all newly included actors who participate under the threat of violence.

The very dramatic experience of the UP and the EPL contrasts with that of Quintin Lame. The difference lies not only in the fact that the department of Cauca was perhaps a less violent region than Urabá or Córdoba, but also the power of the social movement behind Quintin Lame—referred to as "a hegemonic social movement"—was important, because it managed to protect the ex-combatants of Quintin Lame from the incursions of other armed actors. In the case of the M-19, however, there was no regional attachment, because the M-19 had very little in the way of a social or regional base outside major urban areas.

Finally, to understand the various outcomes in terms of incorporation, one must also consider the nature of the armed organization itself and the differences among the organizations in question. Transitioning from a situation of conflict to postconflict is a traumatic experience, not only for the individuals involved but also for organizations themselves. Shifting from a military structure to a political and civilian structure, or from the unified command of guerrilla forces to the competition for leadership that occurs in postconflict politics, can be extremely difficult, particularly because the types of skills politicians need to survive in electoral politics differ greatly from those needed to survive guerrilla warfare. In this sense, all demobilized guerrilla combatants faced similar challenges, as they were unable to use much of their guerrilla past for their civilian future. This generalization notwithstanding, differences again emerged among groups as their members transitioned back into civilian and political life. Members of Quintin Lame found the transition from guerrilla group to social organization and finally to political party much easier than other groups, as they were able to return to a strong social and regional base. Additionally, the capacity and will of the Quintin Lame to work from the bottom up proved to be advantageous to the political transition of the group, a condition that was clearly absent in the case of the M-19. The M-19 fell very rapidly into the pattern of conducting politics from the top down after it launched itself as a national movement with a strong presence in the Constituent Assembly. Later, however, the organization learned the hard way that it must return to the localities to engage in local politics if it wanted to rebuild a national force.

Another crucial distinction among the various groups is the degree to which the entire organization finally decides to demobilize or not; again, the experiences of the UP and the EPL are instructive. There are cases in which the armed apparatus of the guerrillas did not demobilize completely—the case of the UP being the most dramatic because the FARC did not demobilize at all—which ultimately made the political fronts victims of the armed movements' own ambiguity. Although the majority of the EPL demobilized, a small faction named the Caraballos remained actively engaged in warfare. This made the political movement that emerged out of the EPL the target of a political extermination campaign led by regional forces—including the Caraballos, the FARC, and regional elites—in those areas where the newly formed political movement attempted to engage in democratic politics.

In assessing protracted negotiations and peace processes such as Colombia's, apart from recognizing "ripe moments," it is also necessary to consider missed opportunities. When analyzing Colombia over the last twenty-five years or so, the obstacles that have emerged and the increasing difficulty of negotiations become readily apparent. This is in comparison with the negotiations' climate of the early 1980s, when the first major opportunity was missed. The following briefly highlights some of the substantial changes throughout the years.

First and most important to mention are changes in the international system, and particularly the difficulties created during the past decade by the increasing internationalization of justice. This is problematic for cases like Colombia; pardons like the M-19's blanket amnesty in 1982 and individual pardons are now basically impossible to achieve given the international community's drive to impose universal norms and standards with respect to truth and justice. Additionally, it is important to recognize the transformations of the international environment following the September 11, 2001, terrorist attacks. The advent of the so-called war on terrorism, the substantive involvement of the United States in Colombian counterinsurgency efforts, and the discourse of the Uribe administration all contributed to a dramatic shrinking of the space for negotiations. That said, the actions of the guerrillas themselves have led to their loss of credibility.

Domestic changes in Colombia also make negotiations more difficult today than twenty years ago. The first change is, of course, the increasing involvement of both guerrillas and paramilitaries in the drug business, which blurs the lines between political violence and organized crime. These are important domestic matters, but they also transcend the limits of domestic politics, because the drug trade is a transnational business. The fact that guerrillas and paramilitaries are actively engaged in the drug trade has led to the increased participation of the United States in the war and, eventually, in any negotiation process. This may be viewed as a constraint but also as an opportunity. For example, key paramilitary leaders entered into negotiations with the Uribe administration shortly after they were indicted for drug trafficking in the United States and the U.S. government requested their extradition. Many paramilitary leaders were, in fact, extradited to the United States to stand trial on drug-trafficking charges.

Another substantial and perhaps more problematic domestic change concerns the counter-agrarian reform that took place in Colombia beginning in the 1980s, led by paramilitaries in conjunction with the traditional landowning class. The reconcentration of land has created formidable obstacles to agrarian reform; and it is no mystery that much of the violence in Colombia—as in Guatemala—has historically been tied up with the issue of land ownership and distribution. The willingness of the administration of President Juan Manuel Santos to tackle the land issue represents a sea change in Colombian politics. His effort to restore farms to those illegally forced off their land may pay huge dividends to future generations. Successfully addressing the land issue—something central to the demands of the FARC—would further erode what remains of their base of support in rural areas. That said, change will be slow and difficult and it is unclear how far the efforts will advance. The agrarian issue has been made more complicated by the new polarization in the countryside between an illegal peasantry, the *cocaleros,* and an illegal landowning class.

The final domestic change has to do with what has been labeled "negotiation fatigue" in Colombia, particularly after the failure of the negotiations in the Caguán between President Andrés Pastrana (1998–2002) and the FARC. The FARC appeared, then as now, to be uninterested in negotiations. Political reforms since the early 1990s have made the country more democratic; the tolerance of Colombian society for armed options and its willingness to grant the insurgents special treatment have evaporated. The Polo Democrático Alternativo and the Green Party constitute nonarmed and increasingly successful options on the left. Missed opportunities do not come back, and the window has been closing on negotiations with remaining guerrilla groups for some time.

Notes

1. This commentary focuses on guerrilla groups that contest the state, not the paramilitary groups that worked in close collaboration with state forces even if, over time, they gained a great deal of autonomy. The administration of President Álvaro Uribe negotiated the military demobilization of the principal paramilitary group, the Autodefensas Unidas de Colombia, although many former combatants have rearmed and remain heavily involved in drug trafficking.

2. Laurence Whitehead, "Reforms: Mexico and Colombia," in *Democracy in Latin America: (Re)constructing Political Society,* edited by Manuel Antonio Garretón and E. Newman (Tokyo: United Nations University Press, 2001), 67.

Chapter 7

Peace in Peru, but Unresolved Tasks

Carlos Basombrío Iglesias

In 1998, I wrote one of the Peru chapters for the volume *Comparative Peace Processes in Latin America.*[1] This new book continues that discussion and provides an update regarding the context, characteristics, and implications of the strategic defeat of the Shining Path (Sendero Luminoso). To do so is important, despite the time elapsed, as the issue continues to be of concern and is still part of the ongoing agenda of the nation's problems.

As described in the above-mentioned chapter, Peru was near the brink of collapse in the early 1990s. On one hand, there was an economic catastrophe. By 1990, inflation had reached 7,649 percent. Gross domestic product decreased 28.9 percent between 1981 and 1991. The real value of wages decreased 24.6 percent in 1988, 45.4 percent in 1989, and 12.7 percent in 1990. In addition, political violence seemed to have spiraled out of control. Shining Path claimed to have abandoned its strategic defense and proclaimed that it was in a period of strategic equilibrium, the prelude to a counteroffensive with which it would take power.

This situation came about as a result of the failure of Peruvian democracy to adequately face the problem of internal subversion that was, and should have always been, marginal. The theory maintained in *Comparative Peace Processes* was that between 1980 and 1992, tension ensued between two viewpoints and approaches to a solution to the problem: One focused exclusively on repression and military action; and the other, without excluding the first, required a comprehensive political solution. This was understood to be a combination of economic, social, political, and intelligence measures that, of course, included the military. This latter approach would first isolate the members of the Shining Path and then impede their growth among new, impoverished sectors of the population, thereby facilitating actions taken against them while, at the same time, respecting the civilian population, the law, and human rights.

The military-only strategy prevailed, and thus a great paradox was created in Peru. Both the Shining Path and those in society and the state that opposed it simultaneously saw democracy as an obstacle to be removed. The Shining Path had proposed since its inception the need to finish off the institutions of the "bourgeois state." At the same time, there were very early voices in the armed forces, political parties, and the press that claimed that the only way to put an end to the Shining Path was to put democracy on hold.[2] As the Shining Path grew, as a result of the prevailing military logic, democracy was discredited, and there was ever more acceptance of the military's request for a blank check. Yet at the same time, for other citizens democracy was discredited for the opposite reason—for being incapable of punishing those who, professing the need to end the violence, themselves violated the law and civil rights and thereby accelerated the process that they professed to be fighting.

The debate ended on April 5, 1992, when President Alberto Fujimori shut down Congress, intervened in the judiciary, abolished regional governments, concentrated power in the office of the presidency, and began to govern with the support of the armed forces and the intelligence apparatus. Two years after the "self-coup" (*autogolpe*), the Shining Path was already strategically defeated. However, this did not come about as a result of the coup, but because of the capture of Abimael Guzmán—which was the fruit of an autonomous process separate from the prevailing political logic—that changed the balance of the war.[3] Nevertheless, the government cleverly handled the connection between authoritarian government and security, receiving significant levels of popular support that consolidated the regime.

My first chapter in *Comparative Peace Processes* concluded by saying: "Dealing seriously and creatively with these problems, the result of fifteen years of violence and the way it was faced, has become the crucial and pending task for consolidating peace in Peru. Doing so requires the direct questioning of the 'men of war' [*señores de la guerra*] in power. This is a political task of exceptional importance, the result of which, to a large extent, will reflect the type of country that Peru will be at the beginning of the new millennium."[4]

The purpose of this chapter is to examine the country's subsequent political process, how far it has advanced in creating the conditions for peace, and what challenges still need to be met so that peace can prevail.

The Struggle for Democracy

The final years of the Fujimori regime were politically very intense.[5] Fujimori's reelection plans for 2000 were at the heart of the confrontations. Information discovered after the collapse of the regime revealed that his re-reelection was an operation carried out on multiple fronts and directed by Vladimiro Montesinos from the intelligence services, in which all state resources were used illicitly.[6]

The Political Constitution of 1993, approved at the time mainly to permit the reelection of Fujimori in 1995, did not foresee a second reelection. Nevertheless, the Congress, controlled by the regime, approved a law of "authentic interpretation," which maintained that his first term should not count because it had begun before the adoption of the new Constitution, and hence Fujimori could run for yet a third term. The Constitutional Tribunal issued a decision declaring the law inapplicable, and in May 1997, Congress dismissed the three judges who had drafted it.[7] In the months and years that followed, the country's polarization intensified. On the one hand, the government and its supporters used all possible means to impose Fujimori's plan for reelection; on the other, the growing citizen opposition movement found all legal openings closed, one by one.

The most shameful and revealing chapter of this fraudulent abuse of democratic practices took place in 1998, when the opposition began to collect signatures for a referendum to oppose Fujimori's reelection. The referendum law was incorporated into the Constitution by Fujimori's own political coalition, but it required the signatures of 10 percent of the total number of voters to request it. Even so, as an expression of the growing rejection of the regime, organizers quickly obtained 1.5 million signatures, easily surpassing the 10 percent required.

When Congress, dominated by Fujimori's political allies, realized that the number of signatures required would be surpassed, it changed the referendum law again. The amended law required that, in addition to the signatures, it had to be approved by at least forty-eight members of Congress to be implemented. With this move, Congress completely subverted the very idea of the referendum, an expression of direct democracy, by forcing it to go through Congress.[8] Moreover, the new law should have been inapplicable in this case, because it was approved after the start of the collection of signatures. Given that the government had complete control of the electoral apparatus (later, it was revealed that many electoral officials were bribed), the congressional interpretation that the referendum should be approved by Congress prevailed. In the end, sixty-seven members of Congress voted against the referendum and therefore ended any possibility of using legal and institutional means to challenge the reelection. The regime was becoming, day by day, an open dictatorship. Civic discontent continued to grow; 78 percent of the population expressed disapproval of this decision.[9]

In 1999, the regime took a further step in the direction of abandoning all pretense of democracy when it announced Peru's unilateral withdrawal from the Organization of American States' Inter-American Court of Human Rights. The excuse given was that it wanted to avoid that the Court "weaken the antiterrorist struggle" by accepting cases of due process. Nevertheless, it was obvious that the real reason was linked to the fact that the Court could accept complaints that had been presented to it regarding the dismissal of members of the Constitutional Tribunal and the revocation of Baruch Ivcher's Peruvian citizenship in order to take away his ownership of a television channel that was opposed to the regime.[10]

In this institutional setting, Fujimori's campaign for a third term in 2000 was launched. It was fraudulent in every aspect. It is now known that the government had bought off everyone, from the most important television channels to the owners of the so-called *chicha* newspapers, or popular tabloids. Television did not even accept paid advertisements from the candidates in the campaign and, along with the yellow press, carried out a systematic campaign of destroying any candidate who seemed to pose a serious threat to Fujimori.[11] They did it first with Alberto Andrade, then mayor of Lima, who was running strong in the polls; when they achieved that objective, they moved on to Luis Castañeda, who had replaced Andrade as leader of the opposition, and again, they were successful.[12] Finally, they tried it with the candidacy of Alejandro Toledo, but they did not have time to accomplish their goal.

In addition, the intelligence services controlled the electoral agencies and even drafted their decisions. Similarly, public funds were used in the poorest areas to push public opinion toward Fujimori, and there was fraud in the registration of his new political party.[13] The armed forces and political authorities actively participated in the campaign in favor of Fujimori.[14]

The utilization of public funds in the poorest areas to influence the reelection was very important. The patronage relationship was strengthened, symbolically associating social spending with the "Presidency of the Republic" and detaching it from the sectoral administration of the government. At the same time, peoples' fears were manipulated, as they were led to believe that a new president would abandon programs upon which the survival of millions of Peruvians now depended.

Even so, on election night the country was polarized between the two candidates, and the first results showed Alejandro Toledo as the winner. Immediately, television coverage went off the air for two or three hours, and channels began to show old movies instead. When the broadcasts were reestablished, Fujimori was ahead and close to avoiding a second round. In the following days, the government manipulated the results as they were reported from around the country, showing Fujimori close to winning in the first round; however, the strength of street demonstrations frightened the government, and it conceded a second round. Knowing that this round would be just as fraudulent, Toledo ultimately declined to participate. Fujimori stood alone and thereby achieved a third term.

The Crisis and Collapse of the Fujimori Regime

Alberto Fujimori began his third term on July 28, 2000. He did so with little opposition in Congress and with hundreds of thousands of protesters in the streets, participating in a wave of popular demonstrations known as the "March of the Four Suyos."[15] During those days, there were also acts of violence that caused the deaths of innocent people in events that, it was later revealed, the government intentionally instigated in order to blame the opposition.[16] By this time, the regime was an illegitimate government, and thus was increasingly isolated internationally. Even so, there did not appear to be anything that could provoke its final fall, especially given the control that the government had over all public institutions, the open support of the armed forces, and the subordination of leading figures of the mass media.

Nevertheless, events moved quickly. In August, there was an unusual press conference in which Fujimori and Montesinos (who until then had stayed away from the cameras), along with the high command of the armed forces, announced that they had discovered an operation to traffic weapons to the Revolutionary Armed Forces of Colombia (Fuerzas Armadas Revolucionarias de Colombia, FARC). Within days, it became clear that they were trying to hide the fact that the weapons trafficking was being carried out by the government itself, led by Montesinos. In other words, the Colombian guerrillas were receiving arms from Peru, in deals that were probably linked to drug trafficking.[17] These developments were decisive because they finally broke the links that the Fujimori government maintained with some agencies of the U.S. government, whose officials believed until the end that Peru was efficient in the war against drugs.[18]

Days later, the final crisis of the regime exploded when the opposition managed to obtain and broadcast a video taped secretly by Montesinos, intended for subsequent extortion, in which he is seen delivering piles of cash to an opposition congressional representative, Alberto Kouri, so that he would switch parties and join the regime.[19] This was the last straw. Fujimori could not survive this blow, and he announced new elections and sought to distance himself from Montesinos, who after a few days was taken from the country. After two months, in which signs of the corruption that had occurred emerged everywhere, Fujimori himself fled to Japan, taking with him all the evidence he could, including videos that might implicate him in illegal actions.[20]

A New Opportunity for Peace

The Fujimori regime collapsed in the middle of a corruption scandal never before seen in Peru's history. A transitional government was installed, headed by prodemocracy figure Valentín Paniagua, who appointed Javier Pérez de Cuéllar as prime minister (president of the Council of Ministers was the official name); he was the respected former secretary-general of the United Nations, who ran against Fujimori in the 1995 elections. Thus, a substantive change in appreciation for democracy and human rights was produced in the country. Disgusted with what had happened in the 1990s, Peruvians wanted a new form of governance and questioned the methods of the past.

Rapid and profound changes occurred in the country. The Constitutional Tribunal was restored as soon as Paniagua took office. The control and political manipulation of institutions was ended. Freedom of the press returned, and free elections were guaranteed. Peru returned to the jurisdiction of the Inter-American Court of Human Rights, and amicable settlements were reached with the Inter-American Commission on Human Rights. Hundreds of people were arrested, and charges were filed against thousands of individuals who had been involved in acts of corruption. For the first time in the history of Peru, the powerful were brought to justice for their crimes within the framework of the law. Prominent businessmen, broadcasters, police and military leaders, Cabinet ministers, high-level court officials, directors of public agencies, and others were arrested and charged.

In that national climate, a window of opportunity was opened for discussing and confronting the consequences of the country's counterinsurgency strategy. The fact that military commanders—who for all those years had claimed to be the "saviors of the country" in the war against terrorism—now were mostly imprisoned and accused of very serious acts of corruption facilitated a national debate on what had taken place. The majority of the population questioned authoritarianism, the *autogolpe,* and human rights violations. In short, demand was generated for rethinking what had happened and what the country could learn from that experience. This allowed for the possibility of convening a truth commission.

The censure of society was felt inside the armed forces itself, which had been drastically purged of the commanders most involved in past events. Then, in April 2001, a video was released that showed hundreds of officers of the armed forces and National Police signing what is called in Peru "the subjection document" (*acta de sujeción*), in which they committed themselves to defending the Fujimori government against the accusations of human rights violations. The institutional credibility of the armed forces in the country had now reached its lowest point.

The military was forced to apologize to the country, and they accepted the need for a truth commission in a document signed by the commanders in chief of the three branches of the military and the director of the Peruvian National Police (PNP). They recognized that "the terrorist violence . . . was the pretext used by the de facto government, as of April 5, 1992, for giving excessive power to the National Intelligence Service (Servicio de Inteligencia Nacional, SIN) and for submitting not only the armed forces and the Peruvian National Police, but also other institutions to the control of the SIN." They committed themselves "to investigate and denounce events that involve the commission of crimes before the corresponding judicial bodies, and also to collaborate with all of the investigations by the Congress of the Republic, the judiciary and the Public Ministry." They expressed "their commitment to carry out functions within the framework of respect for human rights, the strengthening of moral values and, consequently, to fight firmly and permanently any indication of corruption or misconduct in institutional life." Finally, they expressed their support for "the initiatives related to the formation and installation of a truth commission that would permit national union and reconciliation, based on justice, in a fair and objective understanding of the facts and circumstances in which the effort for national pacification was carried out."[21]

It was a historic document that illustrated the magnitude of the abrupt change that had occurred in Peru. Weeks later, on June 24, 2001, President Valentín Paniagua created the Truth Commission, and months later, President Toledo expanded the number of commissioners and added the objective of reconciliation. Four processes were initiated that should and could have a direct bearing on the consolidation of the peace process in Peru: a national reflection on what happened and its causes, undertaken by a truth commission; a reform of the security forces; punishment of those responsible within the framework of the law; and, finally, the need for reparations for the victims. What follows is a review of the evolution of each of these processes.

The Work of the Truth Commission and Its Impact on the Country

As Carlos Iván Degregori describes it in his commentary after chapter 12 of this volume, without a doubt the work of the Truth and Reconciliation Commission (Comisión de Verdad y Reconciliación, CVR) exemplifies this political juncture. The CVR's process of compiling its report was public, intense, and captured the country's attention. It had the support of many segments of the population although, at the same time, it received intense criticism from others who tried to discredit it.[22]

After eighteen months of intense work, the CVR published a lengthy final report. Among its main conclusions, these are the most noteworthy:

- The bloodiest conflict in Peru's history had grave and long-lasting consequences for the population.

- The deep cultural and social disparities that separate Peruvians meant that the victims were from the weakest and the most marginalized sectors of society.
- The Shining Path was primarily responsible, because of its ideology, the number of its victims, and the extreme cruelty of its acts.
- The country's leaders were not prepared; they relinquished their responsibilities and then did not know how to face this serious blow to democracy.
- The armed forces and the National Police began acting blindly and later were not supervised and therefore committed serious violations of human rights.

Finally, the CVR concluded that reconciliation must be accomplished through new relationships between the state and society in order to overcome the discrimination that underlies the multiple conflicts that have occurred throughout Peru's history. Moreover, reparation for victims, which includes justice, is indispensable for national reconciliation.[23]

The CVR's conclusions had a significant impact on national life. Its report received ferocious criticism from those political segments that felt most affected by its conclusions and, almost unanimously, by the armed forces. Support from the Toledo government, which implemented the CVR, was relatively weak. Nevertheless, in general, its conclusions were well received by public opinion,[24] and even by parts of the population that had not previously been concerned with human-rights-related issues.[25] Its findings and recommendations have become a fundamental benchmark for the country, although most have yet to be acted upon. However, the demands to bring certain cases to justice and the reparations plan for the victims have moved forward and have had an impact.

Security Reform and Its Institutions

The return of democracy provided the opportunity to redefine the role of the armed forces. The Toledo government created a Commission for the Comprehensive Restructuring of the Armed Forces, composed of public figures, civilian experts, and prominent retired soldiers, which delivered its final report on January 4, 2002. It states that the objective of the reform is not only of a technical or bureaucratic nature, but that it is intrinsically linked to strengthening democracy and to the role that the armed forces should have in this process, which is, above all, a political one. The report states "that it means, fundamentally, to place the armed forces in the framework of the rule of law, subject to the authority of the legitimately elected government."

The Commission for the Comprehensive Restructuring of the Armed Forces sought to establish a new type of military-civilian relationship that has an inherent element of civilian control of the armed forces and military abstention from participating in political decisions: "Civil-military relations should be those of a modern democracy, considering that, in a democracy, the armed forces do not intervene in nor put conditions on political decisions; on the contrary, they implement the defense and military policies adopted by the freely elected government."

Another crucial point of the proposed reform, which coincided with the parallel Commission on Restructuring the National Police, was to establish a clear distinction between security and defense at the constitutional level. The need to reform military justice was also emphasized. The Restructuring Commission gave crucial importance to the process of reform and modernization, as described above, and to have a true Department of Defense "that should be defined as responsible for the formulation, direction, coordination and administration of the general strategies of the state insofar as these refer to defense policies." The recommendations of the Restructuring Commission coincided with the proposals that were simultaneously presented by the CVR.

The reform process proved to be extremely difficult to implement in the years that followed the publication of the report. Significant progress was made during the administration of Aurelio Loret de Mola, who had been a member of the Restructuring Commission and was the second civilian minister of defense in the history of Peru.[26]

Perhaps the most significant aspect of the work of Loret de Mola was obtaining congressional approval of a new law for the Ministry of Defense,[27] a qualitative advance over the previous law, which stated that the Ministry of Defense was the "representative body of the armed forces," a definition that undermined its purpose and established a dependent relationship on the armed forces. Under the new law, the armed forces depend functionally, organically, and politically on the Ministry of Defense and are the implementation tool of the ministry. Other important advances were the reduction of the scope of military secrecy to the strictly indispensable and greater transparency in decisionmaking processes and procurements. Also, a new law aimed at greater professionalism for career officers was approved and after some public debate, a Defense White Paper was also published.

After the Ministry of Defense law was approved in mid-October 2002, strong tensions emerged between the ministry and the armed forces, which fought to maintain their autonomy in decisionmaking.[28] Moreover, as the government weakened politically and the reformist spirit faded, President Toledo returned to the former practice of having the military be in charge of the sector.[29] This contributed to the military's success in pressuring to retain autonomy and traditional powers, especially in such sensitive areas as budget management and military justice.[30]

Against all predictions given the poor quality of the debate on these themes during the electoral campaign and the traditional views on the role of the military that were expressed, the government of Alan García took up again the reform initiatives with renewed vigor. The first minister of defense, Ambassador Allan Wagner, incorporated the conclusions of the CVR into his efforts, and he adopted a position of clearly subordinating the military to civilian power. He also proposed a host of modernization and transparency initiatives. In late December 2007, Wagner was replaced by Antero Flórez Araoz; and, as typically occurs in countries like Peru where reforms are linked to individuals rather than to programs of government, old practices began to reemerge. Rafael Rey—perhaps the most notorious leader of the extreme conservative right, a Fujimori supporter in the 1990s, and a member of Opus Dei, a Vatican-affiliated organization often perceived as reactionary—succeeded Flórez as defense minister. Under his leadership, the recurring theme was that the CVR had lied and that trials of members of the military were abuses committed against the men who had saved the country from terrorism.

The other key reform was security, internal order, and the PNP.[31] The Toledo government put a group of civilians in charge of the Interior Ministry who had been actively involved in the struggle for democracy and the defense of human rights.[32] As was the case with the armed forces, a Restructuring Commission of the PNP was created. The commission presented many institutional changes for the police and its mission in society. Of particular significance, the demilitarization of the police was proposed, reaffirming the civilian identity of that institution, maintaining its professionalism, and differentiating it from the military; its mission is to serve society and the people before the interests of the state. The commission also proposed separating the sections on defense and internal order in the Constitution, and to give police and military personnel the right to vote.

In December of 2001, 2002, and 2003, the month in which retirements and promotions are announced, a significant purge of those commanders linked to the dictatorship was carried out, and greater professionalism was sought via changes in educational policies and professional career opportunities. An Office of Internal Affairs was created to aggressively fight corruption. Treating police personnel with dignity was encouraged, as superiors had often mistreated their subordinates. Susana Villarán, subsequently elected mayor of Lima in 2010, was named police human rights ombudswoman, a position created in February 2002 to protect members of the institution from the abuses they endured in the workplace. The rights of woman on the police force were promoted, and the first rule against harassment in the workplace was approved. In general, a zero tolerance policy against human rights violations was adopted.[33]

A democratic counterinsurgency strategy was designed that defined the need for comprehensive action from the state. Civilian authority, specifically the Ministry of the Interior, was made responsible for the development and execution of these policies. Commissioners for peace were created as representatives of the state in the areas of ongoing conflict, with the aim of coordinating public policies in those areas. Sound intelligence gathering was again promoted as a tool to locate and identify subversive groups, and an aggressive policy was instituted for the recovery of members of indigenous populations who had been captured by the Shining Path, in particular the Ashaninkas, who (as was noted in the CVR report) were especially affected during the conflict.

Many other changes were designed and put into practice, but they were abridged by lack of continuity and the almost total lack of political support from the president. In mid-2004, the government's political coalition took control of the Ministry of the Interior. They opted to maintain the status quo rather than continue making changes, and the majority of them ceased. The reform effort came to a premature end. Alan García's years in power were terrible ones for citizen security in Peru. All hints of reform were abandoned. There were many different ministers, all of them heavily criticized. The institutional corruption of the police increased even as its capacity to respond to basic problems deteriorated. By the end of García's term, the deterioration of citizen security and failures in the fight against drug trafficking constituted two of the most negative aspects of his administration.

The Struggle against Impunity

The democratic transition also provided an opportunity for cases of human rights violations and acts of corruption—which often involved the same people—to be brought to trial and for punishment of those found guilty. In both instances, there have been important advances, but, at the same time, tension and notorious setbacks.

With regard to human rights violations during the conflict, the CVR identified 492 presumed perpetrators in the cases it investigated. Of these, 356 were members of the armed forces, and 70 were from the National Police.[34] There is a widespread perception in the country that the CVR made indiscriminate accusations against officers and soldiers that took part in the internal conflict. This is not true.[35] The cases presented by the CVR before the attorney general (*ministerio público*) were generally already known. Thus, 40 of the 47 cases presented had already been previously investigated, and 24 of them had advanced to the prosecution stage, though only 6 had resulted in guilty sentences.

Perhaps even more important than the numbers was that in spite of all the difficulties, the most notorious cases of human rights violations in the 1980s and 1990s were being tried. Peruvians became totally familiar with the names of notorious paramilitary groups such as the Grupo Colina and the Comando Rodrigo Franco. Moreover, places associated in the past with state terrorism—La Cantuta, Barrios Altos—or with military massacres— Accomarca and others—became associated with judicial proceedings. During the García years, and in spite of government hostility toward seeking punishment for the human rights crimes of the past, there were some guilty verdicts in prominent cases such as La Cantuta and Barrios Altos.

With regard to the anticorruption cases, as indicated above, never before in the history of Peru had there been a process more extensive and respectful of the guarantees of defendants than the one initiated in 2000. An anticorruption subsystem was organized, including an Ad Hoc Anti-Corruption Public Prosecutor's Office, and rules were adopted that facilitated the ability of those charged with lesser offenses to provide relevant information in exchange for a reduced sentence. A total of 259 criminal cases against 1,509 people were initiated.[36] As of 2005, $197 million had been repatriated, and an additional $82 million was located in foreign accounts. The García years represented a serious reversal in these areas. The anticorruption system was weakened to the point of caricature. Government corruption increased, and most political observers in the country agreed that the most serious and notorious cases of corruption of the García administration (the "Petroaudios" and "Business Track" cases) would remain in impunity, with the clear complicity of judicial authorities.

An important milestone in the fight against corruption took place in November 2005, with Alberto Fujimori's trip to Chile, his arrest, and, after

long extradition proceedings, his return to Peru two years later to face prosecution on human rights and corruption charges. The trial of Fujimori was
a historic event, and not just for Peru. It represented the first time anywhere
in the world that a president was judged in his own country for human
rights crimes; and this by a legitimate court that provided all the guarantees
of due process. In April 2009, a lower court found Fujimori guilty of murder and kidnapping and gave him the maximum sentence of twenty-five
years in prison. The sentence was upheld in January 2010, and the trials
ended that same year. Fujimori accepted his guilt on all corruption charges
in order to avoid public disclosure of the facts; and he was found guilty of
all counts for which he was extradited from Chile. However, he will not
serve consecutive sentences, because in the Peruvian judicial system, the
longest sentence takes primacy.

Another legal scenario linked to the armed conflict concerned that of the
new trials of previously convicted members of the Shining Path. During
Fujimori's government, the standards of due process were not respected.
Thus, when democracy was restored, the Constitutional Tribunal annulled
all trials and ordered the defendants to be retried. This was a great challenge
for a judicial system that was deluged with cases and was also, by and large,
incompetent. Nevertheless, in three years the Special Anti-Terrorist Court
handled satisfactorily almost all the 1,400 cases, and the process of retrying
those already convicted, including the leadership, was brought to an end.

This is not the situation in other areas, where the extraordinary slowness of the judicial system has become a burden to ending the country's
cycle of violence. In the anticorruption arena, for example, trials advance
very slowly, and many defendants have found in the leniency and favorit-
ism of some courts a way to escape their responsibilities. Peruvian society
thus continues to be trapped in judicial processes that deal with events that
occurred fifteen and even twenty years ago. A national effort is needed so
that these trials can be accelerated and concluded quickly.

The trials of the members of Shining Path have ended and the guilty
remain in jail, with legitimate and firm sentences. The trials of the military
were also to have moved forward in the same manner. As mentioned above,
the CVR presented a group of cases of crimes committed by state agents
that it recommended should be investigated. In some instances, it identified
alleged perpetrators. As a result, investigations were initiated against an
important number of military personnel, although the number is relatively
small compared with the number involved. These trials should have been
carried out in a timely fashion, as they produced enormous unrest in the

armed forces, and the delay was used by authoritarian sectors to question the CVR and, in general, those who promote the defense of human rights. Unfortunately, these cases dragged on into 2010 and authoritarian sectors of the extreme right linked to Fujimori continued to take advantage of the process for partisan electoral purposes.

Reparations for the Victims

In the majority of the postconflict processes in Latin America, a very important subject has been reparations for the victims of violence. In Peru's case, due to the nature of the conflict and by virtue of its cultural, social, and economic characteristics, the victims and the marginalized coincide. The majority of victims were extremely poor, lived in rural areas that were extremely neglected by the state, and suffered multiple hardships. According to the CVR, "reparations constitute the beginning of a process of compensating and providing dignity to the victims; therefore, they have deep ethical and political implications." Reparations imply "reversing the climate of indifference with acts of solidarity that contribute to overcoming discriminatory approaches and habits that are not exempt from racism. Reparations, applied with equity, should generate civic confidence, reestablishing the damaged relations between citizens and the state."[37]

Although progress has been slow, there were some notable advances in the process of providing reparations. In 2005, the Peruvian Congress approved the Comprehensive Reparations Plan (Plan Integral de Reparaciones, PIR, Law 28592) and Supreme Decree 047-2005-PCM. The latter requires all state agencies that have some responsibility for the PIR's implementation to include funding for it in budgets between 2005 and 2010. At the regional level, in Apurímac, Ayacucho, Huancavelica, Huánuco, Junín, San Martín, Pasco, and Ucayali, commissions to design the regional PIR have been created, composed of the regional government, organizations of the victims, and civil society organizations.

That said, the national government's budget for reparations in 2006 was very meager (10 million soles, equivalent to $3 million, which stands in stark contrast to the 100 million soles offered by Toledo in his speech to the country in July 2005). The budget in 2007 and 2008 was only a bit more generous; the coordination difficulties are enormous, and the political interest of the government in the issue has been very low. This was evident in the fact that the High-Level Multi-Sector Commission created to promote the PIR was transferred from the presidential level in the Council of Ministers to the Ministry of Justice.[38] During the García administration, the issue of reparations was a very low political priority, although some collective reparations were made.

Between Toledo, García, and Humala

More than ten years after the fall of the authoritarian regime, the favorable political climate for discussion of the effects of the armed conflict and implementation of the CVR's recommendations had dissipated. The process began with the weakening of the Toledo government that had embodied the transition, promoted the CVR, and accepted its recommendations, but it is also due to the general deterioration of political democracy. Toward the end of the Toledo government, distrust in Congress, the executive branch, the judiciary, and political parties reached about 90 percent in all surveys. A comparison with other Latin America countries shows the magnitude of the disenchantment. According to Latinobarómetro in 2005, in Peru only 40 percent of those polled consider democracy to be preferable to any other form of government, well below the Latin American average of 53 percent and higher only than Paraguay, Honduras, Guatemala, and Brazil. By the end of the decade, surveys fully confirmed these results. According to both Latinobarómetro and the Americas Barometer in 2010, support for democracy was lower in Peru than in any other country in the hemisphere.[39] As Dinorah Azpuru indicates in chapter 2, support for democratic institutions in Peru was lower even than in Haiti before the 2010 earthquake.

Simultaneously, voices emerged in the country, especially within the armed forces and among retired officers, stating that the purpose of the CVR was only revenge against the armed forces, that its conclusions were biased against them, and that all this favored the Shining Path. Some even proposed discussing the possibility of a new amnesty for the military.

This regression toward authoritarianism became stronger during the 2006 presidential election campaign. There was the unusually strong emergence of the candidacy of a retired army commander, Ollanta Humala, who called for a central role of the armed forces in an ultranationalist political project with xenophobic and even warmongering positions. At the same time, Humala faced several grave and credible denunciations for having been directly responsible for serious crimes—including forced disappearances, extrajudicial executions, rape, and torture—when he was military commander of the Madre Mía base in the Alto Huallaga in 1992,[40] one of the bloodiest years of the conflict and in which the most abuses in the area against the civil population were reported.

The desire for authoritarianism was also expressed in the candidacy of Martha Chávez, representing Fujimori supporters. Chávez was one of the people that defended the legitimacy of human rights violations during the government of Fujimori with great energy and frankness.[41] It was also evident in the candidacy of García who, in his campaign speeches, sought to incorporate proposals that attracted the most primitive feelings of the Fujimori electorate, including reestablishment of the death penalty, despite the fact that the Inter-American Convention on Human Rights does not permit it. More revealing still, García nominated as his vice presidential running mate retired admiral Luis Giampietri, who has never hidden his sympathies for Fujimori and who has maintained a position belligerently opposed to everything that is an affirmation of human rights and the work of the CVR. Even Lourdes Flores and Valentín Paniagua voiced criticisms and distanced themselves from the CVR, believing that this would attract support given the spirit of the electoral moment.

At the same time, the election became a time for national reflection. The issues of poverty, racism, and social exclusion that emerged with so much force in the CVR's analysis were placed at the center of the debate of the country's business, intellectual, and political elites, mainly from the shock caused by the overwhelming support received by Humala during the campaign in a large part of the country.[42] It is worth noting that during the Toledo administration, despite the country's healthy economic growth, official sources indicated that extreme poverty only decreased from 22 to 18 percent and the poverty rate from 52 to 48 percent. The way in which the country was polarized in the second electoral round revealed the problems Peru faces. Humala had the most support in the poorest and most marginalized areas, and the opposite occurred on the north coast. This area has modern production linked to exports and, especially in Lima where the middle classes are concentrated, has greater coverage of basic needs and more opportunities in general. The results speak for themselves. In Ayacucho, the historic epicenter of the armed conflict and one of the poorest areas of the country, Humala received 83.4 percent of the vote. In other regions, also devastated by poverty and conflict, the results for Humala were similar—73.8 percent in Apurimac, 73 percent in Cusco, 76.4 percent in Huancavelica, and 76.5 percent in Puno.

Exactly the opposite occurred with García, who increased his vote in the second round with the massive support of voters who feared the consequences of a Humala victory.[43] Thus, García received a large majority in Lima (62 percent), a district that has historically been unfriendly toward him. Because the capital contains almost 40 percent of the population, this was decisive enough to permit a García victory.[44]

Humala returned to the scene in the 2011 presidential elections, striving to project a more moderate image in order to broaden his appeal, particularly among centrist voters and the urban middle class. He and Keiko Fujimori, daughter of the former president, captured a combined total of slightly more than half the vote in the first round of elections held in April 2011, spreading anxiety and uncertainty among the other half of the country who had not voted for them. Former president Toledo, who had been the favorite scarcely two months earlier, ran a lackluster campaign and saw his fortunes plummet.

Two major structural factors helped explain the 2011 electoral outcome. The first was the chasm between Peru's impressive levels of economic growth from 2005 to 2010—among the highest in Latin America—and the ongoing sense of precariousness felt by the majority of the population. Although poverty rates fell, many remained only a few days' salary away from falling once again below the poverty line. The state remained inefficient, incompetent, and unable to address the needs of the majority. Second, the profound crisis of politics endured. Peruvians remained deeply distrustful of politicians in general and of the institutions that support democracy, including parties and the legislature. As mentioned above, public opinion polls indicated that Peruvians were more dissatisfied with democracy than the citizens of any other country in the hemisphere.[45] This, along with a generalized sense of indignation over corruption, made the electorate unpredictable and highly volatile.

The victory of Humala in June 2011 is open to many interpretations, and it is too soon to know what it portends for Peru's future. Yet the very fact that, despite a period of rapid economic expansion, people voted for the candidate who has been most against the "system" reveals the dismal state of politics in Peru.

Will Peace Be Consolidated?

Although there has been notable progress, especially compared with the conclusions of the chapter published in 1999, peace in Peru continues to be, in various ways, an unfinished task. This is so in the most practical and broadest sense. Armed violence has not disappeared, because there still are two small Shining Path groups operating in the Huallaga and the Apurímac-Ene river valleys, areas with difficult terrain that are dominated by an illegal economy, mainly drug trafficking.[46] These groups have a certain level of support from the population in these areas, and they move with relative ease in territory that is difficult for the police and armed forces to patrol. They carry out only sporadic attacks against the security forces, but they cause many casualties.[47]

To recover complete control of the national territory is part of the final effort for achieving peace. It should be carried out via a democratic counterinsurgency strategy that combines different forms of state intervention, directed by civilian authorities, including a sustained intelligence initiative and a stronger military and police presence along with operations in areas currently controlled by drug traffickers and remnants of the Shining Path. It is important to achieve this, not only for security reasons but also for political reasons. The existence of these armed groups, and especially the cruel attacks they perpetrate, keep authoritarian impulses alive in parts of Peruvian society. They also encourage antidemocratic views that question basic liberties and identify the affirmation of human rights as the cause of the problem.

What, if anything, changed during the García years? The balance does not inspire optimism. There was a great deal of hostility at the presidential level toward the CVR and its conclusions, especially those linked to the reparations plan. In its political discourse, the government completely abandoned the fight against impunity for human rights violations[48] and against corruption,[49] even though some trials continued. Even though the country experienced a significant period of economic growth, the government still did not undertake the structural reforms necessary to confront extreme poverty, exclusion, racism, and inequality, conditions to which the truth commission pointed as the underlying causes of the previous conflict. As chapter 2 demonstrates, social expenditures in Peru as a percentage of gross national income are among the lowest in the entire hemisphere, and grew only marginally in the years after the end of conflict. Peru runs the risk that in the end, as during the Toledo government, the country's necessary and vital economic growth will be confused with the solution to these profound problems. In this environment, the danger of new explosions of discontent that can be channeled in any direction, including violence, by caudillos with messianic pretensions will not have disappeared in Peru.

This conclusion and these risks reinforce the argument made in Cynthia Arnson's introductory chapter, to the effect that "the end of conflict and democratization are less clearly, if at all, related. The manner in which conflicts end—not just whether they end—is a decisive influence on postwar political development." In Peru, the end of the conflict was associated with a period of authoritarianism and repression. Except during a very brief period between 2001 and 2003, the population did not associate peace with democratization; rather, Peruvians have actually begun to fear that democratization brings the risk of new forms of violence, an attitude that reinforces the authoritarian sectors of society. This is even more the case given that ongoing state weakness in the postwar period has compromised and at times undermined or derailed the process of democratization. The democratic state in Peru has not been able to guarantee security; in fact, the Shining Path and other threats persist and have grown. Nor has the state been able to provide the population with enough social well-being that would give meaning and substance to the democracy that is proclaimed in discourse.

Notes

1. Carlos Basombrío, "Peace in Peru: An Unfinished Task," in *Comparative Peace Processes in Latin America,* edited by Cynthia J. Arnson (Washington, D.C., and Stanford, Calif.: Woodrow Wilson Center Press and Stanford University Press, 1999).

2. Shining Path was an extremely fanatical and brutal insurgent group that terrorized Peru in the 1980s and 1990s, during the administrations of Fernando Belaunde (1980–85), Alan García (1985–90), and Alberto Fujimori (1990–92, 1992–95, and 1995–2000).

3. Through years of patient, painstaking work, a small specialized police force was able to capture, one by one, almost all of the Shining Path leaders. The final, devastating blow to the organization was the capture of Abimael Guzmán. The police force responsible for the capture of Guzmán and others worked independently of intelligence chief Vladimiro Montesinos.

4. Basombrío, "Peace in Peru," 219. *Señores de la guerra* is an expression that alluded to a type of leader who based his legitimacy on defeating his enemies by force and then used that argument as a justification for staying and exercising power beyond the permissible limits in a democracy.

5. There are excellent works published on the Fujimori regime that can help shed light on the subject, including Carlos Iván Degregori, *La década de la antipolítica: Auge y huida de Alberto Fujimori y Vladimiro Montesinos* (Lima: Instituto de Estudios Peruanos, 2000); Julio Cotler and Romeo Grompone, *Auge y caída de un régimen autoritario* (Lima: Instituto de Estudios Peruanos, 2000); and Catherine Conaghan, *Fujimori's Peru: Deception in the Public Sphere* (Pittsburgh: University of Pittsburgh Press, 2005).

6. On what was learned later on this and other issues see, e.g., the book by Luis Jochamovich, *Vladimiro vida y tiempo de un corruptor y Conversando con el doctor* (Lima: Ediciones El Comercio, 2002).

7. About the actions of the Fujimori coalition in Congress and other cases see, e.g., Henry Pease García, *Así se destruyó el Estado de Derecho* (Lima: Ediciones Congreso de la República, 2000).

8. Of course the number was arbitrary, as there are 120 members of Congress and 48 was not even half, nor two-thirds, but simply the number that the majority knew the opposition could not get.

9. See Carlos Basombrío, "Peor que un crimen fue un error," *Ideele* 111 (September 1998): 1–3.

10. Baruch Ivcher is a powerful television entrepreneur born in Israel and a naturalized Peruvian citizen. Initially, he was an enthusiastic follower of the Fujimori regime, but then for reasons that have never been fully known, he became one of the most serious critics and openly supported the democratic opposition. In Peru, only citizens can own television stations. To eliminate a powerful opposition source, the government used administrative maneuvers to revoke his nationality and took Channel 2 away from Ivcher. The affected party went to the Inter-American Commission on Human Rights, which ultimately ruled in his favor.

11. This was done through the daily and systematic dissemination of false information regarding the supposed points of view of these individuals on highly sensitive matters for the public. Over the long run, this kind of character assassination against opposition leaders bore fruit.

12. Later, Castañeda was able to recover his political space. He was elected mayor of Lima for the 2003–6 term and emerged as a serious contender for the 2011 presidential elections. Alberto Andrade was elected to Congress in 2006.

13. See "Las Elecciones Frankenstein, 830 Razones," in the special supplement of *Ideele* 128 (June 2000).

14. Regarding the role of the armed forces, see Fernando Rospigliosi, *Montesinos y las Fuerzas Armadas: Cómo controló durante una década a las instituciones militares* (Lima: Instituto de Estudios Peruanos, 2000).

15. The old Inca Empire was administratively divided into *suyos*: the Antisuyo, Collasuyo, Chinchaysuyo, and Contisuyo. What the slogan indicated was a march from all the regions of the country to the capital to defend democracy.

16. Within the framework of the megatrials for what happened during the Fujimori government, legal proceedings were launched with respect to the high government officials responsible for these events.

17. See, e.g., Conaghan, *Fujimori's Peru Deception*. Ultimately, in September 2006, Montesinos was sentenced to twenty years in prison for these events.

18. It must be pointed out, however, that the U.S. Department of State and the U.S. Congress were very important allies in the struggle to restore democracy in Peru.

19. In the following months, hundreds of similar videos came to light, involving all sorts of individuals from the political, military, business, and journalist sectors of the country. Montesinos's obsession with documenting on camera all of his corrupt practices later revealed in images, like never before in the history of Latin America—and perhaps the world—the form and levels of corruption that can be reached in authoritarian governments.

20. For more on corruption during that period in Peruvian history, see Alfonso Quiroz, *Corrupt Circles: A History of Unbound Graft in Peru* (Washington, D.C., and Baltimore: Woodrow Wilson Center Press and Johns Hopkins University Press, 2008).

21. These are extracts from this document: "The Armed Forces and the PNP Condemn the 1992 Coup and Reiterate Their Subordination to the President," Lima, April 16, 2001, signed by Police General Armando Santisteban de la Flor, general director of the PNP; Army General Carlos Alfonso Tafur Ganoza, commander in chief of the Army; Admiral Víctor Ramos Ormeño, commander in chief of the Navy; and Air Force General Pablo Carbone Merino, chairman of the commanders in chief and general commander of the Air Force.

22. See the commentary in this volume by Carlos Iván Degregori following chapter 12, which provides more detail about the Peruvian CVR.

23. See "Las 7 grandes verdades de la CVR," *Ideele* 157 (September 2003): 8–43.

24. See "La opinión de la gente," *Ideele* 157 (September 2003): 44–47.

25. In this regard, it is important to note the important support to the work of the CVR and its report provided by the influential group, El Comercio (including *El Comercio* newspaper; the tabloid *Perú 21*; and CANAL N, a cable television channel). In a certain way, the support of El Comercio tipped the balance in favor of the CVR. Its position was not surprising, because the daily newspaper *El Comercio* had a very prominent role in the struggle for the recovery of democracy and has modern and advanced visions in multiple areas and, for many years, has had a very active commitment to human rights.

26. The first was Toledo's vice president, David Waisman, but his tenure was brief and unremarkable.

27. Law 27860, enacted November 11, 2002.

28. This weakened the work of Loret de Mola and, later, of Roberto Chiabra himself, who after having been commander in chief of the Army and who had tense relationship with Loret de Mola, endured the same thing when he was minister and General Graham was commander in chief.

29. Given his advanced age, the last minister of defense, Army General Marciano Rengifo, also had a very traditional view of the role of the armed forces.

30. For additional information, see Carlos Basombrío and Fernando Rospigliosi, *La seguridad y sus instituciones en el Perú del siglo XXI: Reformas democráticas o neomilitarismo* (Lima: IEP, 2006).

31. The author has been an active protagonist in different ways in the processes described in this chapter and therefore does not claim academic distance and objectivity—and even less when referring to the changes in the police and security because he was executive secretary and a member of the Restructuring Commission of the PNP and also vice minister of the interior during the time of these reforms.

32. Fernando Rospigliosi, twice minister of the interior during the Toledo government, had openly confronted the Fujimori regime and was a member of the Pro-Human Rights Association (APRODEH). Gino Costa, who was first vice minister and then minister, came from the Office of the Human Rights Ombudsman (Defensoría del Pueblo) where he was deputy ombudsman, and Susana Villarán, who was named the first police human rights ombudswoman, had previously served as executive secretary of the National Human Rights Coordinating Committee (Coordinadora Nacional de Derechos Humanos) and was later a member of the Inter-American Commission on Human

Rights. In my case, I worked for fifteen years in the Legal Defense Institute (IDL), an institution linked to the struggle for human rights and the restoration of democracy.

33. The numbers of cases of intentional human rights violations committed by members of the police since the return of democracy have been few, and many have been investigated. The number of civilians killed in public order disturbances during Toledo's government was probably the lowest in Peruvian history, despite the fact these were years of extraordinarily violent social protests.

34. All the information in this section was obtained from Defensoría del Pueblo, "A dos años de la Comisión de la Verdad y Reconciliación," in *Informe de la Defensoría del Pueblo* (Lima: Defensoría del Pueblo, 2005).

35. The institutional responsibility of the armed forces was greater than what the CVR indicated. Ricardo Uceda—in an exceptional work of investigative journalism, *Muerte en el Pentagonito* (Lima: Editorial Planeta, 2004)—documents the internal chain of command in the crimes and the creation of death squads within the army, and provides detailed information on hundreds of cases of extrajudicial executions, using as his principal source one of the main perpetrators of the crimes.

36. The source of the information for this paragraph are *Lucha anticorrupción: Urgente necesidad de enmienda,* by Abraham Siles Vallejos, Ronald Gamarra Herrera, Lilia Ramírez Varela, Cruz Silva del Carpio, and Natalia Torres Zúñiga (Lima: Instituto de Defensa Legal, 2005).

37. *Informe final de la CVR* (Lima: CVR, August 2003). (The translation of excerpts into English can be found at http://www.cverdad.org.pe/ingles/ifinal/conclusiones.php.)

38. For additional information, see Coordinadora Nacional de Derechos Humanos, *Informe Anual 2005* (Lima: Coordinadora Nacional de Derechos Humanos, 2006).

39. Corporación Latinobarómetro, *Informe 2005* (Santiago: Corporación Latinobarómetro, 2005); Corporación Latinobarómetro, *Informe 2010* (Santiago: Corporación Latinobarómetro), 71, available at www.latinobarometro.org; Americas Barometer / Barómetro de las Américas, Latin American Public Opinion Project surveys, Vanderbilt University, 2010, available at www.lapopsurverys.org.

40. The complaints were documented and presented to the prosecutor's office by the National Human Rights Coordinating Committee (Coordinadora Nacional de Derechos Humanos). See Coordinadora Nacional de Derechos Humanos, *Contexto de Violencia en la Región Nororiental y Sucesos de la Base Militar "Madre Mía" 1992: El caso del ex Capitán EP Ollanta Humala Tasso* (Lima: Coordinadora Nacional de Derechos Humanos, 2006). The Office of the Public Prosecutor in Tocache, which decided to charge him, investigated Humala. The head of the fourth supraprovincial Court, Miluska Cano, has brought preliminary criminal proceedings for the forced disappearance of persons and torture. Humala claims that this is all political persecution against him.

41. The Fujimori coalition obtained 7.4 percent of the valid votes and was able to elect 13 congressmen out of a total of 120.

42. Very symptomatic of this concern for social exclusion is that CADE 2006—the annual meeting of Peruvian businessmen that is one of the country's most important political forums and that had never paid any attention to these issues—made the principal topic of its meeting "There is no 'we' with someone left out: inclusion and development for everyone."

43. Alan García faced great resistance on the part of voters due to the results of his first government. He came in second in the first round, beating Lourdes Flores (who was

labeled as the "candidate of the rich") in the final stretch by a narrow margin (20.406 vs. 19.979 percent).

44. At the national level, the APRA Party obtained a total of 6,965,017 votes, or 52.625 percent of the valid votes. Ollanta Humala's Union for Peru (Unión por el Perú) obtained 6,270,080 votes, or 47.375 percent. Alan García obtained 1,104,000 votes, more than Humala in Lima, indicating that the capital city was definitive in his elections.

45. The public opinion polls by Latinobarómetro over the years have demonstrated Peruvians' low regard for democracy. See note 39 above.

46. The majority of estimates indicate that there are not more than two hundred armed insurgents in Peru.

47. In December 2005 alone, in two incidents thirteen policemen were murdered in two ambushes by these columns. There were similar attacks in the months that followed.

48. Quite the contrary, the president had an aggressive anti–human rights and anti–CVR rhetoric—for example: "How much blood was provided by those who speak out today? How much effort, sacrifice, or loss of life was provided by those who now raise their voices against the armed forces?" Quoted from "Homage to the Armed Forces," September 22, 2006.

49. Alan García's inaugural speech was full of references to the indignation he felt for the frivolity and lack of austerity of the Toledo Administration, citing numerous examples. He never mentioned, however, the crimes committed by the Fujimori/Montesinos regime.

Chapter 8

The Crisis in Chiapas: Negotiations, Democracy, and Governability

Raúl Benítez Manaut, Tania Carrasco, and Armando Rodríguez Luna

The Mexican state demonstrated a remarkable inability during the twentieth century to devise strategies to address and resolve the political exclusion, poverty, and marginalization of its indigenous peoples. According to the 2010 census, 9.16 million of a total of 108 million people in Mexico speak an indigenous language. In Chiapas, the indigenous population represents 34 percent of the total.[1] The state and its institutions are practically nonexistent in this region; authoritarian and traditional forms of political control are predominant. The statistics given in chapter 2 of this volume help illustrate the vast chasm in social indicators between Chiapas and the rest of Mexico.

The Mexican Constitution was amended in 2001 to include the Indigenous Rights Law.[2] This provision ensures the indigenous population's equality under the law and recognizes the cultural and political rights of indigenous communities. However, the Mexican state has not established the mechanisms needed to make these rights effective. Inequality and injustice predominate in the daily lives of communities and in political relations between indigenous communities and the government at the federal, state, and municipal levels. In other words, the state has not been able to impose the rule of law.[3]

The emergence of the Zapatista Army of National Liberation (Ejército Zapatista de Liberación Nacional, EZLN) as an armed group in 1994, with support from a sector of the indigenous population, generated interrelated dilemmas for the country's democratization process and for national security. Before 1994, the issue of the indigenous as political actors with rights was not included as part of the democratization agenda. The challenge to national security arose from the fact that Chiapas is considered a strategic state; it produces 46 percent of the nation's electricity, 23 percent of its liquefied natural gas, and 40 percent of its sulfur.[4] The state also shares a border with the Guatemalan highlands.

At first, the EZLN uprising on January 1, 1994, presented a military challenge. Once conversations and contact between government representatives and the EZLN leadership had been established on January 12, the conflict became essentially political and called into question the democratization process. Because the country was in the midst of a process of democratic transition, the rebellion had an immediate effect on national political parties and influenced the electoral process at the time. The demands of the Zapatistas—for democracy, justice, work, and land, among other things—resonated within a broader society hungry for an end to Mexico's system of semiauthoritarian, corporatist rule. The Chiapas negotiations played an important role in the midterm elections in 1997 and again in the presidential elections in 2000. By 2006, Chiapas no longer figured in the debates between the principal political parties. Some improvements in living conditions for the indigenous people living in Chiapas helped to reduce the political and social conflict. For example, from 2000 to 2010, the life expectancy for the indigenous population in the state rose from 72.29 to 75.22. Infant mortality rates also dropped in that same period, although, as chapter 2 demonstrates, they remained far above those of the rest of Mexico.[5]

Chiapas: A Weak Link in Mexican Democracy

Governability in rural Mexico has always been the weakest link in the structures that constitute Mexico's political system. Indeed, the greatest weaknesses of Mexican democracy have their origin in the countryside, where the largest fractures and dissidence occur. In Mexico, agrarian reform was for many decades the state's instrument par excellence for regulating conflict. However, the deep crisis of rural Mexico began to have repercussions evident in the breakdown of traditional and authoritarian rural political structures. New social organizations also appeared, seeking open dialogue with the state without the traditional intermediaries characteristic of the previous governments headed by the Institutional Revolutionary Party (Partido Revolucionario Institucional, PRI).

The EZLN is one of the organizations that has not wanted to be institutionalized. In the years following the Mexican Revolution, between 1920 and 1950, state policy toward the indigenous population was assimilationist and integrationist. The National Peasant Confederation (Confederación Nacional Campesina, CNC) and the National Indigenist Institute (known as INI) were the vehicles for implementing these policies and establishing an authoritarian relationship. In 1975, many peasant-indigenous groups broke with the CNC and demanded recognition of their cultural specificity.[6]

In Chiapas at this time, agrarian reform was incomplete and had benefited large landowners. From the 1970s and 1980s onward, indigenous Tzotzil, Tzetzal, and Tojolabal peasants began gradually to take over land.[7] This was seen as a new indigenous movement that not only made claims related to land but, like the EZLN subsequently, also demanded political rights.[8] With the tacit support of the state government, landlords created paramilitary structures called *guardias blancas* (white guards), which contributed to even greater polarization and conflict. It was in this context that the EZLN emerged.[9]

In the 1990s, two unresolved problems compounded the conflict over land. The first was the issue of indigenous rights and constitutional reform.[10] This issue was being debated in other states in Mexico with large indigenous populations, although political conflict in these other areas was not as acute as in Chiapas.[11] The second unresolved issue was environmental, having to do with the form of exploitation of natural resources, their growing scarcity, and the struggle over them.[12]

The poverty, marginalization, and exclusion of Chiapas' indigenous population in 1994 mirrored the social conditions in Guatemala and El Salvador when insurrections broke out in the early 1980s and before. Local representatives of the Mexican political system regulated the conflict in a corporatist fashion; when co-optation was not possible, they turned to the security forces, to paramilitary *guardias blancas,* and to the military to contain peasant and indigenous protests. In Chiapas, the systematic violation of human rights was common.

The agrarian crisis thus coincided with political collapse, as the prevailing PRIista model of control and its defense of large-scale farmers were no longer viable. Autonomous peasant and indigenous groups appeared and Liberation Theology gathered strength, as did the EZLN subsequently. The situation also coincided with a demographic explosion, resulting in uncontrolled migration from the highlands and the Selva Lacandona—the Lacandon Jungle, a rainforest that stretches from Chiapas into Guatemala and the southern Yucatán Peninsula—in search of land. The fragility of the Selva Lacandona as an ecosystem made farming and livestock activities unsustainable. "Neoliberal" agricultural reforms in the 1990s coupled with the opening of markets sent the coffee-growing economy into severe depression.

The EZLN was a leader and a catalyst of the cumulative discontent felt by social protest movements in Chiapas at the time. The strong indigenous orientation of the EZLN defined the course of negotiations with government representatives, civil society, and the international community. The principal issue between 1994 and 2000 was the defense of indigenous rights, a reflection of Chiapas' position as the weak link in Mexico's transition to democracy.[13]

History of the Negotiation Process

The military conflict between the Mexican army and the Zapatistas lasted only twelve days. For maximum effect, the uprising was timed to coincide with the official starting date of the North American Free Trade Agreement (NAFTA) on January 1, 1994. EZLN guerrillas declared war on the Mexican government and took over five towns in eastern Chiapas. During the twelve days of combat, 145 lives were lost. The EZLN accepted the government's call for a cease-fire on January 12, initiating a long process of negotiation. But since the cease-fire, and despite the involvement of numerous mediators and mediation bodies established to broker a compromise, the government and the EZLN have found a comprehensive peace settlement elusive. Indeed, given the length of time that has passed since the initial Zapatista uprising, it appears unlikely that such a broad settlement will ever be reached.

An overview of the negotiations process highlights the different, and for the most part irreconcilable, views of what the talks were meant to accomplish. The first stage of the negotiations, popularly known as the "Conversations in the Cathedral," involved talks between the EZLN representative,

Subcomandante Marcos, and foreign minister and former Mexico City mayor Manuel Camacho Solís. They were mediated by Catholic bishop Samuel Ruiz and took place in the cathedral in San Cristóbal de las Casas in the Chiapas highlands.[14] The "Conversations in the Cathedral" failed to produce significant results because the government and the Zapatistas shared fundamentally different ideas about the scope and dimension of the issues on the table.[15] The EZLN demanded political and economic reforms of a national scope, but the federal government offered changes at only the state and local levels. Amid the impasse occasioned in part by Mexico's mid-1994 presidential election season, the conversations were suspended. Bishop Ruiz created a new mediating body, the National Intermediation Commission (Comisión Nacional de Intermediación, CONAI), in November 1994 to lead a second round of negotiations with the incoming government of Ernesto Zedillo.

In early February 1995, just two months after assuming the presidency, the Zedillo administration attempted a military campaign aimed at capturing Subcomandante Marcos. The campaign failed, generating a backlash in Mexican public opinion and within the EZLN that led to the collapse of the first phase of peaceful negotiations.[16] In a demonstration of the significant political support the EZLN maintained at the time, the Mexican Congress stepped in to create a framework for a new round of negotiations. The Law for Dialogue, Conciliation, and a Dignified Peace in Chiapas created a congressional Commission for Concord and Peace (Comisión de Concordia y Pacificación, COCOPA) and granted EZLN commanders immunity from prosecution as long as the peace process continued.[17]

The new law spawned a second round of peace negotiations in October 1995, involving the government, EZLN, COCOPA, and CONAI. These talks led to a breakthrough agreement in February 1996 in the Chiapas municipality of San Andrés Larraínzar. Known as the San Andrés Accords, the agreement established a framework of constitutional reforms designed to "recognize differential collective rights for indigenous groups within clearly specified territorial boundaries, in accordance with the standards set out by the International Labor Organization Treaty 169 . . . on indigenous rights."[18]

The San Andrés Accords established an acceptable compromise for both parties but ultimately did not resolve the conflict. Largely to avoid a debate over the meaning of self-determination and customary authority in indigenous communities, the government refused to submit to Congress draft legislation proposed by COCOPA to implement the San Andrés Accords.

During much of 1996 and through the end of 1997, paramilitary groups supported by local political authorities and landowners stepped up attacks on the Zapatistas and their perceived sympathizers. Heightened paramilitary activity, at a minimum tolerated by the federal government, culminated in the December 1997 massacre of forty-five women, children, and the elderly inside a church in the town of Acteal. The killings marked the collapse of the peace process centered on the San Andrés agreements, an impasse that lasted for the next three years.[19]

When Vicente Fox was elected in 2000 as the first non-PRIista president in Mexico in seven decades, he made a resolution of the conflict in Chiapas a centerpiece of government policy. Fox removed Mexican troops from conflict zones, ordered the release of Zapatista prisoners, and promised to submit to congress the proposed law on indigenous rights that had been drafted by COCOPA in fulfillment of the San Andrés Accords.[20] To pressure the government to pass the legislation, the Zapatistas initiated the "March of the Color of the Land," known colloquially as the "Zapatour." The march mobilized 1,111 indigenous representatives and culminated with the presence of EZLN commanders in the Congress on March 28, 2001.[21] Shortly thereafter, the Senate approved the Indigenous Rights Law on April 25, as did the House of Deputies on April 28 of the same year. However, the EZLN broke communications with the government, deeming the law a legislative joke because it represented a departure from the San Andrés Accords of 1996 and, in their view, did not reflect the negotiations with COCOPA.

Negotiations at a Stalemate

The on-and-off nature of the negotiations process highlights the difficulties in reaching a compromise in the Chiapas conflict. Since the outbreak of conflict in 1994, it has not been possible to negotiate the EZLN's transition from "military actor" in a state of war to that of political actor fully integrated into the democratic process. The Mexican government has relied on political negotiations based on constitutional changes and the Indigenous Rights Law of 2001 to resolve the conflict. The EZLN has chosen to direct its strategy toward national and international media, seeking greater social support and legitimacy for its cause.

The EZLN's pressure on the Mexican government was initially indirect, in order to evade the army's intense deployment of troops beginning in

1994. The EZLN tried to maintain its presence by convoking alternative forms of social mobilization or by creating alternative community organizations. By obtaining support from nongovernmental organizations, it was able to gain national and international attention. The dilemma for the EZLN lay in either continuing to focus on the indigenous demands unsatisfied by the Indigenous Rights Law of 2001, or taking on the demands of other sectors. The dilemma for the Mexican state lay in creating legislation and finding new forms of political negotiation to rise above the tension with both the EZLN and the so-called autonomous communities in Chiapas.

For more than a decade following the outbreak of conflict, the importance accorded by the Mexican government to security and respect for rule of law was evidenced by the military presence in the State of Chiapas and particularly in zones with a predominantly indigenous population. According to official figures from the National Defense Secretary, in 2000 in the Seventh Military Region, which includes the states of Tabasco and Chiapas, 14,000 troops had been deployed, 10,500 of which were located in the State of Chiapas.[22] By 2005, according to official sources, there were some 20,000 soldiers in Chiapas.[23]

From the time the crisis broke out in January 1994 until 2000, the government's strategy was one of ongoing deterrent military deployment. Its response to the social and cultural demands of the insurrection was very limited. Government efforts to promote private investment, aside from tourism, were not successful. Public investment in farming and in the indigenous agrarian sectors, along with spending on social programs, were unable to resolve the conditions of marginality affecting indigenous peoples. As a result, a political and peaceful solution to the conflict remained stalemated for several years.[24] The EZLN did not recognize the government programs as positive; rather, it considered them to be a mechanism for political co-optation. The government's strategy for modernization—centered on investment in infrastructure—and its social expenditures in the state have had little impact on improving productive opportunities over the long term.

According to official statistics, primary economic sectors in Chiapas (agriculture, livestock, and mining) are the least dynamic sectors of the economy. At the same time, a construction boom occurred between 2000 and 2004. The government's efforts to improve infrastructure in Chiapas were not reflected in an improvement in the quality of life for the state's inhabitants. For example, in 2000, 85.2 percent of the nation had access to piped water; in the State of Chiapas, only 69.3 percent had access and in indigenous communities, a mere 65.7 percent. National coverage for electricity totaled 95.4 percent, in Chiapas 88.4 percent, and 78.5 percent for indigenous communities.[25] As chapter 2 indicates, by the end of the 2000s, social indicators in Chiapas remained abysmally low. The government strategy to defuse the conflict by investing in infrastructure and social programs did not achieve the results expected. The EZLN did not believe that government spending successfully addressed conditions of marginality.

Both parties adopted different strategies. The government approach was minimalist. Particularly after the National Action Party (Partido Acción Nacional) came to power in December 2000, the government believed that the problem could be solved through legislative changes. But its legalistic solution, lacking a political component, was incapable of neutralizing the conflict. The EZLN, by contrast, was maximalist. It believed that by demanding the macroeconomic transformation of the country (to solve structural and historical poverty), it could win overwhelming popular support with which to pressure the government. The EZLN did not measure the "correlation of forces" and maintained—without negotiating—that the solution lay in overcoming poverty and social, political, and cultural exclusion of indigenous peoples. Both parties shunned the idea of negotiation: The government was unwilling to yield and broaden the legal issue to transform it into a political negotiation; and the EZLN refused to reduce its demands and transform itself from a military to a political actor.

Legislation: Necessary but Not Sufficient

In 1989, the International Labor Organization presented member countries with the Indigenous and Tribal Peoples Convention. This agreement sets forth the guarantees necessary for indigenous peoples to be recognized within the legal order of nations as peoples with their own identities, cultures, and customs.[26] Mexico was the first country to ratify this convention in 1990.

To link Mexico to trends in globalization and regionalization, the state negotiated and signed NAFTA and in 1989 began to reform national legislation.[27] Constitutional changes to address indigenous issues included amendments to Articles 4 and 27 in 1992. Article 4 now recognizes Mexico's pluricultural composition based on its indigenous peoples. It affirms that the law shall protect and promote development of indigenous languages, cultures, customs and habits, resources, and unique forms of social organization, and guarantees effective access to state jurisdiction.[28] The amended Article 27 establishes the basis for privatization of the *ejido,* or commonly owned land. It grants *ejidatarios* the right to transfer or sell their plots with the aim of putting more land on the market, "capitalizing the countryside," and promoting small ownership.[29] This modification of Article 27 was a response to the fragmentation of the *ejido* and to the structural scarcity of land for new generations of farmers.

Technical and financial factors (including a lack of loans and investment) have deepened the crisis of the *ejidos*. Having concluded that the *ejido* is not viable, the state has abandoned the *ejido* system.[30] All these factors fostered political rebellion expressed through land takeovers and growing violence. Undoubtedly, Chiapas was the site of the most powerful protests.

The EZLN emerged in this context. For the first ten years, from 1984 to 1994, it took the form of a guerrilla group, concentrating on building a social support base in the migrant villages between the Chiapas Highlands and the Selva Lacandona (the region where the Ocosingo Canyons are located).[31] The EZLN took up arms and on January 1, 1994, called for the overthrow of the political regime in power. This uprising was unexpected and immediately affected Mexico's transition to democracy. Further, the fact that the protest was led by armed guerrillas made it—until the surge of narco-trafficking and related violence in the late 2000s—the single most important challenge to national security to have affected Mexico in twenty-five years.[32] The long-term challenge for the first three administrations facing this conflict (Salinas de Gortari, Ernesto Zedillo, and Vicente Fox) was to resolve the remaining social problems. Political conditions in the state of Chiapas and throughout the country are notably different from what they were in 1994, and the democratization process has advanced on national and state levels. Following a change of government in December 2000, Vicente Fox concentrated on trying to politically convince the Congress that a reform to the Constitution was the solution to the conflict. This proposed constitutional reform, however, ignored the EZLN's principal demand: the recognition of collective rights and the use of natural resources.[33] The EZLN therefore rejected the proposed reform and decided to continue its battle on other fronts. The government of President Felipe Calderón, like its predecessors, continued to ignore one of the principal causes of the uprising: the demand for recognition of indigenousness as a specific identity.

The Two Mexicos and the EZLN

Why are not legal reforms enough? The answer lies in the EZLN's belief that legal reform is incapable of solving the structural problems that gave rise to the rebellion. This is because in economic, political, social, legal, and cultural terms, there are two Mexicos. An urban developed Mexico extends from the center northward, and another rural Mexico lies for the most part to the south. The same duality exists in Chiapas: that of the cities and coast—the modern sector—and the highlands and jungle—the marginal, excluded, and indigenous sector.

Laws are not upheld in southern Mexico. They exist on paper and are not enforced in practice. The EZLN has not wanted to hear about legal reforms, as the government is incapable of upholding the law in rural, marginalized Mexico. The EZLN rebelled in 1994 in an attempt to represent the indigenous population and Mexico's poor and excluded. The formal electoral democracy under construction in the urban and modern sectors of the country has not improved the conditions in which indigenous and marginalized people live. Impoverished Mexico puts no stock in a free market economy and does not trust formal electoral democracy. Thus, the EZLN's "militaristic" discourse, aimed at Mexico's marginalized sector, continues in spite of the cease-fire that has been in effect since the early days of the conflict.

With the EZLN's "rebellion" against the government technically still in effect, there is a need to analyze the organization's ideological and political evolution. The political life of the organization, begun in 1984, can be divided into three periods. During the first period, from 1984 to 1994, the EZLN accumulated social and political power among the indigenous peoples of Las Cañadas de Ocosingo (the jungle in the state of Chiapas), and sought to organize itself as a guerrilla army capable of taking on the government.[34] Clearly, the EZLN's origins were that of a classical guerrilla group of Marxist-Leninist-Maoist orientation, operating in almost total secrecy. The second period began in 1994, when the group's ideological platform changed notably. This was due to political "success" and the sympathy of numerous sectors of Mexican society and even groups abroad. This success was due to the fact that the EZLN's human capital consisted of indigenous peoples. The group was also the first guerrilla organization to recognize and use the potential of the Internet.[35] This second period, from 1994 until the first months of 2001, focused mainly on indigenous issues. It ended with the Zapatour and the passage of the Indigenous Rights Law of 2001, which failed to address key issues of both the San Andrés Accords and the original COCOPA proposal.

The COCOPA proposal recognized indigenous peoples as collective subjects with rights and a degree of autonomy. This would have included recognition of a series of political, economic, and cultural rights; access to and administration of justice; and protections of migrant indigenous peoples. In political matters, the communities were to be considered collective subjects of public law. In economic matters, indigenous peoples were granted the right to collectively access and use natural resources on their lands and territory. Communities would also have had the right to acquire, operate, and administer their own means of education and communication.[36]

The main differences, therefore, between the COCOPA proposal and the government proposal focused basically on the core issue of collective rights, specifically the collective right to free determination, access to natural resources, the indigenous peoples' right to access and operate the means of communication, and the right to develop and access national wealth.[37] The government has never recognized these collective rights; instead, it has directed its legal proposals at individual rights.

The third period began in 2001. Negotiations froze during Vicente Fox's term in office. An ideological and political restructuring took place within the EZLN as the organization refused to accept the government's legitimacy or to recognize the evolution in Mexican democracy. It broke with the "institutional" left, represented by the Party of the Democratic Revolution (Partido de la Revolución Democrática, PRD) and, beginning in 2003, developed several alternative political strategies, including the "Councils of Good Government," which sought de facto autonomy from the federal, state, and municipal governments.[38] The EZLN therefore rejected existing democracy, seeing it as reserved exclusively for developed Mexico and not for the nation's marginalized and excluded.

The Government's Strategy, Paramilitarism, and National Security

The national government's strategy for confronting the EZLN had seven overlapping components: (1) a response to social demands, particularly those of municipalities with the highest indices of poverty and marginalization; (2) the promotion of private investment to stimulate the Chiapanecan economy; (3) the reaffirmation and application of the rule of law; (4) the fostering of intercommunity and intracommunity political consensus building; (5) the provision of humanitarian aid for displaced populations; (6) the support of legislation regarding indigenous peoples and communities; and (7) the forging of a political and peaceful solution to the conflict with the EZLN.[39] From the time the conflict began in 1994, the government began spending huge sums of money on social programs in an attempt to "take the water from the fish"; in other words, to undermine the EZLN's popular support. Simultaneously, the government created structures for dialogue, mediation, and negotiation, which led to the Accords of San Andrés Larrainzar in 1995.

Clearly, the national government proposed to address the conflict in Chiapas through attention to its structural causes as well as through political negotiations. However, the seven kinds of initiatives described above remained at the level of political discourse only; in reality, between 1994 and 1998 the government relied on paramilitary groups to confront the Zapatista communities and on militarization and territorial occupation by the armed forces. The emergence of paramilitary groups created enormous political tension and destroyed the possibility for negotiations. This sullied the image of the government's strategy, as human rights violations became the means of confronting *zapatismo*.

The EZLN thus found justification for its refusal to negotiate, arguing that in reality the government was carrying out a "dirty war." The EZLN considered the negotiations a sham. The government was pursuing two tracks: one aimed at the general public and focused on negotiations and a structural solution; and another aimed at the indigenous communities, involving repression, paramilitarism, and dirty war. This duality had a notable and distorting effect on the transition to democracy between 1994 and 2000. Counterinsurgency in Chiapas looked similar to the strategies pursued in many parts of the world that combined social programs with militarization and even paramilitarization.

Under the Fox administration and following the approval of the Indigenous Rights Law and the resulting Zapatour, the relationship between the parties was characterized by a lack of dialogue and by attempts to find a consensus. Nonetheless, the partial withdrawal of troops in conflict zones and the deactivation of paramilitary groups helped reduce tensions.[40] Governance in the state of Chiapas improved. In the last fifty years of the twentieth century, no governor of Chiapas had finished his term. Pablo Salazar, who took office in 2000, was the first governor to do so, distancing himself from the traditional landholding group in power. The EZLN, for all practical purposes, stepped away from confrontation and returned to building "local alternative power." This proved successful from 2003 onward with the founding of autonomous municipalities known as *caracoles* or "snails." The EZLN's withdrawal and silence was aimed at reestablishing the tattered social and political fabric in communities that had constituted the EZLN's support base. The government contributed to this effort by freeing up political spaces and avoiding direct confrontation.

The EZLN's Political Successes and Errors

The symbolic inauguration of the *caracoles* took place in the town of Oventik on August 9, 2003; according to Subcomandante Marcos, they represented "an organizational effort by the communities to address issues of autonomy as well as build a more direct bridge between the communities and the world."[41] The leftist Mexican intellectual Pablo González Casanova saw the effort as going beyond that, creating "zones of solidarity between localities and similar communities, creating a network of autonomous municipal governments that in turn articulated government networks spanning even broader zones and regions."[42] Each of the *caracoles* included a Junta de Buen Gobierno (Council of Good Government) consisting of one or two delegates from each of the *caracoles'* Autonomous Councils; these juntas were to function as the sole authority administering justice, community health programs, education, housing, land, work, food, commerce, information and culture, and local transportation.

The right to form these autonomous communities had been a demand of the EZLN from the time of the Third Declaration of the Selva Lacandona in June 1994 and was subsequently set forth in the San Andrés Accords signed on February 16, 1996. The Indigenous Rights Law signed by the Mexican Senate on April 24, 2001, however, contained no such provision. Thus, each party, the government and the EZLN, set out in different directions while avoiding direct confrontation.

It is difficult to maintain that the EZLN uprising of 1994 had a negative effect on Mexico's transition to democracy. On the contrary, the uprising injected two new issues into the debate: poverty and indigenous affairs. Both are extremely important in countries with a structural dualism such as Mexico's. In other words, given the existence of two Mexicos, the uprising cast into doubt the notion that democracy could be limited to a change in government through elections.

The EZLN's rejection of liberal-electoral democracy constituted a rare case of nonadherence to the country's institutionality at the same time that a crisis of governability was avoided. The EZLN was a guerrilla group that did not carry out military actions or seek to insert itself in the country's legal framework. The EZLN and the indigenous uprising are no longer a problem for national security. The manner in which indigenous communities and their leaders will participate in the process of Mexico's transition to democracy has remained undefined. On this difficult path, the decision not to participate in the democratic process has worked in favor of the

EZLN's growing isolation. The balance sheet of EZLN successes and failures thus contains many contradictions:

1. The attempt to form a Zapatista National Liberation Front (as opposed to Army) at the end of the 1990s had no echo in the cities. The organization's relationship with broader civil society has been very difficult.
2. The "March of the Color of the Land" or "Zapatour" to Mexico City in 2001 had a great national impact. It forced Vicente Fox's government to reform the political Constitution in order to recognize the rights of indigenous peoples. However, the reform did not conform to the earlier proposal made by COCOPA. The EZLN was unsatisfied and withdrew.
3. Open conflict exists between the EZLN and the leftist PRD. Very close relations from 1994 to 1997 gradually dissipated. During the electoral campaigns of 2000 and 2006, the PRD did not consider the indigenous issue a priority in terms of redefining the relationship between indigenous peoples and the state. Even more telling, during the debates in congress over the San Andrés Accords, the PRD failed to defend the original version of the agreement. The evolution of the EZLN's antiglobalization and antisystem discourse did not help relations with the PRD, whose political platform remained within institutional margins.
4. The EZLN also distanced itself from the wing of the Catholic Church identified with Liberation Theology. The Church and the EZLN had different strategies for putting the indigenous issue on the national agenda. This was evident in the relationship between the EZLN and CONAI. In 1994 CONAI was headed by Samuel Ruiz, the bishop of San Cristóbal de las Casas, who saw CONAI as the mediating body in the search for peace.[43] CONAI's mediation efforts were oriented toward getting the parties to negotiate peace. It was unsuccessful in achieving its objectives given the lack of convergence between the strategies and goals of the government and those of the EZLN. The EZLN has a "prolonged" strategy in which *immediate peace* is less important than a *substantive peace* in which its demands are met without stepping back from what was agreed to by COCOPA. CONAI's mediation discourse focused more on obtaining local and community justice (fighting the local *cacique* structures and repression in general), and less on the EZLN's discourse of antiglobalization and open confrontation with the system.
5. The EZLN's attitude toward the entire national political elite was one of disillusionment and disenchantment. The EZLN rejected the "powers

that be," which made dialogue and negotiations with the government more remote.

6. In 2001, the EZLN's return to the Selva Lacandona following the "March of the Color of the Land" left many questions unanswered. What explained its "strategic retreat?" Had the EZLN accomplished its aims by demonstrating its political power, appearing in Congress, and expressing its ideas regarding the content of the law?

7. Thereafter, the EZLN changed tack and engaged in introspection both strategic and existential. Together with its community support base, the EZLN focused on constructing an "alternative" represented by the *caracoles* and the Councils of Good Government. Externally, the group sought to establish links to antiglobalization networks in Mexico and abroad.

Overall, the EZLN focused on two main projects. One was local, with an indigenous and constructivist perspective that resonated deeply among migrant indigenous peasants uprooted and abandoned by the state. The second project focused on strengthening relations with antiglobalization protest movements. It has been a challenge for the EZLN to orient its actions in both directions. During the 2006 election period, their "Other Campaign" strategy garnered less social and political support than the leadership had expected and provoked open conflict with the PRD. Notably, the EZLN did not support the electoral campaign of PRD candidate Andrés Manuel López Obrador, who lost the election by a very slim margin.

The gap between the EZLN's approach and that of the Mexican state grew increasingly wider, hindering negotiations. Local efforts represented by the *caracoles* and the Councils of Good Government did not necessarily imply confrontation with the state. They did, however, involve clashes with power at the local level, represented by the landlords and "institutional," predominantly municipal, political authorities in Chiapas.

Whither Democracy?

After more than a decade and a half of open conflict between the EZLN and the government, political conditions in Chiapas are notably different. Compared with 1994, political stability is greater and virtually all paramilitary groups have been dismantled. The *caracoles* and Councils of Good Government evidence the more favorable conditions for developing new kinds of political options. Any possible future negotiations between the government and the EZLN will have to take into consideration the active participation and demands of multiple organizations of civil society.

There exist de facto many autonomous forms of political and social organization among the indigenous communities. The implementation of state-sponsored social and economic projects aimed at promoting development, especially in regions where indigenous peoples reside, must therefore necessarily include dialogue and negotiations at a community level and with community organizations. Thus, the EZLN may be able to negotiate at a local level even if it does not do so at a national level.

The Indigenous Rights Law of 2001 does not incorporate all the aspirations of Mexico's indigenous peoples. Therefore, the indigenous issue is still a pending one for state reform in Mexico. In Mexico and throughout Latin America, indigenous movements and governments are debating questions of possible autonomy, territorial rights, and rights over the use of natural resources.

Negotiations between the EZLN and the Mexican government, however, are deadlocked. In Mexico as in the majority of Latin American countries, one of the weaknesses in the process of transition to democracy is the difficulty the state has in negotiating with new types of antisystemic and occasionally violent protest movements. These new forms of contestation eschew existing political and institutional channels and have difficulty maintaining the support of civil society and sustaining themselves and lasting over time. This is particularly true among social and political movements of diverse origin that do not find in existing state structures the spaces needed for dialogue and participation. Their forms of struggle thus tend to radicalize.

At the heart of the conflicts are conditions of marginality and social and political exclusion, leading to confrontational and radical forms of expression. All levels of the state—federal, state, and municipal—have been incapable of responding to, listening to, or negotiating with these movements or of dialoguing and interacting with their leaders. Such is the case of the conflictive relations between the EZLN and the Mexican state, supported by a wide array of power structures. Between 1994 and 2001, the EZLN was the catalyst and articulator of some of the most important expressions of discontent to come out of rural and indigenous Mexico, in this case Chiapas. The impact of the EZLN during those years was felt at a national level. From 2001 onward, however, the EZLN lost its capacity to lead and represent indigenous groups in the rest of Mexico. The EZLN's separated itself from the left, led by the PRD. In addition, the Vicente Fox administration, inaugurated in 2000, was able to dominate and lead the political forces that would deepen the democratic transition. This was when the EZLN's isolation began. It was thought at the time that the democratic transition would strengthen the Mexican state. During the administrations of Vicente Fox and subsequently of Felipe Calderón (2006–), government actions focused on promoting indigenous reforms, particularly of laws at the local level, in the majority of Mexican states with an indigenous population.[44] However, the Mexican state has been unable to create legal or political mechanisms for relating to emerging social movements. This weakness in Mexico's current democracy explains why peace negotiations between the EZLN and the government have reached a standstill. The danger for democracy is that these movements, as in many Latin American countries, are becoming increasingly more radicalized. The government of President Calderón had no concrete proposal for attempting to resolve the EZLN problem, as the indigenous issue gradually vanished from the national scene during Vicente Fox's term in office.[45] The Calderón government reduced the indigenous issue to a question of fighting poverty or promoting cultural rights. The EZLN, for its part, continued to offer to "direct" the antiestablishment social movements, further endangering the possibility of negotiations with the government. There are thus no areas of convergence between the parties that could serve as a basis for returning to the negotiating table. The unwillingness of either the government or the EZLN to negotiate is harmful to democratization in Mexico.

In conclusion, the national security aspects of the 1994 Chiapas crisis have diminished over time as a factor of governability. In Mexican states with a high density of indigenous population (Chiapas, Oaxaca, Yucatán, Hidalgo, Guerrero), the indigenous issue has been dealt with using "liberal" strategies, which is to say that the federal and state governments have made social and economic investments represented by spending on roads, education, housing, and measures to incorporate the indigenous into national society. The issue of rights has been restricted to the cultural arena and so-called customary law, for electing authorities. The Mexican state has not resolved the deeper problems of inequality and exclusion faced by indigenous peoples, but the fact that extreme poverty has been reduced has meant that the conflict has ceased to have violent expressions. The "armed insurrection" of 1994 has been replaced by a movement of communitarian organization (carried out by the *caracoles*). The state government of Chiapas has contributed to this transformation.

Notes

1. Estimates of the indigenous populations are based on data from the Consejo Nacional de Población, "Proyecciones de la población de México 2005–2050," http://www.conapo.gob.mx/index.php?option=com_content&view=article&id=36&Itemid=234; and http://www.conapo.gob.mx/publicaciones/marginabsoluto/IAM1990-2000_docprincipal.pdf.

2. Constitución Política de los Estados Unidos Mexicanos (Political Constitution of the United States of Mexico), updated with the reform published on April 7, 2006, http://www.ordenjuridico.gob.mx/. Changes to the Constitution were made regarding indigenous rights, such as Articles 4 and 27, in 1992. The first refers to the recognition of Mexico's pluricultural composition based on its indigenous peoples and states that the law must protect and promote the development of their languages, cultures, customs, resources, and specific forms of social organization, guaranteeing effective access to state jurisdiction.

3. According to the 2000 census, 6.7 million of Mexico's total 98 million people speak an indigenous language.

4. Luis H. Álvarez, "Chiapas: Dilemas actuales del conflicto y la negociación," in *Chiapas: Interpretaciones sobre la negociación y la paz,* edited by Cynthia Arnson, Raúl Benítez Manaut, and Andrew Selee (Mexico City: Centro de Investigaciones Sobre América del Norte at UNAM and Woodrow Wilson International Center for Scholars, 2003), 75.

5. Consejo Nacional de Población, "Proyecciones de indígenas de México y de las entidades federativas 2000–2010," http://www.conapo.gob.mx/00cifras/indigenas/Proyindigenas.pdf.

6. La Confederación Campesina de México (CNC) was founded in 1938. Since its origin, it has been linked to the PRI.

7. Margarito Ruiz Hernández and Araceli Burguete, "Chiapas: Organización y lucha indígena al final del milenio (1974–1998),"*Asuntos Indígenas* 3 (1998): 26–33.

8. George Collier, "El nuevo movimiento indígena," in *Costumbres, leyes y movimiento indio en Oaxaca y Chiapas,* edited by Lourdes de León Pasquel (Mexico City: CIESAS and Miguel Ángel Porrúa, 2001).

9. Neil Harvey, "Rebelión en Chiapas: Reformas rurales, radicalismo campesino y los límites del salinismo," in *Chiapas: Los rumbos de otra historia,* edited by Juan Pedro Viqueira and Mario Humberto Ruz (Mexico City: CIESAS, UNAM, and CEMCA, 1995), 447–79; Thomas Benjamín, *Tierra rica, pueblo pobre* (Mexico City: Ed. Grijalbo, 1995).

10. Francisco López Bárcenas et al., *Los derechos indígenas y la Reforma Constitucional en México* (Mexico City: Centro de Orientación y Asesoría a Pueblos Indígenas, 2001); and *Autonomía y derechos de los pueblos indios* (Mexico City: Cámara de Diputados, 1998). See also "Memoirs from the Interactive Meeting on Constitutional Reform Regarding Indigenous Issues: Balance and Viewpoints," El Colegio de México, June 2004 (published on CD).

11. Moisés Jaime Bailón, "Los derechos indígenas en México después de las reformas de 2001: Una mirada atrás y otra hacia adelante," in "Memoirs from the Interactive Meeting."

12. "Consenso en estrategia para salvar Lacandona," *Reforma,* June 27, 2003. This is a common problem in many countries with indigenous populations who live in regions

with limited resources. Nieves Zúñiga García-Falces, "Conflictos por recursos naturales y pueblos indígenas," *Pensamiento Propio* 22, no. 10 (July–December 2005). In the case of Chiapas, the deterioration of the Selva Lacandona is critical; the annual rate of deforestation reached 1.6 percent.

13. Not until the Third Declaration of the Selva Lacandona in January 1995 does the indigenous question become a central issue in the Zapatista discourse, stating that "the indigenous question will not be solved without *radical* transformation of the national pact."

14. Background on the peace process is given by Raúl Benítez Manaut, Andrew Selee, and Cynthia J. Arnson, "Frozen Negotiations: The Peace Process in Chiapas, *Estudios Mexicanos* 22, no. 1 (Winter 2006): 138–46.

15. Ibid., 138–39.

16. Ibid., 139.

17. Ibid., 139–40.

18. Ibid., 144–45.

19. Ibid., 143.

20. Ibid., 144.

21. See, e.g., Clandestine Indigenous Revolutionary Committee-General Command Group of the Zapatista Army of National Liberation, "Words from the EZLN on February 24, 2001, in San Cristóbal de Las Casas, Chiapas," Mexico, February 24, 2001, http://www.ezln.org/marcha/20010224a.es.htm.

22. Global Exchange, *Siempre cerca, siempre lejos: Las Fuerzas Armadas en México* (Mexico City: National Center for Social Communication, 2000), 112.

23. Sergio Aguayo Quezada, *El Almanaque Mexicano 2007* (Mexico City: Ed. Aguilar, 2007).

24. See Benítez Manaut, Selee, and Arnson, "Frozen Negotiations."

25. Comisión Nacional para el Desarrollo de los Pueblos Indígenas, "Socioeconomic Indicators of Mexico's Indigenous Peoples," 2002, http://www.cdi.gob.mx/index.php?id_seccion=91. See also INEGI and INI-CONAPO, "Estimates of Indigenous Population Based on Data from the XII General Population and Housing Census 2000."

26. International Labor Organization, "Convention No. 169 on Indigenous and Tribal Peoples," Geneva, June 1989, Articles 7, 9, and 13.

27. Moisés Jaime Bailón, ed., *Derechos humanos y derechos indígenas en el orden jurídico federal mexicano* (Mexico City: National Human Rights Commission, 2003).

28. Constitución Política de los Estados Unidos Mexicanos.

29. Ibid.

30. Tania Carrasco and Augusta Molnar, "Indigenous Peoples and Poverty," in *Mexico: A Comprehensive Development Agenda for the New Era,* edited by Marcelo M. Giugale, Oliver Lafourcade and Ving H. Nguyen (Washington, D.C.: World Bank, 2001).

31. Xóchitl Leyva Solano and Gabriel Ascencio Franco, *Lacandonia al filo del agua,* 2nd ed. (Mexico City: CIESAS, UNAM, and FCE, 2002), 174.

32. Sergio Aguayo, *Chiapas: Las amenazas a la seguridad nacional,* EST-006-86 (Mexico City: Centro Latinoamericano de Estudios Estratégicos, 1987). This analysis in the 1980s signaled the explosive situation in Chiapas due to extremely contrasting social conditions and an increase in confrontations between landowners and the peasant and indigenous populations demanding land, along with conflicts in Central America and the presence of Guatemalan refugees in Mexico.

33. "Transitorios de las reformas constitucionales en materia indígena de 2001," *Diario Oficial de la Federación* (Mexico City), August 14, 2001.

34. This is analyzed in detail by Jan de Vos, "Raíces históricas de la crisis chiapaneca," in *Chiapas: Los desafíos de la paz*, edited by Cynthia Arnson and Raúl Benítez Manaut (Mexico City: Miguel Ángel Porrúa, ITAM, and Woodrow Wilson Center, 2000), 36–40.

35. David Ronfeldt, ed., *The Zapatista Social Netwar in Mexico* (Santa Monica, Calif.: RAND Corporation, 1998), 181.

36. Rodolfo Stavenhagen, "Mexico's Unfinished Symphony: The Zapatista Movement," in *Mexico's Politics and Society in Transition,* edited by Joseph S. Tulchin and Andrew Selee (Boulder, Colo.: Lynne Rienner, 2003).

37. For more details regarding divergences between the COCOPA proposal and the government, see Bárcenas et al., *Derechos indígenas.*

38. Marco Tavanti, *Las Abejas: Pacifist Resistance and Syncretic Identities in a Globalizing Chiapas* (New York: Routledge, 2003). "Las Abejas" are communities allied with the Zapatistas that sought alternatives in the productive and organizational spheres. They were hit hard by paramilitary groups in 1997 to prevent their example from spreading.

39. Coordination for Dialogue and Negotiations in Chiapas, *Chiapas con justicia y dignidad: Memoria, acuerdos, compromisos, acciones y obras* (Mexico City: Secretaría de Gobernación, 2000), 189–91.

40. Both the federal government and the state government led by Governor Pablo Salazar endeavored to bring to justice the leaders of paramilitary groups, particularly those responsible for the December 1997 Acteal massacre, in which forty-five indigenous people were murdered.

41. "Chiapas: La Treceava Estela. Subcomandante Insurgente Marcos," Mexico City, July 2003, http://www.nodo50.org/pchiapas/chiapas/documentos/calenda/chiapas 6.htm.

42. Pablo González Casanova, "Los caracoles zapatistas: Redes de resistencia y autonomía," *Memoria* 177 (CEMOS, Mexico City), November 2003.

43. National Intermediation Commission, *Archivo Histórico Enero de 1994–Julio de 1998* (Mexico City: Edición de Servicios y Asesoría para la Paz, 1998).

44. Diódoro Carrasco and Moises Bailón, eds., *¿Una década de reformas indígenas? Multiculturalismo y derechos de los pueblos indios de* México (Mexico City: Comisión Nacional de los Derechos Humanos, 2009).

45. Rosalía Aída Hernández, Sarela Paz, and María Teresa Sierra, eds., *El Estado y los indígenas en tiempos del PAN: neoindigenismo, legalidad e identidad* (Mexico City: Center for Social Anthropology Research, 2004).

Chapter 9

An Illusory Peace: The United Nations and State Building in Haiti

Johanna Mendelson Forman

In the 30 seconds that it took for an earthquake of 7.0 on the Richter scale to devastate Port-au-Prince on January 12, 2010, the fate of Haiti, a small Caribbean nation of 10 million people, became the rest of the world's concern. The estimated death toll of more than 250,000, with injuries to perhaps double that number, only serves to underscore the fragility of life in the poorest country in the Western Hemisphere.

The sudden loss of 2 percent of any population (and injury to very many more) is overwhelming, but Haiti's experience is worsened by the fact that most of those killed were in and around the nation's capital, Port-au-Prince. A city built to accommodate 50,000 inhabitants, its population had reached almost 3 million as a result of urban in-migration—a factor that itself underscores the lack of opportunity in the rest of country, where poor infrastructure, deforestation, and overwhelming poverty have made even subsistence living virtually impossible.

Even more daunting is that 75 percent of Haiti's population lives on less than $2 a day, and 56 percent (4.5 million people) live on less than

$1 per day. Any recovery from disaster is difficult, but for Haiti it will require a complete rethinking of how to do development. If the mantra before the earthquake hit was to help Haitians go "from misery to poverty," it is hard to find the words that will characterize this attempt to build a new nation. What is clear, however, is that after this latest tragedy Haiti will need to resolve its governance deficits with the help of the international community and also with the help of its citizens if it is to build a state that can provide the basis for security and well-being. Crisis, violence, and conflict have been the norm in Haiti since its independence. From 1804, when Haitian slaves rebelled against France, through most of the nineteenth and twentieth and into the twenty-first centuries, Haitians have suffered the cruel fate of being ruled by tyrants. Led either by the military or rent-seeking elites who exploited Haitian citizens, the country endured insecurity and economic decay. State institutions did not provide justice, education, or health benefits to the majority. Haitian leaders did not opt for participatory processes that laid a foundation for democratic rule. Haiti was a "failed state" long before the term became part of the post–Cold War lexicon.

In 1990, a young priest, Jean Bertrand Aristide, rose to the political stage to become the first democratically elected leader of Haiti. In an election observed and accepted by the international community as free and fair, Aristide defeated a slate of old guard politicians supported by the national elite. Haitian citizens, who yearned for greater freedom and opportunity, were attracted to his charisma. Support of the masses delivered a victory for democracy, something unheard of in Haitian history. The United States reluctantly embraced Aristide's new leadership, recognizing that his election marked a new beginning for Haiti.

But Aristide's victory was short-lived. Nine months after assuming the presidency, his tenure was curtailed by a military coup in September 1991. General Raoul Cedras's military junta reclaimed the state and proceeded to run a brutal regime that was notorious for human rights abuses and poor governance. In exile, Aristide increasingly gained international support and began the political battle to fulfill his role as elected leader.

Haiti was subject to a political roller coaster from 1991 to 2004. It underwent seven UN interventions, the 1994 return of President Aristide to office with the support of a multinational force, and a downward spiral of governance. Despite massive foreign aid from multilateral donors, efforts to pull Haiti together failed. In 2000, when President Aristide was reelected to a second term, the Haitian state was extremely weak. By the time he was forced to leave office again in February 2004, the Haitian state had joined the official ranks of countries included in the Failed State Index.[1]

This chapter examines state building in Haiti as a unique example of how the international community used the vehicle of peacekeeping and diplomacy to construct a capable state. At the end of the Cold War, with few tools to manage weak and fragile states, the international community turned to the United Nations, and its peacekeeping operations in particular, to address the ongoing crisis of security and instability that affected the Haitian state. Given the absence of a hot conflict in Haiti, this story is really about the evolving role of the United Nations in this state-building process.[2] A brief discussion of the Haitian case provides comparisons with other regional state-building efforts.

This chapter also examines the role of the United Nations peace operations that were mandated in 1994 to help create a safe and secure environment and build a Haitian state. It also addresses the more recent role that Latin American nations have played in support of Haiti's development since 2004, when the international community was called upon again to stabilize the Haitian state after its president was forced from office. The growing involvement of Latin American states in peacekeeping efforts in Haiti marks a transition from indifference to increased involvement in hemispheric affairs. The chapter also briefly identifies the role of another tool that supported the UN effort, the Group of Friends of Haiti, which in both the first and second rounds of UN operations contributed to the goal of building Haiti's institutions and engaging donors to contribute to these efforts.

In the wake of the most recent tragedy to befall Haiti—the massive earthquake in January 2010, which created yet another setback in the UN's efforts to leave Haiti more secure—the chapter suggests that long-term peace operations such as this one are more akin to development programs than traditional peacekeeping. In contrast with Latin American nations like El Salvador and Guatemala that were subject to UN-mandated peace processes, Haiti never experienced the type of armed conflict that would justify a formal peace agreement. Nevertheless, Haiti's continued internal conflict exhibited many similarities to post–Cold War cases where violence, human rights abuses, and a weak state created conditions necessitating an international intervention. The continued destabilization of Haiti even after it had its first ever democratic election in 1990 followed only seven months later by a military coup suggested that to build a strong and capable state the international community would have to remain for a long of period of time.[3] This reality ran counter to the nature of international intervention by the UN and donor countries.[4]

During the past seventeen years, the evolving nature of the UN mission in Haiti has also included a much broader integration of UN agencies, which support reforming institutions of governance, reforming the security sector by training a new police force, and creating economic opportunities through training, education, and support of women in Haiti. Today, in the wake of a natural disaster that has undermined the progress made during the past few years, the UN's presence in Haiti is needed more than ever as Haiti struggles to regain basic institutional stability. Its mandate is one of development, and its duration is still unknown. With a yearly cost of more than $800 million, it is clear that such expenses will not be sustainable unless Haitians themselves work with their international counterparts to finally find an exit from this ongoing cycle of UN intervention. The case of Haiti demonstrates that the UN cannot undertake state building alone, but instead needs strong partners to provide resources and support to the government of Haiti to ensure that these efforts are not in vain. With the election of a new government in 2011, finding ways to enable Haiti to become a capable state will be a top priority for the government of President Michael Martelly.

Peace Processes: Where Does Haiti Fit?

The Haitian case is unique within Latin America, because it demonstrates how state building can serve as a form of peacemaking in the context of a failed state, even in the absence of a peace agreement or some form of official document to resolve political differences.[5] Like peace processes that end conflict, these negotiations require a commitment from a range of both domestic and international actors to be successful. Whether formalized by an accord or through a series of power-sharing arrangements, the goal is to resolve conflicts in a given society. By contrast, cease-fires and treaties are more immediate mechanisms to stop violence.

During the past decade, the literature on state building focused on security as the core pillar in the framework for reconstruction. The framework also includes justice and human rights, socioeconomic well-being, and governance.[6] In addition to identifying key tasks to be performed in the short, medium, and long terms, the four pillars demonstrate the complexity of state-building programs in failed or weak states. Research on the success or failure of state building has recognized how difficult it is to achieve gains in governance, economic recovery, or justice if the security sector remains unreformed.

Moving from short- to medium- and long-term transformations as part of a stabilization effort can take at least twenty years.[7] Yet donor nations rarely have the political will to engage for extended periods of time. Most programs have time horizons that do not exceed five years. Herein may lay the first of many problems that has limited the effectiveness of state building in Haiti over the last nearly two decades. The stop-and-go funding of international donors in response to crises in governance has actually been the source of major setbacks in the state's ability to build credible institutions, such as a national police force. This includes the shifting mandates of the UN peace operation.

The quest for stability in Haiti is shaped by an ongoing political, social, and economic dialogue between the international community and the Haitian leadership. It is not based on a formal accord but on a series of attempts to negotiate a transformation of the political and economic order and also reform of the security sector. The process is supported by the ongoing presence of a UN peace operation, the United Nations Stabilization Mission in Haiti (Mission des Nations Unies pour la stabilisation en Haïti, MINUSTAH). Haiti's instability is not caused by rebel armies but by youth gangs and former military personnel that continue to terrorize Port-au-Prince and other urban centers struggling in the absence of state control. Such conflicts are resolved only when there is a political consensus on ending the violence or some dramatic event triggers various actors to be willing to allow for peace.[8] By 2011, the newly-trained Haitian National Police had begun to have an impact on citizen security in Port au Prince.

Some have argued that the Governor's Island Accord, crafted in July 1993 by the Organization of American States (OAS), the UN, and the United States was a form of a negotiated settlement among various parties. The accord laid out steps for a peaceful transition to constitutional government as well as Aristide's return. It was negotiated with parliamentary and political leaders, and included a plan for Aristide to appoint a new prime minister. U.S. funding was used to sweeten the deal. Yet in the end, neither the UN, nor the OAS, nor the Haitians implemented this agreement.[9]

In contrast, during the past seventeen years, Haitians have engaged in a series of informal dialogues about how to end violence and restore the political role of the state. At times, this process has been brokered by the international community, the UN, and the OAS. At other times, it has been mediated by international actors like the United States, Canada, and what has come to be known as the "Friends" process. By themselves, none of these actors has been successful in resolving the ongoing political turmoil that characterizes Haitian politics. However, some progress may be in the offing as of the 2011 presidential elections that gave Haiti a reform-minded executive.

Since the most recent international intervention in February 2004, greater effort has been made to reach out to Haitians. Ownership-creating strategies have been implemented by the UN agencies, the OAS, and other international actors. These attempts sought to open enough political space to allow former President René Préval to create a power-sharing government. Nevertheless, in the absence of a formal political process that brings all interests to the table, the UN presence has substituted for any real strategic effort to produce a lasting resolution to Haiti's internal problems, which are as much political as economic and social.

Even today in the wake of the earthquake, parallel sources of authority actually run the state. The UN's special representative in Haiti and, until recently, the Interim Haitian Reconstruction Commission provide leadership and decisionmaking authority. Governance is de facto, managed by groups of elites who maneuver for their own political and economic gains, using the legislature to support their respective interests in return for financial gain. Similarly, since 2004 security has been maintained by UN peacekeepers, rather than the Haitian state. Though conditions are changing slowly, the high level of corruption, coupled with illicit resources from narco-trafficking, impedes progress in devolving power back to the central government.[10] In the aftermath of the 2010 earthquake, public security concerns remain high, as it is estimated that 60 percent of Haiti's prison population escaped in the chaos of the earthquake. Police forces are straining to meet greater demand to protect vulnerable groups. Rural Haiti remains underserved by the national police.

On the economic front, from the Duvalier regime to Aristide's 1994 government, the Haitian economy was personalized; thus, only a small groups of private citizens controlled services and could buy protection. In this respect, Haiti in 1994 resembled many Sub-Saharan African states, such as Liberia or Sierra Leone, where overwhelming poverty and corrupt leadership made it difficult to control internal conflicts or violent factions.[11] The extreme poverty and inequality that have persisted in Haiti throughout this century and the one just past reinforce the economist Paul Collier's observations that low levels of economic development create opportunities for young unemployed men to join gangs. When there is little to lose, it is easy to make a career in crime or violence an attractive option.[12]

One of the major differences between Haiti and the peace processes in Central America is the reform of the security sector. Both past and recent demobilization, disarmament, and reintegration attempts by the UN and by the Government of Haiti have been only partially successful. In early 1995, as part of the security-sector reforms, President Aristide disbanded the Haitian Armed Forces by decree.[13]

In an attempt to restore state control over security, the new Haitian National Police force was developed to replace the one that rose from the demobilized army in 1995. The small force of 5,000 men was inadequate for the size of the country, unable to support basic police functions, and very susceptible to corruption. By the time the UN returned in 2004, it was apparent that one of its primary tasks would be to set up a new police force. Today the challenge once again is creating a police force that is capable of providing for public order and citizen security. The UN estimates that it will take until 2012 to reach the desirable number of police (11,000), and the gap in public safety is still wide, given the absence of any rural civil defense force.[14]

Although willing, the UN was unsuccessful in disarming the population, let alone the armed forces. A short-term training effort in 1995, supported by the U.S. Agency for International Development, was intended to reintegrate former soldiers. Though it provided some benefits to soldiers, there was no follow-up program. The U.S. government was also unwilling to pay additional pensions or support to former soldiers. The result of these early decisions was to unleash a rather large group of angry and unemployed former soldiers that were capable of disrupting stabilization efforts.[15] This ongoing discontent came to a head in February 2004, when former army veterans were instrumental in the violence that led to the breakdown in public order, and the flight of President Aristide from the country. With access to weapons and no police deterrent, they had little incentive to sit at a negotiating table. Attempts at any negotiations were unsustainable because of the proliferation of other armed groups.[16]

In contrast to Haiti, El Salvador, Guatemala, and to some extent Nicaragua reformed and downsized their militaries, created an independent police force, and provided for some degree of citizen security. Unlike the situation in El Salvador, Guatemala, or Nicaragua, where guerilla leaders were transformed into politicians with political parties, Haitian political leaders and their respective parties relied on gangs to threaten public order in the advent of a political stalemate. Security-sector reform in Central America is still incomplete, but progress has been made in some countries for more democratic governance. Some countries have also experienced new levels of sustained economic growth, which have been attributed to the improved security climate. But citizen security still remains imperiled by narco-traffickers and common crime.

In the Central American countries, where human rights abuses were committed by the security forces and rebels, reconciliation took many forms, from tribunals mandated in accords to ad hoc government commissions. Despite the diversity of these efforts to bring closure to the past, efforts were made to engage victims and their families. Several stalled attempts in Haiti to produce some form of human rights commission have never succeeded, despite the presence of the UN and OAS. Even though the UN and OAS initially provided for joint monitoring of human rights abuses after the 1991 coup, through the International Civilian Mission in Haiti (Mission Civile Internationale en Haïti, known as MICIVIH),[17] their effort did not result in a truth commission report.[18]

Although there is no silver bullet in making peace, what is evident from the cases of the last decade is that implementation strategies coupled with sustained financing of the security sector are essential to bringing about lasting results. In Haiti, all types of programs were tried—to reform the security forces, create a working judiciary, and restore economic and social development. Yet, unlike other state-building efforts in the region, Haiti was in need of an initiative that could mobilize democratic governance, a social project that Haitian leadership is still debating today.

The presence of MINUSTAH in Haiti underscored the importance of the UN in helping the government of Haiti by providing security that the state was still not able to maintain throughout the country. After the earthquake, the burden of security still remained a UN function, in spite of ongoing training of the Haitian National Police. There was tremendous hope after the earthquake that Haitians would actually have a dialogue about a more stable future, but this still remains an elusive goal for the majority of Haitians who remain homeless and have become even more vulnerable to crime as the country tries to rebuild. As of this writing, there is a new debate about whether the army, a much reviled institution, should be restored. President Martelly vowed to recreate the Haitian armed forces but the international donor community remained cool to the process.

Haiti as a Stabilization and Reconstruction Poster Child: The UN Role

Central America represented many firsts for the international community in seeking to resolve an internal conflict in the post–Cold War era. The UN intervention in Haiti triggered a different set of firsts. At the end of the Cold War, chaos ensued in many parts of the developing world. Weak governance and internal conflict made many civilians victims of instability and violence. State building and postconflict reconstruction efforts, now called stabilization efforts, emerged as strategies for moving nations from chaos to normalcy. The UN Security Council authorized peace operations that addressed the collective threat to peace and security arising from failed states. In the early 1990s, the UN experience in Haiti became a model for other UN operations in Africa and South Asia because conditions in Haiti foreshadowed those of many subsequent cases of state failure.[19]

The UN operation in Haiti can be best described as developmental peacekeeping. This type of peacekeeping operation concentrates efforts on postconflict reconstruction through an integrated approach to the work that other UN agencies perform in the field. The greatest challenge of this type of operation in a place like Haiti is the length of such a mission given the enormous needs that Haiti faces. In the thirteen Security Council Resolutions since February 2004, the UN mission has been extended to embrace not only the security conditions on the ground but also to provide Haiti with the tools needed to build capacity in governance, improve the rule of law, support economic growth, and address issues such as the sexual abuse of women and the impact of armed violence on children. As Haiti continues to recover from this natural disaster, the UN will remain in the country to ensure a transition to a more stable environment.[20] The evolution of the UN's operations in Haiti underscores how its role has adapted to the country's ever-changing political environment.[21]

At the start of its seventeen-year presence, the UN entered Haiti under the authority of Chapter VII of the UN Charter (see table 9.1). A Chapter VII operation is invoked when the situation is deemed to be a threat to international peace and security, and authorizes intervention by force. In Haiti, however, there was not as much need for an active peace operation—which entails the separation of forces, creation of a cease-fire, and demobilization and reintegration—as there was for a development effort.

In countries that are either failed or fragile states, success in mitigating conflicts is often ephemeral.[22] In these countries, the main task for this new generation of UN operations is holistic development, as opposed to strictly security-sector reform.[23] The creation of MINUSTAH in 2004 was part of an evolving concept of peace operations that is not only about rebuilding failed states but is also focused on launching democratic rule through deeper engagement with political leaders and civil society.

Table 9.1. UN Missions in Haiti, 1993–2007

Mission	Year, Resolution	Chapter of UN Charter	Cost	Objective and Mandate
Joint UN-OAS Civilian Mission (MICIVIH)	1993, General Assembly OAS 47/20B	Chapter VII		To observe the human rights situation in Haiti
Multinational Force in Haiti (MNF)	1994, UN Security Council (UNSC) Resolution 940			To help end military leadership
UN Mission in Haiti (UNMIH)	1995, UNSC Resolution 975	Chapter VI	$315,794,700	To assist the democratic government to sustain a stable environment, professionalize the armed forces and create a separate police force, and establish an environment conducive to free and fair elections
UN Support Mission in Haiti (UNSMIH)	1996, UNSC Resolution 1063	Chapter VI	$62,100,000	To assist the government in the professionalization of the police, maintenance of a secure and stable environment conducive to the success of efforts to establish and train an effective national police force, and to coordinate activities of the UN system in promoting institution building, national reconciliation, and economic rehabilitation
UN Transition Mission in Haiti (UNTMIH)	1997, UNSC Resolution 1123	Chapter VI	$20,600,000	To assist the government of Haiti by supporting and contributing to the professionalization of the Haitian National Police
UN Civilian Police Mission in Haiti (MIPONUH)	1997, UNSC Resolution 1141	Chapter VI	$20,400,000	To assist the government in the professionalization of the National Police
International Civilian Support Mission in Haiti (MICAH)	2000, UN General Assembly Resolution A/54/193	Chapter VI		To consolidate the results achieved by MIPONUH and its predecessor missions of the United Nations in Haiti as well as by the International Civilian Mission in Haiti (MICIVIH)

Mission	Date, Resolution	Chapter	Budget	Mandate
Multinational Interim Force (MIFH)	2004, UNSC Resolution 1529	Chapter VII		To contribute to a secure and stable environment for the deployment of the stabilization mission and of humanitarian workers
UN Stabilization Mission in Haiti (MINUSTAH)	2004, UNSC 1542 (renewed)	Chapter VII	$1,430,400,000	To ensure a secure and stable environment within which the constitutional and political process in Haiti can take place
UN Stabilization Mission in Haiti (MINUSTAH)	February 2007, UNSC Resolution 1743	Chapter VII		To continue support for the political process, and to specifically address gang violence, humanitarian needs, and development
UN Stabilization Mission in Haiti (MINUSTAH)	October 2007, UNSC Resolution 1780	Chapter VII		To continue support for institution building, with the government of Haiti leading the efforts to develop security and social inclusion, and to coordinate development with international donors
UN Stabilization Mission in Haiti (MINUSTAH)	October 2008, UNSC Resolution 1840	Chapter VII		To continue to support governance, stability, and democracy in Haiti, specifically reaffirming approval for the recent government General Policy declaration under Prime Minister Michèle Pierre-Louis
UN Stabilization Mission in Haiti (MINUSTAH)	October 2009, UNSC Resolution 1892	Chapter VII	$500,000,000	To continue to support the government of Haiti in its efforts to strengthen state institutions and provide logistical assistance during the upcoming elections in 2010

Sources: UN documents.

The First Period of UN Involvement, 1990–2000

When the UN first became involved in Haiti in 1990, it did so in the name of democracy. The Department of Political Affairs was charged with helping Haiti prepare for what was slated as its first democratic elections. The UN, working alongside the OAS, had the support of the United States and other donors. The successful democratic process that resulted in Aristide's victory was hailed as a new era for Haiti, and neatly coincided with the overall wave of democratization and electoral transitions taking place in the hemisphere. But this optimism was premature.

In September 1991, seven months after taking office, President Aristide was overthrown by a military coup and forced into exile. The UN worked from a distance with the OAS to restore democratic governance and return Aristide to the presidency. In September 1994, under a UN-mandated multilateral intervention led by U.S. forces, the military government in Haiti was forced to leave. The justification for this Chapter VII operation was the restoration of democracy.

The UN returned to Haiti under a peace operation mandate to restore an elected government, and to provide security and stability for the state. How it would achieve these goals was managed by U.S. planners, and the time frame for their actions is significant for two reasons. First, it represents the evolving doctrine of military operations other than war, which emphasized the political nature of peace operations, and became the precursor to what are now called stability operations. Second, because the U.S. planners had very specific events as conditions for the departure of the multilateral force, the UN Mission in Haiti was considered by most to be a short-term effort to stabilize the country. It was also a political mission, led by the United States. The UN, along with bilateral donors, suggested a democratization course and set a timeline for exit. By 1995, the United States had turned over its military responsibility to the UN, whose mission was to stabilize security, create a new police force, and eventually demobilize the army. The mission was also downgraded by the Security Council to one arising from Chapter VI of the UN Charter, where the UN was in Haiti by invitation of the government.

If one looks at the mandate for UN peace operations in 1994, Security Council Resolution 940 had simple objectives: to help end the military leadership and reinstall the democratically elected president. Once a civilian government was in place, the U.S. military planners defined their exit strategy without the benefit of a doctrinal definition. They relied on the traditional conflict termination model that focused on the end of military actions and a transition to civilian authorities. Security Council Resolution 975 went further, however, stating that once the security situation was stabilized, the mission would help create a new police force and establish an "enabling environment for elections." This was especially problematical for U.S. troops because the Department of Defense rejected any policing role for American troops. Thus, the goal of the mission was dependent upon other civilian agencies of donor governments and the UN to recruit and train a new Haitian police force that would provide Haitians with internal security, and more important, allow the U.S. forces to leave.[24]

UN Security Council Resolution 975 also served as the basis for an exit strategy. The benchmarks would be a secure and stable environment that would allow social and economic development, free elections, and a peaceful transition of responsibility to the government of Haiti. Still, it was clear that to maintain a secure and stable environment it was necessary for elections to be held so that a planned force reduction could take place by 1996. It also became apparent that a time- or event-driven strategy alone would not offer the UN troops enough flexibility for a gradual transition of internal security to the government of Haiti.[25]

If one accepts the argument that the UN's intervention in Haiti was really a fully owned U.S. operation under the cover of a multilateral arrangement, then it is easy to write off the early exit as a political decision that disregarded the needs of the Haitians, or the broader mandates of development that the Security Council endorsed.[26] Still, somewhere between the notion of leaving Haiti after an election and the creation of a new police force lies a less cynical view that argues that Haiti seemed to be heading in the right direction, and that the peace operation had achieved its goals.

This UN Mission between 1994 and 2000 was plagued with domestic and international problems. These included a difficult political environment in Haiti that reflected the polarization of different factions even after the reinstallation of President Aristide that was never resolved by dialogue or consensus building.

This absence of Haitian ownership made it difficult to ensure acceptance of what appeared to be an externally driven state-building process. For example, in 1995, at the insistence of the international community, but especially the United States, there was a premature push for presidential elections. Aristide had only served one year of the remainder of his interrupted mandate. The elections of 1995, in which Aristide was prohibited by law from running, created destabilizing internal conflicts in a country where the ideological polarization of political factions from the years of military rule had not yet been resolved. Moreover, for the average Haitian who had experienced high expectations on the return of their president in 1994, it was now evident that the slow pace of change in the economy, the delays in forming a new police force, and the lack of success in creating effective institutions of justice for the nation's citizens had resulted in a complete stalemate in the political arena.

Even with the election in 1996 of Aristide's political ally, René Préval, Haitians did not feel as if there was real competition. The perception was rather that of an imposition of a leader driven by the schedules of a peace operation. By July 1997, due to protests over legislative elections, Haitian prime minister Rosy Smarth resigned, leaving the government paralyzed and curtailing international donor support. This crisis led to debates in the UN Security Council about the continued presence of UN forces in Haiti, with many countries, including the United States expressing ambivalence about renewing the mission. Nevertheless, the UN's mandate was renewed.

By the end of 1999, a Security Council mandate was no longer possible. The United States pulled out its last troops. Aristide was reelected to the presidency in 2000, for a second time when on-the-ground security assessments described a deterioration of human rights and political stability.[27] Controversy over this election led to an opposition boycott, which undermined Aristide's legitimacy from the start of his second term and created political tensions that were never resolved. Aristide's opposition included members of the small middle class and traditional business elites who were hostile to his progressive economic agenda.

The Second Period of UN Involvement, 2004–10

A month-long uprising by anti-Aristide rebels in February 2004 forced the resignation of President Aristide. The uprising represented the culmination of a situation that had been allowed to fester in Haiti despite all the resources and initiatives to rebuild Haiti. Some attribute this breakdown to the failure of the UN missions of the last decade to actually transform Haiti—its institutions, its politics, or its economic base—when it was most needed.[28] Others observers attributed this to the UN's inability to facilitate a political consensus, thus preventing external actors from framing a definite and achievable exit strategy.[29] What it really represents is a case in which the UN, forced to play a moderating role in such a fragile state, could no longer reconcile the political differences on the ground that are essential for building a sustainable peace.

After Aristide's departure, the UN's primary mission was to reinforce the interim government led by acting prime minister Gerard Latortue. No effort was made to arrest the rebellious troops that forced Aristides's ouster. In 2004, UN Security Council Resolution 1542, which created the United Nations Stabilization Mission in Haiti, known, again, as MINUSTAH, did not suggest a strategy for political reconciliation, and the national dialogue process it mandated did not result in a broad-based dialogue about Haiti's future among civil society groups and political parties. The main goal of the peacekeeping operation was to oversee new elections, which, after multiple postponements, finally occurred in February 2006, bringing back René Préval to a second term as president.[30]

This new government, the result of a long-delayed electoral process, actually offered hope to many Haitians seeking an end to the chaos of the interim government that had been created after Aristide. Préval was able to form a government that included representatives of many political factions, a unique occurrence in Haiti's long and tortured political history. Like his predecessors, his government faced the tremendous challenge of overcoming insecurity due to criminal activities arising from Haiti's role as a major drug transshipment state, and from the urban youth gangs who terrorized thousands of residents of the capital's largest slum, Cité Soleil. If Préval was to succeed in building institutions—from the rule of law, to schools and health care, to jobs—he would need MINUSTAH to provide the requisite security for the time being.

In December 2006 and January 2007, the Haitian government, working with MINUSTAH, undertook what can only be characterized as an urban military expedition to rid Cité Soleil of its gang leaders. By routing out some of the worst offenders, the UN forces actually were able to liberate many parts of the city from criminals who used the warren of slum housing to hide kidnap victims (a very lucrative business) and to threaten poor women and children. Though there were some civilian deaths in this operation, the peacekeepers were successful in their mission, in part because the Préval government made it clear that they were operating on his orders. This effort was mostly successful, as records indicate that kidnappings have declined, and the residents of these areas are now able to move about with greater safety. Peacekeepers still remain posted in and around these slums to ensure that new gangs do not return.

Nevertheless, for Haitians MINUSTAH is the subject of much debate and frequent derision. Government leaders, from the president down, recognize that the UN presence is needed, given the corrupt police, and the challenge of security sector reform in this poverty-stricken country.[31] Yet Haitians believe that MINUSTAH represents another occupation force on their soil. This is ironic because it is not a U.S.–led mission, but one that is led by Brazil, and staffed today with soldiers from seventeen Latin American countries.[32] Newspaper editorials in Port-au-Prince continue to exploit the UN's presence as a way to stir up fierce nationalism whenever something goes wrong. In April 2008, when food riots broke out in Port-au-Prince, UN forces made the difference in protecting the elected leader from the mobs.[33] Although Préval and his Cabinet have come to accept and work with MINUSTAH, building trust between the Haitian government and the UN mission has taken time and diplomacy that could be considered part of what some have called a transition process required for exit.[34]

As Haiti attempts once again to work with the UN to create a new police force, until the state is able to train and deploy a full complement of police, a corps of 11,000 men and women, it will still require MINUSTAH's support. The estimated time frame for a new police force to be completely mobilized is 2012.

Until 2008, Haiti was making progress on a number of fronts based on socioeconomic indicators. In April 2008, a series of food riots, due to the increasing cost of basic commodities such as corn and rice, resulted in the resignation of Haitian prime minister Jacque Edouard Alexis. President Préval was unable to find a suitable replacement, as the National Assembly rejected candidate after candidate he put forward. It was not until August 2008 that Michele Pierre Louis was finally named as a replacement. The following month, three devastating hurricanes hit Haiti. The flooding and destruction killed thousands; one of the country's secondary cities, Gonaïves, was buried in mud; and much of the progress that had been made was quickly undermined by this unforeseen natural disaster. These events led to a greater focus on development, with the UN naming former U.S. president Bill Clinton to become the UN special envoy to Haiti to help restart the economic reconstruction.

In most of its work in Haiti since 2004, the UN has operated alongside the state, serving as the security force to prevent violence but also to help develop institutions of governance such as a judiciary, or a police, and provide humanitarian aid to citizens through feeding and health programs. What has eluded the UN in recent years has been any effort to establish benchmarks that would allow for the mission's departure. William Durch has suggested that it is difficult for the UN to measure success until after it has left a country.[35] If this observation is correct, then the question becomes whether the UN has learned any lessons from its first intervention in Haiti that might apply to its current mission. The seven UN missions, including the current one, all lead to the question of whether the UN will ever be able to leave Haiti—given the overwhelming development and governance challenges that still remain, and the massive humanitarian crisis brought about by the earthquake.

One outcome of this new UN focus on Haiti was that for the first time there was a greater engagement of the Haitian private sector, the Haitian state, and the UN. There was a greater sense of hope, and this optimism for Haiti was reinforced by support in the United States for better trade agreements on textiles, thus helping to create new jobs in the Haitian assembly sector. By the end of 2009, it appeared for the first time that there had been progress in building a more viable state. It is this situation that made the January 12, 2010, earthquake a greater tragedy. Just as Haiti was showing positive signs of development, everything was suddenly halted as the worst natural disaster of the Western Hemisphere engulfed the poorest country in the region. After assessing the damage, the economist Paul Collier, who wrote a more positive report about Haiti's future after the natural disasters of 2009, still expressed his belief that Haiti could overcome its widespread poverty with stable governance and private investments in the textile assembly and agricultural industries. Haiti's proximity to the United States, its abundant and cheap labor, and its peaceful neighborhood give it the potential to become a viable nation.[36]

Friends of Haiti and a Regional Security Opportunity

Throughout the course of the UN's efforts to rebuild a Haitian state, a parallel process emerged to help guide the UN role in this area. Haiti became the beneficiary of modern multiparty diplomacy that during the past two decades was adopted as a way to resolve conflicts. Such diplomacy took the form of Groups of Friends, which were used to support the more formal conflict resolutions operations of the UN and in the OAS.[37]

The First Group of Friends, 1994–2000

In 1994, a Group of Friends for Haiti—comprising the United States, Canada, France, Argentina, and Venezuela—was created to assist the UN secretary-general. The mechanism established a neutral space for dialogue between the various political groups in Haiti and the five national government "friends." The group was small enough to act in concert to convince other countries to engage in the state-building activities needed to increase diplomatic engagement. As a recent study on Friends processes correctly points out, the Friends were not a substitute for political negotiations to resolve deep divisions in Haiti.[38] Nevertheless, those nations that participated helped to continue the conversation about issues and grievances among the affected parties in Haiti.

A parallel Friends process was also convened in August 2000 by the former OAS secretary-general, César Gaviria. This OAS group included Argentina, the Bahamas, Belize, Canada, Chile, the Dominican Republic, Guatemala, Mexico, the United States, and Venezuela, plus France, Germany, Norway, and Spain—all of which have permanent observer status. This group focuses mainly on governance and election issues.

The Second Group of Friends, 2004 to the Present

A similar Group of Friends at the UN emerged out of the 2004 intervention in Haiti. This new group included the United States, Canada, France, Chile, and Brazil, and the latter two countries had seats on the Security Council. By 2011, the Friends had added Costa Rica, Mexico, Peru, and Uruguay. Venezuela, part of the original Friends group, was no longer included, although the government of President Hugo Chávez supported Haiti through economic assistance in the form of oil to run its power plant.

At the UN the reactivation of this smaller Group of Friends in 2004 permitted a multinational force to receive the UN's blessing through Security Council Resolution 1529. These countries arrived in advance of the peace operation that followed three months later. Moreover, along with the United States and Canada, both Friends groups have remained central to policy development for the UN in Haiti: The Security Council's renewal of MINUSTAH's mandate continues due to the efforts of this group. The Friends also pushed a more development-oriented focus in October 2007 when Security Council Resolution 1780 recognized both security and development as essential to long-term progress in Haiti. They also reinforced the importance of rebuilding a new police force to provide the Haitian people with security and stability. The new police force should be in place by the end of 2012, in spite of the setbacks caused by the 2010 earthquake.[39]

Latin American Participation in MINUSTAH:
State Building Revisited

What distinguishes this recent intervention in Haiti from the one in 1994 is that Latin American nations have gone beyond participation, in peace operations globally, to leading the mission in this hemisphere. The MINUSTAH military mission is headed by Brazil and includes troops from seventeen countries in the hemisphere, comprising approximately two-thirds of the total force.[40] Participation in MINUSTAH demonstrates an important shift in the way the governments of Latin America view the UN's role in peacekeeping in the Americas and how peacekeeping has emerged as an important regional state-building project.[41]

Another aspect of regional participation in Haiti is the new dynamic of civil-military cooperation that has evolved under the current UN intervention. Starting in May 2005 with a meeting in Buenos Aires, the vice ministers of foreign affairs and defense of Argentina, Brazil, Chile, and Uruguay have met to discuss ways to strengthen the regional contribution to MINUSTAH. This effort, known as the 2 × 4 process, represented an important step in civilian-military cooperation in Latin America, bringing together ministers of foreign relations and defense together to address multilateral issues of regional concern. The group expanded in August 2005 to a 2 × 7 group, adding Ecuador, Guatemala, and Peru. These nations reaffirmed their commitment to a democratic Haiti and to continued support of MINUSTAH. Finally, meeting in Lima in February 2011, the group expanded to nine countries, 2 × 9, adding Bolivia and Paraguay to the mix—all troop contributors. These countries remain central to the UN's peace operations in Haiti in support of security and development efforts.[42]

The emergence of regional defense ministerial meetings to address conditions in Haiti may also represent a transitional role of Latin American states as guarantors of regional security. Neither the United States nor Canada was included in these regional defense ministerial meetings on Haiti, a departure from the first UN intervention in 1994, when both the United States and Canada played central roles in the peace operations. Today, the leadership of Brazil, Chile, and Argentina in MINUSTAH also reflects the emergence of regional leadership in security and democracy building. This is not to say that the U.S. role in rebuilding Haiti has been eclipsed by troop-contributing countries, but it does represent a reduction in the reliance on U.S. dominance in security matters that characterized the last decade of the twentieth century. The absence of the United States from these consultations suggests a new age of regional security arrangements that look toward Latin American governments for setting a hemispheric security agenda, and that see building capable states in the Americas as the core function of foreign engagement.

The impact of the Haiti UN Mission on democratic processes in other countries throughout the region has gone far beyond the ranks of the armed forces. According to press reports from Chile, Brazil, and Bolivia, it has stimulated important and open discussion among civilian leaders about the role of the military in Latin America and the costs associated with peace-keeping.[43] Greater Latin American participation in peace operations has also given many troop-contributing countries an opportunity to serve on the new Peacebuilding Commission, which was created out of the 2005 UN Reform process.

Brazil's defense and foreign policy has made state building in Haiti a top priority, doubling the number of military officials stationed in Haiti since the earthquake. Its presence in peacekeeping missions in Haiti has increased international acknowledgment of Brazil's involvement in multi-lateral politics.

Saving Haiti: Lessons Learned

Today the Haitian state remains very fragile, in spite of elections at both the national and local levels. These participatory processes are new, and are difficult given constitutional requirements that force frequent elections in a country that can hardly sustain the government it has elected. Haiti remains the poorest country in the Western Hemisphere.[44] It has the dubi-ous distinction of being alone among states of the Western Hemisphere to have experienced a decline in per capita gross domestic product during the past forty years to roughly half to two-thirds of what it was in 1965.[45] State institutions in Haiti have never really functioned outside Port-au-Prince. The justice system, despite millions of dollars having been invested in capacity building, is still under construction. Haitian executive ministries are only now getting capable staffs and operating budgets. The security sector, reformed after the first UN intervention in 1994 when the Haitian army was demobilized and disbanded, has never been effective in providing for citizen security in spite of the new Haitian National Police force, which was created to replace the army and is still a work in progress.

Unlike earlier UN models of postconflict reconstruction that focused on maintaining security, MINUSTAH also addressed the endemic poverty and development needs that were at the root of Haiti's governance challenges. Its mandate is one of state building rather than of providing only for the security of Haitians. Before the 2010 earthquake, MINUSTAH had talked about ending the mission in 2011 when the Haitian National Police had been fully trained and had reached a goal of 11,000 officers. That goal has now been overtaken by events as the enormous rebuilding tasks of the post-earthquake environment have compelled the UN to continue its security mandate and its institutional strengthening role.[46]

The UN mission in Haiti also raises questions about exit strategies in such prolonged crises of security and governance. The earlier history of UN peace operations in the years immediately after the Cold War tended to ignore the longer-term development issues to build capacity in weak states. Recent scholarship on exit strategies confirms that UN departures should be viewed as a process, with commitments based on long-term needs of security, the rule of law, political leadership, and community development.[47] In accordance with the renewed understanding of state building, the Haitian mission focused more on maintaining security and also supporting the capacity building of the Haitian government, only exiting when stability returns.

The once-reviled UN was tolerated after its peacekeepers, in December 2006, helped to remove violent gangs that had overtaken Haiti's largest slum, Cité Soleil. This operation, done with Haitian civilian police support, marked a greater collaboration between international and local security forces. Until the earthquake, it was thought that President René Préval achieved what we could call a form of political reconciliation, power sharing, and confidence building that had eluded Haiti in the past. Elections had been scheduled for both the legislature and the presidency. But all this unraveled after January 12, 2010.

Although it is still in its early stages, there has been some real progress in engaging the business elite. This cooperation arose from an earlier natural disaster, the hurricanes of 2008. Business groups recognized that their future would require a greater commitment to working with a more modern and transparent state. It is also clear that the private sector is aware of how transnational problems—such as drug trafficking, corruption, and the concomitant criminal activity, problems that cannot be overlooked by a peacekeeping mission—can undermine business. How this affects the future of governance is still unclear because the earthquake has unleashed a new dynamic about the need for sustainable growth, something that is only possible if there are institutions and rules of the game that allow investments in Haiti to grow. Certainly after the earthquake, with the huge amount of resources destined for Haiti ($5.9 billion has been pledged for the first five years), including a greater commitment to private investment partnerships, the real test of how the private sector embraces reforms is essential for the stability of the Haitian state. This will be one of the decisive indicators of progress for the government installed in May 2011.

Epilogue

Haiti is at a crossroads. The earthquake's impact on the entire society created a giant chasm between the citizens of Haiti and their leaders. President Préval, who barely survived the disaster, failed to provide any real leadership in the days and weeks following the earthquake. As millions of Haitians were displaced, it fell to the UN, bilateral donors, and the community of nongovernmental organizations to support the state. Although the damage to the weak Haitian state was overwhelming (twenty-eight of twenty-nine ministries collapsed), there was little communication with the people.

President Préval's term, which ended in 2011, and the legislature, whose legal status ended in March 2010, became the subject of strong international debate about whether elections could be held when almost 1.3 million people lived around the capital in outlying tent cities. Although the Government of Haiti along with the UN created an International Haitian Reconstruction Commission in April 2010, headed by Prime Minister Jean-Max Bellerive and UN Special Envoy Bill Clinton, to provide a structure for governance and decisionmaking, it has to date not produced the results or demonstrated the leadership that Haitians so long for at this time.

On November 28, 2010, the UN and OAS provided technical support to the government of Haiti to hold presidential elections. President Préval was barred from reelection, but his party, UNITE, did support a candidate, Jude Celestin, who was handpicked to carry on Préval's vision. There were eighteen other candidates. After a turbulent election day, with many allegations of fraud, three candidates emerged, although only two would face a runoff. The three finalists were Mirlande Manigat, the former senator and wife of past Haitian president Leslie Manigat; Préval's candidate, Celestin; and Michel Martelly, also known as "Sweet Mickey," who had taken third place on the first vote. Although Manigat's lead was clear, the other two candidates vied for second and third place. Documented fraud and public protests led to a recount where the OAS determined that the frontrunners were actually Manigat and Martelly. A successful runoff election on March 20, 2011, led to a Martelly win. He assumed the presidency in May, but governs with a divided legislature. Nevertheless, Haitians are cautiously optimistic about the new government, for which state building will be a priority.

In the foreseeable future, Haiti will still need the UN, and the UN will need Haiti. Similarly, Haiti will also need the OAS and its friends in the hemisphere to support reform in governance. The Group of Friends, both at the UN and at the OAS, will continue to provide expert guidance along this transition. As the political scene is clarified, it will test the limits of the UN's ability to work in partnership with such a weak state. What is clear, however, is that the UN mission will remain in Haiti way beyond its envisioned exit in 2011. Haiti's long road to peace and stability, interrupted by natural disasters in 2008 and then again 2010, points to the need for rethinking how to support the citizens of Haiti in the absence of a strong institutional government. The needs of Haitians for jobs, housing, sanitation, and health care are enormous. (Just before the ill-fated elections, Haiti experienced a cholera epidemic that has killed more than 4,000 people to date and is still raging in many rural areas.)

What lies ahead for Haiti if the UN does not remain in the country may indeed be a situation where violence overtakes the nation and where any progress that had been made in creating a capable state is overturned. The best one can hope for is the greater involvement of peacekeepers from Latin America, and the internationalization of peacekeeping in Haiti. This provides a strong basis of support for sustaining the country until a political solution is found and Haiti can again begin its long climb back to the status quo ante.

Notes

1. In *Foreign Policy*'s "Failed State Index 2007," Haiti ranked 11th, between the Central African Republic and Pakistan, out of 177 countries analyzed using twelve indicators of state failure.

2. The term "state building" is used in this chapter, instead of "peace building" because it is a more accurate description of what the UN and other actors are trying to accomplish in Haiti. There is no strong consensus on the definition of peace building, let alone the best practices for achieving it. Former UN secretary-general Boutros Boutros-Ghali defined peace building expansively as "action to identify and support structures which will tend to strengthen and solidify peace in order to avoid a relapse into conflict" in his *Agenda for Peace,* but as Michael Barnett and his colleagues point out, the operational meaning of peace building varies significantly across multilateral, regional, and national agencies. See Thomas J. Biersteker, "Prospects for the UN Peacebuilding Commission," Disarmament Forum, www.unidir.org/pdf/articles-art2630/pdf.

3. Roland Paris and Timothy Sisk, "Managing Contradictions: The Inherent Dilemmas of Postwar Statebuilding," International Peace Academy, November 2007.

4. This chapter does not examine the role of the OAS in Haiti, though references to joint UN-OAS collaboration appear throughout. A separate study would be needed to document how the OAS, as a regional organization, provided an important and substantive role in the case of Haiti.

5. For a more in-depth discussion of peace processes in Latin America, see Cynthia J. Arnson, ed., *Comparative Peace Processes in Latin America* (Washington, D.C., and Stanford, Calif.: Woodrow Wilson Center Press and Stanford University Press, 1999).

6. "Play to Win: Final Report of the Bi-Partisan Commission on Post-Conflict Reconstruction," Center for Strategic and International Studies and Association of the U.S. Army, Washington, D.C., 2003. This report became the basis for the U.S. government's approach to state building. It discusses a strategic approach toward failed states, adopting the goal of enabling them to successfully rebuild following conflict.

7. Nicole Ball and Tammy Halevy, "Making Peace Work: The Role of the International Development Community," Overseas Development Council, 1996. This paper describes the work of a reconstruction as a twenty-year-plus effort, in spite of donors' attempts to only support five-year intervals.

8. For a good description of a case of where low-intensity warfare resulted in a long process of political negotiation, see Rose J. Spaulding, "From Low-Intensity War to Low-Intensity Peace: The Nicaraguan Peace Process," in *Comparative Peace Processes,* ed. Arnson, 32.

9. U.S. Department of State, "The Governor's Island Accord: Victory for Diplomacy," dispatch, July 26, 1993.

10. William Reno, "Shadow State and the Political Economy of Civil Wars" in *Greed and Grievance: Economic Agendas in Civil Wars,* edited by Mats Berdal and David M. Malone (Boulder, Colo.: Lynne Rienner, 2000). After the earthquake an emergency body, the Interim Haiti Reconstruction Commission, was created to help manage the sorting out of projects and strategies needed for rebuilding the state. The commission is codirected by the prime minister, Jean-Max Bellerive, and by UN special envoy to Haiti, former U.S. president Bill Clinton.

11. Paul Collier, "Doing Well Out of War: An Economic Perspective," in *Greed and Grievance,* ed. Berdal and Malone.

12. For a more in-depth analysis of Haitian gangs, see Henry F. Carey, "Militarization without Civil War: The Security Dilemma and Regime Consolidation in Haiti," *Civil Wars* 7, no. 4 (Winter 2005): 330–56. Carey also makes comparisons to the security sector and reform in El Salvador and Guatemala.

13. Haiti's 1987 Constitution still enforces and mandates an armed forces, despite the demobilization; see Title XI, Chapter 1, of the Constitution, http://pdba.georgetown .edu/Constitutions/Haiti/haiti1987.html. In 2012 President Martelly proposed the reinstatement of former soldiers who were demobilized in 1995.

14. The UN still believes that it will be able to reach its goal of training 10,000 to 11,000 new police, although the nation lost many police during the 2010 earthquake.

15. Johanna Mendelson Forman, "Beyond the Mountains, More Mountains: Demobilizing the Haitian Military," in *Peacemaking and Democratization in the Western Hemisphere,* edited by Tommie Sue Montgomery (Coral Gables: North-South Center Press at the University of Miami, 2000).

16. John Darby and Roger MacGinty, *Contemporary Peacemaking* (New York: Palgrave MacMillan, 2003), 1–2.

17. The International Civilian Mission in Haiti (MICIVIH) was established in February, 1993, under President Aristide, with the mandate to observe human rights in Haiti.

18. William O'Neil, "Human Rights Monitoring versus Political Expediency: The Experience of the OAS/UN Mission in Haiti," *Harvard Human Rights Journal* 8 (1995).

19. "In keeping with this holistic understanding of human security, developmental peacekeeping is defined as a post-conflict reconstruction intervention which aims to achieve sustainable levels of human security through a combination of interventions aimed at accelerating capacity building and socio-economic development which will result in the dismantling of war economies and conflict systems and replacing them with globally competitive peace economies. Developmental peacekeeping has two features, which distinguish it from current definitions of peacekeeping. The first feature, which distinguishes developmental peacekeeping from current approaches, is the focus on human security. Traditional definitions focus on the application of security and military apparatus in ensuring the security of the state, as opposed to the security of individuals and communities." Nozizwe Madlala-Routledge and Sybert Liebenberg, "Developmental Peacekeeping: What Are the Advantages for Africa?" *African Security Review* 13, no. 2 (2004).

20. For a complete list of all Security Council resolutions on Haiti, see "Haiti: UN Documents," *Security Council Report,* December 22, 2010, http://www.securitycouncil report.org/site/pp.aspz?c+gkKWLeMTIisG&b_2713083.

21. On January 19, 2010, the UN Security Council adopted Resolution 1908 to express sympathy and solidarity to those affected by the devastating January 12 earthquake and to reaffirm the previous resolutions on Haiti.

22. Jean-Paul Azam, Paul Collier, and Anke Hoeffler, "International Policies on Civil Conflict: An Economic Perspective," unpublished paper, December 14, 2001, 2.

23. See Espen Barth Eide et al., "Report on Integrated Missions: Practical Perspectives and Recommendations," Independent Study for the Expanded UN ECHA Core Group, May 2005; and Richard Gueli and Sybert Liebenberg, "The Concept of Developmental Peace Missions: Implications for the Military and Civilians," *Conflict Trends* 3. Also see United Nations Peacekeeping, http://www.un.org/Depts/dpko/dpko/faq/q1.htm.

24. Robert Perito, "Police in Peace and Stability Operations: Evolving US Policy and Practice," *International Peacekeeping* 15, no. 1 (February 2008): 55. Perito notes that the U.S.–led Haiti operation was influenced by the earlier failures of the UN peace operation in Somalia, where "mission creep" ultimately resulted in the death of U.S. military personnel.

25. Kevin C. M. Benson and Christopher B. Thrash, "Declaring Victory: Planning Exit Strategies for Peace Operations," *Parameters,* Autumn 1996, 4.

26. Sarah Kreps, "The 1994 Haiti Intervention: A Unilateral Operation in Multilateral Clothing," *Journal of Strategic Studies* 30, no. 3 (2007): 471; Benson and Thrash, "Declaring Victory," 4.

27. See Sebastian von Einstedel and David M. Malone, "Peace and Democracy for Haiti: A UN Mission Impossible," *International Relations* 20, no. 2 (2006): 160.

28. Ibid., 164.

29. See Chetan Kumar, "Sustaining Peace in War-Torn Societies: Lessons from the Haitian Experience," http://www.cissm.umd.edu/papers/files/Kumar/pdf.

30. As of 2008, MINUSTAH was the only UN Peace Operation in the Americas. There were 9,012 uniformed personnel, of which 7,082 were soldiers, 1,930 were police, and another 500 were international civilians.

31. Marc Lacey, "Occupation Army (?): Haitian President Shifts to UN in Fighting Gangs," *International Herald Tribune,* February 10, 2007.

32. The MINUSTAH military mission is headed by Brazil and includes troops from fifteen countries in the hemisphere, comprising approximately two-thirds of the total force. Participation in MINUSTAH demonstrates an important shift in the way the governments of Latin America view the UN role in peacekeeping and the way peacekeeping has emerged as an important mission for the region's armed forces.

33. Few thought that Préval would be ousted, like so many other elected Haitian leaders have been, before his term ended in 2011. He became the only leader to win a democratic election, serve a full term, and peacefully hand over power when he first served as president from 1996 through 2001. But underscoring the fragility of his government, national security commission head Patrick Elie said Préval could easily have been toppled by protesters who sought to storm the national palace in May 2008. The only thing preventing that was the UN peacekeeping force, said Elie; Reuters, November 2011.

34. See Dominik Zaum, "The Norms and Politics of Exit: Ending Postconflict Transitional Administrations," *Ethics and International Affairs* 23, no. 2 (2009): 189–208.

35. William Durch, "Exit Strategies and Peacekeeping," paper presented at "Exit Strategies and Peace Consolidation," a conference at Robert Schuman Center, a project of the Center for International Studies of the University of Oxford, European University Institute, Florence, November 30, 2007.

36. Paul Collier, "Haiti: From Natural Catastrophe to Economic Security," Report for the Secretary General of the United Nations, Department of Economics, Oxford University, January 2009, available at http://www.focal.ca/pdf/haitcollier.

37. For the best in-depth study of the Friends process, see Teresa Whitfield, *Friends Indeed?* (Washington, D.C.: U.S. Institute of Peace, 2007), and specifically her chapter on Haiti, 105–34.

38. Ibid., 279, 281.

39. Organization of American States, Press Release E-203/01, http://www.oas.org/OASpage/press2002/en/press2001/october01/203.htm.

40. Of the eighteen peace operations of the United Nations, Latin American nations participate in fourteen.

41. Susanne Gratius, *Brazil in the Americas: A Regional Peacebroker?* Working Paper 35 (Madrid: Fundación para las Relaciones Internacionales y el Diálogo Exterior, 2007), 19–20.

42. Reuniones Ministeriales, RESDAL, http://www.resdal.org/haiti/haiti-crisis-reuniones-up.html.

43. A 1995 study on Latin American contributions to peace operations, based on interviews done with Chilean and Argentine soldiers, revealed an important impact on the individuals who had served in foreign missions. These soldiers learned new skills through participation in international missions. They also gained a broader worldview by experiencing different cultures and challenges of other nations far away from home. And participation in these international peacekeeping forces engaged Latin American soldiers in a more modern form of civil-military relations working through a UN chain of command in the field. Antonio Pala, "The Increased Role of Latin American Armed Forces in UN Peacekeeping: Opportunities and Challenges," *Airpower Journal,* Special Edition, 1995.

44. United Nations Development Program, *Human Development Report 2007: Climate Change and Human Development—Rising to the Challenge* (New York: Palgrave Macmillan, 2008). Nicaragua, another country that did not have a written peace accord, is the second-poorest country in the region.

45. Institut Haitien de Statistique et d'Informatique, 2005, 19.

46. Paris and Sisk, "Managing Contradictions."

47. See Zaum, "Norms and Politics of Exit."

Chapter 10

Europe's Role in Fostering Peace in Central America and Colombia

Markus Schultze-Kraft

This chapter presents a comparative analysis of Europe's role as an external actor in the peace process in Central America in the 1980s and its contribution, during the past decade, to efforts to end the long-standing internal armed conflict in Colombia. Because neither Central America nor Colombia has ever been a geopolitical or economic priority for European countries and because both are clearly within the U.S. sphere of influence, it seeks to explain how and why Europe nonetheless assumed a role in encouraging peace on the Central American isthmus and helping to overcome the conflict in Colombia.

The views expressed in this chapter do not necessarily reflect those of the Institute of Development Studies at the University of Sussex, with which the author is affiliated. The author wishes to thank Cynthia Arnson, Julia Gorricho, Wolf Grabendorff, Adrianus Koetsenruijter, and two anonymous reviewers for their valuable comments on earlier drafts of the chapter. Of course, he is solely responsible for any errors or faults of interpretation the reader might encounter.

In Central America in the 1980s, a number of Western European states—in particular France, Spain, and West Germany—and the European Economic Community (EEC) became involved in supporting a political settlement of the antiregime wars in Nicaragua, El Salvador, and Guatemala, primarily because of domestic security considerations in the Cold War setting. Faced with President Ronald Reagan's hard-line policy toward the Sandinista regime in Nicaragua, which they did not share, Europeans were apprehensive about the negative impact of the Central American crisis on East-West and North-South relations. Increasing Cuban and Soviet involvement in Central America in reaction to Reagan's policy of propping up the counterrevolutionary contras in Nicaragua and the government armed forces in El Salvador made European governments and the EEC acutely aware of the dangers this policy could eventually entail for their own security. Particularly in the West German administrations of Helmut Schmidt and Helmut Kohl, there was a perception—in hindsight perhaps somewhat exaggerated—that an invasion of Sandinista Nicaragua by the United States could seriously shake Western Europe's security architecture and even trigger a military response by the Soviet Union and its allies in the heart of Europe.[1]

However, seeking not to unduly antagonize the United States,[2] the peace engagement in Central America of, first, a number of socialist or social democratic and then Christian democratic governments took the form of low-key diplomacy; support for regional peace initiatives, especially the Contadora group but then also the Central American peace plan (Esquipulas II); political backing of the UN's mediation efforts; and assistance in strengthening the region's emerging democratic regimes and overcoming pervasive social injustice. This reflected the European conviction that the conflicts could only be ended through political means and the eradication of their political and socioeconomic roots. Arguably, Europe's engagement proved to be surprisingly effective as it helped prevent an escalation and prolongation of the antiregime wars, pave the way for their political settlement, and reduce the threat of Soviet military action against Western Europe. It also prompted Europe as a bloc—for the first time since the 1950s—to take a markedly different stance on an international policy issue than the United States.

Since the late 1990s, European peace engagement in Colombia has followed a comparable approach to that in Central America, though it has been broader and institutionally more structured and, in the post–Cold War setting, has not been driven by security concerns. From 1999 to 2002, a number of European countries actively engaged in the ultimately unsuccessful peace negotiations between the government of Andrés Pastrana (1998–2002) and the Revolutionary Armed Forces of Colombia (Fuerzas Armadas Revolucionarias de Colombia, FARC), the country's largest insurgent organization. As on the isthmus, this involvement was based on the premise that the Colombian conflict has deep political and socioeconomic roots and can only be resolved politically. It also grew out of European disagreement with Plan Colombia—a multi-billion-dollar aid strategy for Colombia devised by presidents Bill Clinton and Pastrana that ultimately focused heavily on military measures to fight the insurgents and drug trafficking.

Prompted by Plan Colombia, the European Union developed its "own" Colombia policy. This policy of European engagement in Colombia, which differs in many ways from the U.S. approach, focuses on helping to alleviate the armed conflict's impact on the humanitarian and human rights situation; strengthening Colombia's state institutions; and encouraging development, reconciliation, and the building of peaceful conflict resolution mechanisms at the local and regional levels. However, Europe neither seeks to build a counterweight to U.S. policy nor openly opposes it. Within the framework of the Group of Twenty-Four, which includes the United States, European countries have also been involved in promoting dialogue between, on the one hand, the right-wing and U.S.-aligned government of Álvaro Uribe (2002–10) and the Colombian state institutions, and, on the other, the country's vibrant civil society and human rights organizations. This effort continued during the government of Juan Manuel Santos (2010–).

This engagement shows that since the days of the EEC in the 1980s, European integration has progressed to include twenty-seven member states, making the EU a more powerful actor on the international scene that likes to portray itself as a "global actor" and "civilian power."[3] Although the bloc has clearly gained in institutional strength and economic weight, the EU's expansion has also taken its toll on the internal political cohesion of the bloc, epitomized by the failure in the mid-2000s to adopt a Constitution for Europe. In consequence, Europe continues to be a long way from speaking with a single voice in international affairs, and its interventions to help end armed conflicts abroad are consequently still limited.[4] This is as true for Colombia as for other world regions where Europe does not have priority security, economic, or other interests.

Peace has thus far been elusive in Colombia, despite Plan Colombia, the Uribe administration's "democratic security policy," and Europe's broad peace support policy. Comparing its engagement in Central America and

Colombia shows that Europe has rather consistently given priority to political conflict resolution approaches. Whereas its intervention on the isthmus was above all prompted by deep concern for its own security in the Cold War, in the more intractable conflict setting of Colombia, the European contribution has been financially and institutionally more solid but politically also less committed, and hence comparatively less effective.

Central America

The antiregime wars in El Salvador, Guatemala, and Nicaragua unfolded during the last stage of the Cold War.[5] All three were ended through an interplay between political and military factors after the fall of the Berlin Wall in November 1989. With the election, in February 1990, of Violeta Chamorro, the candidate of the center-right National Opposition Union (Unión Nacional Opositora), and the signing of the "Transition Protocol" with the outgoing Sandinista administration,[6] Nicaragua was the first of the war-torn countries to demobilize its irregular force, the Nicaraguan Resistance (Resistencia Nicaragüense, the "contras"), and implement a far-reaching military reform. The Salvadoran peace accords, brokered in less than two years with UN mediation between the government of Alfredo Cristiani of the right-wing Nationalist Republican Alliance (Alianza Republicana Nacionalista) and the insurgent Farabundo Martí National Liberation Front (Frente Farabundo Martí para la Liberación Nacional), followed in January 1992.[7] In December 1996, President Álvaro Arzú of the rightist National Advancement Party (Partido de Avanzada Nacional, PAN) and the Guatemalan National Revolutionary Unity (Unidad Revolucionaria Nacional Guatemalteca, URNG) signed a final peace agreement after eight years of intermittent and partially UN-mediated negotiations under four consecutive governments.[8] The UN monitored the polls and the contra demobilization in Nicaragua, and large UN human rights observation and peacekeeping missions were deployed to both El Salvador and Guatemala before the signing of the peace accords, accompanying their implementation during the years after the wars had ended.[9]

In a nutshell, Central America's pacification was the outcome of a combination of military struggle and political negotiations between the armed contenders in the three countries. But, in the final stage of the Cold War, it was clearly also influenced by outside actors. These included the Contadora group,[10] the Cuban government under Fidel Castro, which under increasing pressure owing to the structural political and economic changes in the Soviet Union started withdrawing its support for Sandinista Nicaragua toward the end of the 1980s,[11] along with the UN and, ultimately, the United States. By all accounts, ending the antiregime wars on the Central American isthmus was a remarkable achievement considering the ideological divides between the warring parties, the ferocity of the conflicts and their deep political and socioeconomic roots, and the high stakes of external powers in the Cold War setting.

Hard-Line U.S. Policy and the Socialist Response from Western Europe

Following the ousting of the dictator Anastasio Somoza in 1979 and the establishment of the Sandinista regime in Nicaragua, the U.S. administration of Jimmy Carter, which had attempted anything short of large-scale military aid for the National Guard to keep the Sandinista National Liberation Front (Frente Sandinista de Liberación Nacional, FSLN) out of power, changed course and began pursuing a policy of moderation vis-à-vis Managua.[12] Despite substantial development and humanitarian and some military assistance for the Sandinistas from Havana as well as economic, technical, and food aid from Moscow, Washington was careful not to repeat the "errors of 1959–1960 when U.S. hostility drove the Cuban Revolution into alliance with the Soviet Union."[13] The main goal of U.S. policy in the early days of the revolution was to avoid the radicalization of the Sandinista regime and to restrain Nicaraguan support for the insurgent FMLN in El Salvador.

This situation changed dramatically when Ronald Reagan took office in January 1981.[14] Using as a pretext intelligence reports on Nicaraguan arms flows to the Salvadoran guerrillas, which were strongly criticized in the U.S. press and by academics for being inaccurate and exaggerated,[15] Reagan adopted a hard-line foreign policy toward the Sandinistas. In this endeavor, he unsuccessfully sought support from U.S. Western European allies, and eventually "unleashed the CIA-supported contras [Nicaraguan counterrevolutionaries]."[16] Faced with the FMLN's "final," if unsuccessful, offensive in 1981, the United States also began channeling large sums of military assistance to the government armed forces in El Salvador, tarnished by serious human rights abuses, to contain the "spread of Communism" on the isthmus. Cuba and the Soviet Union and its allies, in turn, started providing Managua with the means to build up the highly effective Popular Sandinista Army (Ejército Popular Sandinista). "During 1981–82," write Theodore Schwab and Harold Sims, "USSR military involvement expanded considerably. . . . Soviet vessels brought 10,000 tons of armament each year, including tanks, antiaircraft guns, armored cars, artillery, and other ordnance. . . . During 1983, Soviet military aid increased dramatically, as arms shipments doubled, reaching 20,000 tons per year."[17] The stage was set for the contra war, which lasted throughout the 1980s, devastated Nicaragua, and had strong repercussions for El Salvador's conflict and, to a lesser degree, in Guatemala.

In Western Europe, many had greeted the Sandinista revolution enthusiastically, perceiving it "to represent the dawning of a new epoch in Latin American and Third World politics in general."[18] On the left, there was still deep disillusionment over the 1973 putsch against the socialist President Salvador Allende in Chile,[19] and the most outspoken political support for the Sandinistas came from the Socialist International, trade unions, and university student committees. Adopting a markedly different stance than the Reagan administration, the socialist or social democratic governments of France (François Mitterrand, 1981–95), West Germany (Helmut Schmidt, 1974–82), and Spain (Felipe González, 1982–96) but also of smaller European countries, such as Austria (Bruno Kreisky, 1970–83) and Sweden (Olof Palme, 1982–86), emphasized the internal socioeconomic and political causes of the Nicaraguan revolution and the antiregime wars in El Salvador and Guatemala. They maintained that any solution to the crisis had to be political. Accordingly, these governments focused mostly on helping to overcome deeply rooted social injustice and promote inclusive, pluralist, and democratic political regimes as a means to end the conflicts. This strategy had its roots in the deep concern of Western European decisionmakers, especially in Bonn, for the security of the continent in the Cold War setting.[20] In consequence, it aimed at preventing Nicaragua from moving toward the Soviet and Cuban camps and supported the Sandinistas' early adhesion to nonalignment as part of the attempt to reduce the threat of Soviet military action in Europe—perceived to be real—in response to Washington's hard-line policy of containing the "spread of Communism" in Latin America.

Though Europe's Christian Democratic parties were more inclined to share the perception dominant in the United States and tended to stress more the role of outside socialist or Communist actors in the Central American crisis, the German Christian Democratic Union, for example, as well as the Christian Democratic World Union coincided with their socialist and social democratic counterparts in the interpretation that the Central American crisis was predominantly rooted in structural internal problems.

Furthermore, in the early 1980s several European "Christian and Social Democratic parties [had] had close contacts in Central America for more than a decade so some European politicians were stunned when the United States failed to use these channels but instead asked West Europeans to support a policy they [found] hardly convincing—and only after the policy had already been established."[21]

Torn between not wanting to jeopardize the transatlantic alliance with the United States while at the same time not supporting its hard-line policies and aiming at strengthening internal democratic structures in Central America, the socialist and social democratic governments of the larger Western European countries fell short of devising an integrated policy vis-à-vis Central America but, ultimately, helped prevent the further deterioration of the political and military situation on the isthmus. France under Mitterrand was most outspokenly critical of Reagan's policy. "A key political signal from Europe," writes Blanca Antonini, a former official of the UN mission in El Salvador, "came from the joint declaration issued in August 1981 by France and Mexico on El Salvador. With strong backing from the Socialist International, the declaration recognized the FMLN-FDR, [an alliance formed by] the armed rebels and its moderate [democratic] allies, . . . as legitimate political interlocutors. The declaration called for negotiations with the insurgents and [the] restructuring of the government and the army."[22] In another act of defiance of U.S. policy toward Central America, in 1983 Mitterrand sent a shipload of weapons to Nicaragua. In the final analysis, however, French support was insufficient in light of the Sandinistas' needs and failed to prevent Nicaragua from moving closer to the Cuban/Soviet camp and the antiregime wars on the isthmus taking their course.

The administrations of Schmidt and González, in turn, were more cautious. Although they shared the view that the Central American crisis had structural internal causes and ultimately could only be resolved by political means, they avoided criticizing Washington openly because both countries were politically and strategically more dependent on the United States. Until 1982, when Chancellor Helmut Kohl of the Christian Democratic Union took office and West German aid to Nicaragua was temporarily wound down in line with British Prime Minister Margaret Thatcher's policy of not intervening in matters and world regions where the United States was dominant, Bonn preferred low-key diplomacy and provided assistance through multilateral or political party channels.[23] Spain, which was still emerging from its democratic transition, was economically weak, and had other foreign policy priorities, such as entering the EEC and the North Atlantic Treaty Organization (NATO). Although not hiding its disagreements with United States about policy toward Central America, the González government resolved not to push any Spanish initiatives unilaterally but to support, after its foundation in 1983, the Contadora group.[24]

Christian Democratic Governments in Central America, Regional Peace Initiatives, and the EEC

The election of Christian Democratic governments in El Salvador and Guatemala in 1984 and 1986, respectively, prompted European Christian Democratic parties to increase political and financial assistance for Central America. The German Konrad Adenauer Foundation, for example, established close ties with the governments of José Napoleón Duarte (1984–88) in El Salvador and Vinicio Cerezo (1986–90) in Guatemala, and helped establish the influential think tank Instituto Centroamericano de Estudios Políticos in Guatemala.[25] By 1984, at the height of the antiregime wars that had not been contained either by Reagan's hard-line policy or by the "soft" intervention of several European countries, the EEC also began to make an appearance on the Central American scene.

The often-espoused argument that the European bloc's involvement in Central America was prompted by its "wish to play a role in the safeguarding of international peace and to differentiate its foreign policy from that of the United States" is certainly in part true.[26] In the 1980s, the EEC expanded to twelve member states, incorporating Greece in 1981 and Spain and Portugal in 1986, and began to show the first signs of intending to assume the role of a "civilian power" in international politics. This is reflected, for instance, in the European Council's 1983 Stuttgart declaration on European union.[27] However, in the 1980s Europe as a bloc was still a fledgling international player and its geopolitical priorities were centered mostly on the continent itself and its immediate neighborhood. Its peace involvement in Central America, therefore, must have come as a surprise to many, not least in the United States. Although this resoluteness of the European stance on the Central American isthmus—unknown since the beginning of European integration in the 1950s—arguably contributed to making Reagan shelve his plan to invade Sandinista Nicaragua, it was primarily propelled by domestic, in particular West German, Cold War security concerns; did not aim at building a "counterweight to the traditional influence of the United States in the region";[28] and never had the reach and political and economic weight to justify the plain interpretation that Europe's engagement was a "success story."[29]

In 1984, the EEC launched the "San José dialogue," which helped bring together the Central American governments and the members of the Contadora group, initially integrated by Colombia, Mexico, Panama, and Venezuela and later joined by Argentina, Brazil, Peru, and Uruguay. The Contadora group had been formed in 1983 and dovetailed with European policy toward the isthmus because it aimed at providing Latin American political support for a negotiated solution to the crisis on the isthmus. Having been opposed by Washington, it was ultimately superseded by the 1987 Central American peace plan designed by presidents Oscar Arias of Costa Rica and Vinicio Cerezo of Guatemala, known as Esquipulas II, which focused on national reconciliation, democratization, and free elections, and thereby helped lay the foundations for the end of the contra war in Nicaragua, the transition from Sandinista rule to the Chamorro government, and the peace negotiations in El Salvador and Guatemala. The San José dialogue provided a "forum for debating issues of interest to the region and acted as a sounding board for Europeans,"[30] lending international legitimacy to the regional peace initiative that was kept alive in the midst of full-out war. It also gave it some additional room to maneuver when the hard-line policy of the Reagan administration, mired in the Iran-Contra scandal and faced with increasing domestic criticism, began to crumble.[31]

The End of the Central American Crisis and European Support
for Postconflict Reconstruction

In the final analysis, peace in Central America was achieved through political negotiations between the governments of Nicaragua, El Salvador, and Guatemala and the contending irregular forces on the basis of Esquipulas II.[32] At the request of the parties, the UN secretary-general played an important role as mediator in the negotiations in El Salvador and Guatemala, as well as in the verification of the 1990 general elections in Nicaragua and the implementation of the peace accords.[33] Europe accompanied this process, not least through the involvement of the new EEC member, Spain, as part of UN secretaries-general Javier Pérez de Cuéllar's and Boutros Boutros-Ghali's "groups of friends" in El Salvador and Guatemala;[34] and by deploying police personnel under the UN umbrella, above all from Spain. However, a major shift in the correlation of forces in favor of negotiated settlements of the conflicts originated in the change of government in

Washington, with President George H. W. Bush abandoning his predecessor's policy of propping up irregular forces in Nicaragua and the inefficient and illegitimate armed forces in El Salvador. Under pressure from Congress and with the end of the Cold War approaching, the White House was compelled to pay more attention to the Salvadoran army's abysmal human rights record, epitomized by the killing of six Jesuit priests on the campus of the Central American University in 1989, and end funding the contras.

Although a secondary player in the final settling of the antiregime wars in Central America, Europe assumed an important role in postconflict reconstruction during the 1990s. The region's share in EU bilateral official development assistance more than doubled between 1991 and 1996, increasing from 18 percent to almost 40 percent.[35] In 1996, Germany made a large aid contribution to Nicaragua, and in 1999 the EEC announced a five-year, $210 million aid plan for the reconstruction of Central America.[36] The reasons behind this European reconstruction engagement are reflected in the analysis of a former Dutch ambassador to Costa Rica: "The real work actually only began when peace agreements were signed. Peaceful conditions had to be kept alive and people had to be helped to get over the consequences of war. Often great effort had to be put into laying the foundations of societies so that conflict would not reerupt."[37]

Colombia

Despite numerous and, at times, prolonged negotiation efforts undertaken by six consecutive governments since the early 1980s—which produced the successful demobilization of several smaller guerrilla groups in the early 1990s and the disbanding of the paramilitary United Self-Defense Forces of Colombia (Autodefensas Unidas de Colombia, AUC) during President Álvaro Uribe's first term (2002–6)—peace has thus far been an elusive goal in Colombia.[38] In 2010, after the ultimately failed talks with the FARC under President Andrés Pastrana (1998–2002) and eight years of "democratic security policy," Uribe's flagship strategy of regaining control of large swaths of territory, protecting infrastructure and expanding the presence of the state, Colombia's largest insurgent organization continued to pose a not small security challenge for the new government of President Juan Manuel Santos.[39] In addition, the talks with the smaller National Liberation Army (Ejército de Liberación Nacional, ELN), which were held from late 2005 through to the end of 2007, failed to produce agreement on a cease-fire and negotiation agenda. New armed groups and paramilitary successor organizations with strong links to drug-trafficking networks and organized crime began emerging in several parts of the country in the later stages of the demobilization of the AUC, which was officially ended in mid-2006.[40]

With some notable exceptions, such as the facilitation and mediation efforts of UN Secretary-General Kofi Annan and a number of European and Latin American countries during the peace process with the FARC, the challenge of crafting peace has basically been assumed by the Colombians themselves. Since the mid-1990s, external actors have come to play a progressively more important support role in Colombia—the United States has been focusing on strengthening the government armed forces and fighting drug production and trafficking; and Europe, Canada, and some Latin American countries have been accompanying peace efforts and providing development and humanitarian assistance. Yet external political commitment to ending the internal armed conflict has been less pronounced than was the case in Central America.

European peace engagement in Colombia since the 1980s can roughly be divided into three, qualitatively distinct phases. From the mid-1980s to the mid-1990s, it was limited to incipient support by some European governments for the counternarcotics efforts of the administration of Virgilio Barco (1986–90), which was followed by broader economic and technical cooperation agreements signed during the governments of César Gaviria (1990–94) and Ernesto Samper (1994–98).[41] At the end of the latter's government, Germany and the German Catholic Church along with Spain played a role in facilitating ultimately unsuccessful talks with the ELN.[42] Increasing violence in the country and the associated humanitarian crisis, reflected above all in rapidly growing numbers of internally displaced persons, and human rights violations also prompted the EU to provide more aid to Colombia.

With the launch of the peace process with the FARC under Pastrana in early 1999, Europe started assuming a more prominent, strictly peace-related role, which lasted until the breakdown of the negotiations in February 2002. During this second phase, several European states actively accompanied the peace talks with the insurgents in the demilitarized zone (DMZ) in the south of Colombia. Confronted with Plan Colombia, a multi-billion-dollar U.S.-Colombian strategy to end the conflict and drug trafficking devised under presidents Bill Clinton and Andrés Pastrana, the EU was prompted to develop its "own" peace policy toward Colombia, in many ways different from the U.S. approach.

The third phase of European peace engagement in Colombia has been under way since President Álvaro Uribe took office in August 2002. After overcoming the frustration with the failure of the peace talks with the FARC and smoothing over initial tensions with the new, strongly U.S.-aligned Colombian government, mostly over human rights and drug policy issues, this phase has been characterized by the continuation of the EU's peace support strategy, in particular implementation of the "peace laboratories," and only limited support for government-ELN talks in Cuba and the demobilization and reinsertion of the paramilitary AUC. In addition, the EU and its member states started participating in the Group of Twenty-Four, a novel forum for coordinating international support for Colombia and enhancing dialogue between, on the one hand, the Colombian government and state institutions, and, on the other hand, civil society that grew out of a 2003 Uribe administration initiative supported by British prime minister Tony Blair.

Supporting the Peace Talks with the FARC, Disagreement with Plan Colombia, and the EU's Alternative Colombia Policy

When President Andrés Pastrana took office in August 1998, his main goal was to reach a peace agreement with the FARC. To this end, he established a vast DMZ, the *zona de despeje*,[43] encompassing five municipalities in the south of Colombia, as had been requested by the insurgents. The talks in the DMZ had a bad start when FARC commander Manuel Marulanda did not show up at the inauguration ceremony in January 1999, allegedly because of concerns for his security, and never reached the stage of substantive and structured negotiations. Arguably, the government ill-judged the FARC's disposition, or rather lack thereof, to reach an agreement and entered the process without sufficient prior preparation and clarity as to its negotiation strategy. The insurgents, in turn, perceived the talks as a unique opportunity to gain domestic and international visibility and political status, and used the DMZ as a platform to strengthen their military capability and financial base through drug trafficking and kidnapping. Aside from the fallout of the continued armed struggle and the atrocities committed by the insurgents throughout the process, it was the FARC's steady request to the Pastrana administration to take tough action against the paramilitaries, which did not occur, that time and again stopped the parties from moving toward substantive negotiations.

These difficulties notwithstanding, outside actors saw the peace initiative as a real opportunity for Colombia and were eager to contribute to it. This was particularly the case for the UN and several European and Latin American countries. The Clinton administration first voiced support for the negotiations and, in December 1998, even sent a State Department delegation to Costa Rica to establish contact with FARC envoys. However, after the guerrillas' murder of three American citizens in early 1999, it began focusing on Plan Colombia. In December 1999, UN secretary-general Annan appointed the Norwegian diplomat Jan Egeland as his "special adviser for international assistance to Colombia." Upon the initiative of Egeland, who was struggling with a mandate all too unspecific to allow him to efficiently assume the role of facilitator between the parties and in his search for building bridges was interested in taking the "guerrillas out of the jungle into the modern world,"[44] in 2000 several European governments provided assistance in the visit of a FARC delegation to the continent. Both EU and non-EU ambassadors (those of Norway and Switzerland) formed part of a group of facilitating countries of the peace talks established in April 2001 and frequently visited the DMZ.[45] The UN and several European and Latin American countries shared the premises that "there was no purely military solution to the Colombian conflict; that the peace process initiated by the Pastrana government, while imperfect, warranted diplomatic and political, as well as financial, support; and that the depth of the humanitarian crisis and the extent of suffering inflicted on the civilian population as a result of the conflict demanded a response from the international community."[46]

After the talks had come to a complete standstill and Pastrana threatened with ending the peace process in January 2002, the ambassadors of several countries, among them EU members France, Italy, Spain, and Sweden as well as non-EU Switzerland and Norway, and James LeMoyne, who had replaced Egeland, engaged in a last-minute attempt to save it.[47] The FARC accepted the presence of LeMoyne and the ambassadors during six days of intense talks between the parties, and an agreement on the continuation of talks was achieved.[48] One month later, in the midst of a FARC military offensive geared at strengthening the insurgents' position at the negotiation table, a guerrilla commando hijacked a commercial airplane and abducted Senator Eduardo Gechem, who was among the passengers. That same day, President Pastrana gave an angry speech on national television and declared the end of the peace process, holding FARC commander Marulanda personally responsible for the failure.[49]

European participation in Pastrana's peace initiative has to be seen in relation to disagreement with Plan Colombia, which spurred what since

2000 has evolved to become Europe's "own" broad peace support policy toward Colombia. As mentioned above, opposition to the joint U.S.-Colombian plan, a multi-billion-dollar strategy devised under presidents Clinton and Pastrana that originally included a broad spectrum of measures to remedy the weaknesses of the Colombian state and fight poverty and drug trafficking but soon was focused heavily on military and counterdrug measures, became manifest as early as July 2000 during the first of three consecutive international donor conferences in Madrid, followed by meetings in Bogotá in October 2000 and Brussels in April 2001. According to the Colombian political scientist Socorro Ramírez, "for high-ranking European officials Plan Colombia was an unacceptable improvisation. Although the Colombian government wished that [the plan] would be medium to long-term and announced it as a strategic state project geared at correcting structural imbalances, initially it conceived it only for one year. [Plan Colombia] had not been approved by [Colombia's] State Council [Consejo de Estado], nor was it based on consensus with the different political sectors and the [Colombian] Congress. It did not form part of the National Development Plan [Plan de Desarrollo Nacional]."[50]

The European Parliament adopted a critical stance vis-à-vis Plan Colombia, which in 2001 translated into the blocking of the disbursement of $320 million in EU aid for Colombia, but both the European Commission and the Council of Ministers, although divided over the issue, generally looked at it more favorably, showing in particular an inclination to support the plan's social components. On the eve of the international donor conference in Brussels, EU external relations commissioner Chris Patten wrote: "The international community has given indications of its readiness to show solidarity with the Colombian people. Europe—from its standpoint as an area of peace, stability, and economic growth—also wishes to show its great concern with Colombia."[51] With the exception of the Spanish government of José María Aznar, the EU member states generally did by no means think highly of the plan.[52] In consequence, the Pastrana administration failed to obtain the expected substantial financial commitment from Europe, $1 billion for social and economic programs. Ultimately, only $366 million were raised between the EU and individual member states, with Spain with $100 million on top.[53]

A corollary of this struggle over Plan Colombia was that the EU, faithful to its claim of being a global actor, found itself prompted to design a different strategy toward Colombia. A Colombia country strategy paper for the period 2000–2006 was drawn up, and $110 million in aid was approved in addition to nonprogrammed humanitarian aid.[54] The EU assigned priority to "the promotion and defense of human rights, the reduction of socio-economic disparities and institution building."[55] Its flagship peace support intervention in Colombia during this period would be the peace laboratories, an aid program aimed at tackling the socioeconomic root causes of the conflict and building a "culture of peace from below" by strengthening communities and local and regional institutions, improving democratic governance, and encouraging peaceful conflict resolution.[56] Announced in October 2000, the first peace laboratory was launched in the Middle Magdalena Valley on March 25, 2002, five days after the breakdown of negotiations between Pastrana and the FARC. A second one was approved in late 2003 and a third one in March 2006.[57] The funds allocated to the three peace laboratories for the period 2000–2012 add up to roughly $120 million, in addition to some $270 million in EU humanitarian aid, in particular for internally displaced persons, and other peace and reconciliation efforts, including for human rights protection, that were disbursed from 2001 through to 2006.[58]

Coming to Terms with the Uribe Administration, the Group of Twenty-Four, and Low-Key Peace Diplomacy

The breakdown of the peace negotiations with the FARC and Álvaro Uribe's taking office in August 2002 dealt a blow to the idea that well-meaning peace diplomacy of a heterogeneous and large group of European and other actors, including the UN special envoy, could help achieve tangible results.[59] Particularly, because the FARC had shown a patent unwillingness to engage seriously in peace negotiations, but also because the space for such initiatives was reduced proportionally to the ever closer relations between Colombia and the United States under Uribe, as epitomized by Plan Colombia and a shared emphasis on "hard" counterinsurgency and counterdrugs measures.[60] After the September 11, 2001, terrorist attacks on the United States, and the U.S. Congress's approval to use Plan Colombia funds also for fighting Colombia's illegal armed groups, deeply involved in drug trafficking, the thrust of Washington's "war on terrorism" discourse and policy was systematically adopted by Colombian policymakers.

In Europe, the impact on world politics of 9/11 translated into the EU's decision to put, first, the AUC and the FARC (May and June 2002) and then the ELN (April 2004) on its newly established list of terrorist organizations. Although this was part of European recognition of the substantially changed world political setting after the terrorist attacks, a consensus on the issue was not achieved easily within the EU.[61] It also did not mean that Europe was prepared to enroll fully in Washington's and Bogotá's war on "narco-terrorism" in Colombia. Europe's "own" peace strategy toward Colombia was designed as an alternative course of action to U.S.-Colombian policy and has been followed by the EU and its member states since 2002.

Between December 2002 and November 2007, the European Council issued five conclusions expressing tacit support for the Uribe administration's policies.[62] In the beginning, it approved of Uribe's efforts to "reform the country's institutions and develop a fully functioning democratic state throughout the territory of Colombia, based on the respect for human rights and the welfare and security of all citizens."[63] Solidarity with Colombia's fight against terrorism and drug trafficking was also expressed. Following the international donor conferences held in London (July 2003) and Cartagena (February 2005),[64] the council acknowledged the "reduction in overall numbers of murders and kidnappings in Colombia" but also underscored the "need to respect the rule of law, international humanitarian law, and international human rights instruments to which Colombia has subscribed."[65]

Reacting to the negotiations between the Uribe administration and the paramilitary AUC, which unfolded from mid-2003 through to mid-2006, and the lack of a government rapprochement with the insurgent FARC and ELN, the Council began to call for a "comprehensive peace strategy," a "legal framework for the process of disarmament, demobilization, and reintegration [DDR] of the illegal armed groups," and a "humanitarian agreement."[66] Though the paramilitaries' constant violation of the unilaterally declared cease-fire was condemned, the government-AUC negotiations were cautiously welcomed, as was the Colombian Congress's passing of the Justice and Peace law (Law 975 of 2005, JPL) in June 2005, which was greeted as "a significant development, because it provides an overall legal framework for DDR in Colombia."[67] In November 2007, the Council reiterated its support for the JPL and acknowledged the steps taken by the Uribe administration to implement it "in a transparent and effective manner."[68]

Although this evolution in the EU Council's stance vis-à-vis Colombia reflected some political support for the Uribe administration, which, however, was not equally shared by all member states, it also showed growing insistence on the respect for international law, the importance of the UN's role in Colombia—in particular its Human Rights Office— and the primacy of a comprehensive negotiated solution to the conflict.

As mentioned above, during this period substantial European energies and resources, including those of the expanded and, at the time, more active and visible European Commission delegation in Bogotá, were channeled into the peace laboratories and other, more indirect peace support activities. Among these were bilateral programs of several EU member states geared at strengthening Colombian state institutions—including the justice system and the police—and civil society and human rights organizations, as well as support for fighting drug trafficking.

Active participation in the Group of Twenty-Four (G-24), also known as the "London-Cartagena process," has permitted the EU and its member states to regularly exchange information on their policies with other international actors, including the United States, contribute to strengthening dialogue between the Colombian government and state institutions, on one hand, and civil society on the other, and smooth over relations with the Uribe administration. The G-24 was formed after the July 2003 international conference in London, which had been called for by President Uribe and first was conceived as a Colombia donor meeting. It met with the support of the Colombian president's allies, British prime minister Tony Blair and U.S. president George W. Bush,[69] who at that moment were compelled to deal with the deep divide that had opened up over the Iraq war between the United States and the United Kingdom, on one hand, and several European states, in particular France and Germany, on the other. Reportedly upon U.S. instigation, Blair seized the opportunity presented by Uribe to make London the seat of a meeting with the purpose of contributing to peace in Colombia through enhanced cooperation between the EU and its member states, the United States, and several other countries and international organizations.[70] Through this move the British and U.S. governments hoped to defuse transatlantic tensions and reward the Uribe administration, which had supported the allied invasion of Iraq.

The group was originally integrated by twenty-four states—all fifteen EU members in addition to Argentina, Brazil, Canada, Chile, Japan, Mexico, Norway, Switzerland, and the United States—and the Inter-American Development Bank and the World Bank. The United Nations Development Program in Bogotá assumed the role of secretariat. With the EU's eastward enlargement and the incorporation of twelve new member states, the G-24 today theoretically agglomerates thirty-six states. In practice, however, only a dozen EU countries, those with a diplomatic representation in Colombia, participate in the meetings on a regular basis.[71] Bringing together the Colombian government and civil society and the international community, the group has fostered a tripartite dialogue focused on six thematic blocs: strengthening of the rule of law and human rights protection, alternative development, reinsertion of demobilized members of irregular armed groups, regional peace and development initiatives, and forests and the natural environment. International and national follow-up conferences were held in Cartagena in February 2005 and 2007 and in Bogotá in November 2007. Since then, activities have continued, mostly in the form of seminars on different thematic issues, but no further conference has been held.

Although it is true that regular information sharing between its members has been improved and dialogue between the different sectors has become more fluid,[72] the G-24 has so far proved to be too heterogeneous to make a decisive contribution to development and peace in Colombia.[73] After a relatively productive initial period between July 2003 and February 2005, when the so-called Cartagena consensus was achieved, the G-24 entered a phase of stagnation.[74] The tripartite discussions about the six thematic blocs turned sterile and failed to produce concrete results.[75] The G-24 has found it difficult to develop a unified course of action and influence Colombian actors, both in the government and civil society, in the quest for peace and development. According to a senior EU official in Bogotá, in case of disagreement between the Colombian government and civil society over a particular issue, such as the national human rights plan, the G-24 does not have the means and does not seek to "impose a solution."[76] Considering that the group does not aspire to play the role of a protagonist but rather, as expressed by the Canadian ambassador and temporary G-24 president in the February 2007 follow-up meeting in Cartagena, that of a facilitator of dialogue between "Colombians who ultimately are responsible for achieving peace," this should come as no surprise.[77]

On the level of the individual EU member states, since 2004 the Netherlands and Sweden have supported the Colombia Peace Support Mission of the Organization of American States, charged with verifying paramilitary disarmament, demobilization, and reintegration in Colombia. Spain and France, and non-EU Switzerland, played a role in trying to bring about a swap of hostages held in FARC captivity and insurgent prisoners (the above-mentioned "humanitarian agreement"). In December 2005, the French, Spanish, and Swiss governments launched a joint proposal for negotiations of a hostages/prisoners swap with international facilitation in two municipalities in Valle Department, which failed to bear fruit, however. Shortly after taking office in May 2007, President Nicolas Sarkozy stepped up the French initiative to bring about a "humanitarian agreement" and achieve the liberation of former Colombian presidential candidate Ingrid Betancourt, a Colombian-French citizen abducted by the FARC in February 2002, as well as another 50 hostages. Coordinating his moves with Sarkozy, President Uribe unilaterally released more than 150 FARC prisoners, among them the insurgents' "foreign minister," Rodrigo Granda, who had served as a French contact in earlier attempts to free Betancourt, but the insurgents failed to respond with the release of hostages. Following the FARC's unilateral release of several politician hostages in early 2008 and the government's successful Operación Jaque in July, in which Betancourt, 3 U.S. contractors, and 11 other hostages were freed, President Uribe ended all international facilitation, including that of France and Switzerland.[78] In 2009 and 2010, the FARC released another 8 civilian, military, and police hostages but the government refrained from pursuing a hostages-for-prisoners swap to free other security forces personnel who as of this writing in mid-2011 remain in FARC captivity.

The talks between the Uribe administration and the ELN, which were held in Cuba from late 2005 through to the end of 2007, were accompanied by Norway, Spain, and Switzerland. In early 2007, upon an ELN request, the group of countries was expanded to include Canada, Italy, Japan, Sweden, and the Netherlands. This enlargement of international accompaniment was short-lived, however, because the Uribe administration was far from embracing it wholeheartedly.[79] Ultimately, the dialogue failed to produce any substantial progress on a cease-fire, and the negotiation agenda came to an end in December 2007.[80]

Comparing Europe's Role in Crafting Peace in Central America and Colombia

Comparing the cases of Central America and Colombia helps explain Europe's role in encouraging peace in Latin America as well as the varying degrees to which its polices have been effective. The main factors that have shaped European peace engagement on the Central American isthmus and its broader, politically less committed peace support involvement in Colombia are (1) the nature of the conflicts; (2) the political configuration in the conflict countries and their respective regional environments; (3) the global political setting and the interests of other external powers; and (4) basic European foreign policy interests, including security concerns, and the evolution of European integration.

Even when including Guatemala, the antiregime wars in Central America were much shorter than the Colombian conflict, and though they had deep internal political and socioeconomic roots after the Sandinista revolution, they were also heavily determined by the global confrontation between the two superpowers. The end of the Cold War was pivotal for the pacification of Nicaragua, El Salvador, and Guatemala because it prompted the end of the ideologically driven confrontation between the contenders in the three countries and the drying up of military assistance from the United States, the Soviet Bloc, and Cuba. First the Contadora initiative and then the Central American peace plan Esquipulas II helped address the conflicts' underlying political causes by emphasizing political democracy as opposed to the military dictatorships and political exclusion that had existed before.

Although in its origins it was also motivated by internal political factors, such as the violent confrontation between the Conservative and Liberal parties in the late 1940s and 1950s and the closing down of political space in the years following the establishment of the National Front government in 1958, since the early 1980s Colombia's conflict has progressively lost its "political-ideological nature"; this is also true in the eyes of external actors, whose political and strategic stakes have never been as high in Colombia as they were in Central America. The persistence and intractability of Colombia's conflict is arguably much more related to the notorious weakness of the state, the emergence of two powerful groups of irregular armed actors (insurgents and paramilitaries), and their direct participation in the drug trade, along with socioeconomic inequity and pervasive poverty. Despite intermittent Mexican and Venezuelan facilitation of talks with the insurgents in the past, no regional peace initiative has existed and is in sight. As such, the Colombian conflict is more complex and intractable than the antiregime wars in Central America, and peace support efforts by outside actors are consequently more difficult.

The institutionally and economically emerging European bloc—which was primarily concerned with East-West relations and the impact of the Central American crisis on its own security; which in the Cold War setting of the 1980s was heavily dependent on the United States; and which was motivated by the wish to help overcome social injustice and the illegitimate and authoritarian political regimes that were perceived to be at the root of the conflicts—for the first time since the 1950s focused its still-limited foreign policy capabilities on preventing the U.S. invasion of Sandinista Nicaragua and supporting dialogue between the Central Americans. Although, in the final analysis, these goals were achieved, they were pursued in a rather patchy fashion by several European countries and the EEC through political party channels and support for the Contadora group, the Central American peace plan, and the UN's activities on the isthmus. In the final stages of the peace process Norway, Spain, and Sweden participated in the UN secretary-general's "groups of friends" in El Salvador and Guatemala but there was no European strategy to facilitate, let alone mediate, in the negotiations between the parties to the conflicts. These tasks were assumed first and foremost by the UN, but as geopolitical and domestic conditions changed at the end of the 1980s also by the United States. Once the job was done, the Europeans appeared more prominently on the stage and provided generous aid and political initiative in the verification of the implementation of the peace agreements and the reconstruction of a Central America devastated by war.

Regarding the Colombian conflict, Europe's position is different in the sense that during the past two decades the EU has grown and become a more powerful actor on the world scene, aspiring to be a "global actor" and "civilian power." This notwithstanding, the EU's enlargement has mired the bloc in internal political difficulties, and without a Constitution for Europe the EU continues to be a long way from speaking with a single voice on foreign policy. The Lisbon Treaty of 2007, which was established after the failure of the European constitutional project and entered into force in December 2009, has not helped to remedy this situation. Despite 9/11, Europe's peace support intervention in Colombia has clearly not been primarily related to security considerations. Nor has it predominantly been related to the drug problem, which Europe does not perceive as a big security issue, or of much concern for North-South relations.

Europe—faithful to its adhesion to multilateralism, acutely aware of the overpowering influence of the United States in Latin America and around the world, and with increasing but comparatively still limited economic interest in the region[81]—has not attempted to oppose American policy in Colombia, to build a counterweight to it, or, even less so, to take the lead in encouraging peace. Instead of supporting Plan Colombia, which was perceived as too much focused on "hard" military and counterdrug measures, Europeans designed their own broad peace support strategy toward Colombia, including the EU's peace laboratories and large humanitarian aid as well as a myriad of bilateral programs of the member states aimed at strengthening Colombia's governance and institutions. Reflecting a degree of continuity of Europe's approach to the Central American crisis, European engagement has been driven by the perception that Colombia's embattled democratic institutions ought to be strengthened, that urgent action is needed to alleviate the humanitarian crisis, and that any solution to the conflict will be political and long term. In contrast to the earlier days of the crisis on the isthmus more than two decades ago, however, Europe has not shown comparable political commitment to peace in Colombia, basically because there are no priority security or other interests at stake.

As in Central America, the EU and some of its member states have also made consistent efforts to strengthen dialogue between Colombians and enhance the peaceful settlement of the conflict. During the peace process with the FARC under President Pastrana, this took the form of political support for the negotiations and the hands-on mediation effort together with the UN's James LeMoyne and a handful of other countries just before the breakdown of the talks in February 2002. Since 2003, the principal forum for such dialogue-enhancing activity has been the G-24, in which a group of European countries is attempting to bridge gaps between the Colombian government and civil society in coordination with other countries, including the United States. The G-24 has only to a small degree filled, alongside the Colombia Peace Support Mission of the Organization of American States, the void created by the withdrawal of the UN secretary-general's special envoy to Colombia in 2004. The current chances of a renewed UN engagement in brokering peace are slim at best.

Looking ahead, it should be asked what else can be expected regarding Europe's broad but politically largely noncommittal peace support involvement in Colombia. Whereas in Central America, Europe was a rather effective junior player in a game dominated by the UN, the United States, and the Central Americans, especially toward the end of the 1980s, in Colombia it could perhaps be the other main outside player next to the United States. During the past two decades, Europe as a bloc has gained in weight and influence on the international scene, even though its domestic political problems and the limitations it is facing owing to Colombia's strong alignment with the United States, which has continued under President Juan Manuel Santos, are undoubtedly obstacles to a larger European role. However, the engagement of other external actors—the UN, the United States, and Colombia's Latin American neighbors—has either been reduced (in the case of the UN), is set to continue but is reaching its limits (the United States), or is not being brought to bear or has become increasingly antagonistic (Latin America). Plan Colombia did not produce the expected breakthrough in the fight against drugs—though it contributed to a reduction in the cocaine flow from Colombia and the weakening of the insurgents—and is being wound down by the administration of President Barack Obama. Therefore, Europe's "soft" and long-term peace engagement, which is focused on aiding the establishment of the political and socioeconomic conditions for a negotiated settlement with the insurgent FARC and ELN, could make a significant contribution to overcoming the protracted conflict. For this to become a real possibility, however, it will be necessary to increase above all Europe's political commitment and to try to bring in friendly Latin American countries, especially Brazil. Although remote, in the absence of other, more promising policy alternatives, such an effort would be worthy of receiving more attention—in Brussels and Europe's capitals, but indeed also in Bogotá and Washington.

Notes

1. Alain Rouquié cites Hans-Dietrich Genscher, then the foreign minister of the Federal Republic of Germany, who was concerned that just as the 1962 Cuban missile crisis the Central American situation could potentially have a dangerous global impact, especially in Germany: "Making the Russians backtrack on Central America could require the withdrawal of the North American troops from the Federal Republic of Germany." Alain Rouquié, *Guerras y paz en América Central* (Mexico City: Fondo de Cultura Económica, 1994), 268 (translation by the author); author's interview with the Latin America expert Wolf Grabendorff, Bogotá, December 2007.

2. The different approaches to the Central American crisis on the part of the United States and Western Europe have been described as one of the "most serious transatlantic misunderstandings" in the 1980s. Arguably, the socialist government of France most actively and openly opposed the hard-line policy of President Ronald Reagan (1981–89) toward the isthmus. See below. Rouquié, *Guerras y paz,* 269–71.

3. The "civilian power" concept is a key element of the EU's international policy-making framework. Analogously to Europe's own integration mechanisms, it refers to the primacy of "civilian" as opposed to coercive or military intervention abroad. The foreign policy of the EU as a "civilian power" seeks to be fully compatible with international law, adheres to multilateralism, and is focused on strengthening democracy, human rights, and a just social order throughout the world. See Katharina Holzinger et al., *Die Europäische Union: Theorien und Analysekonzepte* (Paderborn: Ferdinand Schöningh, 2005), 256–65.

4. Nikolas Busse, "Institutionelles Lifting," *Frankfurter Allgemeine Zeitung,* October 17, 2007; Volker Perthes and Stefan Mair, eds., *European Foreign and Security Policy: Challenges and Opportunities for the German EU Presidency* (Berlin: Stiftung Wissenschaft und Politik, 2006). See also Helmut Schmidt, *Die Mächte der Zukunft: Gewinner und Verlierer in der Welt von morgen* (Munich: Wilhelm Goldmann Verlag, 2006), 200–222.

5. Guatemala's civil war, the longest in the isthmus, started in the early 1960s, but the heaviest fighting between the insurgents and government armed forces took place in the early 1980s, when presidents Romeo Lucas (1978–82) and Efraín Ríos Montt

(1982–83) resorted to a scorched earth policy that left thousands of civilians dead. Markus Schultze-Kraft, *Pacificación y poder civil en Centroamérica: Las relaciones cívico-militares en El Salvador, Guatemala y Nicaragua en el posconflicto* (Bogotá: Grupo Editorial Norma, 2005), 68–70; Edelberto Torres-Rivas, "Guatemala: Desarrollo, democracia y los acuerdos de paz," *Revista Centroamericana de Ciencias Sociales* 3, no. 2 (December 2006): 11–48.

6. After the Sandinista National Liberation Front's (FSLN) defeat in the February 25, 1990, polls, Defense Minister Humberto Ortega, General Joaquín Cuadra, and Comandante Jaime Wheelock started negotiations about the transfer of power with the government-elect of Violeta Chamorro. At the heart of the talks—which on the part of the incoming government were led by the designated minister of the presidency, Antonio Lacayo—was the future of the Popular Sandinista Army (Ejército Popular Sandinista, EPS) and the demobilization of the contra. The counterrevolutionary troops were still armed and while concentrated in camps in Honduras as well as inside Nicaragua were perceived as a serious and continuing threat by the EPS high command and the FSLN. The "Protocol on the Transfer of Executive Power of the Republic of Nicaragua" was signed on March 27, 1990, by the two parties—with OAS secretary-general João Baena Soares, the UN secretary-general's personal representative, Elliot Richardson, and former U.S. president Jimmy Carter acting as witnesses. Among the "Transition Protocol's" key provisions were the timetable for the disarming, demobilization, and reintegration of the contras and the Chamorro administration's pledge not to interfere with the internal affairs of the EPS, including the chain of command and EPS-designed programs of troop reduction and military conversion. Schultze-Kraft, *Pacificación,* 253–63.

7. Among the many texts, see Jack Child, *The Central American Peace Process, 1983–1991: Sheathing Swords, Building Confidence* (Boulder, Colo.: Lynne Rienner, 1992); Tricia Juhn, *Negotiating Peace in El Salvador: Civil-Military Relations and the Conspiracy to End the War* (New York: St. Martin's Press, 1998).

8. Among the many texts, see Schultze-Kraft, *Pacificación;* Rachel Sieder, ed., *Central America: Fragile Transition* (Basingstoke, U.K.: Palgrave McMillan, 1996); Torres-Rivas, "Guatemala."

9. The United Nations Observer Mission in El Salvador (known by its Spanish name as ONUSAL) was established in 1991. Its mandate ended in 1995, when the much smaller UN Mission in El Salvador (known as MINUSAL) was charged with providing good offices to the parties and continuing verification of the implementation of pending points of the 1992 peace accords. The United Nations Mission for the Verification of Human Rights and of Compliance with the Commitments of the Comprehensive Agreement on Human Rights in Guatemala (known as MINUGUA) was established in 1994 and stayed in the country until 2004.

10. The Contadora group was formed in 1983 by a number of Latin American countries—including Colombia, Mexico, Panama, and Venezuela—and sought to contribute to a political solution of the Central American crisis. For further details, see below.

11. Author's interview with Grabendorff.

12. William M. Leogrande, "The United States and Nicaragua," in *Nicaragua: The First Five Years,* edited by Thomas W. Walker (New York: Praeger, 1985), 425–27.

13. Ibid., 426.

14. Ibid., 425–46; Theodore Schwab and Harold Sims, "Relations with the Communist States," in *Nicaragua,* ed. Walker, 447–66.

15. See, e.g., the comment by Thomas W. Walker in footnote 19 of "Relations," by Schwab and Sims, in *Nicaragua,* ed. Walker, 463.

16. Schwab and Sims, "Relations," 452.

17. Ibid., 454.

18. Schultze-Kraft, *Pacificación,* 209–10.

19. Author's interview with a former Dutch ambassador to Costa Rica, Bogotá, February 2007.

20. Writing from the perspective of a French diplomat-scholar, Alain Rouquié acknowledges the importance of Western European security concerns but also assigns weight to political factors. After Vietnam, according to the author, Europe had lost much of its faith in the "capacity of the United States to understand and resolve the problems of the Third World." Therefore, in Central America, Europe wanted to "serve as a bridge between the West and the radicalized and 'anti-imperialist' political movements [of the region] by offering them a non-hegemonic Western alternative. In other words, Europeans [were] ready to oppose the United States [if this had been] necessary to 'salvage' the West" (translation by the author). Rouquié, *Guerras y paz,* 268–69.

21. Wolf Grabendorff, "West European Perceptions of the Crisis in Central America," in *Political Change in Central America: Internal and External Dimensions,* edited by Wolf Grabendorff, Heinrich-W. Krumwiede, and Jörg Todt (Boulder, Colo.: Westview Press, 1984), 289.

22. Blanca Antonini, "Peace Processes in Central America and Colombia: A European Perspective," unpublished manuscript prepared for the Woodrow Wilson Center, 2006.

23. Nadia Malley, "Relations with Western Europe and the Socialist International," in *Nicaragua,* ed. Walker, 489.

24. Ibid.: 489–90.

25. Author's interview with a senior European diplomat formerly posted to San José, Bogotá, February 2007.

26. Susanne Gratius, "Spielt Europa in Lateinamerika noch eine Rolle?" *Aus Politik und Zeitgeschichte* 15 (September 2003): 44.

27. European Council, "Solemn Declaration on European Union, Stuttgart, 19 June 1983," *Bulletin of the European Communities* 6/1983 (June 1983): 24–29.

28. Wolf Grabendorff, "La estrategia birregional y sus limitaciones en un mundo unipolar," *Nueva Sociedad* 189 (January–February 2004): 106–7.

29. Ibid., 44; Sabine Kurtenbach, *Europe and the Colombian Conflict,* Working Paper (Washington, D.C.: Inter-American Dialogue, 2005), 1.

30. Antonini, "Peace Processes."

31. The Iran-Contra scandal, which broke in late 1986, refers to the selling of weapons by members of the Reagan administration to Iran, at the time a declared enemy of Washington. The funds were then illegally used to equip and support the Nicaraguan contras.

32. For details on the three peace processes and the importance of the military and political variables in each case, see Schultze-Kraft, *Pacificación,* 209–408.

33. The OAS's International Support and Verification Commission (CIAV) monitored, together with the UN Observer Group (ONUCA), the contra cease-fire and troop concentration in 1990.

34. Through his special envoys to El Salvador and Guatemala, the UN secretary-general played an important facilitating role in the peace negotiations. The secretary-general's "group of friends" were composed of Colombia, Mexico, Spain, the United States, and Venezuela in El Salvador; and Colombia, Mexico, Norway, Spain, Sweden,

Venezuela, and the United States in Guatemala. Oslo served as the site of an important encounter between representatives of the Guatemalan government, URNG, and the National Reconciliation Commission (CNR) in March 1990. The result of the meeting was the Basic Agreement on the Search for Peace by Political Means, a key accord in Guatemala's peace process. Europeans also helped in fomenting the important role of civil society, epitomized in the Civil Society Assembly (ASC), in Guatemala. See Schultze-Kraft, *Pacificación,* 278–408.

35. In 1991–92, Central America's share of European bilateral ODA was roughly 18 percent; in 1993–94, it increased to more than 20 percent, and in 1995–96 to almost 40 percent. Throughout the 1990s, Germany was the top European donor in Latin America. In 1996, its total aid for the region was twice that of the United States. Christian Frères, "The European Union as a Global 'Civilian Power,'" *Journal of Interamerican Studies and World Affairs* 42, no. 2, Special Issue: The EU and Latin America: Changing Relations (Summer 2000): 63–85; the citation here is on 72, 74.

36. Ibid., 74.

37. On the basis of the UN General Assembly's Resolution 48/161 of December 20, 1993, which called on all political groups in Nicaragua to advance toward democratic consolidation, reconstruction, and reconciliation, the governments of Canada, Spain, Mexico, the Netherlands, and Sweden formed the Nicaragua Support Group in May 1994. It worked until 1996, when Arnoldo Alemán replaced Violeta Chamorro in the presidency and failed to show an interest in the support group. Frans van Haren and Kristjan Guy Burgess, "Lessons from the 'Support Group for Nicaragua,'" *Peace and Conflict Monitor,* available at www.monitor.upeace.org; author's interview with a senior European diplomat, Bogotá, February 2007.

38. The first attempt to reach a negotiated solution with the FARC dates back to the government of Belisario Betancur (1982–86). It was followed by the demobilization of the M-19, the Popular Liberation Army (Ejército Popular de Liberación), the Quintin Lame Armed Movement (MAQL), the Revolutionary Workers' Party (PRT), the Socialist Renovation Current (CRS), the Garnica front, and militias in the city of Medellín during the administrations of Virgilio Barco (1986–90) and César Gaviria (1990–94). Barco and Gaviria also held talks with the Simón Bolívar Guerrilla Coordinating Instance, in which the ELN and FARC participated and which were supported by Venezuela and Mexico. President Ernesto Samper (1994–98) attempted to establish talks with the ELN but failed; President Andrés Pastrana failed to negotiate a peace agreement with the FARC (see below); and President Álvaro Uribe established talks with the paramilitary AUC, which produced their formal demobilization in 2006, and the ELN, which did not prosper.

39. Juan Manuel Santos, a former defense minister of Uribe, was elected with 69 percent of the votes in the runoff poll on June 20, 2010. He represents the continuity of Uribe's security, but not political project.

40. Among the larger groups are Rastrojos, Paisas, and Ejército Revolucionario Popular Antisubversivo de Colombia (ERPAC). Author's interviews in Bogotá, Pasto, Tumaco, and Santa Marta, February and March 2007 and January 2010; International Crisis Group, *Colombia's New Armed Groups,* Latin America Report 20 (Brussels: International Crisis Group, 2007); International Crisis Group, *Improving Security Policy in Colombia,* Latin America Briefing 23 (Brussels: International Crisis Group, 2010).

41. See Philippe de Lombaerde et al., "EU Policies towards the Colombian Conflict: Policy Coordination and Interregionalism," United Nations University, http://www.cris

.unu.edu/sbook.175.0.html?&tx_ttnews[tt_news]=109&cHash=c47f6287b12fe7a853a 79798a2be3759, 2.

42. See International Crisis Group, *Colombia: The Prospects for Peace with the ELN,* Latin America Report 2 (Brussels: International Crisis Group, 2002).

43. As a matter of fact, Pastrana not only withdrew the government troops and police from the *zona de despeje* but all other state institutions also ceased to work in the area, including the attorney general's and public prosecutor's offices and the ombudsman. This left the population of the five municipalities under complete FARC control, a grave mistake that caused Pastrana much repudiation.

44. Cynthia J. Arnson and Teresa Whitfield, "Third Parties and Intractable Conflicts: The Case of Colombia," in *Grasping the Nettle: Analyzing Cases of Intractable Conflict,* edited by Chester A. Crocker, Fen Osler Hampson, and Pamela Aall (Washington, D.C.: U.S. Institute of Peace Press, 2005), 252.

45. The group was integrated by Canada, Cuba, France, Italy, Mexico, Norway, Spain, Sweden, Switzerland, and Venezuela. In June 2000, another "group of facilitating countries" had been created for peace talks with the ELN, including Cuba, France, Norway, Spain, and Switzerland. Those talks never got off the ground, however, and were overshadowed by the peace process with the FARC, even after its failure.

46. Arnson and Whitfield, "Third Parties," 252.

47. The ten facilitating countries were Canada, Cuba, Spain, France, Italy, Mexico, Norway, Sweden, Switzerland, and Venezuela.

48. International Crisis Group, *Colombia's Elusive Quest for Peace,* Latin America Report 1 (Brussels: International Crisis Group, 2002), 23–24.

49. Ibid., 25.

50. Socorro Ramírez, "Actores europeos ante el conflicto colombiano," in *Nuestra guerra sin nombre: Transformaciones del conflicto en Colombia,* edited by IEPRI (Bogotá: Grupo Editorial Norma, 2006), 80–81.

51. Chris Patten, "Colombia: An Engagement with Peace," *El Espectador,* October 24, 2000.

52. Joaquín Roy, *European Perceptions of Plan Colombia: A Virtual Contribution to a Virtual War and Peace Plan?* Implementing Plan Colombia Special Series (Carlisle, Pa.: Strategic Studies Institute, 2001), 10–11, 17–20.

53. It is still unclear whether these funds were disbursed in the end. See Ramírez, "Actores europeos," 85; Roy, *European Perceptions,* 2; and Joaquín Roy, *Europe: Neither Plan Colombia, nor Peace Process—From Good Intentions to High Expectations,* Working Paper 11 (Miami: Dante B. Fascell North-South Center, 2002), 9.

54. Patten, "Colombia."

55. Ibid.

56. International Crisis Group, *Uribe's Re-election: Can the EU Help Colombia Develop a More Balanced Peace Strategy?* Latin America Report 17 (Brussels: International Crisis Group, 2006), 18–20.

57. The second peace laboratory covers sixty-two municipalities in Norte de Santander, Antioquia, Cauca, and Nariño departments; and the third is located in the Montes de María region and Meta department. Ibid., 13.

58. On December 22, 2005, EU commissioner for external relations and European neighborhood policy Benita Ferrero-Waldner stated that "with this package [€1.5 million for peace and reconciliation] we intend to help Colombia provide support for vulnerable groups and reconciliation activities. EU actions will range from awareness

raising, legal advice to victims and support to the affected communities, part of a robust, longer-term programme for Peace and Development in Colombia," "Colombia: EU Commission Releases €1.5m for Peace and Reconciliation," Brussels, December 22, 2005; see also "European Commission Provides €12 million of humanitarian assistance to the victims of conflicts in Colombia," Brussels, 28 March 2006; "EU Humanitarian Assistance for Victims of the Internal Conflict in Colombia," Brussels, March 10, 2005; "EU Humanitarian Aid to Victims of Internal Conflict in Colombia," Brussels, April 2, 2004; and "EU Humanitarian Aid for Internally Displaced People in Colombia," Brussels, February 9, 2004.

59. In effect, it was not until well into 2003 that European actors overcame the disorientation and, perhaps, frustration caused by President Pastrana's 180-degree turn in February and May 2002, announcing first the end of the peace process with the FARC and then proceeding to stop the rapprochement with the ELN. Author's interviews with senior European diplomats, Bogotá, January–March 2003.

60. One of the first "victims" of this political evolution was the figure of the UN secretary-general's special envoy to Colombia. Following the breakdown of the talks with the FARC, James LeMoyne continued in the post during the Uribe administration, but tensions soon flared up. LeMoyne was reluctant to subscribe to the new government's interpretation of the armed conflict, perceived as a terrorist threat, and made this publicly known in media interviews. In early 2004, Colombia suggested to the UN that the figure of special envoy was not needed anymore, and LeMoyne's mission was ended. Though a comparatively low-level position for a peace and development adviser was created and filled in the United Nations Development Program in Bogotá in early 2007, since 2004 the UN has not played any significant role in helping with the establishment of peace negotiations with the insurgents.

61. The EU's decision to put the FARC and ELN on its list of terrorist organizations (established in December 2001), which since May 2002 has included the paramilitary AUC, was not an easy one. Allegedly, France and Sweden first objected to the FARC's inclusion (although this was later denied by Swedish government sources), which finally occurred in June 2002; and Belgium reportedly stopped the ELN's inclusion, which only proceeded in April 2004. The decision to include the FARC came after the II EU-LAC summit in May 2002 in Madrid, apparently at the request of the Spanish EU presidency, and the Bojayá massacre committed by the FARC that same month. See De Lombaerde et al., "EU Policies," 10–11; and Roy, *Europe: Neither Plan Colombia, nor Peace Process.*

62. EU Council conclusions on Colombia, December 10, 2002, January 26, 2004, January 13, 2004, October 3, 2005, and November 20, 2007.

63. EU Council conclusion, Brussels, December 10, 2002.

64. See this section below.

65. EU Council conclusion, Brussels, January 26, 2004.

66. EU Council conclusions, Brussels, December 13, 2004, and October 3, 2005.

67. EU Council conclusion, Brussels, October 5, 2005; EU Presidency declaration on the start of talks between the Government of Colombia and the AUC paramilitary groups, Brussels, June 30, 2004.

68. EU Council conclusion, Brussels, November 20, 2007.

69. EU Council conclusion, Brussels, October 5, 2005; EU Presidency declaration on the start of talks between the Government of Colombia and the AUC paramilitary groups, Brussels, June 30, 2004.

70. Confidential diplomatic note; author's interview with Grabendorff.

71. Author's interview with a senior EU diplomat, Quito, March 2007.

72. Confidential diplomatic note.

73. Author's interview with a senior EU diplomat, Quito, March 2007.

74. The "Cartagena consensus" refers to the rapprochement between the Colombian government, civil society and human rights organizations, and entrepreneur associations on key issues, such as the protection of human rights and the improvement of the security situation in the country.

75. In illustration, differences between the Uribe administration and Colombian human rights organizations regarding the elaboration of the National Action Plan for Human Rights and International Humanitarian Law (PNADH, in Spanish), a long-standing issue that was incorporated into the agenda of the "London-Cartagena process," could not be bridged. In the context of the ongoing armed conflict and the associated human rights violations, many nongovernmental organizations did not have enough faith in the government's commitment to the defense and protection of fundamental rights and sought instead to obtain funds from international donors to strengthen their own organizations and networks. Some European countries gave money, and others were disconcerted by the lack of unity of action and the apparent impossibility of making substantial headway in the pressing matter. After much haggling, a committee integrated by representatives of the government, the public prosecutor (*procurador general de la nación,* PGN), the ombudsman (*defensor del pueblo,* DP), and civil society organizations was established in September 2006 and charged with elaborating the plan. As of this writing, no discernible progress has been made. Author's interview with a European diplomat, Bogotá, March 2007.

76. Author's interview with a senior EU diplomat, Bogotá, March 2007.

77. Talk given by the Canadian ambassador to Colombia, Mathew Levin, during the inauguration of the Cartagena conference on development and human rights in February 2007.

78. The government used information retrieved from the computers of "Raúl Reyes," a senior FARC commander who was killed in a Colombian military raid on his base camp in Angostura, Ecuador on March 1, 2008, to publicly charge that the Swiss and French facilitators were pro-FARC, had carried out errands for the insurgents since 2000 and had achieved nothing with their facilitation. See International Crisis Group, *Ending Colombia's FARC Conflict: Dealing the Right Card,* Latin America Report 30 (Brussels: International Crisis Group, 2009), 17–19, 24.

79. Author's interview with a European diplomat, Bogotá, March 2007.

80. See International Crisis Group, *Colombia: Moving Forward with the ELN?* Latin America Briefing 16 (Brussels: International Crisis Group, 2007).

81. In the period 1999–2008, trade between the EU and Latin America doubled. Imports from Latin America increased from $53.3 billion (€42.5 billion) to $128.3 billion (€102.4 billion). EU exports to Latin America grew from $65.4 billion (€52.2 billion) to $108.3 billion (€86.4 billion). Nevertheless, in 2007 imports from Latin America only amounted to 6.4 percent of EU world imports; and exports to Latin America were 6.6 percent of EU world exports. In comparison, the respective figures for the Association of South East Asian Nations countries are 7.3 percent and 8 percent, and for South Korea 3.4 percent and 3.4 percent. Eurostat and World Trade Organization figures, http://ec.europa.eu/trade/creating-opportunities/bilateral-relations/statistics/.

Chapter 11

Political Transition, Social Violence, and Gangs: Cases in Central America and Mexico

José Miguel Cruz, Rafael Fernández de Castro, and Gema Santamaría Balmaceda

For most of Central America and Mexico, violence continues to be a major problem of the transition to democracy. El Salvador, Guatemala, and Honduras—the so-called Northern Triangle of Central America—endure levels of violence higher than at any point in their history and some of the highest rates of crime in the world. Although posttransition Mexico has lower levels of violence than Central America's Northern Tier, violence in states such as Chihuahua, Sinaloa, and Guerrero is at record levels, even by Central American standards. Much of the violence in Central America has been attributed to youth gangs and organized crime linked to drug trafficking that emerged in the region following the moment of political transition.

However, the phenomenon of youth gangs is not new. The presence of gangs as local actors in the network of urban violence in Central America

The authors wish to thank Raúl Benítez Manaut and Alejandro Díaz-Domínguez for their help during several stages of this project. They would also like to thank Cynthia Arnson for her comments and patience while the project was being completed.

and certain parts of Mexico has been manifest for several decades, and gang presence has multiple expressions: neighborhood defense groups, the use of graffiti, and delinquent activity. What is new is the attention given to gangs by the media in recent years, the policies designed to combat them in Central America, and the recent transformation that the "gang problem" has undergone. In the case of Central American gangs known as *maras*,[1] they have been transformed from what we refer to here as "traditional gangs" to truly transnational organizations that *work with* or *act as* organized forms of crime.[2]

The presence of gangs is related, on the one hand, to the social context of the countries in which they emerge; and, on the other, to policies developed to fight them.[3] Social networks and social capital can help to contain the phenomenon, whereas a culture associated with violence or a legacy of extended civil war may do just the opposite, acting as detonators. The state, its institutions, and the political responses they generate play a fundamental role in resolving or aggravating the conditions that give rise to juvenile violence, particularly gang-related violence.

This chapter examines the role of states in the development of the youth gang problem. We contend that in order to understand the evolution of the so-called *maras* in northern Central America, we must look at the shortcomings in processes of political transition and how these lay the groundwork for later state responses that have aggravated the problem of youth violence. Thus we concentrate on those Central American countries that are being affected by gangs and compare them with Mexico, which has also undergone a political transition—although with its own unique characteristics—but whose gang problem is not of the same dimension and magnitude as that in Central America.

In contrast to Central America, where *maras* present a major security challenge on their own, gangs in Mexico can only be considered a major security threat when they come into contact with other forms of organized crime, particularly drug-trafficking cartels. This is the case of Los Mexicles and Los Aztecas, a new type of gang linked in their entirety to two of the most powerful and well-organized drug cartels, the Sinaloa Cartel and the Juárez Cartel. In Central America, gangs have been autonomous from drug-trafficking organizations; their major criminal activity does not revolve around drugs but rather, extortion rackets.[4] In other words, in Central America, as of 2010, gangs shape most of the security agenda; in Mexico, that is done by drug trafficking. Moreover, Mexican gangs in general continue to observe more traditional patterns, so that gang membership represents a transitional, temporal, and exclusively juvenile activity grounded and limited by the boundaries of the barrio or local neighborhood. As we explain below, Central American gangs were "born transnational," so to speak, whereas Mexican gangs—and only some of them—went beyond the barrio very recently and only as an effect of the transformation of drug trafficking in Mexico. As in Central America, Mexico's gang problem has been recently shaped, in an indirect and unintended manner, by the state responses and policies associated with drug trafficking. The importance of the Mexico–Central America comparison becomes more apparent if we consider that Mexico also forms part of the northern Central American region comprising Guatemala, Honduras, and El Salvador, an area with intense migration toward the United States. Furthermore, Mexico is a stop along the way for members of Central American *maras* entering and leaving the United States.[5]

This chapter is divided into four sections. First, it presents a brief summary of Central American gangs. Second, it provides an analysis of the phenomena of political transition in Mexico and Central America. Third, it examines general patterns of violence in the region. Fourth and most important, it shows the impact of states on the gang phenomenon, especially in Central America. The chapter closes by emphasizing the importance of institutionalizing public safety in order to keep open the possibility of achieving democratic regimes that fully respect the rule of law.

Maras in the Spotlight

Until very recently, there has been serious disinformation regarding urban violence and gangs in the region, their scope, and their effects on governance. The media has exaggerated their presence, inflating a phenomenon that is, by its very nature, sensationalist. Some governments have inflated the numbers of gang members or suggested possible links between them and terrorist groups in other parts of the world in order to justify heavy-handed policies applauded in Washington as models for coping with the problem.[6]

The attention garnered by the *maras* in the international media can be explained by the fact that gang members are young people who employ extreme and flamboyant violence in their initiation rituals and when confronting rival gangs. Their possible links to organized crime are also of interest, especially the possible links to drugs and arms traffickers, and in the case of southeastern Mexico, migrant traffickers (who control traffic and the extortion of Central American migrants heading for the United States). U.S. military analysts have raised alarms by suggesting possible links between the *maras* and international terrorist groups.[7] Despite these allegations, no empirical evidence exists to indicate that Central American *maras* appeared and reproduced as part of an American gang-led plot of transnational expansion or as part of a strategy on the part of Mexican drug cartels to sponsor *mara* membership.[8] The recent penetration of Mexican cartels in Central America has opened opportunities for circumstantial alliances and business between drug traffickers and some *mara* cells. However, both phenomena continue operating under different dynamics, with the *maras* more engaged in extortion rackets and homicides than in transnational drug trafficking.[9] Any detailed account of organized crime in Central America and Mexico should be able to differentiate between these two expressions of violence in the region.

Assessing the number of gang members in Central America and Mexico is complex and elusive. *Maras* are constantly changing, and their structures and ways of operating are in constant transformation. They have experienced significant changes in the last twenty years; what started as disconnected bands of street youth have become well-structured racketeering organizations in some countries. In any given year, their numbers change due to shifting alignments, incarcerations, or deaths. Trustworthy data are thus hard to obtain. INTERPOL uses one of the most conservative estimates and calculates that a total of approximately 60,000 young people belong to the *maras* (14,000 in Guatemala, 36,000 in Honduras, and 10,500 in El Salvador).[10] In Mexico, the secretary of public safety confirmed in early 2005 the presence of 5,000 *mareros* in twenty states throughout the country.[11] However, it appears that 98 percent of them were concentrated in Chiapas, specifically in the Soconusco area (where the city of Tapachula is located). An empirical investigation of the *maras* in which these authors participated, carried out by the Transnational Network of Analysis, found no basis for the Mexican government's concern with the proliferation of Central American *maras* throughout the country.[12]

The emergence of the Central American *maras* is not due to one single cause; rather, it is the result of many social, ecological, and political factors acting together in complex fashion. Likewise, and aggravating the problem, the growth of gangs and the increase in the violence they perpetrate cannot be attributed to one single factor. Diverse studies in Central America and Mexico point to migration, poverty, social exclusion, a past marked by military conflict and authoritarian governments, a lack of social capital, a culture of violence, rapid urban expansion and disorder, dysfunctional families, and a lack of opportunities as some of the factors behind Central American youth gangs.[13]

All these factors and others are partially responsible for the *mara* phenomenon, but none of them alone can explain its seriousness or fundamental characteristics. For example, migration has played an undeniable role in the spread of the phenomenon, but migration alone has not always led to the emergence of gangs, particularly the Central American *maras*. Equally inexplicable is why Mexican gang members who formed gangs in Los Angeles starting in the 1940s (the White Fence, Barrio Maravilla, and Eighteenth Street gang that later became a Central American *mara*) never flourished in Mexican territory.

This chapter focuses on one of the factors that, until now, has rarely been analyzed in the growing literature on Central American *maras* or even in the general literature about gangs: the state's role in handling the gang problem, and its link to processes of political transition since the early 1990s.[14] The basic premise is that *maras* are not only a product of migration processes, social exclusion, problematic family ties, and cultures of violence but are also the result of actions taken by governments to fight them—and that the manner in which governments have tackled the problem is directly linked to unique processes of political transition in these countries.

Political Transitions:
The Importance of Sociopolitical Context

The defining characteristics of Central America's sociopolitical history during the past thirty years are the lengthy processes of war and subsequent transition to peace that three of the five countries in the region experienced. Protracted wars in Guatemala and El Salvador, and the revolutionary and counterrevolutionary conflicts in Nicaragua, turned Central America into one of the continent's most unstable regions in the 1970s and 1980s. Although there was no actual combat in Honduras and Costa Rica, the conflicts in neighboring countries created political instability in those relatively pacific societies.

Throughout most of the twentieth century, the majority of Central American countries were ruled by authoritarian governments. As Edelberto Torres-Rivas argues in chapter 4 of the present volume, except for the political opening in Guatemala in the 1940s, which was ended by the coup of 1954 sponsored by the U.S. Central Intelligence Agency, societies had no opportunity to experiment with democratic or semidemocratic regimes, contrary to what happened in the rest of Latin America. In both Guatemala and El Salvador, different conditions and processes led to the escalation of armed conflict and internal wars between leftist guerrillas and military regimes. In Nicaragua, as Shelley McConnell chronicles in chapter 5, following the Sandinista revolution against the Somoza dictatorship, the United States among other actors sponsored a counterrevolutionary war aimed at toppling the Sandinista regime. Political transitions and the establishment of formal democracies came at the end of these wars, with the signing of peace agreements and the celebration of relatively free and fair elections.[15]

Although, between the 1980s and 1990s each country in Central America followed its own course of political transition, they all share at least some characteristics. As Ricardo Córdova Macías and Carlos G. Ramos indicate in chapter 3, postwar political transitions in Central America were three-dimensional, involving (1) a transition from war to peace; (2) a transition from a military to a civilian government; and (3) a wider transition from authoritarian to democratic regimes, something that also occurred in Honduras.

Probably the most remarkable characteristic of the political transitions in Guatemala, El Salvador, and Nicaragua is the progression from varying degrees of civil war to political peace. In all three cases, the transitions were profoundly shaped by the resolution of armed conflicts. In Guatemala and El Salvador, the end of armed conflict was intrinsically linked to reform processes included in peace treaties; these reforms substantially transformed the state security apparatuses, demilitarizing the police institutions and placing the military under civilian control. In Nicaragua, the Sapoá Treaty, signed in 1988, established conditions that led to definitive elections in 1990.[16]

In Guatemala and El Salvador, the army was required to relinquish control of the internal security institutions and dissolve existing networks of civilian collaborators that had played a fundamental role in the control, repression, and dissemination of government violence.[17] Both countries created a new police force headed by civilians, and the military was to wield considerably less power than before the peace agreements.[18] In Nicaragua, the processes of demilitarization and reduction of the Sandinista Peoples' Army (Ejército Popular Sandinista, EPS) led to a dismantling of the internal security system. The Interior Ministry's intelligence offices were closed, the Sandinista Popular Militias were dismantled, and the EPS and Sandinista police force were reduced in number (the latter was renamed, and its members included former contra combatants).

The political transitions in Central America not only removed the army from a position of direct power; they also created legions of unemployed former soldiers with extensive military experience. This, together with inadequate programs of retraining and reinsertion, would have important consequences for Central American postwar societies.[19] The signing of the peace agreements and the formal separation of the army from the internal security apparatus cleared the way for the creation of democratic institutions and the establishment of civilian, democratically oriented regimes.

Although there has been extensive debate among researchers regarding the type and quality of Central America's new democracies,[20] all seem to agree that the postwar transitions led to regimes that consistently opted for democracy for the first time in their country's histories.[21] This created additional challenges for the small, poor Central American nations. A new kind of institutional practice and political culture were required. Lacking a democratic memory, new rules had to be built on authoritarian notions and institutions.[22] This was a difficult task, made still more difficult by the fact that the institutions to be reformed or created were drawn from during the period of conflict.

For example, the new police institutions comprised important percentages of members of the old institutions. In Guatemala, nearly 11,000 members of the new police force came from the old force and had been trained by former military commandos. In El Salvador, 40 percent of the new police institution was supposed to be made up of former policemen and guerrilla combatants.[23] In Nicaragua, the police force remained practically identical following the Sandinistas' loss in postwar elections.[24]

In contrast to the Central America cases, where the boundaries of the political transitions can be more sharply delineated and the military played a major role during the authoritarian regimes, the Mexican transition toward an electoral and procedural democracy took place as a scattered sequence of reforms in the electoral arena, without any premeditated attention to reforming the security apparatuses as part of the democratic opening. One of the most salient differences with Central America is that the Mexican transition was not marked by a single event and did not break radically with the immediately previous political order. Instead, the political transition in Mexico was part of a long-term, gradual, and somehow scattered process that took place even during the years of rule under the Institutional

Revolutionary Party (Partido Revolucionario Institucional, PRI). This process would culminate—not begin—in 2000, with the presidency of the Vicente Fox of the National Action Party (Partido Acción Nacional).[25]

The most important difference between the Central American transitions and that of Mexico concerns the transformations of the security apparatuses and the role played by the military. In Mexico, the withdrawal of military forces from the political arena was never a central issue for democratic transition; military institutions were always under civilian control, and the former professed an unequivocal loyalty to the president and the civilian leadership.[26] In addition, the reform of the Mexican political system never deliberately took up the issue of transforming the police forces, despite their utterly corrupt character and the pervasive and complex extortion rackets that reached into the upper institutional echelons.[27] However, as electoral changes brought more party competition, and as political forces other than the PRI came into local, regional, and federal governments, the reform of police institutions attached to the old bureaucracy and the dismantling of the patron-client networks around them became a by-product of the political transition, however sluggish and uneven.[28]

In Mexico, the breakdown of patronage networks contributed to the rise of criminal violence and insecurity through two processes: first, through the appearance of renewed conflicts in the various bureaucracies and among the political forces that stalled the efforts to deepen reforms in the police institutions;[29] and second, through the collapse of the protection pacts between local authorities and criminal organizations.[30] Attempts to dismantle the old structures of clientelism that infused the security institutions led to violent competition among drug traffickers and criminal organizations aimed at establishing new systems of protection and control. Local youth gangs, then, became important in Mexico, as they were used to fight in the drug wars.

Violence, Crime, and Insecurity

Mexico: Reconfiguration of Crime and the Use of Violence

Crime and violence are indeed serious problems in Mexico; the state has been unable to resolve the grave public security challenges that have an impact on citizens' quality of life and potential economic growth. In states such as Baja California, Chiapas, Guerrero, Oaxaca, and the Federal

District of Mexico City, homicides account for between 20 and 30 percent of total violent deaths each year.[31] In spite of increasing media attention focused on *maras*[32] and other gangs such as Los Mexicles and Los Aztecas[33] in certain Mexican states, violence in Mexico does not originate in juvenile gangs, but is instead rooted in other forms of organized crime, mainly drug trafficking.[34] The problems of governance and violence in cities such as Ciudad Juárez, Tijuana, Nuevo Laredo, and Matamoros seem to indicate that since the drug cartels consolidated their presence in Mexico in the 1980s, the rule of law and territorial control have steadily deteriorated in certain regions, perhaps even jeopardizing governance in the country. It is precisely with respect to drug trafficking, not youth gangs, that the social fabric and the state apparatus—the two "containers" of violence in Mexico—cease to function effectively.[35]

The year 1994 is commonly identified as a turning point marking a sustained increase in public insecurity. However, there is no convincing or consistent evidence of an increase in crime and violence beginning at this time. Available statistics are often contradictory and inconsistent from one source to another. Statistics from the National Public Security System and the National Institute of Statistics and Geography (Instituto Nacional de Estadística y Geografía, INEGI) regarding homicides (often used as indicators of more comprehensive criminality) from 1980 to 2003 reveal that the number of homicides remained relatively stable. Furthermore, these statistics reflect only two significant increases in 1985 and 1992, and a tendency toward a significant decrease between 1997 and 2003.[36] Other reports on common criminality in Mexico based on the Sixth Presidential Report of Vicente Fox's government suggest a noticeable reduction in all types of crime between 1997 and 2006. According to the Judicial System of Statistics of INEGI, the number of criminals registered and prosecuted in 2003 under federal jurisdiction was 32,287; in 2008 the number was 34,856. There was no significant variation in the years in between, where numbers averaged less than 32,000. Moreover, regarding criminal acts associated with juvenile gangs or *pandillerismo,* INEGI reported a total of 29,167 cases for 2008, based on data from the municipal police. Although the number is significant, it appears less dramatic when compared with the total of 45,407 cases of domestic or intrafamily violence, a subject that typically is ignored by the media and in public discourse.[37] However, figures for the so-called federal jurisdiction, which includes crimes linked to drug trafficking, do show an increase of around 75,000 crimes per year at the end of the 1990s, rising to almost 90,000 in 2005.[38]

Figures from the Citizens' Council for Public Security and Criminal Justice indicate that the general rate of intentional violent crime (homicide, kidnapping, rape, aggravated assault, and violent theft) rose from 148 per 100,000 inhabitants in 1989 to 475 in 2006.[39] The same source indicates that one of the most rapidly increasing crimes in Mexico in recent years is kidnapping; the annual average rose from 90 in the years prior to 1993 to 600 in the years following 1997. Furthermore, in terms of perceived security and performance indicators for public security systems in Mexico City and the State of Mexico, a recent study showed that during 2005 and 2006, "at least one member in one fourth of all households . . . had been a [crime] victim, one or more times." In indexes of perception of insecurity (which run from 1 to 10, with 10 indicating the highest degree of security), Mexico City scored lower than 5.5; trust in police and justice institutions (on the same scale of 1 to 10) scored less than 4.[40]

These statistics suggest that, in spite of uncertainty generated by the disparity in data in Mexico, we can easily identify an area of growth in crime: violence linked to organized crime and drug trafficking. For example, in cities like Acapulco and Nuevo Laredo, homicide rates between 2003 and 2005 doubled, usually as a product of intensified drug-trafficking wars among traffickers themselves and against security forces.[41] These violent episodes, which seem to repeat themselves periodically, have had a significant impact on how Mexicans perceive the problem of public security, above all by creating the sensation that violence generated by drug trafficking encompasses all forms of Mexican criminality and violence.

Public perception of insecurity, therefore, has intensified significantly in Mexico in the last twenty years. At least three factors help explain the reality of intensified insecurity in Mexico: the economic crisis of 1994; the gradual political transition in Mexico, which included dismantling the PRI-style state apparatus, characterized by highly institutionalized and centralized control of decisionmaking; and the transformation of regional routes for drug trafficking as a result of the higher risk associated with the Colombia–Caribbean–South Florida route and the consequent emergence of Mexico as a key point for trafficking, distribution, and, most recently, consumption.[42]

The economic crisis of 1994 generated a significant increase in levels of public insecurity the very same year that Mexico announced it would begin economic integration with North America by putting the North American Free Trade Agreement into effect.[43] The year 1994 also saw the public emergence of the Zapatista National Liberation Army in Chiapas, one of the most influential and attention-getting guerrilla groups in Mexico's recent history, and the reappearance of guerrilla groups in other southern states such as Guerrero and Oaxaca. Criminal operations in general became more sophisticated—with the increase, for example, in the number of bands of kidnappers, drug traffickers, and human traffickers. Two high-profile political murders also seriously affected the public perception of security: the assassination of Luis Donaldo Colosio, the PRI's presidential candidate; and that of José Francisco Ruiz Massieu, the PRI's national leader.[44]

As discussed in chapter 8 by Raúl Benítez Manaut, Tania Carrasco, and Armando Rodríguez Luna, the Chiapas uprising in 1994 was the result of worsening economic conditions in the state linked to the implementation of land reform, the modernization of agriculture, and the marginalization of indigenous communities.[45] Nevertheless, although the indigenous uprising had a serious impact on the Mexican public's consciousness, which until then had seen as very remote the possibility of armed conflict within national borders, the crisis in Chiapas had relatively little to do with generating criminal violence, at least when compared with conflicts in neighboring Central American countries. A little more than a decade after the uprising, data on victimization due to violence in Mexico indicate that Chiapas is the state with the lowest crime rate.[46] Nonetheless, the Chiapas uprising contributed to the erosion of the public's perception of the Mexican government's ability to maintain a certain level of control.

During the 1990s, the PRI lost its hegemonic power; both the state apparatus and practices of co-optation that had been used to control levels of violence were slowly dismantled. Different actors in organized crime took advantage of the power vacuums left as a result of the reshuffling of power relationships. The genealogy of the recent increase in drug-related violence, for example, can be traced back to the different breakdowns of these preexisting pacts.[47] Moreover, in recent years a series of anticorruption and police reforms have severely undermined the preexisting linkages between corrupt state officials and criminal organizations.[48]

Finally, the past twenty-five years have witnessed a deterioration of the Mexican police and justice system. In the 1990s, the Ministry of the Interior observed that "there were close to 900 armed criminal gangs, more than 50 percent of which were comprised of current or retired law enforcement officers."[49] The most paradigmatic cases concern those of the Zetas and La Línea recruits, members of elite military antidrug squads recruited by drug traffickers.[50]

The efforts of President Fox's government to stop corruption and impunity never translated into real changes during his six-year term. The clearest reforms were the creation of the Ministry of Public Security and the professionalization of those employed by the security apparatuses, with help from the armed forces (this latter tendency had already been seen in the "militarization" of police forces in the Federal District government). However, impunity and corruption have continued to be the norm, and it has been impossible to successfully implement the triad that would guarantee better performance from security forces in Mexico: professionalization, better education, and higher pay.[51] Diane Davis has cited security dynamics used in the Federal District as a model to argue that the manner in which the democratization process was carried out in Mexico created competition between parties that, "together with the decentralization of the state and the fragmentation of coercive apparatus, exacerbated intra-governmental and bureaucratic conflicts"; these, in turn, prevented the police reforms needed to provide public safety and improve citizens' trust in institutions.[52]

With all these different factors affecting levels of violence in Mexico, there is no solid evidence that youth gangs like the Central American *maras* play a dominant role in the violence or levels of insecurity in Mexico. Although certain violent events can be associated with Central American–type *maras*,[53] they play a very insignificant role in Mexico's criminal violence as compared with the violence generated by drug trafficking and larger-scale organized crime. In fact, the *maras*' presence reached its highest point (in both government security programs and public opinion) in 2004, but it was confined to Mexico's southern border, specifically to the city of Tapachula in Chiapas.[54] Even there, the *mara* phenomenon took a different form. In about 2005, according to data from the Secretaría de Seguridad Pública, the majority of youth in the *maras* were young Mexicans and not Central Americans.[55] Even more important, the *maras* in Mexico adopted the characteristics of Mexican gangs—which, generally speaking, are less violent and have adopted a more fluid structure.[56]

The presence of Mexican gangs such as Los Mexicles and Los Aztecas continues to be an exception to the rule, and their presence is directly linked to the development and transformation of drug-trafficking cartels in Mexico since the mid-2000s. These gangs serve as a reservoir of armed men willing to carry out the most violent acts on behalf of the cartels. In this sense, the emergence and development of Mexican gangs can be interpreted as an indirect and unpredictable effect of the Mexican government's policies against drug trafficking since 2000. In contrast to Central American *maras*, whose transition from traditional gangs to organized forms of crime took place within an already-existent gang structure, Mexico's gangs seem to have emerged or consolidated themselves only as a result of confrontations among drug-trafficking organizations in Mexico. It is too soon to predict whether the presence of these gangs will change the way that other gangs—most of which continue to be local, transitory, and not necessarily linked to organized crime—operate in the country. It is not at all impossible that a "gang problem" would emerge in Mexico as a security threat in and of itself, linked to or parallel to the problem of drug trafficking.

Central America: From Political to Social Violence to Organized Crime

Immediately following the signing of the peace agreements in Central America, statistics measuring levels of crime and violence began to deteriorate. Beginning in the mid-1990s, El Salvador, Guatemala, and Honduras published statistics on violence that placed them at the same level as Colombia. A study sponsored by the Inter-American Development Bank found that El Salvador had homicide rates of more than 100 deaths per 100,000 inhabitants during the early years of the postwar period.[57] Another Bank publication reported that in the years following the peace agreements, Guatemala reached the astonishing level of almost 150 violent deaths per 100,000 inhabitants.[58] An analysis of crime victimization in Latin America, based on data in a Latinobarómetro survey, revealed that nearly 50 percent of households in Guatemala, El Salvador, and Venezuela reported that some family member had been the victim of a violent crime over the course of one year.[59] The same survey showed that almost all Latin American countries had household victimization indexes of more than 30 percent.

By the end of the first decade of the 2000s, Central America was the most violent region in the world outside countries at war. Rates of homicide in Guatemala, El Salvador, and Honduras (the so-called Northern Triangle) are higher than the regional average, while Nicaragua is below the average.[60] Costa Rica is the exception in the region.

Violence and social crises are not unknown in the history of Central American nations affected by crime in the 1990s. As we saw above, during the twentieth century Central American societies were governed by military or authoritarian regimes that used violence to neutralize and control political opposition and thus guarantee their own permanence.[61] Following the civil wars, violence continued to shape the lives of Central Americans, especially those in Guatemala and El Salvador. Public opinion surveys showed that once the wars were over, people became increasingly worried about new forms of violence.[62]

The increase in violence in Central America is manifest not only in the numbers of violent deaths and murders; it also appears in the form of common street crime, robbery, and assault. To Central Americans, these are the most visible forms of a larger crime wave. According to the 2010 edition of the Americas Barometer Democracy Survey, nearly 25 percent of people in Guatemala and El Salvador, as compared with 19 percent in Nicaragua, were victims of common crime in 2009.[63] All in all, statistics have shown a clear increase in violence during the posttransition years. For example, the Nicaraguan National Police recorded a total of 30,086 felonies in 1991; five years later, in 1996, this figure had risen to 54,983; and in 2002, the total number of felonies was more than 90,000.[64] Although Nicaragua has managed to reduce homicide rates since the early 2000s, and by 2009 was closer to Costa Rica than to the rest of Central America in terms of violent deaths, overall figures for property crime remain relatively high.[65]

In El Salvador, crimes processed by the Attorney General's Office increased from 20,812 in 1994 to 40,410 in 1998. In 2000, more than 31,000 of the cases brought before the authorities involved violent crimes (homicides, assaults, damage, and extortion). In fact, the increase of homicides has been so significant throughout the 2000s in El Salvador that by 2009, the country's murder rate approached the figures of the immediate posttransition period, with 72 homicides per 100,000 inhabitants, the highest in the Western Hemisphere.[66] By 2010, the homicide rate in Honduras exceeded that of El Salvador.[67]

However, not all Central American nations exhibited the same types of violence. Delinquency and common violence affect Central American societies in different ways. Generally speaking, whereas Guatemala and El Salvador differ from Nicaragua in terms of global violence, they are also marked by serious problems with organized crime (kidnapping, bank robbery, drug-trafficking networks) and *maras*.[68] In Guatemala, although state violence decreased following the peace treaties, agents of the state continue to be an important source of public insecurity,[69] together with organized crime, gangs, and common criminals. Other forms of violence include striking levels of public lynchings.[70] In El Salvador, by contrast, violence by state agents has been less of a problem. Rather, organized crime, youth gangs, routine common delinquency, and killings by hired assassins are the main aspects of violence in El Salvador, the smallest country in the region.[71] Despite differences in the forms of violence in Central American nations, countries of northern Central America have shared similar demographic conditions that have given rise to violent youth gangs, or *maras*.

The penetration of drug cartels into Central America and the transformation of the region into a major transshipment route following the disruption of Caribbean routes in the late 1990s have also transformed the dynamics of violence in Central America and contributed to the soaring rates of homicides. Although *maras* have not taken over the key drug-trafficking activities in the region, and the major drug-related activity in Central America remains the transportation of drugs between South America and Mexico, youth gang cells have become a frequently used asset in resolving internal disputes over the control and protection of transportation routes.[72]

The *Maras* and Government Responsibility

The *maras,* though not solely responsible for Central American violence, contribute significantly to the crimes of homicide, robbery, and extortion in Guatemala, El Salvador, and Honduras. Data from the Salvadoran police attributed more than 30 percent of all murders in the country to the *maras,* a total of more than 700 homicides per year;[73] more significantly, 70 percent of extortion cases were credited to youth gangs.[74]

The Central American civil wars, widely cited by government agencies and the media as responsible for the army of youths prepared to use intense violence, cannot alone explain the fact that hundreds of young people join gangs. Although certain publications have pointed to the connection between the armed conflicts and the current gang phenomenon,[75] none of the original studies of Central American gangs showed any evidence that children and young people who had fought in the civil wars in El Salvador and Guatemala (Honduras did not experience civil war during the 1980s) had become members of the *maras.*[76] Nor did later studies find any organic link between the *maras* and former combatants.[77] Perhaps the best evidence for this lack of connection is the fact that Honduras, which did not experience civil war, has developed a serious problem with *maras* and gangs, almost on a par with El Salvador and greater than the problem in Guatemala. Conversely, Nicaragua, which suffered from a prolonged armed conflict during the 1980s, has not produced *maras* like its neighbors to the north.[78] It is not the case that the Central American wars in general have nothing to do with the later emergence of gangs. Rather, the armed conflicts contributed by creating other conditions that later favored the unique development of the Central American *maras.* The wars were responsible for the exile and later migratory returns that helped disseminate gang culture, exacerbating the preexisting culture of violence in Salvadoran society, and they facilitated access for young people to all kinds of firearms.[79]

The *mara* phenomenon emerged toward the end of the 1980s. Indeed, the first systematic study of the subject was done in Guatemala in 1986.[80] Since that time, gang membership has significantly increased, the *mara* phenomenon has spread to other regions, and *mara* methods of operation have intensified.[81] For many years, governments in northern Central America paid no attention to the problem, allowing the phenomenon to expand relatively slowly and silently.[82]

Government attitudes changed in the early 2000s, when hard-line and zero-tolerance plans went into effect in the three countries of northern Central America. Generally known as *mano dura* (firm-hand or iron-fist) policies,[83] these programs declared war on gangs and introduced an environment in which state force was the main means of confronting the problem.[84] In response, the gangs redesigned their operations; they reorganized their structures more vertically, rigidly, and violently and began to recognize leadership that allowed for formal communication with other gangs and with organized crime.[85] Consequently and paradoxically, the *mano dura* and zero-tolerance policies that have dominated in northern Central America have aggravated the gang situation. By the middle of the 2000s, gangs had become a clear threat to security in the region. They no longer constitute only a circumstantial risk to those living in the urban communities where they operate; they also have become—or are in the process of becoming—groups involved in organized crime whose main motivation is the illegal control of resources and persons in particular communities. The exercise of violence has become the most common and definitive characteristic of their actions.[86]

Although the factors that gave rise to the gang phenomenon in Central America are diverse and their interaction in local contexts is very complex, the dimensions and nature of the phenomenon cannot be explained without considering how states have responded to the violence and criminality of the *maras*.[87] States have responded in two ways. One response is framed by the legality and formality of institutions devoted to justice and security. The second—less evident but probably much more decisive in the war against the *maras*—is illegal and covert; it is not entirely controlled by the formal instruments of state power, although it is facilitated by them. The second response is a direct product of the failure to establish transparent institutions of public security during the period of postwar political transition.

Legal Responses

Legal responses guided by the institutional framework can be divided in two types of policies. One is the development of zero-tolerance and *mano dura* policies aimed at gangs and youths suspected of being involved in violence; the other involves the development and implementation of government-sponsored programs for the prevention of youth violence. The former is clearly defined, but with differences in implementation in Guatemala, El Salvador, and Honduras. The latter is found primarily in Nicaragua.[88] (Mexico's response has been different; there, the state has all but ignored youth gangs, partly due to the overwhelming problems of drug trafficking and organized crime.) *Mano dura* policies consist of police programs that have identified the *maras* and young people associated with them as Public Enemy No. 1, deserving of repression, control, and incarceration. Preventive programs include projects that define these youths as a vulnerable population who must be attended to, stimulated, protected, and monitored as necessary. Prevention programs do not obviate the need for law enforcement aimed at young people operating outside the law, but also provide prevention efforts, aid, and rehabilitation for young people at risk.

Governments with *mano dura* gang policies have implemented specific prevention, rehabilitation, and reinsertion programs for gang members, especially following the resounding failure of zero-tolerance policies. Similarly, the Nicaraguan government and state institutions have at times succumbed to the temptation of excessive repression of *mareros* when conditions seemed out of control. However, in northern Central America the emphasis has been, above all, on repression, whereas Nicaragua (and also Costa Rica) has favored a more integrated approach. Under the repressive model, the success or failure of state action is assessed by the number of young gang members who have been captured and incarcerated. Under the Nicaraguan model, the most important indicator is the number of young people enrolled in preventive programs organized by the police and the Ministry of Youth.[89]

The implementation of *mano dura* policies in northern Central America was inspired by the zero-tolerance model adopted in several North American cities, especially New York, at the beginning of the 1990s.[90] This model became attractive because of its apparent success in reducing levels of criminality in the United States, but also because U.S. agencies such as the Federal Bureau of Investigation, the Drug Enforcement Administration, and several big-city police departments cooperated extensively with area governments on questions of security.[91] The model was implemented, however, based on a unique interpretation of its doctrine and mechanisms. More important, it was applied by institutions suffering from serious defects of control, supervision, and efficiency. That is, the *mano dura* policies were implemented through weak, inefficient institutions with a strong authoritarian legacy from their military past.

In addition, *mano dura* policies were created not only to combat crime by the *maras* but also as a political ploy to win votes in elections and to help governments gain legitimacy among populations disenchanted with their performance. The first example of this political manipulation took place in Guatemala during the presidential campaign of Alfonso Portillo (2000–4), who later implemented Plan Escoba (the "Broom Plan") in 2000 aimed at controlling gangs. In Honduras, President Ricardo Maduro (2002–6) implemented zero-tolerance plans (first called "Libertad Azul," or "Blue Freedom"), which included broad sweeps by police and military forces to pursue and incarcerate gang members. Under these programs, gang members were even accused of being terrorists and suspected of having links with Middle Eastern terrorist organizations.[92] Zero-tolerance programs were also part of the electoral platform of the "officialist candidate" in the 2005 Honduran elections. It was in El Salvador, however, that the electoral aims of the *mano dura* policies were most evident. The government of conservative President Francisco Flores presented its first *mano dura* policy nine months before the 2004 presidential elections.[93] Thirteen months later, following the official party's reelection, the new Salvadoran government led by President Antonio Saca (2004–9) promoted the Super Mano Dura Plan, a continuation of previous policy. The effort at Super Mano Dura was launched in the context of another electoral campaign, this time for mayors and for deputies in the Legislative Assembly.

Mano dura policies were essentially plans for police intervention based heavily on military strategy. Honduras and El Salvador both approved laws or legal reforms allowing security forces to pursue and capture youths suspected of belonging to a gang, without evidence or formal procedures. Both administrations used the plans as linchpins for government efforts; both moved to reclaim the involvement of national armies in antigang operations; and both developed operations that allowed for the capture and mass incarceration of gang members, thus saturating and overpopulating the penitentiary system. For example, in El Salvador a 2005 report by the National Civilian Police detailed how, between July 23, 2003, and July 8,

2005, the police captured 30,934 gang members. Although the majority of these arrests represented different captures of the same person (gang members were arrested, freed after 48 hours, and then arrested again), the figure reflects the volume of antigang police activity that took place in a relatively short period of time.[94] In Honduras, operations aimed at incarcerating gang members resulted in a much smaller number of gang members in prison. According to a 2009 report, approximately 5,000 persons were incarcerated in a two-year period, having been accused of forming part of "illegal associations," a legal category allowing for the jailing of gang members. Almost a quarter of these gang members were arrested in the first five months (between August and December 2003), with some 277 gang members incarcerated per month.[95] The intensity of operations in Honduras, whose legal system permitted longer prison sentences for gang members, initially reduced both the number of gang members on the streets and the number of subsequent arrests. But human rights conditions deteriorated as these policies were implemented.[96]

In contrast, Nicaragua's approach to gangs was rooted more in a communitarian-based deterrence strategy, described by some police authorities as a "social accord" (*concertación social*).[97] The Nicaraguan police paid attention to the fact that, whereas "zero-tolerant" New York reduced crime to the same extent as "community-oriented" San Diego, the latter managed to do so with significantly fewer arrests and even reduced the number of complaints against the police for human rights abuses. Some critics of the Nicaraguan Police argue that their policy was possible because of the links between gangs and some Sandinista police cadres. Those cadres used youth gangs as "shock troops" during periods of social turmoil to pressure the administrations of presidents Arnoldo Alemán (1997–2002) and Enrique Bolaños (2002–7) over contentious political issues.[98] Although this is a plausible explanation, it is also true that the Nicaraguan Police adopted a completely different strategy to confront gangs than police forces in the rest of the region. In some way, the Nicaraguan approach was closer to Mexican tactics of clientelistic co-optation than to the Northern Triangle's total war on gangs.

Extralegal Responses

It is impossible to understand the magnitude of the phenomenon of violence in northern Central America, to which the *maras* contribute, without appreciating that a substantial portion of the extralegal violence and "social cleansing" has been facilitated by the consent and even at times the direct participation of agents of the state. This participation is, for the most part, enabled by the institutional weakness that characterized the reforms that emerged from political transitions and peace processes. These transitions were compromised by the same political elite that signed the peace treaties and formally approved the reforms.[99] Although in Guatemala, El Salvador, and Honduras many reforms were implemented to strengthen and institutionalize public security, including the creation of new police forces, these institutions preserved many of their former practices. This is primarily because the elite retained the same military commanders in public security institutions, even if they no longer formally served as members of the armed forces. Many of those responsible for serious human rights violations retained their positions following the transitions, and their influence in power structures continued.[100] This meant that politically motivated illegal armed groups survived and transformed themselves into organized crime groups and clandestine groups operating from within the structures of the state.[101]

These groups, along with actors with links to particular governments, later actively participated in the maelstrom of violence unleashed against the *maras* as part of the *mano dura* policies.[102] *Mano dura* and zero-tolerance policies in the region opened the door to extralegal responses by facilitating three developments related to the war on gangs. First, security institutions allowed their internal control and supervision systems to slacken; the persecution of gangs led to the violation of the fundamental human rights of those arrested. In Honduras, the government was indifferent to the ways that zero-tolerance policies were implemented and disinclined to control the abuses by its own agents or to prevent the involvement of external actors in operations of social cleansing. A U.S. State Department report on human rights in Honduras in 2005 cited extralegal assassinations and summary executions of those suspected of belonging to gangs committed by members of police and security forces.[103] There have also been massacres within prisons, resulting in the murders of more than 170 incarcerated gang members in one year, murders that were probably committed with the participation of the authorities.[104] Other reports on human rights have made similar findings for Guatemala and El Salvador.[105]

Second, the authorities responsible for *mano dura* policies used rhetoric that made it possible for armed groups engaged in social cleansing to increase their activities against young people suspected of gang membership. Several reports from Casa Alianza Honduras, an organization dedicated to the protection of children and youth rights, indicated that approximately 70 percent of murders committed against youths under the age of twenty-three years are carried out by unknown assassins in what resemble death squad operations. Casa Alianza's December 2006 report stated that "bloody events show that the assassins planned the deaths, kidnapping their victims in unmarked vehicles and carrying out executions on vacant lots, shooting at vital body parts to ensure the victim would die. . . . This pattern of executions is repeated over and over again, with only slight variations."[106] A report from the Forensic Institute of El Salvador in 2005 stated that 59 percent of the more than 3,800 murders committed that year were by unknown assailants, many of them bearing the marks of summary executions.

Official statements and speeches announcing the antigang programs emphasized the need for all-out war on gangs and delinquent youths, while criticizing the respect for and observance of the rights of suspects. Generally speaking, the message was that human rights were an obstacle to combating gangs. A statement by former president Ricardo Maduro of Honduras sums up this position:

> Given the 6 million Hondurans with their hands tied in the face of gang violence, whose human rights are more important? Those of the innocent citizens representing the vast majority of the population, or those of the criminals violating the rights of others? As soon as the Anti-Maras Law goes into effect, we'll storm the streets to do what the Honduran people have demanded: freedom from the yoke that *maras* have placed on them.[107]

This type of rhetoric created a climate that certain sectors in Central America interpreted as ripe for social cleansing activities against gang members. That is, certain sectors of society, including some with links to state apparatuses, interpreted the call for a war on gangs as a license to exterminate young people associated with them.

Finally, the *mano dura* offensive allowed actors other than those linked to the state apparatus to participate in the war on gangs. Businessmen became involved at various levels in financing illegal groups, civilians seeking retribution in the form of social cleansing participated, and an economy of crime developed wherein assassins were contracted to eliminate enemies. During the period of *mano dura,* violence generated by other members of society was attributed to youth gangs, which became scapegoats for all forms of crime.[108] A survey in Guatemala in 2006 found that nearly one-third of the population supported this type of vigilante justice and 43 percent of the population supported the social cleansing taking place at the time.[109] The 2010 Americas Barometer revealed that in El Salvador, 52.6 percent of all citizens supported the idea of authorities acting outside the law as long as they captured the delinquents; in Honduras 46 percent of the population agreed with these tactics.[110] These attitudes were interpreted by authorities and civilians as signifying tacit approval for the excesses committed in the war on gangs and thus contributed to the general climate of social confrontation in which the violence increased.

To summarize, *mano dura* programs exacerbated the conditions that unleashed agents of violence who were not demobilized through public security reforms during political transitions. At the time when *mano dura* programs were launched in northern Central America, security institutions still faced problems with internal corruption, links with organized crime, human rights violations that were not adequately investigated, and political leadership that, in some cases, had turned the issue of security and security institutions into an electoral instrument, publicly scorning the commitment to human rights and civil liberties. These factors transformed *mano dura* programs into a consummate vehicle for reversing the progress in public security reforms and for eroding state institutions.

In response to the policy, gangs prepared for an all-out war against governments already suffering from serious problems of political legitimacy. For the gangs, this war never had a political agenda; rather, gang members faced offensives by the state by punishing those they suspected of collaborating with the government or simply by increasing their violent actions. It is beyond the scope of this chapter to detail how the gangs prepared for or waged this war.[111] Undeniably, however, the transformation of Central American gangs from 2000 onward into groups bordering on organized crime is, to a large extent, a product of the way Central American governments chose to confront them.[112]

By contrast, youth gangs in Mexico were never singled out as a target for government security programs. With the exception of some limited initiatives in the area of Chiapas, the Mexican state never had as a cornerstone of public security policy a war against youth gangs. To the extent that youth gangs stayed out of major drug cartel activities, they were spared inclusion in the war against drugs carried out by the Mexican state. Thus, their need for the kind of violent transformations that took place in Central America has been less urgent.

Conclusion

Some criminologists believe that youth gangs are not sui generis, but rather are a product of complex interactions within an environment in which public policy and the state play fundamental roles.[113] This interpretation is especially important in understanding the Central American *maras*. The phenomenon of youth street gangs occurs throughout the Mesoamerican region, including Costa Rica and Nicaragua; nevertheless, gangs in these countries and in Mexico did not evolve in the same way as those in Guatemala, El Salvador, and Honduras. In northern Central America, traditional gangs have evolved into confederations of youths capable of high levels of violence and, in some cases, with fairly well-organized structures.

What, then, is the common denominator among these countries in recent years? This chapter has argued that migration, poverty, and armed conflict have not, in and of themselves, determined the current characteristics of *maras* in northern Central America. Factors such as migration explain the transnational character of the phenomenon, but it is necessary to look for local variables to explain why gangs play a more important role in some countries than in others. The case of Mexico illustrates that an issue such as migration explains the phenomenon up to a point, but then local variables become significant. For example, Mexico has a long history of sending migrants and also being a point of transit or settlement for migrants from elsewhere. Even so, Central American–type gangs have not become relevant factors in violence and organized crime in Mexico. In fact, in two of the cities most affected by migration—Tapachula, on Mexico's southern border in Chiapas; and Tijuana, on the northern border—there are few signs of a *maras* presence. Studies of the *maras* by the Transnational Analysis Network (a group of academics in which the authors of this chapter participate) show that the presence of gangs is quite marginal. In the case of Tapachula, those *maras* that do exist have been brought under control by the security operations of the Chiapas government. Further, Hurricane Stan destroyed the rail lines that had transported Central American migrants and had been a favorite target of youth gang members.[114] Mexican local gangs have a greater presence, although the levels of violence associated with them are much lower; and compared with other actors in organized crime (particularly those linked to drug-trafficking networks), they pose a considerably lower threat to public security. Gangs such as Los Mexicles and Los Aztecas, whose organization and rationale are linked to but also dependent upon the main drug cartels in Mexico, continue to be an exception to the rule: They constitute a security threat only to the extent that they reinforce the presence and violence of drug-trafficking cartels. In Nicaragua, a country that is among the poorest not only in Central America but in all Latin America and that lived through a devastating civil war lasting more than a decade, gangs have more traditional characteristics and continue to provide hundreds of young people from poor neighborhoods with an identity, protection, and a sense of belonging.[115] Thus, Nicaragua further demonstrates that variables such as poverty or the status as a postwar society have less explanatory power; more important are the institutional responses by the state (in the Nicaraguan case, less repressive and more focused on prevention).

In Guatemala, El Salvador, and Honduras, the common denominator associated with the *maras* is a repressive government response carried out through programs that formally and informally violate the public security institutions that have already been weakened in the wake of political transitions. These repressive programs were made possible in part by the failure of reforms to establish transparent and professional institutions independent of electoral agendas. This does not mean that other countries in the region have not had problems with the institutionalization of public security; rather, in northern Central America, the democratic transitions were unable to uproot certain practices and structures from the past, which in the end determined how the new institutions would respond to public security challenges. As Frances Hagopian argues, the type of authoritarian regime determines the possibilities available to posttransition regimes.[116] In Central America, this meant a reliance on militarized responses; the use of informal actors not always under strict government supervision; human rights violations permitted by the political leadership; and, finally, the extermination of gang members just as rebels had been dealt with in the past.

The Mexican case is distinct. Lacking Central America's history of violent repression, Mexico has a more intact social fabric and an alternative way of integrating legal and illegal activities. Historically, the state and governmental institutions have more effectively absorbed the criminal networks of informal protection, making unrestrained violence less essential to the state's project of public order and security. These are fundamental factors for understanding the specific trajectory of gangs and of juvenile violence in general. The seventy-two years of dominance by the PRI left a legacy of state presence in practically all areas of social life. Numerous authors have detailed how the PRI co-opted different actors from the business world, farming communities, and working-class sectors, to resolve conflicts and prevent potential crises of governance from "overflowing" without the need for radically repressive mechanisms. The corruption and co-optation of PRI governments were not just tools for sustaining the system itself, as Jesús Silva-Herzog Márquez affirms; they were also critical to the operation of a system of "rewards and punishments" that kept illegality within the framework of the institutionalized state.[117]

These structures apparently began to dissolve with the change of power during Mexico's political transition, but the public security problems caused by the transition are different from those in Central America. The end of corporatism in Mexico led, instead, to conflicts within state public security institutions. Organized crime, much more powerful than the Central American gangs, has taken advantage of these conflicts. This has led to less widespread but equally severe violence, which is less street based but just as threatening to the consolidation of a democratic state. In other words, Mexico, with its unfinished transition to democracy and out-of-control drug trafficking, faces a serious problem of dissolution of its public institutions and social fabric. This situation could very well lead to a more fertile ground for increasingly violent youth gangs like those in northern Central America.

In Central America, the recent penetration of drug cartels has added even more violence to that already exercised by increasingly powerful gangs, social cleansing groups, and rogue police and military officers. In Mexico, violence has been unleashed as the informal mechanisms of protection of the old regime have been dismantled, without a solid institutional framework to substitute for it. In both Mexico and Central America, the challenge is clear: Public security must be institutionalized in order for democracy and the rule of law to be consolidated. Violence is a symptom of state weakness and of the failure to institutionalize important democratic reforms. In Central America, such weakness manifests itself in the war on gangs; in Mexico, it is manifest in the war on drugs.

Notes

1. When speaking of "Central American gangs," we generally refer to the gangs operating in the Northern Triangle of Central America (Honduras, Guatemala, and El Salvador), commonly known as "*maras*." The gangs in Nicaragua and Costa Rica, as explained further on, display different characteristics.

2. The *maras* constitute one of most dangerous threats to peace in the region since the end of the Central American civil wars, but they are not the only threats. See Ana Arana, "How the Street Gangs Took Central America," *Foreign Affairs* 84 (2005): 98. José Miguel Cruz has defined *maras* as a vast network of groups of people associated with the identity franchises of two street gangs that had their origins in the city of Los Angeles, but whose development no longer depends on the U.S. dynamics. See José Miguel Cruz, "Central American *Maras:* From Youth Street Gangs to Transnational Protection Rackets," *Global Crime* 11 (2010): 379–98. In the case of Mexico, it could be claimed that the "gang problem" also experience a recent shift, from the predominant presence of traditional gangs to the recent emergence of gang organizations with a function, structure, and rationale completely linked to drug trafficking and the development of intercartel and state-cartel warfare. However, it is too soon to determine the nature and scope of this new type of gang in Mexico or to predict the impact they will have on other juvenile gangs that continue to operate under a more traditional scheme. The authors carried out the research for this chapter precisely when the Zetas and gangs like Los Aztecas, Los Mexicles, and the Artistas Asesinos (Killer Artists) began to appear.

3. See José Miguel Cruz, *Street Gangs in Central America* (San Salvador: UCA Editores, 2007); and Cruz, "Central American *Maras.*"

4. See María Santacruz Giralt, *Seconds in the Air: Women Gang-Members and Their Prisons* (San Salvador: UCA Editores, 2010).

5. Jeffrey Passel of the Pew Hispanic Center states that nearly 80 percent of illegal migration to the United States originates in Mexico and Central America. See Jeffrey Passel, "Estimates of the Size and Characteristics of the Undocumented Population," Pew Hispanic Center, http://pewhispanic.org/files/reports/44.pdf.

6. See Jerry Seper, "Al Qaeda Seeks Tie to Local Gangs; Salvadoran Group May Aid Entry to the U.S.," *Washington Times,* September 28, 2004.

7. See Max G. Mainwaring, "Gangs and Coups D'Streets in the New World Disorder: Protean Insurgents in Post-Modern War," *Global Crime* 7 (2004): 505.

8. See Centro de Estudios y Programas Interamericanos, "Red Transnacional de Análisis sobre Maras," Instituto Tecnológico Autónomo de México, http://interamericanos.itam.mx/maras/vinculos.html. The most recent empirical research on Central American gangs conducted by the UCA in El Salvador shows a clear distinction made by gang members between them and drug-related organized crime. See Santacruz Giralt, *Seconds in the Air.*

9. Steven S. Dudley, *Drug Trafficking Organizations in Central America: Transportistas, Mexican Cartels, and Maras* (Washington, D.C.: Woodrow Wilson Center and Trans-Border Institute, University of San Diego, 2010).

10. INTERPOL, "Fenómeno de las pandillas en la región centroamericana y la importancia de la cooperación internacional," http://www.cicad.oas.org/Crimen_Organizado/ESP/Reuniones/Tapachula2005/Presentaciones/Interpol%20-%20El%20Salvador%20-%20Fenomeno%20de%20las%20Pandillas%20o%20Maras%20en%20C%20A.pdf.

11. Chiapas Secretaría de Seguridad Pública, *Escenarios de la Mara Salvatrucha (X3) y Barrio Dieciocho (XV3)* (Chiapas, Mexico: Unidad de Prevención del Delito y Política Criminal, 2005).

12. See Centro de Estudios y Programas Interamericanos, "Red Transnacional."

13. Ibid. See also ERIC, IDIES, IDESO, and IUDOP, *Maras y pandillas en Centroamérica, Volume I* (Managua: UCA Publicaciones, 2000).

14. One notable exception to this is John Hagedorn, *A World of Gangs: Armed Young Men and Gangsta Culture* (Minneapolis: University of Minnesota Press, 2008).

15. There has been a lot of discussion regarding when political transitions in each of the Central American countries began and ended. For practical reasons, here we use the date of peace agreements in Guatemala and El Salvador, and the 1990 elections in Nicaragua as central events in these transitions. This does not mean that transitions began or ended with these events, only that the events substantially define the nature of political changes that followed in each of the countries.

16. Edelberto Torres-Rivas, "Foundations: Central America," in *Democracy in Latin America: (Re)Constructing Political Society,* edited by Manuel Antonio Garretón and Edward Newman (New York: United Nations University Press, 2001), 99–125.

17. Rachel Sieder, "War, Peace, and Memory Politics in Central America," in *The Politics of Memory: Transitional Justice in Democratizing Societies,* edited by Alexandra Barahona de Brito et al. (Oxford: Oxford University Press, 2001), 161–89.

18. However, in El Salvador the government began to use the army in the mid-1990s to aid the police in public security tasks, renewing the practice of involving the military in fighting crime. This collaboration increased in the hard-line campaigns against the *maras* that began in 2003 with the adoption of Joint Patrol Units, small patrols made up of members of the police and the army. Guatemala followed generally the same pattern.

19. Charles Call, "Democratization, War, and State-Building: Constructing the Rule of Law in El Salvador," *Journal of Latin American Studies* 35 (2003): 827–62.

20. See Cynthia J. Arnson, ed., *Comparative Peace Processes in Latin America* (Washington, D.C., and Stanford, Calif.: Woodrow Wilson Center Press and Stanford University Press, 1999); and Terry Lynn Karl, "The Hybrid Regimes of Central America," *Journal of Democracy* 6 (1995): 72–86.

21. Garretón, Newman, and Torres-Rivas thus refer to them as "foundational democracies." See Garretón and Newman, *Democracy.*

22. José Miguel Cruz, *¿Elecciones para qué? El impacto de la cultura política salvadoreña en el ciclo electoral 1999–2000* (San Salvador: Facultad Latinoamericana de Ciencias Sociales–Programa El Salvador, 2001).

23. Gino Costa, *La nueva Policía Nacional Civil de El Salvador (1990–1997)* (San Salvador: UCA Editores, 1999).

24. The figures on Guatemala and Nicaragua come from Jack Spence, *War and Peace in Central America: Comparing Transitions toward Democracy and Social Equity in Guatemala, El Salvador, and Nicaragua* (Brookline, Mass.: Hemisphere Initiatives, 2004).

25. Luis Rubio and Susan Kaufman Purcell, eds., *Mexico under Fox* (Boulder, Colo.: Lynne Rienner, 2004).

26. Raúl Benítez Manaut, "Seguridad y defensa en México: Proceso de toma de decisiones y amenazas," in *Reforma de las fuerzas armadas en América Latina y el impacto de las amenazas irregulares,* Latin American Program Reports on the Americas 20, edited by José Raúl Perales (Washington, D.C.: Woodrow Wilson International Center for Scholars), 49–57.

27. Chappell Lawson, "Mexico's Unfinished Transition: Democratization and Authoritarian Enclaves in Mexico," *Mexican Studies* 16 (2000): 267–87.

28. Diane Davis, "Undermining the Rule of Law: Democratization and the Dark Side of Police Reform in Mexico," *Latin American Politics and Society* 48 (2006): 55–86.

29. Ibid.

30. Richard Snyder and Angelica Durán-Martínez, "Does Illegality Breed Violence? Drug Trafficking and State-Sponsored Protection Rackets," *Crime, Law and Social Change* 52 (2009): 265–73.

31. These statistics were presented by INEGI for 2002 to 2005.

32. See, e.g., "Invaden México pandillas centroamericanas," *El Universal,* December 19, 2003.

33. According to media sources, the gang known as Los Aztecas works directly with the Juárez Cartel and collaborates with La Línea, the main armed group of the cartel. They are located in Juárez, Chihuahua, but allegedly also operate in and recruit some of their members from El Paso and other cities in Texas (i.e., Dallas and Austin). The gangs known as Los Mexicles and the Artistas Asesinos (Killer Artists) work with the Sinaloa cartel. They operate also in Juárez and allegedly across the border (i.e., El Paso, San Diego, and Los Angeles). As is usually the case with statistics related to crime, estimates of the number of members of each gang vary widely, from 5,000 to 7,000 in the case of Los Aztecas and to 3,000 to 5,000 for Los Mexicles.

See "Las cárceles de Juárez, el otro infierno," *Milenio* online, March 8, 2009, http://impreso.milenio.com/node/8541717; "Drugs and Violence: Mexico . . .," BBC News, September 3, 2010, http://www.bbc.co.uk/news/world-latin-america-11174174; and "Death Toll in Juarez . . .," *New York Times,* October 24, 2010, http://www.nytimes.com/2010/10/25/world/americas/25mexico.html?scp=2&sq=gangs mexico drug cartels&st=cse.

34. See Laurie Freeman, *State of Siege: Drug-Related Violence and Corruption in Mexico—Unintended Consequences of the War on Drugs,* WOLA Special Report (Washington, D.C.: Washington Office on Latin America, 2006); and John Bailey and Jorge Chabat, *Transnational Crime and Public Security: Challenges to Mexico and the United States* (La Jolla: Center for U.S.-Mexican Studies, University of California, San Diego, 2002).

35. According to Perea Restrepo, gangs in Mexico differ from their Central American counterparts in terms of the greater social ties they continue to hold with certain institutions or social groups that exist outside the gang, such as the family, the school, or the work space. Accordingly, the gang is just one among many parallel spaces of conviviality and identity formation. This, claims Perea, is explained by the key role played by the symbolic and institutional presence of the state, the nation, and the community. The police forces of the state are usually feared and therefore obeyed by gang members; the nation is present in the form of symbolic celebrations that link the gang with other members of the community; and, finally, the "barrio" mediates and limits the criminal and violent behavior of the gang. See "Caso Mexico," developed by Carlos Mario Perea Restrepo at the Centro de Estudios y Programas Interamericanos, "Red Transnacional de Análisis sobre Maras," Instituto Tecnológico Autónomo de México, http://interamericanos.itam.mx/maras/diagnosticos.html. Also see Carlos Mario Perea Restrepo, "El frio del miedo: Violencia y cultura en Mexico," *Revista CIDOB d'Afers Internacionals* 81 (2008): 17–43.

36. Arturo Arango and Cristina Lara, "El homicidio en México," in *Seguridad Pública en México* (Mexico: CrisAda Editorial, 2007).

37. INEGI, "Resultados de la Encuesta Nacional de Gobierno, Seguridad Publica y Justicia Municipal," 2010, 275; available at www.inegi.org.mx.

38. Raúl Benítez Manaut, "Seguridad nacional y gobernabilidad en México: Criminalidad y fronteras," in *Conocer la guerra, construir la seguridad: Aproximaciones desde la sociedad civil,* edited by Ana Maria Tamayo (Lima: IDL, 2008).

39. José Antonio Ortega, ed., "Seguridad ¡Ahora!" (Mexico City: Consejo Ciudadano para la Seguridad Pública, 2007), http://www.seguridadjusticiaypaz.org/dmdocuments/SEGURIDADAHORA%20_FULL.pdf.

40. IDE and Seguridad Ciudadana, "Índices de Desempeño del Sistema de Seguridad Pública y Justicia Penal," Reporte 2005–6, http://www.seguridad-ciudadana.org/CIDE-Seguridad%20Ciudadana%20(Documento%20para%20medios).pdf.

41. Freeman, *State of Siege.*

42. Snyder and Durán-Martínez, "Does Illegality Breed Violence?"

43. Angel Gustavo López-Montiel, "The Military, Political Power, and Police Relations México City," *Latin American Perspectives* 27 (2000): 79.

44. Raúl Benítez Manaut, "México: Seguridad ciudadana, conflictos y orden público," *Revista Nueva Sociedad* 191 (2004): 103.

45. See Neil Harvey, "Rebellion in Chiapas: Rural Reforms and Popular Struggle," *Third World Quarterly* 16 (1995): 39.

46. Instituto Ciudadano de Estudios sobre la Inseguridad, "Homicidios del orden común, 1997–2010: Total y por cada 100,000 habitantes," http://www.icesi.org.mx/documentos/estadisticas/estadisticasOfi/denuncias_homicidio_1997_2010.pdf.

47. Freeman, *State of Siege.*

48. According to Snyder and Durán-Martínez, these reforms have decentralized, democratized, and multiplied the number of law-enforcement actors, diminishing the possibility of racketeering on both ends and increasing the possibility of intra-cartel and state-cartel warfare and violence. See Snyder and Durán-Martínez, "Does Illegality Breed Violence?"

49. López-Montiel, "Military, Political Power, and Police Relations," 106.

50. Freeman, *State of Siege.*

51. Ibid, 110.

52. Davis, "Undermining the Rule of Law."

53. Manaut, "México."

54. Gema Santamaría, "Maras y pandillas: Límites de su transnacionalidad," *Revista Mexicana de Política Exterior,* no. 81 (2007): 101, http://portal.sre.gob.mx/imr/pdf/04GemaS.pdf.

55. Rodrigo Sigfrid, "Las políticas de mano dura en Guatemala, Honduras y El Salvador, y su repercusión en el incremento de la presencia mara en la frontera sur de México," thesis, Instituto Tecnológico Autónomo de México, 2006, 39–40.

56. Perea-Restrepo, "Frio del miedo."

57. José Miguel Cruz et. al., "De la guerra al delito: Evolución de la violencia en El Salvador," in *Asalto al desarrollo: Violencia en América Latina,* edited by Juan Luis Londoño, Alejandro Gaviria, and Rodrigo Guerrero (Washington, D.C.: Inter-American Development Bank, 2001), 173–204.

58. Mayra Buvinic, Andrew Morrison, and Michael Shifter, *Violence in Latin America and the Caribbean: A Framework for Action* (Washington, D.C.: Inter-American Development Bank, 1999).

59. Alejandro Gaviria and Carmen Pagés, *Patterns of Crime Victimization in Latin America,* Working Paper 408 (Washington, D.C.: Inter-American Development Bank, 1999).

60. United Nations Development Program, *Informe sobre desarrollo humano para América Central 2009–2010: Abrir espacios a la seguridad ciudadana y el desarrollo humano* (Bogotá: United Nations Development Program, 2009).

61. Torres Rivas, "Foundations."

62. José Miguel Cruz, "The Peace Accords Ten Years Later: A Citizen's Perspective," in *El Salvador's Democratic Transition Ten Years after the Peace Accords,* Latin American Program Reports on the Americas 6, edited by Cynthia Arnson (Washington, D.C.: Woodrow Wilson Center for International Scholars, 2003), 13–36.

63. Mitchell Seligson, Elizabeth Zechmeister, and Diana Orcés, *Political Culture of Democracy, 2010: Democratic Consolidation in the Americas during Hard Times* (Nashville: LAPOP, 2010).

64. Policía Nacional de Nicaragua, *Anuario Estadístico 2002* (Managua: Policía Nacional, 2002).

65. United Nations Development Program, *Informe sobre desarrollo humano para América Central 2009–2010.*

66. Diego Murcia, "2009, el año más violento desde 1992," *El Faro,* January 3, 2010, http://www.elfaro.net/es/201001/noticias/820/.

67. Instituto Universitario de Democracia, Paz y Seguridad, "Observatorio de la violencia: Mortalidad y otros, Enero–diciembre 2010," *Boletín* 20 (marzo 2011): 4.

68. See Charles Call, *Sustainable Development in Central America: The Challenges of Violence, Injustice and Insecurity,* CA 2020: Working Paper 8 (Hamburg: Institute for Latinoamerika-Kunde, 2000); and Caroline Moser and Ailsa Winton, *Violence in the Central American Region: Towards an Integrated Framework of Violence Reduction* (London: Overseas Development Institute, 2002).

69. Jennifer Schirmer, *The Guatemalan Military Project: A Violence Called Democracy* (Philadelphia: University of Pennsylvania Press, 2000).

70. Carlos A. Mendoza, *Ausencia del Estado y violencia colectiva en tierras mayas: Una aproximación cuantitativa al fenómeno de los linchamientos en Guatemala (1996–2002)* (Guatemala City: Facultad Latinoamericana de Ciencias Sociales–Programa Guatemala, 2007).

71. This does not mean that state representatives were not responsible for any violence. However, compared with the situation in El Salvador's past, nongovernmental actors are responsible for a large part of the violence. See UN Office on Drugs and Crime, *Crime and Development in Central America: Caught in the Crossfire* (New York: United Nations, 2007).

72. Dudley, *Drug Trafficking Organizations.*

73. Edith Portillo, "Maras no son la principal causa de la violencia según la misma PNC," *Periódico digital El Faro,* www.elfaro.net/Programas/Buscar/DetalleNota.php?IDNota=2047%20.

74. Oscar Iraheta, "El setenta por ciento de las extorsiones son cometidas por maras,"*El Diario de Hoy,* August 19, 2009.

75. See, e.g., Steven Boraz and Thomas Bruneau, "Are the *Maras* Overwhelming Governments in Central America?" *Military Review* 86 (November–December 2006): 36. See also Andrew Grascia, "Gang Violence: Mara Salvatrucha—'Forever Salvador,'" *Journal of Gang Research* 11 (2004): 29.

76. See Deborah Levenson, "On Their Own: A Preliminary Study of Youth Gangs in Guatemala City," *Cuadernos de investigación de AVANCSO* 4 (2008). See also Sandra Argueta et al., "Diagnóstico de los grupos llamados 'maras' en San Salvador: Factores sociales que prevalecen en los jóvenes que los integran," *Revista de Psicología de El Salvador* 43 (1992): 11–89.

77. Daniel Lederman, "Ciencia, investigación y políticas públicas: El curioso caso del crimen y la violencia en América Latina," paper prepared for international conference "Crimen y Violencia: Causas y Políticas de Prevención," sponsored by World Bank and the Universidad de los Andes, Bogotá, May 4–5, 2000.

78. José Luis Rocha, "Mareros y pandilleros ¿Nuevos insurgentes criminales?" *Revista Envío* 293, http://www.envio.org.ni/articulo/3337.

79. José Miguel Cruz, "Beyond Social Remittances: Migration and Transnational Gangs in Central America," paper presented at Conference "How Migrants Impact Their Communities," Frederick S. Pardee Center for the Study of the Longer-Range Future, Boston University, Boston, 2009.

80. Levenson, "On Their Own."

81. Cruz, "Central American *Maras.*"

82. Bureau for Latin American and Caribbean Affairs, U.S. Agency for International Development, *Central American and Mexico Gang Assessment* (Washington, D.C.: U.S. Agency for International Development, 2006).

83. In El Salvador, this was the official name given to the first of this type of programs. The second stage of the program, implemented by President Antonio Saca, was called the "Super *Mano Dura.*"

84. UN Office on Drugs and Crime, *Crime and Development.*

85. José Miguel Cruz and Marlon Carranza, "Pandillas y políticas públicas: El caso de El Salvador," in *Juventudes, violencia y exclusión: Desafíos para las políticas públicas,* edited by Javier Moro (Guatemala City: MagnaTerra Editores, 2006), 133–75.

86. United Nations Office on Drugs and Crime, *Crime and Development.*

87. Cruz, *Street Gangs.*

88. Bureau for Latin American and Caribbean Affairs, U.S. Agency for International Development, *Central American and Mexico Gang Assessment.* See also José Miguel Cruz, ed., *Maras y pandillas en Centroamérica, volumen IV: Las respuestas de la sociedad civil organizada* (San Salvador: UCA Editores, 2006), 401–47.

89. Wendy Bellanger, "La sociedad civil ante la violencia juvenil en Nicaragua," in *Maras y pandillas,* ed. Cruz, 329–400.

90. Elana Zilberg, "Fools Banished from the Kingdom: Remapping Geographies of Gang Violence between the Americas (Los Angeles and San Salvador)," *American Quarterly* 56 (2004): 759.

91. In mid-2007, the first Transnational Anti-Gang Center in the region opened in San Salvador, with direct aid from the U.S. Federal Bureau of Investigation in the form of agents and resources. See "Agentes del FBI iniciaron labor contra las pandillas," *El Diario de Hoy,* August 26, 2007.

92. "Al Qaeda Seeks Tie to Local Gangs."

93. Jeannette Aguilar, "La mano dura y las 'políticas' de seguridad," *Estudios Centroamericanos (ECA)* 667 (2004): 439–50.

94. Jeannette Aguilar and Lissette Miranda, "Entre la articulación y la competencia: Las respuestas de la sociedad civil organizada a las pandillas en El Salvador," in *Maras y pandillas,* ed. Cruz, 37–144.

95. Tomás Andino and Guillermo Jiménez, *Violencia juvenil, maras y pandillas en Honduras: Informe para la discusión* (Tegucigalpa: Interpeace, 2009).

96. As the number of gang members on the street decreased, the police captured more people, especially adolescents and children, who were not involved in gangs. This

aggravated the human rights situation for young people and adults in Honduras. See Rachel Harvey, *Del papel a la práctica: un análisis del sistema de justicia juvenil en Honduras* (Tegucigalpa: Save the Children and Casa Alianza, 2005). Also see Andino and Jiménez, *Violencia juvenil.*

97. Francisco Bautista, "El papel de la policía ante la seguridad ciudadana y la violencia juvenil," paper presented at seminar "La responsabilidad penal juvenil desde las perspectica de los derechos humanos," Ciudad de Guatemala, Guatemala City, 2004.

98. See José Luis Rocha, *Lanzando piedras, fumando piedras: Evolución de las pandillas en Nicaragua 1997–2006* (Managua: UCA Publicaciones, 2007).

99. See Rachel Nield, *Sustaining Reform: Democratic Policing in Central America* (Washington, D.C.: Washington Office on Latin America, 2002). See also José Miguel Cruz, "Violence, Citizens Insecurity, and Elite Maneuvering in El Salvador," in *Public Security and Police Reform in the Americas,* edited by John Bailey and Lucía Dammert (Pittsburgh: University of Pittsburgh Press, 2006), 148–68.

100. William D. Stanley, *Protectors or Perpetrators: The Institutional Crisis of the Salvadoran Civilian Police* (Washington, D.C.: Hemisphere Initiatives, 1996).

101. See Antonio Cañas and Héctor Dada, "Political Transition and Institutionalization in El Salvador," in *Comparative Peace Processes,* ed. Arnson, 69–96. See also Adriana Beltrán, *The Captive State: Organized Crime and Human Rights in Latin America* (Washington, D.C.: Washington Office on Latin America, 2007).

102. International Human Rights Clinic, *No Place to Hide: Gang, State, and Clandestine Violence in El Salvador* (Cambridge, Mass.: Human Rights Program at Harvard Law School, 2007).

103. See "Honduras: Country Reports on Human Rights Practices," Bureau of Democracy, Human Rights, and Labor, U.S. State Department, http://www.state.gov/g/drl/rls/hrrpt/2005/61732.htm.

104. Andino and Jiménez, *Violencia juvenil.*

105. See "Guatemala: Country Reports on Human Rights Practices," Bureau of Democracy, Human Rights, and Labor, U.S. State Department, http://www.state.gov/g/drl/rls/hrrpt/2005/61729.htm; and International Human Rights Clinic, *No Place to Hide.*

106. Casa Alianza Honduras, "Monthly Analysis of the Problem of Violence against Honduran Children, December 2006," January 2007, available at www.casa-alianza.org.

107. Víctor Meza, *Honduras: Hacia una política integral de seguridad ciudadana* (Tegucigalpa: CEDOH, 2004), 167.

108. Aguilar and Miranda, "Entre la articulación y la competencia."

109. Elin Cecilie Ranum, "Pandillas juveniles transnacionales en Centroamérica, México y Estados Unidos Diagnóstico Nacional Guatemala," Instituto Tecnológico Autónomo de México, http://interamericanos.itam.mx/maras/Diagn%F3stico%20 Guatemala%20Final.pdf.

110. Seligson, Zechmeister, and Orcés, "Political Culture of Democracy."

111. Some of these processes were already outlined by Cruz and Carranza, "Pandillas y políticas públicas"; and by Cruz, *Central American Gangs.*

112. Perhaps one of the events that best exemplifies this process is the massacre perpetrated by a group of gang members from the Mara Salvatrucha in Chamelecón, Honduras, in December 2004. The aggressors opened fire with automatic weapons on a bus, killing 28 and wounding another 10. The criminals left a note at the scene of the crime saying that the attack was in response to policies of persecution against gangs. Six months later, in May 2004, an apparently planned fire set in the San Pedro Sula prison

took the lives of 104 gang members. Human rights organizations and family members claimed that prison guards ignored the prisoners' cries for help after the fire broke out and that some even fired upon the imprisoned gang members. See Ismael Moreno, "Insecurity, Criminality, Hidden Powers, and Visible Roots," *Envío* 312 (2007).

113. Lorine Hughes, "Studying Youth Gangs: The Importance of Context," in *Studying Youth Gangs,* edited by James F. Short Jr. (Lanham, Md.: Altamira Press, 2006), 37–45.

114. Chiapas Secretaría de Seguridad Pública, *Escenarios.*

115. Recently, Rodgers described how drug trafficking has begun to transform the nature of gangs in Nicaragua. However, comparatively speaking, it can still be argued that Nicaraguan gangs display less violent characteristics. See Dennis Rodgers, "Living in the Shadow of Death: Gangs, Violence and Social Order in Urban Nicaragua, 1996–2002," *Journal of Latin American Studies* 38 (2006): 267–92.

116. Frances Hagopian, "After Regime Change: Authoritarian Legacies, Political Representation, and the Democratic Future of South America," *World Politics* 45 (1993): 464–500.

117. Jesús-Silva Herzog Márquez, *El antiguo régimen y la transición política en México* (Mexico City: Planeta / Joaquín Mortiz, 1999).

Chapter 12

Why Truth Still Matters: Historical Clarification, Impunity, and Justice in Contemporary Guatemala

Victoria Sanford

The eyes of the buried will close together on the day of justice, or they will never close.

—Miguel Ángel Asturias

Background

As World War II came to an end, Guatemala was in the midst of its first experience with democracy following the end of the dictatorship of General Jorge Ubico.[1] The Democratic Spring (1944–54) that followed the Ubico regime was an attempt at a capitalist revolution designed to break the feudal relations that defined the country's agro-export economy. Both nationalist and democratic, the government sought to integrate all Guatemalans, including the Maya, into a new, modern capitalist economy. When Jacobo Árbenz was elected in 1952, he instituted a national land reform program expropriating fallow land from large landholders, including the

United Fruit Company. Although landless and land-poor peasants greeted this redistribution of land with much enthusiasm, the United Fruit Company, Guatemalan elites, and the U.S. government called it Communism. Ultimately, through the prism of the Cold War and the economic interests of key advisers, the Eisenhower administration justified the 1954 overthrow of the democratically elected government of Árbenz orchestrated by the U.S. Central Intelligence Agency. This military coup set the stage for the next three decades, which saw twelve different generals and military juntas leading the Guatemalan government (sometimes through fraudulent elections and sometimes through coups) until the 1985 election of civilian president Vinicio Cerezo.[2]

The 1960s saw the growth of the Guatemalan guerrilla movement begun by a small group of disgruntled army officers who attempted a coup d'état against the corrupt and unpopular government of General Miguel Ydígoras Fuentes in November 1960. This failed coup led to the development of an armed insurgency. In 1966, the army began a series of coordinated attacks in urban and rural areas, including mass disappearances of urban activists critical of the regime and indiscriminant bombing of villages believed to support guerrilla operations in Zacapa and Izabal. Thousands of civilians were killed or disappeared during this first counterinsurgency campaign between 1966 and 1968. Counterinsurgency violence and surveillance practices established in these campaigns would be used by the army to attack the guerrillas and control the civilian population for the next thirty years.[3]

In 1978, the Guatemalan army garnered international attention when it opened fire on a group of unarmed Q'eqchi' Maya peasants protesting for land and killed dozens of men, women, and children in what became known as the Panzós massacre. That same year, the Guatemalan army also began a selective campaign of political disappearance and assassination in Guatemala City and other urban and rural centers.[4] In tandem, it accelerated the construction of military bases throughout rural Guatemala. Before 1979, the army had divided the country into nine military zones, each with a large army base in its center. By 1982, the army had designated each of the twenty-two departments as a military zone, accompanied by multiple army bases in municipalities and army garrisons in villages throughout the country.[5] Forced recruitment into the Guatemalan army ensured the requisite number of troops for this extension of the military infrastructure.[6] In 1982, troops were increased from 27,000 to 36,000.[7] This expanded army presence was accompanied by an acceleration of army violence, from selective urban and rural assassinations and disappearances to extreme urban repression and multiple village massacres, which ultimately led to genocide.[8] This armed conflict continued, with varying degrees of intensity, until the signing of the peace accords by the Guatemalan government and the Guatemala National Revolutionary Unity (Unidad Revolucionaria Nacional Guatemalteca, URNG) guerrillas on December 29, 1996. At the time of the signing of the accords, the URNG had 2,500 official combatants and the army had about 60,000 soldiers and more than 270,000 civil patrollers under army command.

Introduction

The Commission for Historical Clarification (Comisión para el Esclarecimiento Histórico, CEH), Guatemala's truth commission, was established by the Accord of Oslo on June 23, 1994, and enacted in January 1997 following the official signing of the peace accords by the Guatemalan government and the URNG. Thus, the Guatemalan CEH, like the Salvadoran Truth Commission that preceded it, formed a part of the peace process and negotiations carried out between government and guerrilla forces. The Salvadoran and Guatemalan truth commissions represented a new type of search for truth in Latin America, where *Nunca Más* (Never Again) reports about human rights violations under military regimes had previously been produced in Brazil, Uruguay, and Paraguay by church and human rights organizations—thus viewed as an alternative or oppositional historical interpretation. Argentine and Chilean truth commissions were initiated under presidential sponsorship following democratic elections in the postauthoritarian period and were seen as the new official history. United Nations sponsorship of the Salvadoran commission and heavy involvement of United Nations Office for Project Services and the international community in organizing, staffing, and funding Guatemala's independent commission lent an official stamp to the "truths" produced and, in the Guatemala case, reinforced the independence of the CEH.[9]

Understanding the Salvadoran commission is key to understanding the mandate of the CEH because the Oslo Accord that established the CEH was being negotiated shortly after the release of the Salvadoran Truth Commission's report. The Salvadoran commission sought to investigate all "serious acts of violence" that occurred between 1980 and 1991, and had caused an impact on the society necessitating that the "public should know the truth." The commission received more than 22,000 denunciations of grave human rights violations, 7,000 of which were made directly to it. The Salvadoran commission also offered a new vision of the work of truth commissions by naming the perpetrators of these violations. Among those named were the prominent guerrilla leader Joaquín Villalobos for ordering the assassination of the beloved Salvadoran poet Roque Dalton and former major Roberto D'Aubuisson for ordering the assassination of Archbishop Óscar Romero, who had become an icon of the struggle for peace.[10]

The framework of the CEH was being negotiated while the Salvadoran left and right dealt with the political fallout of having prominent leaders named as perpetrators. Thus, it is not surprising that the Guatemalan army and the URNG both agreed that institutional responsibility would be assigned for human rights violations, but individual perpetrators would not be named. Though envisioned as an independent commission, the majority of the CEH investigative staff moved from the United Nations Mission in Guatemala (MINUGUA) offices to the CEH. Indeed, many of the MINUGUA staff had previously worked for the UN Mission in El Salvador (ONUSAL) and also for the Salvadoran Truth Commission. Still, unlike the Salvadoran commission, the CEH included a significant number of Guatemalan nationals on its staff, many of whom formerly worked with human rights nongovernmental organizations. Although it has been suggested that truth commissions are more successful when staffed by internationals,[11] the experience of the CEH, like that of the Guatemalan Forensic Anthropology Foundation (Fundación de Antropología Forense de Guatemala, FAFG), suggests that a combination of internationals and nationals works extremely well. In the Guatemalan experience, the presence of internationals was important to the security of the nationals and also to demonstrate the international visibility of the work. Still, when internationals arrive to conduct sensitive human rights research, it is critical to local involvement that nationals are included in the project because everyone knows that when the going gets tough, internationals have passports to get going. The presence of fellow citizens encourages potential participants (and especially local officials) to come forward. As one local leader explained, "If they haven't killed him for doing his work, they probably won't kill me for talking to him. That's how we decided to participate."[12]

In spite of their differing approaches, each of these commissions benefited from being official and they shared a belief in the moral obligation to reveal truths to heal painful pasts. Like the Salvadoran commission, the CEH envisaged its mission as an integral contribution to reconciliation following extreme state violence. Common to all the truth commission reports from the Southern Cone through Central America was the insistence on keeping a focus on the underlying social inequalities that had brought so much violence. Thus, labor rights, agrarian reform, access to justice, citizen security, respect for human rights, and meaningful participation of civil society were among the final recommendations of each commission.

In 1995, as the first president of the new South Africa, Nelson Mandela appointed the Truth and Reconciliation Commission (TRC) to investigate the crimes of apartheid and empowered the commission to grant amnesty to individual perpetrators in exchange for information.[13] The TRC began its investigation in 1995 and published its report in 1998.[14] During the tenure of the CEH's investigation, educated Guatemalans interested in the CEH talked about the TRC as much as they did about the CEH, both lamenting and resigning themselves to what many perceived as a "weaker" truth commission in Guatemala. That TRC hearings were televised, and the commissioners granted subpoena powers seemed almost a fantasy. In Guatemala, many thought the more expansive powers of the TRC would mean more justice for black South Africans. Many doubted that the CEH would be able to collect evidence; and even after the evidence was collected, many (including CEH investigators) doubted the political will of the CEH to assign legal categories to the violations committed by the Guatemalan state. Hearteningly, the CEH carried out a thorough and comprehensive investigation, followed by painstaking legal analysis, which concluded that "acts of genocide" had been committed by the Guatemalan army.[15]

In South Africa, amnesty was traded for truth, in the sense that the TRC granted amnesty to perpetrators who came forward to offer their version of events. The risk in this trade-off is that institutional structures of violence become secondary while individual perpetrators, their crimes, and their victims become the focus of the atrocities of the previous regime (this is all the more true when hearings of perpetrator "confessions" are televised). Although academic and policy debates about transitional justice emanating from the South African experience have tended to cast truth and justice as counterplots and overshadow other goals and potential affects of truth commissions, the Latin American experience is different. In Latin America, at the founding of the Salvadoran commission, there was much hope that it would be able to do more than the Argentine and Chilean commissions because it had been mandated to name the names of perpetrators. This led many human rights activists in Guatemala to believe that the Guatemalan Truth Commission would have an even stronger mandate than the Salvadoran one. As truth commissions were established in Latin America, truth was seen as a path to justice rather than its alternative.[16] And though it may have been an imperfect justice, it did not preclude ongoing efforts to prosecute perpetrators in Argentina, Chile, El Salvador, and Guatemala. Indeed, in all these countries, human rights nongovernmental organizations continue to push cases in domestic courts.[17]

Although the CEH did not have sweeping powers to grant amnesty, did not hold televised public hearings, and did not name names, the CEH investigative process and report (like the archbishop's *Nunca Más* report that preceded it) made a significant contribution to truth and justice. To understand both the short- and medium-term impact of the CEH report, we need to look at the CEH process from the investigative period to the release of the report and consider its impact on human rights, truth, and justice in Guatemala from local, regional, national, and international spaces. In this chapter, I offer an overview of the CEH mandate and findings as well as an analysis of the role played by the CEH report in local, regional, and national human rights cases. Specifically, I address army culpability for genocide of rural Maya and also review illustrative urban cases of human rights violations. I conclude with responses to the report's release and some reflections on why truth still matters in twenty-first-century Guatemala.

The CEH Mandate

The mandate of the CEH was to (1) bring to light with objectivity, fairness, and impartiality the human rights violations and violent acts that caused suffering to the Guatemalan people; (2) produce a final report containing the results of the investigation that includes analysis about the violence; and (3) formulate specific recommendations to strengthen peace and harmony in Guatemala, with a particular focus on ways "to preserve the memory of the victims, foster a culture of mutual respect, observe human rights, and strengthen the democratic process."[18] To carry out its mandate, the CEH had offices in fourteen different rural areas that were known to have suffered greatly during the violence.[19] Additionally, there were several mobile investigative units as well as the offices in Guatemala City. Between September 1997 and May 1998, CEH investigators visited some 2,000 communities taking 500 collective testimonies and 7,338 individual testimonies. Most communities were visited on multiple occasions, and many received ten or more visits. The CEH interacted directly with more than 20,000 people who supported its work by providing information. More than 1,000 of these people were current or former members of the Guatemalan army and other state entities. Additionally, the CEH collected testimonies outside Guatemala. It also became a depository for important documents, including thousands of declassified U.S. State Department and Central Intelligence Agency documents on Guatemala. Upon completion of the field research phase, the CEH then concentrated on the analysis and presentation of data collected up until the official release of the report *Guatemala: Memoria del Silencio* (Memory of Silence), in February 1999.

Published in 1998, the archbishop's *Guatemala: Nunca Más* report, also known as the REHMI (Proyecto Interdiocesano de Recuperación Histórico; Interdiocesan Project for the Recuperation of Historical Memory) report, played a key role in the work of the CEH. This report was a far-reaching investigation utilizing the infrastructure of the Catholic Church in munici-palities throughout the country. Research for REHMI was conducted in 1996 and 1997, with the final report being written and published in April 1998. The CEH began its field investigation as REHMI investigators were concluding their own. In fact, many REHMI investigators went on to work with the CEH. Although the existence of the REHMI project was largely due to a lack of confidence in the official CEH, given what was perceived as a weak mandate that would not name names, in fact the REHMI project became an important foundation for the CEH. Not only was the final report a useful resource, but the very fact that REHMI investigators had previ-ously worked in communities provided an opening for the CEH. Indeed, the CEH's access to survivors and witnesses was largely the result of previ-ous investigative work conducted in rural communities and support given to community members by REHMI and also by MINUGUA. The willing-ness of witnesses and survivors to come forward was also increased by the signing of the peace accords, the demobilization of civil patrols, and the reinsertion of the guerrillas into civil society—each of which took place before most CEH investigations in rural communities. Thus, for example, the REHMI report covers the Panzós massacre and names eight victims based on the testimonies of four survivors, whereas the CEH report names fifty-three victims based on testimonies of more than two hundred survi-vors. Although both reports are largely based on survivor testimonies, the CEH had more access because it followed the REHMI project.

It should also be noted that Bishop Juan Gerardi, who led the REHMI investigation, was bludgeoned to death two days after he released the REHMI report on April 24, 1998. Although there have been some arrests and convictions in his murder case, the exact circumstances of his killing remain a mystery. One international observer suggested that the killing of the bishop was strategic on the part of the army because public discourse is around 'Who killed the bishop?' instead of who killed and disappeared the thousands of Guatemalans listed in the REHMI report.[20]

The CEH's Findings

The 1999 release of the Report of the Commission for Historical Clarification provided evidence of Guatemalan army massacres in 626 Maya villages and raised the number of documented dead or disappeared to more than 200,000. Additionally, it documented that in the course of what had come to be referred to by rural Maya as La Violencia (The Violence), 1.5 million people were internally displaced and 150,000 were driven to seek refuge in Mexico. Significantly, the CEH attributed blame to the Guatemalan army for 93 percent of the human rights violations and the guerrillas for 3 percent. It further identified 83 percent of the victims as Maya and 17 percent as ladino.[21] The army's violations were so severe and systematically enacted against whole Maya communities that the CEH determined that the army had committed acts of genocide against the Maya.[22] This finding of genocidal acts continues to affect Maya struggles for justice and accountability and also to frame political and juridical debates.

At the height of La Violencia, the army's justification of massacres in rural Maya communities rested upon its claims that it was, in the words of former military dictator Efraín Ríos Montt, "scorching Communists."[23] Moreover, the transnational nature of the Guatemalan army's campaign against the Maya was revealed in an October 5, 1981, Department of State memorandum classified as "secret." The author of the memorandum acknowledged that then-dictator General Romeo Lucas García believed that "the policy of repression" was "working," and the State Department official writing the memo described the "extermination of the guerrillas, their supporters and sympathizers" as the measure of a "successful" policy of repression.[24] The Guatemalan army used ground troops and aerial forces to saturate the mountain with firepower in its attempt to exterminate the unarmed Maya men, women, children, and elderly who had fled the massacres and destruction in their communities.

In late 1982, before a meeting between U.S. president Ronald Reagan and General Ríos Montt, a confidential U.S. State Department document reported that in "March 1982, the current President Ríos Montt came to power as expected" and pointed out that "he quickly consolidated his power" and began "to implement a rigorous counterinsurgency offensive."[25] Nevertheless, the State Department officer writing the memo acknowledged that "Ríos Montt does not have a strong base of power. . . . We would like to be able, therefore to support Ríos Montt over the short term."[26] At the same time, the document acknowledged "that the military continues to engage in massacres of civilians in the countryside."[27]

The CEH finding of genocidal acts, rather than genocide, though ambiguous, is nonetheless significant. In addition to pointing out the specific and varied roles of the executive, judicial, and legislative branches of the Guatemalan government in violating the human rights of its citizens, the CEH attributed direct responsibility to the state and its agents for the construction of the counterinsurgency state and for the state's complete failure to comply with its obligation to investigate and prosecute human rights violations. At the public presentation of the CEH report in February 1998, CEH president Christian Tomuschat stated:

On the basis of having concluded that genocide was committed, the Commission also concludes that, without prejudice to the fact that the participants in the crime include both the material and intellectual authors of the acts of genocide committed in Guatemala, State responsibility also exists. This responsibility arises from the fact that the majority of these acts were the product of a policy pre-established by superior order and communicated to the principal actors.[28]

Finding Genocide in Guatemala

Five years after the CEH findings of genocidal acts, on April 29, 2004, the Inter-American Court of Human Rights condemned the Guatemalan government for the July 18, 1982, massacre of 188 Achi-Maya in the village of Plan de Sánchez in the mountains above Rabinal, Baja Verapaz.[29] In this judgment, and for the first time in its history, the Court ruled that genocide had taken place and attributed the 1982 massacre and the genocide to Guatemalan army troops. Beyond the importance of this judgment for the people of Plan de Sánchez, the Court's ruling is particularly significant, for in the judgment key points include a declaration that there was genocide in Guatemala, which was part of the framework of the internal armed conflict when the armed forces of the Guatemalan government applied their National Security Doctrine in their counterinsurgency actions. Moreover, the Court placed responsibility for the genocide during the regime of General Efraín Ríos Montt.

Two years and some months after the Inter-American Court's ruling, the Spanish Court issued an international arrest order charging various former generals and military officials with genocide, terrorism, torture, assassination, and illegal detention. Those charged included General Efraín Ríos Montt, head of state through military coup from March 1982 to August 1983; General Oscar Humberto Mejía Victores, head of state through military coup from August 1983 to January 1986; General Fernando Romeo Lucas García,[30] president of Guatemala from 1978 to March 1982; General Ángel Aníbal Guevara Rodríguez, minister of defense under Lucas García; Donaldo Álvarez Ruiz, minister of the interior under Lucas García; Colonel Germán Chupina Barahona, director of the National Police under Lucas García; Pedro García Arredondo, chief of Command 6 of the National Police under Lucas García and later director of the National Police; and General Benedicto Lucas García, Army chief of staff during his brother's reign.[31] Years later, none of these military officers had been extradited. They filed numerous appeals to slow the process and continue to make public justifications and/or deny any knowledge of human rights violations.

On October 30, 2007, the Guatemalan Court of Appeals denied the final appeal of former director of the National Police Pedro García Arredondo and General Ángel Aníbal Guevara Rodríguez. According to the U.S.-based Center for Justice and Accountability (CJA), "The decision upheld the legality of the arrest warrants and extradition requests issued by the Spanish National Court. As a result, extradition proceedings may move forward to transfer the defendants to Spain to stand trial for genocide."[32] CJA lawyers note that although "Ríos Montt has filed a separate appeal challenging the validity of the extradition treaty; . . . the arrest warrant pending against Ríos Montt and the other defendants remain valid" given this recent ruling. Although none of them has been jailed, the country of Guatemala is now their jail because INTERPOL agreements bind any country receiving a visitor on INTERPOL's international arrest order list as being immediately extraditable. Still, they continue to argue that self-granted amnesties give them immunity from prosecution as they live with impunity in Guatemala.[33]

Civil Patrols

In its comprehensive investigation, the CEH found that 18 percent of human rights violations were committed by civil patrols. These patrols, also referred to as Civil Self-Defense Patrols (Patrullas de Auto-Defensa, PACs), were army-controlled units of civilian men who were forcibly recruited and required participation of all men in rural communities. The CEH noted that 85 percent of violations committed by patrollers were carried out under army order.[34] It is not insignificant that the CEH found that one out of every ten human rights violations was carried out by a military commissioner, the local army-appointed PAC leader, and that though these commissioners often led patrollers in acts of violence, 87 percent of the violations committed by commissioners were in collusion with the army.[35]

Plan Victoria, developed under Ríos Montt, increased the centrality of the PACs to army strategy.[36] Less than one month after Ríos Montt's coup, the army began an intensified and systematic forced recruitment of Maya into the PACs.[37] This further systematized the inclusion of civil patrols in the counterinsurgency begun under Lucas García. Following the departure of army detachments from model villages in the late 1980s, the army continued to maintain tight surveillance and control of the community through the continuing structure of PACs led by army-appointed military commissioners within the community. For the majority rural Maya, participation in the PACs was required for personal and familial security, and performed under duress. Even a 1991 U.S. State Department memo noted that "credible reports say that those who refuse to serve in the civil patrols have suffered serious abuse, including death."[38] Moreover, the PACs attacked nascent civil society organizations and especially human rights groups. As late as 1992, Christian Tomuschat, a United Nations expert on Guatemala who as noted above would later lead the CEH, concluded that "the civil patrols have become an institutionalized element of uncontrollable violence."

Thus, long after the soldiers left the army garrisons in Maya villages, the military structure of the army continued to be reproduced by the PACs under army orders. The apparent decrease in actual army activities masked the militarization of communities systematically implemented and rigorously maintained by the army-controlled PACs throughout Maya communities. In 1995, there were 2,643 civil patrols organized and led by the army. In August 1996, when the demobilization of civil patrols began, there were 270,906 mostly Maya peasants registered in civil patrols.[39] This is significantly less than the 1 million men who were organized into civil patrols in 1981. Taking into account the population at the time and adjusting for gender and excluding children and elderly, this means that in 1981, one out of every two adult men in Guatemala was militarized into the army-led civil patrols.[40]

Urban Truths

In addition to the significance of the CEH concluding that the Guatemalan army committed genocide, the CEH also acknowledged the disproportionate amount of suffering inflicted on Guatemala's urban rights activists:

> The massacres that eliminated entire Mayan rural communities belong to the same reality as the persecution of the urban political opposition, trade union leaders, priests and catechists. These are neither perfidious allegations, nor figments of the imagination, but an authentic chapter in Guatemala's history.[41]

Indeed, these memories of urban violence are as fresh to its survivors as the massacres are in Maya communities. And though 87 percent of the 200,000 dead or disappeared were indigenous, 17 percent (or 34,000) were urban ladinos.[42] University students and professors, union leaders and activists, land rights activists, catechists, priests, nuns, teachers, doctors, nurses, and anyone else who made professional or political claims for social justice were systematically targeted by the army regimes in Guatemala. Raúl Molina Mejía, rector of the public University of San Carlos (USAC) in Guatemala City in 1980, wrote: "The assassination of Oliverio Casteñeda and the massacre at the USAC, like the Spanish Embassy massacre, are as important as 626 villages."[43] Indeed, the CEH included each of these cases among its illustrative cases in the twelve-volume report.

USAC student leader Oliverio Castañeda de León was machine-gunned in broad daylight by Guatemalan soldiers in downtown Guatemala City on October 20, 1978: "According to eyewitnesses, among those present was police chief Germán Chupina Barahona, who may have been on hand to coordinate the attack."[44] After being elected general secretary of the university student association in May 1978, Castañeda de León played a key role in organizing several of the largest urban marches in Guatemalan history, integrating peasants, workers, and students in protest against the government. A national march in Guatemala City protesting the May 29, 1978, army massacre of dozens of unarmed peasants in Panzós and a general strike in September 1978 are among the key historic events in which he played a leadership role. He was one of 492 students and professors killed or disappeared during the internal armed conflict.[45] His assassination remains in impunity. The USAC student association was renamed in his honor.

Just as the 1978 assassination of Oliverio Castañeda brought attention to urban violence against intellectuals, the 1980 Spanish Embassy massacre—which took the lives of several dozen peasant land rights protesters, including Rigoberta Menchú's father—demonstrated the army's zero-tolerance policy for protest and drew international attention to state brutality. Instead of dialoguing with the protesters, the government responded to the peasant occupation of the Spanish Embassy by sending hundreds of security forces to seize control of the embassy. Police forces launched incendiary devices into the embassy, trapped the protesters inside, and refused to allow firefighters or anyone else to help them escape the fire. Thirty-seven people burned to death as a result of the police fire-bombing the embassy. Like the Spanish Civil Guard investigation that preceded it, the CEH concluded that "agents of the state" were responsible for "the arbitrary execution of those inside the Spanish Embassy," and that "the very highest levels of authority of the government of Guatemala are the intellectual authors of this extremely grave violation of human rights." Moreover, dispelling arguments put forth by army apologists, the CEH specifically noted that "the hypothesis that victims self-immolated has no foundation."[46]

In addition to the Castañeda de León and Spanish Embassy cases, the CEH report includes other significant urban cases. One that has recently received international attention is the forced disappearance of fourteen-year-old Marco Antonio Theissen on October 6, 1981, when three heavily armed men dragged him out of his family's home and away from midday lunch with his mother, Emma Theissen Álvarez. Ignoring the pleas of his mother, the armed men bound and gagged Marco Antonio and threw him in their pickup truck. Emma made note of the vehicle license number. Years later, this information helped to identify the pickup as an official vehicle of the Guatemalan army. Indeed, it was in the collection of information about army vehicles during the course of the CEH investigation that army ownership of the vehicle was confirmed based on the license plate number.

After Marco Antonio's 1981 disappearance, his family searched the country until March 1984 when, under threat of death, they were forced to seek asylum in the Ecuadorian Embassy, abandon their homeland, and give up their search. Though unable to continue their physical search, the family filed a claim against the Guatemalan government in the Inter-American Court system. Twenty-three years later, the whereabouts of Marco Antonio remain unknown, and his case has become emblematic of the 5,000 children who "disappeared" during the internal armed conflict.[47]

The case made international news when, in July 2004, the Inter-American Court ruled that the Guatemalan state must locate and return the remains of Marco Antonio to his family as well as investigate his disappearance with the goal of identifying, trying, and sentencing the material and intellectual authors of his forced disappearance. Further, the Court ordered the Guatemalan government to hold a public ceremony calling international attention to the state's responsibility for Marco Antonio's disappearance, to designate an educational center in Guatemala City with a new name recognizing the thousands of children who were disappeared during the internal armed conflict, and to prominently display a plaque in memory of Marco Antonio at the site. The Court also mandated the state to develop an expedited procedure that allows relatives of the disappeared to obtain a death certificate declaring the presumption of death from forced disappearance, which would allow survivors to access death benefits, pensions, inheritance rights, and the right to remarry without divorcing the disappeared spouse in absentia. The Court further obligated the Guatemalan government to establish a system for tracking genetic information of the disappeared and to pay nearly $700,000 in damages to Marco Antonio's surviving family members. These orders of the Court are consistent with the CEH's recommendations for dignifying the memory of the victims and providing reparations.

Marco Antonio's case is one of the cornerstone rulings in a series of recent Inter-American Court judgments against the Guatemalan government. These cases represent different types of human rights violations committed by the Guatemalan state against its citizens during the dictatorships of the early 1980s and the ongoing impunity that endured into the postwar period of the 1990s. For example, in 2003, the court condemned the Guatemalan state for the brutal 1990 stabbing and assassination of the Guatemalan anthropologist Myrna Mack Chang, the 1985 assassination of the U.S. journalist Nicolas Blake, and the 1992 disappearance of the guerrilla leader Efraín Bámaca Velásquez. During 2004, the Court condemned the Guatemalan state for the 1993 machine gun assassination of the congressional deputy, newspaper publisher, and leading presidential hopeful Jorge Carpio Nicolle. As mentioned above, in 2004, for the first time in its history, the Court condemned a member state for genocide in the case of the 1982 army massacre of 268 Maya peasants in the village of Plan de Sánchez. There is no doubt that the CEH report played a role in the Inter-American Court's rulings on these cases because they reflect both the findings and recommendations of the CEH.

The National Response to the Report's Release

Following the 1999 release of the CEH's final report, which also found that the guerrillas had committed 3 percent of the human rights violations, guerrilla leaders were forced to publicly come to terms with violence committed against civilian populations. Though its members were just as apt to use the same types of reservations and justifications as the army, although through a different ideological lens, the URNG publicly apologized to the Guatemalan people. The army, which the CEH found responsible for 93 percent of human rights violations, remained silent—despite the CEH's urging that both armed actors had a moral obligation to make an apology for their atrocities.[48] Then Guatemalan president Álvaro Arzú fell in line with the army, denying "that there was a genocide during the armed conflict, disagreeing for the first time with the Commission for Historical Clarification."[49] At the same time, President Bill Clinton affirmed the CEH's finding with his unequivocal condemnation of past U.S. intervention and support for four decades of Guatemalan state terrorism: "For the United States, it is important that I state clearly that support for military forces and intelligence units which engaged in violence and widespread repression was wrong, and the United States must not repeat that mistake. We must, and will, instead, continue to support the peace and reconciliation process in Guatemala."[50] Despite the recalcitrance of the Guatemalan army and president, these reluctant and limited acknowledgments of responsibility represent the intersection, or perhaps clash, of political space with new public space for memory.

Throughout Guatemala, human rights organizations and local Maya organizations continued to organize and mobilize for truth and justice. Many communities took advantage of the political space created by the presence of the CEH investigators and the REHMI or FAFG investigators to push for justice at the local level. CONAVIGUA (the national Maya widows' organization), FAMDEGUA (Families of the Disappeared of Guatemala), CERJ (Comité Étnica Runujel Junam), CALDH (Centro de Acción Legal de Derechos Humanos), and GAM (Grupo de Apoyo Mutuo) continued to work at the local level, supporting legal cases built on local initiatives of survivors seeking the exhumation of clandestine cemeteries, proper burials, truth-telling, and court hearings. At the national level, they continued to push for the recognition of rights violations and redress for victims. The FAFG has conducted 1,132 exhumations of clandestine cemeteries,[51] and there are now as many cases stagnating in local Guatemalan courts. Of all the cases involving massacres, the first one to make it to full court proceedings in the Guatemalan court system was a case against three local PAC military commissioners who were found guilty, whereas no charges were ever brought against the intellectual authors or those who gave the orders. Indeed, one could argue that this prosecution had a chilling effect on PAC members and commissioners coming forward with evidence because it demonstrated that they would be afforded no protections or immunities despite the forced nature of PAC membership.

One former FAFG leader commented that the army has allowed the exhumations because they move nowhere in the courts. Although the court system was reorganized following the peace accords and now has an adversarial legal system with a prosecutor, public defender, and judge, these officers of the court receive little to no protection when they have high-profile rights cases; there are incidents of threats, intimidation, and "accidents" that have happened to those who have sought to push forward rights cases that implicate the army and its officers. Considerably more than a decade-and-a-half after the peace accords, human rights advocates, including the FAFG, continue to receive death threats. Attacks on human rights workers continue to cause fear throughout Guatemala, especially in isolated rural communities. In 2005, there were 224 documented attacks against rights workers.[52] In 2006, more than 300 human rights defenders were attacked; the number fell slightly in 2007, but was still close to 200.[53] In 2008, the attacks rose to 220, and by the end of 2009, 353 human rights defenders had been attacked. In 2010, 294 human rights workers suffered violent attacks.[54]

Why Truth Still Matters

Truth still matters in Guatemala because we can make connections between practices and discourses of violence in the past and present. Indeed, there is a particular lexicon that we can trace from the 1980s to the present. In the 1980s, the military regimes blamed the victims by calling them subversives, threatened anyone who opposed the repression, claimed amnesty for any crimes committed by the army, blamed the guerrillas for any killings or disappearances, and pled ignorance to the violence engulfing the country. In the 1990s, the army blamed the massacre victims for causing the massacres, claimed the victims and survivors were subversives, threatened anyone who sought exhumations, claimed amnesty for any crimes committed, blamed the guerrillas for all violence, and pled ignorance for obvious army violence. After the Spanish Court issued its arrest warrant, the generals claimed that the Spanish judge was an ETA terrorist, threatened witnesses, claimed amnesty for any crimes committed, blamed the guerrillas for massacres, and pled ignorance. It is impunity that ties the past to the present.

Against this backdrop of genocide and impunity, Guatemalans find themselves living in an incredibly violent country with an astronomically high homicide rate. Between 2001 and 2005, five years of "peacetime," there were 20,943 registered murders in Guatemala. If the number of murder victims continues to rise at the current rate, more people will die in the first twenty-five years of peace than died during the thirty-six-year internal armed conflict and genocide that took the lives of 200,000 Guatemalans. And there is no more justice today than there was twenty years ago. Of the 5,338 murders registered by the national police in 2005, only eight were brought to justice.[55] According to the United Nations, the number of homicides in 2008—6,292—was almost double the number at the time of the signing of the peace accords in 1996. The rate of impunity for murders stood at 98 percent.[56] Although the impunity rate hangs at 98 percent, homicides continue to rise. In 2009, there were 10,859 registered homicides in Guatemala.[57]

The international community can play a positive role in ending impunity in Guatemala by supporting human rights groups, the human rights ombudsman (Procuraduría de Derechos Humanos), and the International Commission Against Impunity in Guatemala (Comisión Internacional Contra la Impunidad en Guatemala, CICIG), a formal commission jointly established in 2007 by the United Nations and the Guatemalan government. CICIG's mandate is to investigate and disarticulate clandestine organizations by working with the Guatemalan justice system to bring what are now openly referred to as "the parallel powers" to justice.[58]

In June 2010, after three years of leading CICIG's struggle against impunity in Guatemala, Dr. Carlos Castresana resigned citing the lack of political will to end impunity and urging the president to fire then newly named attorney general Conrado Reyes. Castresana cited Conrado Reyes's ties to organized crime. Additionally, Castresana seized the moment of his resignation to hold a press conference and denounce high-ranking current and former officials in various government entities who were linked with drug traffickers and were the intellectual and/or material authors of a number of crimes under investigation by CICIG.[59]

Within the month, the UN had named Costa Rican attorney general Francisco Dall'Anese Ruiz as the new director of CICIG. This appointment was applauded by many because Dall'Anese Ruiz had a record of successfully prosecuting drug traffickers in Costa Rica.[60] At the same time, Conrado Reyes lost his post as attorney general when the Constitutional Court annulled his appointment.[61] His departure opened some space with the Prosecutor's Office (Ministerio Público, MP) to pursue high-impact cases in tandem with CICIG. It is hoped by many that this opening will lead to the processing of human rights cases that have stagnated in the MP for more than a decade.

Indeed, recent examples of the possibilities of building the rule of law and achieving justice include the June 17, 2010, arrest of retired general Héctor López Fuentes on charges of genocide during his tenure as army chief of staff; the July 24, 2010, arrest of former police chief García Arredondo for his participation in forced disappearances in the 1980s; and the 6,060-year prison sentences issued against former elite army corps members Daniel Martínez, Manuel Pop, and Reyes Collin y Carlos Carías on August 2, 2011, for their participation in the 1982 massacre of 201 civilians in the village of Dos Erres. On January 26, 2012, a Guatemalan judge ruled that Efraín Ríos Montt must stand trial for genocide and crimes against humanity in Guatemala. Rather than plead guilty or not guilty, Ríos Montt told the judge, "I prefer to hold my silence."

Diplomatic missions, concerned citizens, and international aid groups can support the heroic efforts of brave Guatemalan prosecutors and the work of CICIG by tying international assistance to ending impunity. Specifically, the international community can exert pressure on the MP to move forward on all homicide cases; on the National Civilian Police (Policía Nacional Civil) to conduct unbiased investigations; on the medical examiner's office to complete a consistent forensic protocol on all murder victims regardless of appearance and to include sexual assault as a standard protocol in murder investigations; and on the Guatemalan government to cooperate with both the Spanish Court and the extradition of the generals for trial in Spain and also moving forward on the prosecutions of hundreds of human rights violations cases currently stagnating in the court system. It can also support the dismantling of impunity by full investigation and disclosure on the role of parallel powers in the state, accompanied by the prosecution of those responsible.

Notes

1. Jim Handy, *Gift of the Devil: A History of Guatemala* (Boston: South End Press, 1984).

2. Victoria Sanford, *Buried Secrets: Truth and Human Rights in Guatemala* (New York: Palgrave Macmillan, 2003), 57. See also, Nick Cullather, *Secret History: The CIA's Classified Account of Its Operations in Guatemala, 1952–54* (Stanford, Calif.: Stanford University Press, 1999).

3. Patrick Ball, Paul Kobrak, and Herbert F. Spirer, *State Violence in Guatemala, 1960–1996: A Quantitative Reflection* (Washington, D.C.: American Association for the Advancement of Science and Centro Internacional para Investigaciones en Derechos Humanos, 1999), http://shr.aaas.org/guatemala/ciidh/qr/english/chap2.html.

4. For an excellent analysis of urban political movements, see Deborah Levenson-Estrada, *Trade Unionists against Terror: Guatemala City 1954–1985* (Chapel Hill: University of North Carolina Press, 1994); Susanne Jonas, *The Battle for Guatemala. Rebels, Death Squads and US Power* (Boulder, Colo.: Westview Press, 1991); Jonathan Fried, ed., *Guatemala in Rebellion: An Unfinished History* (New York: Grove Press, 1983); and Eduardo Galeano, *País Ocupado* (Mexico City: Nuestro Tiempo, 1967). For a comparative analysis of Latin American movements, see Arturo Escobar and Sonia Álvarez, eds., *The Making of Social Movements in Latin* America (Boulder, Colo.: Westview Press, 1992). For more on urban state terror in Guatemala, see Gabriel Aguilera Peralta, *Dialéctica del Terror* (Ciudad Universitaria Rodrigo Facio, Costa Rica: Editorial Universitaria Centroamericana, 1981); and Figueroa Ibarra, *El Recurso del Miedo* (San José: Editorial Universitaria Centroamericana, 1991). See also Juan Corradi, ed., *Fear at the Edge: State Terrorism in Latin America* (Boulder, Colo.: Westview Press, 1992). For an eloquent fictional portrayal of urban life during La Violencia, see Arturo Arias, *After the Bombs* (Willimantic, Conn.: Curbstone Press, 1990).

5. Tom Barry, *Guatemala. The Politics of Counterinsurgency* (Albuquerque: Inter-Hemispheric Education Resource Center, 1986), 36. For excellent maps of military bases in Guatemala, see also Commission for Historical Clarification (CEH), *Guatemala: Memoria del Silencio,* vols. 1–12 (Guatemala City: CEH, 1999), 2:524–25.

6. See Victoria Sanford, "The Moral Imagination of Survival: Displacement and Child Soldiers in Colombia and Guatemala," in *Troublemakers of Peacemakers? Youth and Post-Accord Peacebuilding,* edited by Siobhan McEvoy (Notre Dame, Ind.: University of Notre Dame Press, 2006).

7. Jennifer Schirmer, *The Guatemalan Military Project: A Violence Called Democracy* (Philadelphia: University of Pennsylvania Press, 1998), 47.

8. CEH, *Guatemala: Memoria del Silencio,* 7:10. Although the CEH provided comprehensive documentation of Guatemalan army human rights violations throughout the country, international and national human rights groups had been reporting these violations for years. See, e.g., Americas Watch (AW), *Closing Space: Human Rights in Guatemala* (New York: AW, 1988); AW, *Clandestine Detention in Guatemala* (New York: AW, 1993); Amnesty International (AI), "Guatemala: A Government Program

of Political Murder." *New York Review of Books,* 19 March 1981: 38–40; AI, *Guatemala: The Human Rights Record* (London: AI, 1987); Shelton Davis and Julie Hodson, *Witness to Political Violence in Guatemala. Impact Audit 2* (Boston: Oxfam America, 1982); Ricardo Falla, ed., *Voices of the Survivors: The Massacre at Finca San Francisco,* Report 10 (Cambridge, Mass.: Cultural Survival and Anthropology Resource Center, 1983). See also Arturo Arias, "Changing Indian Identity: Guatemala's Violent Transition to Modernity," in *Guatemalan Indians and the State,* edited by Carol Smith (Austin: University of Texas Press, 1990), 230–57; and Martin Diskin, *Trouble in Our Backyard: Central America and the United States in the 1980s* (New York: Pantheon Books, 1983).

9. The governments of Austria, Belgium, Canada, Denmark, Germany, Italy, Japan, the Netherlands, Norway, Sweden, Switzerland, the United Kingdom, the United States, and the European Union funded the CEH. The government of Argentina also provided support. The American Association for the Advancement of Science, the Ford Foundation, and the Soros Foundation also provided support.

10. Juan Hernández-Pico, "Gerardi Case: Justice for a Just Man," *Envío* 20, no. 239 (2001): 36–44.

11. Gregory Jowdy, "Truth Commissions in El Salvador and Guatemala: A Proposal for Truth in Guatemala," *Boston College Third World Law Journal,* Spring 1997.

12. Interview by the author, tape recording, Rabinal, Guatemala, July 29, 1994.

13. The South African TRC was the second truth and reconciliation commission to be established. Although "TRC" is frequently used to discuss truth commissions, only the South African and Chilean commissions were TRCs. The other commissions were truth commissions.

14. Truth and Reconciliation Commission of South Africa Report, 2003, http://www.info.gov.za/otherdocs/2003/trc/. See also Robert I. Rotberg and Dennis Thompson, eds., *Truth v Justice: The Morality of Truth Commissions* (Princeton, N.J.: Princeton University Press, 2000).

15. CEH, *Guatemala Memory of Silence: Conclusions and Recommendations* (Guatemala City: CEH, 1999); CEH, *Guatemala: Memoria del Silencio.*

16. Juan Hernández-Pico and Lawrence Weschler, *A Miracle, a Universe: Settling Accounts with Torturers* (Chicago: University of Chicago Press, 1998).

17. On October 9, 2007, the Reverend Christian von Wernich was sentenced to life in prison for his participation in murder, torture, and kidnapping during Argentina's Dirty War; see Alexei Barrionuevo, "Argentine Priest Receives Life Sentence in 'Dirty War' Killings," *New York Times,* October 10, 2007. At the time of his death in December 2006, General Augusto Pinochet had been indicted in three human rights cases and was under investigation for several dozen other cases, and on October 4, 2007, Pinochet's widow and seventeen of his military and civilian collaborators were indicted for misappropriation of public funds; see Pascale Bonnefoy, "Chilean Court Orders Arrests of Pinochet Kin and Close Allies," *New York Times,* October 5, 2007. In Guatemala, there are now more than 300 massacre cases sitting in domestic courts, and four of these cases were paradigmatic cases of the CEH.

18. CEH, *Guatemala: Memoria del Silencio,* 1:24.

19. Ibid., 1:33.

20. Author's interview, June 5, 2007; the international observer requested anonymity.

21. CEH, *Guatemala: Memoria del Silencio,* 5:42.

22. CEH, *Guatemala: Memory of Silence—Conclusions and Recommendations* (Guatemala City: CEH, 1999); CEH, *Guatemala: Memoria del Silencio.*

23. George Black, *Garrison Guatemala* (London: Zed Books, 1984), 11.

24. U.S. Department of State, "Secret Memorandum: Reference—Guatemala 6366," October 5, 1981, 1–2; declassified January 1998.

25. U.S. Department of State, "Confidential Action Memorandum to the Secretary of State: Subject—US Guatemala Relations: Arms Sales," unclassified; no month or day are specified, but the text indicates that it was written before December 4 and after November 2, 1982, 1.

26. Ibid., 2.

27. Ibid., 3.

28. Jan Perlin, "The Guatemalan Historical Clarification Commission Finds Genocide," *ILSA Journal of International and Comparative Law* 6 (2000): 396. See also Bernard Duhaime, "Le Crime de Génocide et le Guatemala: Une Analyse Juridique," *Recherches Amérindiennes au Québes* 29, no.3 (1999): 101–6.

29. See Corte IDH, *Caso Masacre Plan de Sánchez vs. Guatemala,* Sentencia de 29 de abril de 2004, serie C, no. 105, http://www.corteidh.or.cr/pais.cfm?id_Pais=18.

30. General Fernando Romeo Lucas García appears to have died in Venezuela shortly before the arrest order was issued. The Spanish Court included him in the arrest warrant because his family did not produce a death certificate.

31. *El Periódico* (Guatemala), July 8, 2006.

32. Center for Justice and Accountability, "Guatemala Court Denies Appeal of Defendants Facing Genocide Charges in Front of Spanish National Court," press release, October 30, 2007, http://www.cja.org/cases/Guatemala_News/PR_Guatemala_Court_Decision_10_2007.pdf.

33. On February 28, 2012, a Guatemalan tribunal responded to the Spanish extradition request and issued arrest warrants and ordered preventive detention for Ángel Aníbal Guevara Rodríguez, Germán Chupina Barahona, Oscar Mejía Victores and Pedro García Arredondo who were charged with crimes against humanity related to the Spanish Embassy massacre and the assassination of eight Spanish priests. On February 6, 2012, a hearing on another charge against García Arredondo for the 1981 disappearance of Edgar Saenz Calito was suspended when García Arredondo's lawyer failed to present himself to the court. On September 11, 2011, the Guatemalan court suspended the hearing against Mejía Victores on charges of genocide due to medical claims that Mejía Victores was not well enough to stand trial. In addition, since 2009, there have been five significant prosecutions for assassinations and massacres in El Jute, San Martin Jilotepeque, Tuluche, and Dos Erres as well as the prosecution of police commanders for the 1984 disappearance of student leader Fernando García.

34. CEH, *Guatemala: Memoria del Silencio,* 2:226–27.

35. Ibid., 2:181.

36. For excellent analysis on the history and systematic incorporation of PACs into military strategy, see CEH, *Guatemala: Memoria del Silencio,* 2:158–234; Oficina de Derechos Humanos del Arzobizpado, *Nunca Más* (Guatemala City: Oficina de Derechos Humanos del Arzobizpado, 1998), 2:113–58.

37. Ejército de Guatemala, *Las patrullas de autodefensa civil: La respuesta popular al proceso de integración socio-económico-político en la Guatemala actual* (Guatemala City: Editorial del Ejército, 1984), 16.

38. Alice Jay, *Persecution by Proxy: The Civil Patrols in Guatemala* (Washington, D.C.: Robert F. Kennedy Foundation, 1993), 23.

39. CEH, *Guatemala: Memoria del Silencio,* 2:234.

40. Ibid., 2:226–27.

41. Ibid., 2:12.

42. "Ladino" is a term used to reference non-Maya or individuals of mixed Spanish and indigenous ancestry as well as indigenous people who no longer practice indigenous customs, wear traditional clothing, or speak indigenous languages.

43. "Opinión de los lectores: Masacre en la USAC," *Prensa Libre,* July 16, 2005, http://www.prensalibre.com/pl/2005/16/lectura_opin.html.

44. Paul Kobrak, "1978: The Popular Movement," in *Organizing and Repression in the University of San Carlos, Guatemala, 1944–1996* (Washington, D.C.: American Association for the Advancement of Science, 1997), http://shr.aaas.org/guatemala/ciidh/org_rep/english/part2_8.html.

45. "Calle en Homenaje a Oliverio Castañeda," *Prensa Libre,* October 10, 2003, http://www.prensalibre.com/pl/2003/octubre/20/70721.html; http://shr.aaas.org/guatemala/ciidh/org_rep/espanol/part1_2.html.

46. See "Caso Illustrativo 79," *Guatemala: Memory of Silence,* online report, http://hrdata.aaas.org/ceh/report/english/intro.html; and Victoria Sanford, "Between Rigoberta Menchú and La Violencia: Deconstructing David Stoll's History of Guatemala," *Latin American Perspectives* 26, no. 6 (November 1999): 39.

47. Amnesty International, "Where Are the Children Who Disappeared in El Salvador and Guatemala?" http://web.amnesty.org/wire/October2004/ElSalvador.

48. CEH, *Guatemala: Memoria del Silencio,* 5:61.

49. Jan Perlin, "The Guatemalan Historical Clarification Commission Finds Genocide," *ILSA Journal of International and Comparative Law: International Practitioner's Handbook* 6, no. 2 (Spring 2000): 411.

50. Mark Gibney and David Warner, "What Does It Mean to Say I'm Sorry? President Clinton's Apology to Guatemala and Its Significance for International and Domestic Law," *Denver Journal of International Law and Policy* 28, no. 2 (2000): 223.

51. Personal communication with the FAFG, October 4, 2010.

52. Movimiento por los Derechos Humanos, "El Terror Se Expande," 2005, 1.

53. See http://www.humanrightsfirst.org/defenders/hrd_guatemala/hrd_guatemala.asp.

54. See "Se Registran 294 ataques contra defensores de derechos humanos en 2010," http://cerigua.org/la1520/index.php/nota-diaria/37-derechos-humanos/639-se-registran-294-ataques-contra-defensores-de-derechos-humanos-en-2010.

55. Procuraduría de Derechos Humanos de Guatemala, *Informe de muertes violentas de mujeres* (Guatemala City: Procuraduría de Derechos Humanos de Guatemala, 2005), 8.

56. Presentation of Ana Isabel Garita (chief of mission, International Commission Against Impunity in Guatemala, Woodrow Wilson Center), "Governance in Guatemala," Washington, June 4, 2009, http://www.wilsoncenter.org/events/docs/Garita%20Presentation%20PDFs.pdf.

57. Ministerio Público, Memoria de Labores, 2010, http://u.filepak.com/r8cc_MP-ML2010.pdf, 74.

58. Ana Lucía Blas and Martín Rodríguez P., "Día decisivo para Cicig," *Prensa Libre,* August 1, 2007, http://www.prensalibre.com/pl/2007/agosto/01/178656.html.

59. See http://www.bbc.co.uk/news/10263494.

60. See http://noticias.emisorasunidas.com/noticias/nacionales/reacciones-tras-nombramiento-de-nuevo-jefe-de-cicig.

61. See http://www.bbc.co.uk/news/10299442.

Commentary: "Eppur Si Muove"— Truth and Justice in Peru after the Truth and Reconciliation Commission

Carlos Iván Degregori

Between 1980 and 1999, Peru experienced the most violent internal armed conflict of its entire history as a republic.[1] In 2001, after the fall of Alberto Fujimori, the transition government appointed a Truth and Reconciliation Commission (Comisión de Verdad y Reconciliación, CVR) to reconstruct the history of the conflict. The CVR labored for two years, issuing its final report in August 2003.

The CVR gathered evidence from nearly 17,000 witnesses throughout the country, conducted nearly 2,000 open interviews—hundreds of them in prisons—and spoke with the principal political and military leaders of the 1980s and 1990s. The CVR was the first such body in Latin America to hold public hearings. And although it was not empowered to offer amnesty in exchange for sincere confessions, as occurred in South Africa, part of its mandate—unlike that of Guatemala's Historical Clarification Commission—was to further the cause of justice by bringing to light crimes and human rights violations committed during the conflict. The CVR benefited from the experience of its "older siblings" in Guatemala, El Salvador,

Chile, and Argentina, and was born in the latter stages of the "Democratic Spring" of human rights that flourished in the world between the fall of the Berlin Wall and the terrorist attacks of September 11, 2001. I wonder whether a truth commission would have succeeded—if, indeed, it could even have existed—in Peru after the events of 9/11.

Before the CVR began its work, the common perception was that the conflict had resulted in about 25,000 victims. The CVR produced new numbers that stunned public opinion. New data put the number of deaths at nearly 70,000, more than 60 percent of which had occurred in rural areas. More than 90 percent of the killings took place in eight of the most deeply impoverished Andean and Amazonian regions, especially Ayacucho, where the conflict began. More than 70 percent of the victims spoke Quechua or another native tongue as their first language, although—according to the 1993 National Census—the number of native Quechua speakers in Peru was less than 20 percent of the population.

Extrapolating from these figures, if the violence throughout the country had reached the same intensity that it did in Ayacucho, the number of victims would have been approximately 700,000. Even more dramatic, if the violence had reached the same levels that it did among the Asháninka people of the central rain forests, the total number of victims would have approached 2 million. In Peru, the victims of violence were mainly poor, rural, indigenous people who were both physically and emotionally far removed from the Lima metropolitan area. In this aspect, the Peruvian case more closely approximates what happened in Guatemala than what occurred in the Southern Cone.

Although there are similarities with the Guatemalan case, there are also significant differences. First, as documented by the CVR, the Shining Path (Sendero Luminoso) was the principal perpetrator of abuse; it was responsible for roughly 50 percent of all victims, a unique case in Latin America. Second, in contrast to Guatemala as well as the Southern Cone, the most intense part of the conflict took place between 1980 and 1992, a period of democratic rule; indeed, Peru's 1979 Constitution was the most progressive in the history of the republic. One of the CVR's conclusions (borrowed from an earlier Amnesty International report) was that beginning in 1983, Peru's civilian governments began to abdicate democratic authority. They sent the armed forces to fight the Shining Path, and looked the other way when it came to human rights violations.

A crucial component of this relinquishing of authority was the abdication of judicial power. This worked in favor of impunity for the military (and to a lesser extent, the police); at the same time, judicial authorities acquiesced to threats and blackmail from the Shining Path, which succeeded in turning the country's jails into what it called "shining trenches of combat."[2] This constituted one of the reasons that more than 70 percent of Peruvians favored trading democracy for security, and supported Alberto Fujimori's "self-coup" in April 1992.

Explaining the Conflict

In working to explain the conflict, the CVR decided to focus primarily on the Shining Path's explicit decision to launch a so-called people's war against the state. The members of CVR considered factors such as structural violence and poverty as background that could have created favorable conditions for insurgency, but in no way were these sufficient to explain the terrible violence that convulsed the country. The fact that, during those years, structural factors were often invoked as a pretext for violence supports the CVR's conclusion that political will played an important role. The Shining Path itself argued, "Why so much fuss over our bringing a few reactionaries to justice, when many more people in our country are dying of starvation, and more children are dying of malnutrition?" Political violence, however, requires a political organizer. This was not a spontaneous eruption of violence, or a social movement that included isolated episodes of violence, but rather the actions of a political organization that took up arms.

Most important, the CVR emphasized the Shining Path's political will because as a party, it rose up not just against the state but also against the mainstream of Peru's major contemporary social movements. These movements had significantly changed the face of the nation during the preceding decades (1950s to 1970s)—a process carried out in a generally peaceful fashion—while working against the predominant political forces of those decades in Peru. Following the approval of the 1979 Constitution, the general elections of 1980 drew unprecedented voter turnout.

The CVR's final report takes up the question of why the Shining Path decided to work against these trends. In this commentary, however, I focus on a different matter: Although political will is an important element in explaining how armed conflicts begin, it does not explain how they expand and endure. To understand what happened in Peru, one must also look at historical, structural, and institutional factors and examine how they interacted with actors in the social and political arenas. In this regard, a number of persistent disparities and inequalities that contributed to the outbreak and prolongation of the conflict are worth mentioning.

First, economic inequality—the chasm between rich and poor—was much more important than the existence of poverty itself. Second is the divide between Lima and the rest of the country, which, both then and now, is much too centralized. Third is the divide between the coast, on the one hand, and the mountainous highlands and the Amazonian jungle regions, on the other. These latter two divisions are not only geographical but also hierarchical, and are intertwined with ethnic and racial divisions between the *criollos* (those of European descent), the *mestizos* and *cholos*[3] (who were of mixed race), and indigenous people.

These divisions of class, region, and ethnicity were interwoven with two new divisions that assumed prominence during the 1970s and 1980s: the gender gap and the generation gap. Young people and women in particular were increasingly well educated, with many of them gaining access to some secondary education, but they faced limited opportunities in the workplace. These old and new divisions created profound mistrust and, particularly, a sense of grievance that was experienced, to differing degrees, within what one might term "subordinate" groups. Certain elements within these groups were particularly sensitive. For reasons I shall not detail here, this included provincial intellectuals and educated young people, especially those of Andean and/or indigenous descent. At the same time, the processes of modernization (many of which were frustrated or frustrating) brought about a collapse of the economic and discursive structures that had "normalized" these divisions—that is, the differences between citizens and noncitizens, or between first- and second-class citizens. The land reforms of the 1970s were particularly relevant in this regard. It is against this background of delegitimization of the traditional structures, forms of authority, and discourse that one must understand not only the social movements of the 1960s and 1970s, but also the Shining Path, which saw in this environment a "window of opportunity" for its totalitarian project.

Peru, however, was not Mao Zedong's China, as Abimael Guzmán, the top leader of the Shining Path, supposed. The fact that his movement survived and grew during the 1980s was due to the state's initial response of indiscriminate repression, which was not only ineffective but also counterproductive, inasmuch as it made the Shining Path appear in many places as the lesser of two evils.

Ultimately, however, the Shining Path was defeated—in a span of time that has proven insufficient to defeat the Revolutionary Armed Forces of

Colombia (Fuerzas Armadas Revolucionarias de Colombia, FARC), and without reaching the levels of Guatemala's "genocide," a word used by the Guatemalan Historical Clarification Commission in reference to the early 1980s. History finally caught up with the Shining Path, whose fight could be described as a constant *fuite en avant*.[4] Despite what one might call the postcolonial reactions of the state at the beginning of the conflict, the transformations of the previous decades had altered the country's social and political profile. The changes included migration;[5] mass schooling; the development of the market, the transportation system, and the communications media; the expansion and densification of the social networks that linked city and countryside; and new forms of social organization in urban and rural areas (unions, campesino federations, communal enterprises, women's organizations, etc.).

Nor was Peru Central America. Following the adoption of the 1979 Constitution, representative democracy existed to a significant degree. There was broad freedom of the press (indeed, until 1989 the Shining Path itself was able to sell its newspaper at corner newsstands), as well as legal protection for political organizations. In this context, the authoritarianism/totalitarianism of the Shining Path was increasingly perceived as intolerable. Thus, it was easier for the Shining Path to construct its so-called new state in those areas where the processes of change and the social networks cited earlier were weaker. This included the Asháninkas of central Amazonia; some rural parts of Ayacucho; certain public universities (particularly in their dining halls and dormitories) that highly resemble what Foucault would call "total institutions"; and frontier societies like the coca-growing areas of the Huallaga River, where the organized social sector was composed of drug traffickers, and where entire populations were pushed into illegality.[6]

The Shining Path had no economic program to offer farmers, save for complete self-sufficiency and subsistence that made sense only in theory; when the concept was actually put into practice, some of the agricultural fields turned literally into killing fields. Additionally, the Shining Path showed a total lack of understanding of Andean culture and especially its forms of justice. For example, the Shining Path imposed capital punishment with impressive frequency. Aside from the ethical questions raised by this practice, it caused the profound disarticulation of poor families, who could not afford to lose hard-working family members for reasons that were essentially ideological. This blindness, I believe, was one of the decisive reasons for the Shining Path's ultimate defeat.

Thus, the first turning point in the conflict came when major sectors of the peasantry decided to ally themselves with the armed forces. In the late 1980s, the military replaced its strategy of indiscriminate repression with another, more selective one, although human rights violations did not end altogether. (For three years, between 1989 and 1991, Peru ranked first in the world in the number of people detained and subsequently "disappeared.") At the same time that the armed forces were homing in on the targets of their repression through a strategy that I would call "authoritarian but not genocidal," the Shining Path was stepping up its own indiscriminate repression of campesinos, especially Quechuas. Many peasants became sufficiently fed up with the Shining Path that they joined the *rondas campesinas* (peasant self-defense patrols) sponsored by the military. Neither the CVR nor I deny that there was at times a high level of coercion involved in the *rondas*. However, unlike the civil patrols in the Guatemalan case, the Peruvian peasantry had much more opportunity, capacity, and room to maneuver. Strange as it may sound, in its own authoritarian way the repressive apparatus of the state learned more quickly than did Peru's civilian governments and political parties.

The second turning point came in 1992, when an antiterrorist police force was able to capture Abimael Guzmán without firing a single shot. The final, ironic chapter came one year later, when Guzmán—who had been ridiculing the guerrillas in El Salvador, Nicaragua, Colombia, and Guatemala for accepting peace negotiations—sent letters from prison to president Alberto Fujimori asking for a peace accord. This demoralized his followers, and sowed the seeds of discontent among the rank-and-file membership.

The Postconflict Era, and Truth and Justice

Although the Peruvian government ultimately won the war, during the 1990s it did not want, nor in the subsequent decade did it know how, to win the peace. Sometimes winning a war is easier than winning the postwar period, as has been demonstrated in other parts of the world.

Fujimori did not want to win the peace. He and his intelligence adviser, Vladimiro Montesinos, needed the threat of the Shining Path to inject fear into society—something they did systematically. They attempted to construct a "hegemonic memory," an official history that claimed, among other things, that human rights violations had been the unavoidable price of defeating terrorism, and that it was best to forget the past and look to the future.

Neither did President Alejandro Toledo (2001–6) know how to win the postwar era. He was yet another political "outsider" with a great sense of respect for the economic elites (who hardly acted in an honorable fashion during the conflict and were not interested in solving the subsequent problems). He also had great respect for the armed forces, which—as Carlos Basombrío explains in chapter 7—were in an extremely weak position and could have been subordinated to civilian authority during those years. What happened instead was a fairly rapid regression to "business as usual." An important moment of opening created by the first transitional government of Valentín Paniagua (2000–2001), and marked by the establishment of the CVR, was thus lost.

It took an almost Herculean effort on the part of Peru's economic and political elites to ignore or dismiss the CVR's recommendations. Many of the government's cautious steps toward the implementation of those recommendations—specifically those referring to reparations for victims— died in the offices of the Ministry of the Economy, sacrificed on the altar of macroeconomic stability and a balanced budget. A great opportunity to reckon with the recent past and strengthen and improve the quality of Peru's democracy was therefore lost. I consider the greatest error the inability of Peru's citizens to recognize themselves as members of a postconflict society and to act accordingly, as evidenced by the lack of interest in making reparations, in pursuing justice, and in undertaking or continuing the indispensable institutional reforms.

The great refusal to accept the role that racism and ethnic discrimination have played in Peruvian politics is an important reason for the emergence and victory of the presidential candidate Ollanta Humala, the country's third "outsider," who has openly and frequently emphasized race and ethnicity in his discourse.

Truth and the Struggle for Memory

The CVR posited a new reading of Peru's history during the period of armed conflict, a way of contesting the "official history" constructed in the 1990s, and thereby struggling against collective amnesia—or, in judicial language, against amnesty and impunity. The CVR's new approach to understanding the history of the conflict became one of those processes that the Argentine social scientist Elizabeth Jelin calls "struggles for memory,"[7] struggles that are not easily or rapidly won, regardless of how much empirical evidence is presented.

With the benefit of hindsight one can conclude that, although social movements can trigger memory and exert pressure against those who would defend forgetting, in the constant interaction between state and society, the role of the state, of political and economic elites, and of the communications media are key in the struggle to keep memories alive.

In spite of massive press attacks against the CVR just before the release of its final report, nearly 60 percent of the Peruvian public agreed with its work and findings. Many groups of students, teachers, Christians, Christian teachers, local authorities, minor political parties, and certain journalists voiced support for the final report, and nearly a year later, nearly 50 percent of the public still approved of its findings. This kind of passive support, however, did not translate into social pressure for justice and reparations. Victims' organizations multiplied during the years of the CVR's work, growing from three or four in 2001 to more than a hundred by the middle of the decade. But the majority are small, rural, dispersed throughout the nation, and have little symbolic capital; their leaders are women of Andean or indigenous descent. In a society as stratified as that of Peru, they are unable to wage a sustained or media-savvy battle like that pursued by the Mothers of the Plaza de Mayo in Argentina.

Thus, unless the government, political parties, and the communications media assume at least part of the postconflict agenda as their own, unless the social variable of the postconflict period becomes part of their strategies, the situation will tend to deteriorate. Violence does not disappear, but rather mutates and metamorphoses into social violence, common crime, and insecurity (as in Central America), or into new political violence, at first rhetorical and then real. It is noteworthy that in the first round of the presidential elections in 2006, Humala obtained the majority of votes in areas of the country hit hardest by the armed conflict, where people felt the most neglected and disillusioned with the postconflict period.[8] In the 2011 elections as well, Humala drew his greatest support from the poorest areas of Peru, especially the rural highlands.

The Battle for Justice

The CVR contributes to transcending what has frequently been seen as the dichotomy or trade-off between truth and justice. The opening of trials does not necessarily jeopardize democracy or peace; indeed, the last decade has shown that quite the opposite is true. Limiting the idea of justice simply to the opening of trials against perpetrators of human rights abuse, one can affirm that the CVR contributed to what the political scientist Kathryn Sikkink and the attorney Ellen Lutz have called "the justice cascade."[9] For example, after a long period in which the judicial branch showed no inclination to deal with the seventy-plus cases submitted to it by the CVR (forty of these cases were new), a number of judges in 2005 began to initiate proceedings against senior officials accused of serious human rights violations during the years of internal armed conflict. Why did this happen, in light of the absence of any judicial reform worthy of the name and if, as I maintained above, the promising moment of transition had been lost? There are five main reasons. First, judicial bodies such as the anticorruption and antiterrorist courts (*salas*) continued to function in more or less decent fashion. Second, human rights organizations had more experience and a longer tradition of pushing cases forward in the legal arena than they did, say, in the area of reparations. Third, the Ministry of Justice was not the Ministry of the Economy or the Ministry of Finance, which served as giant aircraft carriers for the government and its implementation of neoliberal reforms. Fourth, even after the setbacks following 9/11, the international context continued to be favorable to human rights trials. Fifth and finally, one needs to emphasize the role of individual judges—both male and female—who dared to open trials.

The reaction of the armed forces and especially of the army to judicial proceedings was to close ranks around longtime comrades, some of them retired, who had been implicated in serious human rights violations during the 1980s and 1990s. Faced with this circling of the wagons, the principal candidates in Peru's 2006 presidential elections hastened to promise amnesty to the military, even though no one in the armed forces had yet been sentenced. (Candidate Lourdes Flores, displaying more intelligence but in the same spirit, offered pardons.) Amnesty laws were proposed but not passed in 2008, and in 2010 President Alan García passed an executive decree law that amounted to a sweeping amnesty for human rights abusers. Domestic and international protests, however, resulted in the revocation of that law, and trials continue today.

Despite all this, what we can call the "battle for justice" continues. Trials are continuing, there are courts specifically dedicated to dealing with these cases, and the courts are conducting themselves properly, including in the new trials of terrorist leaders. The Inter-American Court of Human Rights ordered such cases to be reopened in light of the legal chaos created by the legislation of the Fujimori years. After a proper trial, the head of the Túpac

Amaru Revolutionary Movement (Movimiento Revolucionario Túpac Amaru, MRTA) was sentenced. That sentence, while severe, is a far cry from the iron-fisted and sometimes hysterical approach promoted by certain political candidates.

Most important, after a fifteen-month trial that relied on several arguments made by the CVR in its Final Report, former president Fujimori himself was convicted and sentenced for crimes committed in the course of the war against the Shining Path. The verdict was announced on April 7, 2009, and Fujimori was sentenced to twenty-five years in prison for his involvement in numerous killings by a government-directed death squad known as the Grupo Colina.[10] Fujimori's conviction was historic, not only for Peru but also for all Latin America. Not only did Peruvian judges demonstrate their professionalism and independence; the Fujimori case also represented the first time in Latin America that a former head of state was extradited back to his home country and then tried, convicted, and sentenced for serious human rights violations.[11] Several months later, in July 2009, Fujimori was also found guilty of embezzlement, after he admitted to having illegally paid his intelligence chief, Vladimiro Montesinos, $15 million in state funds. He was sentenced to an additional seven and a half years.

Despite this victory for justice, other aspects of the future remain uncertain. (I have not even touched on the subject of access to justice for indigenous peoples in a pluricultural country, or on the microlevel processes of reconciliation that have been taking place in many rural communities.) The case of the CVR and its report remind me of the title of the Chilean cinematographer Patricio Guzmán's film, *Chile, Obstinate Memory*. The CVR has put forward an "obstinate agenda" that will not disappear even though the most important political actors attempt to ignore or quash it. The issues return, sometimes in perverse ways, to the center of political life. Before the Fujimori verdict, this is precisely what occurred during the 2006 electoral campaign; after the main candidates had rushed to offer amnesty, ranting and raving against both the report and the members of the CVR themselves, reports surfaced that the leading candidate in the polls, Humala, was possibly the very same "Captain Carlos" who had perpetrated atrocities in the coca-growing zones of the Huallaga region in the early 1990s. The very candidates who had been attacking the CVR's report suddenly began hurling it as a weapon against Humala.

As long as Peru fails to reckon with its past and fails to advance further on the path of reconciliation, the subject is destined to reemerge, like the proverbial skeletons in the closet. This was evident in the context of the

2011 presidential elections, in which Humala emerged as the front-runner to face Fujimori's daughter, Keiko, in a second-round contest. The ghosts of the past intensely shaped the electoral debate, with new accusations of Humala's role in human rights violations and charges that Keiko would surely pardon her father—and likely work out a deal to end trials against members of the armed forces—if she were to be elected president. Humala won the election by just a few percentage points, revealing underlying divisions and polarizations. How the post-CVR agenda fares under Humala remains to be seen; he has promised to deliver the long-awaited individual reparations for which victims have been waiting, but he has been largely silent on the question of justice. Peru's "battles over memory" shall surely continue into the near future.

Notes

1. The phrase starting the title of this commentary, "Eppur si muove"—literally, "And yet it moves"—is said to have been uttered by the Italian scientist and philosopher Galileo Galilei after the Inquisition found him guilty of heresy. Galileo's "crime" was having written a book defending the Copernican theory that the Sun, not the Earth, was the center of the universe. In modern usage, the term generally indicates that truth, even truth that is denied, rests on facts and is not subject to manipulation based on ideology, religion, or governmental authority.

2. See José Luis Rénique, *La voluntad encarcelada: Las "luminosas trincheras de combate" de Sendero Luminoso del Perú* (Lima: Instituto de Estudios Peruanos, 2003).

3. In the Andean region, the word "*cholo*" is generally a pejorative term for a person of mixed race.

4. The French term *fuite en avant* refers in politics to the acceleration of a process that cannot be controlled and is evolving in a dangerous or reckless fashion. It is sometimes translated as a "headlong rush."

5. As the conflict spread to new areas of the country, all those who could, fled to the cities. The number of displaced persons grew to more than 600,000 at the height of the conflict.

6. An entire section of the national territory was declared lawless. However, because of the 1969–75 land reform, there were no strong rural actors (particularly landowners) capable of supporting the emergence of paramilitary forces, as occurred in Colombia and El Salvador.

7. Elizabeth Jelin, *Los trabajos de la memoria* (Madrid: Siglo XXI, 2002). See also Elizabeth Jelin, Judy Rein, and Marcial Godoy-Anativia, *State Repression and the Labors of Memory* (Minneapolis: University of Minnesota Press, 2003).

8. Humala's support was strongest in the southern and central Andes, including Ayacucho, the birthplace of Sendero Luminoso, as well as the Amazonian regions.

9. Ellen Lutz and Kathryn Sikkink, "The Justice Cascade: The Evolution and Impact of Foreign Human Rights Trials in Latin America," *Chicago Journal of International Law* 2, no. 1 (Spring 2001): 1–34.

10. See Jo-Marie Burt, "Guilty as Charged: The Trial of Former Peruvian President Alberto Fujimori for Grave Violations of Human Rights," *International Journal of Transitional Justice* 3, no. 3 (2009): 384–405.

11. General Augusto Pinochet of Chile was extradited to Chile from the United Kingdom, but he never stood trial for the hundreds of cases of murder, torture, and disappearance of which he was accused.

Chapter 13

Conclusion

Cynthia J. Arnson

This book's review of democratization in countries that have endured internal armed conflict in Latin American has been, overall, a sobering exercise. In contrast to the optimism that surged in the wake of political settlements to the Central American wars in the early and mid-1990s, an assessment of the situation in seven conflict and postwar countries in the region shows decidedly mixed results. The chapters included in this volume reveal the difficulties of overcoming conflict and consolidating peace through broad processes of institutional reform, the adoption of mechanisms of social inclusion, and the strengthening of the rule of law.

What Edelberto Torres-Rivas described in chapter 4 as the "interplay of light and shadow" invites us to acknowledge real progress in many arenas. Latin America's ideologically driven guerrilla conflicts that cost hundreds of thousands of lives, resulted in widespread suffering and violations of human rights and international humanitarian law, and destroyed or delayed prospects for growth and human development are largely a thing of the past. In Colombia and Peru, remnants of insurgent organizations remain militarily active and strong in remote border areas, sustaining themselves through links to the drug trade but lacking in popular support or sympathy. Since the late 1990s, Colombia has made major strides in the security arena. The leadership of the main guerrilla group, the Revolutionary Armed Forces of Colombia (Fuerzas Armadas Revolucionarias de Colombia), has been decimated and its ranks have been thinned by desertions, while overall the number of homicides, kidnappings, and massacres has declined dramatically. The government of President Juan Manuel Santos, who took office in mid-2010, has looked to couple military advances with an ambitious effort to redress structural inequalities in rural areas and provide reparations to victims of violence. In El Salvador, the candidate of the former Frente Farabundo Martí para la Liberación Nacional (FMLN) guerrillas won the presidential elections in 2009, breaking the twenty-year hold of the conservative Nationalist Republican Alliance (Alianza Republicana Nacionalista, ARENA) party and taking office in a peaceful transfer of power. Satisfaction with democracy jumped more than 10 percentage points in El Salvador as a moderately left-wing president expanded social programs and pledged to govern with pragmatism, efficiency, and transparency.[1] In Peru, courageous judges pressed ahead with court cases against perpetrators of wartime violence and corruption. The most relevant case was the prosecution of former president Alberto Fujimori, which represented the first time in Latin American history that a former head of state was extradited, tried, and sentenced in his native country for human rights abuses and corruption committed during his time in office. In 2011, Haiti saw the opening of a new window of opportunity following its presidential elections; the achievement of greater political stability and the willingness of the international community to continue supporting the country's post-earthquake reconstruction offered hope that Haiti would progress in achieving long-standing development and institutional goals.[2]

In all the countries considered in this book, the process of constructing or strengthening the mechanisms and institutional architecture for electoral, procedural democracy showed significant advances. Freedom of expression expanded, despite persistent threats and attacks against journalists reporting on sensitive issues such as organized crime. The ideological spectrum of views expressed in the media and political spheres broadened considerably. Levels of poverty in most cases decreased, as they did throughout the hemisphere, but the deep inequalities characteristic of the prewar and wartime eras for the most part remained stubbornly high. Most disturbing, new forms of violence emerged, some rooted in past exclusions and others in the incomplete reforms contemplated as part of the democratic transition or the increased presence of transnational drug-trafficking mafias. By the end of the first decade of the twenty-first century, El Salvador and Guatemala, along with neighboring Honduras, had the world's highest levels of homicides except for those countries in an open situation of war.[3] This surge in violence has hobbled a slowly emerging civil society and undermined citizenship. It has also further eroded the legitimacy of democratic institutions.

As was noted in chapter 1, the introduction, and was ratified in subsequent chapters, making generalizations across such a wide variety of countries is extremely difficult—even perilous. Historical context and specificity matter; for every broad-brush generalization one could make, there is at least one, if not multiple, exceptions. Thus, many elements vary dramatically from context to context—the causes, geographic reach, and intensity of Latin America's internal armed conflicts; the type of settlement of each conflict; the changing goals of and levels of support for insurgents; the relative strengths of the actors who make peace possible and define the course of postwar competition; the quality of political leadership; the strength of civil society; the ability to advance justice and postconflict reconciliation; the degree and nature of international involvement; the capacity of state institutions to uphold the rule of law or advance social welfare; and the role of state and nonstate actors in the reproduction of violence. To attempt to compare all seven cases examined in this book with respect to each of these elements would raise untold methodological and practical difficulties. One also faces the perennial problem of taxonomy, "apples and oranges," in attempting to lump together such a wide range of disparate cases. But to argue that everything is context specific and contingent is also unsatisfactory. What follows, therefore, is a series of reflections on a number of recurring themes and salient factors affecting the quality of peace and the nature of democracy in conflict and postwar settings in the region.

First, in considering processes of democratization that are conditioned by internal armed conflict, what is notable is the degree to which Latin American conflict countries have fared worse than their authoritarian but nonconflict counterparts with respect to many indicators of democratization and social well-being. Despite significant strides in procedural democracy, conflict societies overall perform worse with respect to key measurements of support for democracy as an abstract idea and satisfaction with democratic performance. As noted in chapter 2, trust in democratic institutions, though problematic throughout the hemisphere, is lower for the group of conflict/postwar countries examined in this book. Tolerance for the democratic rights of opponents—which is critical to the emergence of a "culture of peace" that fosters respect for differences within a common set of rules of the game—is also lower.[4] In 2010, public opinion polls across Latin America demonstrated that support for democracy "as the best system of government" and satisfaction with democracy was far lower in postconflict countries than elsewhere in the hemisphere.[5]

On the socioeconomic front, the situation is not much better. Human development indicators in conflict/postwar societies are worse, and government social expenditures as a percentage of gross domestic product are lower. There is no necessary causal relationship between these lower social indicators and armed conflict (although high levels of poverty and inequality and large numbers of unemployed young men are considered significant risk factors for conflict worldwide).[6] What the indicators suggest, however, is that conflict/postwar countries in Latin America overall have been unable—and in some cases unwilling—to "win the peace" by resolving their core problems of political and socioeconomic exclusion. These exclusions themselves reflect difficulties in transforming the way political power is exercised, and on whose behalf.

One pattern that emerges from this comparative review is that when preexisting democratic institutions are weak or nonexistent, postwar politics tends to reproduce the polarization and cleavages of the war; in addition, state institutions are more easily captured by partisan interests. Thus in Nicaragua, as chapter 5 demonstrates, the transfer of conflict from the military to the political arena—a desired outcome of most peace processes—has split the country's politics along pronounced Sandinista-versus-anti-Sandinista lines. A political pact of convenience between the Sandinistas and a faction of the Liberal Party has led to institutional and constitutional reforms that have made Nicaragua's electoral system the most exclusionary in Latin America and subjected other branches of government, particularly the judiciary, to partisan control.

Likewise, in El Salvador, chapter 3 shows how wartime polarization between the FMLN guerrillas and the ARENA party became etched into the postwar political system, as parties or movements that had been organized around wartime goals were ill equipped to assume the tasks of postwar transformation. These divisions grew deeper over the years, diminishing possibilities for dialogue and compromise to address the country's most critical challenges. Finally, in Peru, as indicated in chapter 7, the profound crisis of politics before and after the defeat of Sendero Luminoso was manifest in widespread disdain for democratic institutions and for politicians in general. Party alliances and the electorate remained volatile and unpredictable, allowing a series of political "outsiders" to run against the system and win elections by capitalizing on a generalized repudiation of the political class and democracy in general.[7]

A second broad pattern has to do with the limitations of formal democracy in the postwar period in overcoming structural inequalities and dualities between urban and rural, and indigenous and nonindigenous, populations. The conflict resolution literature teaches that effective, transparent social service delivery—the provision of a range of public goods such as education, access to safe drinking water, and health care—is critical to establishing the legitimacy of postwar governance institutions.[8] Addressing social deficits, however, raises questions not only of institutional capacity but also decisions made at the political level. In Chiapas, as noted in chapter 8, the national security aspects of the 1994 crisis diminished (if not disappeared) over time as a factor of governability. This was due not only to the Zapatistas' own self-inflicted political isolation but also to the fact that political leaders, particularly at the regional level, invested government resources in overcoming the most extreme levels of poverty. That said, and as much as the Chiapas uprising had a catalytic effect on Mexico's democratic transition, it had little effect on resolving the deeper problems of the inequality and exclusion of indigenous peoples. The urban, developed north and center of Mexico continue to contrast with the rural Mexico of the south; this duality is replicated even within Chiapas, where a modern sector has taken root in the cities and coastal areas and marginalization persists in the highlands and jungle areas.

The Peruvian case exposes a different dynamic. In Peru, geography and ethnic and racial divisions also coincide, separating Lima from the rest of the country and particularly from the rural highlands. These latter areas constituted the epicenter of the war; they also provided overwhelming backing in 2006 and 2011 for the political "outsider" Ollanta Humala. Humala's electoral base in the Altiplano reflected the failure of several postwar governments, elites, and political parties to spread the fruits of Peru's dynamic economic growth beyond the areas of the coast, and in particular Lima.[9] As chapter 2 demonstrates, social expenditures in Peru as a percentage of gross national income are among the lowest in the entire hemisphere, and have grown only marginally in the years since the end of conflict. Almost two decades after the "strategic defeat" of Sendero Luminoso, the World Bank's Human Opportunity Index ranked Peru thirteenth out of seventeen countries in the region, the lowest score in all of South America.[10] Although the poverty rate declined in urban areas, particularly in and around the capital, it remained at 60 to 70 percent of the population in the rural highlands.[11] As chapter 7 argues and as Carlos Iván Degregori so eloquently states in the commentary on chapter 12, Peru's greatest error since the early 1990s was "the inability to recognize ourselves as a post-conflict society and to act accordingly."

Similarly, in Guatemala, the marginalization and impoverishment of the country's majority indigenous population has continued well beyond the formal conclusion of the internal armed conflict. Poverty rates among Guatemala's indigenous peoples are among the worst in the hemisphere, as is tax revenue as a percentage of gross domestic product. Elites justify their resistance to raising the tax rate in support of social goals by pointing to real and perceived corruption, inefficiency, and lack of transparency in government spending. However, debates over fiscal reform also mask deeper and unresolved struggles about a realignment of power in the postwar period. Colombia and El Salvador, and to some extent Nicaragua and Haiti, also exhibit patterns of growth and increased well-being in urban areas against a backdrop of continued poverty and social exclusion in rural areas.

Another theme that emerges across the cases examined in this book is the importance of security and security-sector reform as a prerequisite for other aspects of state building. The Weberian emphasis on the state's ability to recapture a monopoly on the legitimate use of force reemerges as a precondition for virtually every other effort to establish inclusive and effective governance institutions and promote economic and social development.[12] Security is one of the major public goods that states must provide, and states acquire legitimacy in the eyes of the population to the extent that they protect civilians from real or threatened violence.[13]

The attention given to security and to security-sector reform reverberates across these pages. Creating security forces devoted to protecting the citizenry rather than to predation, organized thuggery, or the direct exercise of political power has been a priority of the international community in Haiti, and was central to the reforms envisioned in the peace accords in El Salvador and Guatemala. In Colombia, asserting military control over parts of the national territory dominated by guerrilla and paramilitary groups was the central objective of the government of President Álvaro Uribe, and was backed with significant assistance from the United States under Plan Colombia. In Peru, the transitional government that took power following the implosion of the Fujimori government made police reform an important marker of the break with the authoritarian, corrupt past. Whatever the success or failure of these efforts, numerous public opinion polls confirm that security is a central demand of citizens, and that support for democracy diminishes when citizen security is absent.[14] However, the cases explored in this book also demonstrate that paying attention to the way that the use of force is legitimized through adherence to the rule of law is as essential as asserting that security is a minimum condition for the achievement of other goals. The security gains of the Uribe administration in Colombia, for example, were marred by significant erosions in democratic practice, as reflected in scandals over political spying by state agencies, the killing of innocent civilians, and the paramilitary infiltration of politics.[15]

To the extent that actors who use violence explicitly attack the state, seek to replace it, or fill its vacuums of power, the state appears as a "victim," a weak actor whose capacities and legitimacy need to be bolstered by national as well as international action.[16] But as several of the chapters in this book indicate, certain forms of illegitimate violence are themselves embedded in the state, making it difficult to construct or transform institutions devoted to security, justice, and accountability. In wartime Guatemala, a state unconstrained by legal authority practiced state terrorism ("acts of genocide," in the words of Guatemala's truth commission). As chapter 4 indicates, although state-sponsored violence in Guatemala diminished in the years following the signing of the peace accords, the state continued to be an important source of public insecurity. State structures involved in counterinsurgency survived the end of the war, constituting "parallel powers" beyond the reach of civilian authority and involved in ongoing acts of violence and criminality. In Colombia, for decades the state fomented, participated in, and turned a blind eye to paramilitary violence unleashed on the civilian population in the name of fighting the guerrillas. Overcoming conflict and building democratic legitimacy in such circumstances involves establishing mechanisms of accountability to control, weaken, or dismantle state structures responsible for the illegitimate exercise of power and violence. Building the legitimate capacity of states (at the national and local levels) and rooting out sources of illegitimate power and authority are complementary but separate tasks. If anything, the chapters in this book attest to the difficulty of simultaneously building security institutions and subjecting them to the rule of law.[17]

Not all the violence that compromises democratic legitimacy is overt. As chapter 6 demonstrates, regionally based clientelistic politicians, drug traffickers, and demobilized paramilitaries in Colombia used threats, intimidation, and extortion to manipulate and subvert electoral processes. The infiltration of political institutions in an effort to corrode and control the state from within exploded into public view in Colombia's "parapolitics" scandal of 2008, which is described in chapter 6. The Colombian judicial system made substantial progress in investigating and prosecuting those involved. But the ability to penetrate, corrupt, and control politics at the national and regional levels remains a structural weakness in many cases in which institutions of accountability are weak or absent and criminal groups possess the financial resources to finance candidates and campaigns for public office.

Perhaps no feature of the various cases explored in this volume is more disheartening than the capacity of violence to transform and reproduce itself. As noted in the commentary on chapter 12, violence does not disappear, but rather, it "mutates and metamorphoses" into other forms of insecurity. Not all manifestations of violence in the postwar period are rooted in the history of internal armed conflict; the Chiapas uprising, for example, despite its contribution to Mexico's democratic transition, bears no connection to the wave of bloodletting linked to narco-trafficking in Mexico that between 2006 and 2011 claimed more than 40,000 lives.[18]

Rather, patterns of transition and the extent or absence of institutional reform play key explanatory roles in the reproduction of violence. As chapter 11 indicates with respect to El Salvador and Guatemala, wartime migratory patterns, the proliferation of firearms, and inadequate patterns of reintegration of former combatants contributed to the explosion of gang violence and soaring rates of homicide. Exacerbating the problem, however, were state policies of *mano dura* and the failure of the democratic process to establish effective public security institutions or to root out the authoritarian and repressive practices of the past. One case that stands out in stark contrast is Nicaragua, where the professionalization and depoliticization of the armed forces and police, together with networks of social solidarity created during the Sandinista period, kept postwar violence to a minimum.[19] Similarly, in Colombia, national police reform together with municipal policies to invest in poor neighborhoods, improve urban infrastructure, and foster a culture of respect for the law reduced levels of violence in several major cities. In Mexico, chapter 11 posits that the country's gradual transition to democracy unfolded independent of any effort to reform security institutions, even as the patronage networks and informal rules that had served to control levels of violence were altered or dismantled. This process led to the eruption of violent competition among drug traffickers and criminal organizations striving to establish new systems of protection and control. In turn, the penetration of Mexican drug cartels into Central America and the transformation of the region into the principal transshipment route for illegal narcotics entering the United States have worsened Central America's already-staggering levels of homicides. By 2011, the World Bank identified drug trafficking as the "main single factor behind rising levels of violence in the region," and noted that the area's weak institutionality is an impediment to crime punishment and prevention.[20]

The fact that Latin America as a region has the highest levels of homicide in the world and that much of it is unrelated to a previous history of civil war invites us to explore the causal factors behind violence more deeply.[21] El Salvador, Guatemala, Honduras, and Venezuela have some of the highest murder rates in the world, while the rates in Chile, Bolivia, Argentina, Peru, and Uruguay are among the lowest. Within countries, national averages may mask the intensity of violence in certain areas, such as cities on the U.S.-Mexico border. These differences aside, during the last twenty-five years, rates of violent crime have increased in most Latin American cities while rates of property crime have at least doubled.[22]

What is striking is that many of the explanations for cycles of violence in postwar settings apply equally to other areas, particularly cities. Indeed, some theorists posit that violence in contemporary Latin America reflects not a failure of democratic institutions but the basis on which those institutions function.[23] Other explanations point to such factors as the absence of employment or educational opportunities for youth in general and young men in particular; rising levels of informality and inequality; the way that globalization has fostered illegal markets as well as unprecedented demand for cheap consumer goods; the failure of police reform and the involvement of state agents in violent criminal behavior, including social cleansing; the growth of organized crime and its sophistication in penetrating state institutions; and the weaknesses of judicial systems at all levels, from judges to courts to the penitentiary system.[24] Despite the similarities between postwar and nonconflict cases, several factors serve to magnify the problem of violence in conflict settings: the availability of firearms due to incomplete programs of disarmament, and inadequate retraining and reinsertion programs for demobilized soldiers and combatants.

Also consistent for both conflict and nonconflict cases are the effects of violence on social relations and democratic citizenship. As the anthropologist Tani Adams has noted, citizens adapt to situations of chronic violence and impunity by adopting survivalist tactics—with a wide range of perverse social consequences.[25] Fear, apathy, and withdrawal from the public sphere have a negative impact on both the formation of social capital and the possibilities for collective action. In the absence of protection or justice, citizens turn to alternate authorities, including criminal groups, and tolerate or demand repressive measures that violate the rule of law. The severity of the social consequences of violence underscores how important it is to consider the construction not only of institutions but also of citizenship as fundamental to the process of democratization.[26]

As chapter 12 and the commentary following it indicate, truth commissions can contribute to the construction of citizenship by dignifying and contributing to reparations for victims of state violence, and by developing a detailed narrative of responsibility for violent acts. And over time, the record throughout Latin America suggests that truth commissions can contribute to the national and international processes whereby perpetrators of abuse are brought to justice.[27] However, when the political and military authorities and societies at large reject the conclusions of truth commissions and fail to assume responsibility for their recommendations, the implications for citizenship are less positive. Amid ongoing marginalization and continued violence, the existence of an "official story" may be less relevant for the individual, village, or neighborhood whose existential condition remains unaltered by a truth-telling exercise.[28]

Finally, the chapters in this book indicate how difficult it is for the international community to contribute to conflict resolution and democratization in the absence of domestic leadership. Undoubtedly, the situation in such countries as Haiti and Guatemala would be much worse without international assistance and presence. But the meager results there of decades of effort to build institutions and enhance the rule of law underline the centrality of local actors in carrying forward a process of transformation. Capacities can be built and reinforced at the national as well as local levels, but the desire to effect change is extremely difficult to generate from the outside. In other words, unless both governmental ands economic elites are invested in reform—and are willing to accept the implications, fiscal and otherwise, of achieving it—there is little that external actors can ultimately achieve. Conversely, outside support is most decisive when it is paired with national and municipal leadership, as it was in Colombia with respect to the security gains during the Uribe years. When governments and elites are not monolithic, international support for key reformers can prove important in preserving their space for maneuvering. At the same time, as chapter

10 indicates, domestic actors can take advantage of varying goals and priorities in the international community to advance their own agendas. The divergent approaches to conflict resolution taken by the United States and European Union in Central America, and to a lesser extent in Colombia, reflect this pattern.

Ultimately, the international factors involved in postwar democratization are not limited to foreign governments or multilateral institutions. Transnational criminal organizations, aided and abetted by the globalization of commerce and communications, prey on and further undermine weak institutions, constituting a source of alternative power and a factor of disintegration perhaps more powerful than combined domestic and international efforts to strengthen a democratic state and the rule of law.[29]

The presence of such existential threats obliges us to consider the interplay between national and international actors and processes in defining the possibilities for democratization in postwar settings. As much as this review of conflict cases in Latin America has reconfirmed the connection between the legitimate exercise of state authority and the prospects for peace and democratization, it has also exposed the multiple forces involved in state formation that work against a democratic outcome. Further research is needed to untangle the ways that power and authority are exercised at various levels in ways that constrain political agency and make an impact on institutional autonomy. Much more precision is needed about what kinds of transformations are functions of political will and technical capacity, and which impediments are more structural in nature. Moreover, characterizing the persistent weaknesses and failures of state institutions is far easier than devising politically viable strategies for improving their contributions to governance. If we know that parallel powers in some cases reside within the state but in others impinge on its ability to carry out effective public policy, what can be done to confront or reduce their shadow? If war reflects the breakdown or absence of social pacts, how can they be constructed in deeply divided societies? If states are both a source of the problem and part of the solution, how can the exercise of legitimate over illegitimate forms of authority best be privileged? If citizens' trust is affected by corruption and criminality, how can the opportunity structures behind both be diminished? By posing all these questions in extremis, and in striving for concrete solutions, conflict and postwar countries help define an important future agenda for research on democratization throughout Latin America.

Notes

1. Latin American Public Opinion Project (LAPOP), *The Political Culture of Democracy, 2010: Democratic Consolidation in the Americas in Hard Times* (Nashville: Vanderbilt University, 2010), http://www.vanderbilt.edu/lapop/ab2010/2010-comparative-en-revised.pdf.

2. Between 1986 and 1990, Haiti had five different governments; between 2006 and 2011, President René Préval was the sole head of state.

3. United Nations Development Program, *Informe sobre desarrollo humano para América Central 2009–2010: Abrir espacios a la seguridad ciudadana y el desarrollo humano* (Bogotá: United Nations Development Program, 2009).

4. Michael Edwards, Libby Marden, et al., "Political Tolerance in the Americas: Should Critics Be Allowed to Vote?" *Americas Barometer Insights: 2011,* no. 67, http://www.vanderbilt.edu/lapop/insights.

5. According to Latinobarómetro in 2010, Guatemala, El Salvador, Mexico, Paraguay, Peru, and Nicaragua, in that order, had the lowest levels of support for the statement that "democracy may have problems, but it is the best system of government." According to the LAPOP 2010 survey, satisfaction with democracy was lowest in Haiti, followed by Mexico and Peru. See Corporación Latinobarómetro, *Informe 2010* (Santiago: Corporación Latinobarómetro, 2010), 48; and LAPOP, *Political Culture,* 105. The low levels of support for democracy in Mexico appear related to the high levels of violence associated with drug-trafficking cartels and the state's policies for confronting them.

6. Paul Collier, "Doing Well Out of War: An Economic Perspective," in *Greed and Grievance: Economic Agendas in Civil Wars,* edited by Mats Berdal and David M. Malone (Boulder, Colo.: Lynne Rienner, 2000), 93–98; World Bank, *Crime and Violence in Central America: A Development Challenge* (Washington, D.C.: World Bank, 2011), 18–21; World Bank, *World Development Report 2011: Conflict, Security, and Development:* (New York: Oxford University Press, 2011), 1–8; Ravi Kanbur, *Poverty and Conflict: The Inequality Link,* Coping with Crisis Working Paper (New York: International Peace Institute, 2007).

7. I am grateful to Dinorah Azpuru for pointing out that, by late 2011, and despite the fact that armed conflicts ended a decade and a half ago in most of Latin America, the top political leadership in five of the seven countries considered in this book was linked in one way or another to the armed conflict. These included former guerrilla comandante Daniel Ortega in Nicaragua, retired army general Otto Pérez Molina in Guatemala, former colonel Ollanta Humala in Peru, former defense minister Juan Manuel Santos in Colombia, and former guerrilla fighter Salvador Sánchez Cerén, El Salvador's vice president. What is striking about these cases is not only the enduring imprint of war on the national consciousness, but also the variety of ways that conflict-era personalities and issues (security and exclusion) continue to dominate the political system. In El Salvador, the Frente Farabundo Martí para la Liberación Nacional (FMLN) party had scored significant parliamentary and mayoral victories for fifteen years before gaining the presidency in 2009. But the legacy of wartime polarization was such that only when the FMLN reached outside its ranks for a presidential candidate did it succeed in winning over a majority of voters. Ollanta Humala and Otto Pérez Molina were also deeply polarizing figures, whose parties served as personalistic vehicles amid the weakness

and fragmentation of the party system. Although allegations about their wartime conduct hovered over their respective campaigns, they appear to have won at least partly because of, not despite their military past. In Colombia, even a committed democrat such as Santos won as the candidate of the "U" party, which had been created by his predecessor Álvaro Uribe outside the traditional party system. His victory reflected the electorate's desire for a continuation of the security polices of the Uribe administration, of which Santos had been a key architect. In Nicaragua, as described above, the Sandinistas entered a marriage of convenience with smaller parties in order to enact electoral reforms that favored their continued dominance of politics. The merging of the Frente Sandinista de Liberación Nacional party, the state, and the caudillo-like figure of Daniel Ortega reproduces a long-standing pattern in Nicaraguan politics, sustained by the weakness of the opposition and its inability to address the needs and interests of the country's poor majority.

8. World Bank, *World Development Report 2011,* 121–42. Employment and job creation are considered critical, although to what extent they are provided by the government, international community, private sector, or some combination, is often murky and, in the Latin American context, highly contested.

9. The cleavages remain stark and politically relevant, even though at the national level, indicators of poverty and inequality improved. See United Nations, *Millennium Development Goals: Achieving the Millennium Development Goals with Equality in Latin America and the Caribbean—Progress and Challenges* (New York: United Nations, 2010), 35; and Luis F. López-Calva and Nora Lustig, eds., *Declining Inequality in Latin America: A Decade of Progress?* (New York and Washington, D.C.: United Nations Development Program and Brookings Institution Press, 2010), 1–24.

10. José R. Molinas, Ricardo Paes de Barros, et al., *Do Our Children Have a Chance? The 2010 Human Opportunity Report for Latin America and the Caribbean* (Washington, D.C.: World Bank, 2010), 55.

11. "Un crecimiento excluyente que congela la desigualdad," *Otra Mirada,* informe no. 444, April 11, 2011, http://www.otramirada.pe.

12. The "softening" of state sovereignty and the emergence of alternative sources of authority in the security, political, and economic realms is the subject of *Ungoverned Spaces: Alternatives to State Authority in an Era of Softened Sovereignty,* edited by Anne L. Clunan and Harold A. Trinkunas (Stanford, Calif.: Stanford University Press, 2010).

13. See, e.g., Vanda Felbab-Brown, "The Complexities of the Drug-Conflict Nexus," Brookings Institution, March 23, 2011.

14. See chapter 2 of the present volume; LAPOP, *Political Culture,* 78–86; and Corporación Latinobarómetro, *Informe,* 11–15.

15. Cynthia J. Arnson and Arlene B. Tickner, "Colombia and the United States: Strategic Partners or Uncertain Allies?" in *Contemporary U.S.-Latin American Relations,* edited by Jorge I. Domínguez and Rafael Fernández de Castro (New York: Routledge, 2010), 164–96.

16. Economists have identified several ways that internal armed conflict weakens the state, including by impeding its ability to collect taxes and deliver public goods such as infrastructure. See Mauricio Cárdenas, Marcela Eslava, and Santiago Ramírez, "Revisiting the Effects of Conflict on State Capacity: A Panel Data Approach," Brookings Institution, Latin American Initiative, January 12, 2011, http://www.brookings.edu/papers/2011/0112_state_capacity_conflict_cardenas.aspx.

17. Over time, paramilitary links to the Colombian state diminished and the major paramilitary group formally demobilized; rearmed paramilitaries continue, however, to be major actors in the drug trade and a source of significant violence in the countryside.

18. For official statistics on homicides in Mexico, see Secretaría de Gobernación, México, "Incidencia Delictiva Nacional, fuero común," http://www.secretariadoejecutivo.gob.mx/es/SecretariadoEjecutivo/Incidencia_Delictiva_Nacional_fuero_comun. The estimates of civil society organizations are higher.

19. A number of commentators have raised concerns about a repoliticization of the police during the period after Daniel Ortega's return to the presidency in 2006.

20. World Bank, *Crime and Violence,* ii–iii.

21. The region has 27 percent of the homicides in the world, but only 8.5 percent of the world's population. See United Nations Development Program and Organization of American States, *Nuestra Democracia* (Mexico City: Fondo de Cultura Económica, 2010), 182.

22. Marcelo Bergman, "El crecimiento del delito en Latinoamérica: Delicuencia organizada, mercados ilegales y estados fallidos," Consejo Mexicano de Asuntos Internacionales, *Cuadernos* no. 9, September 2010, 3.

23. Enrique Desmond Arias, "Conclusion: Understanding Violent Pluralism," in *Violent Democracies in Latin America,* edited by Enrique Desmond Arias and Daniel M. Goldstein (Durham, N.C.: Duke University Press, 2010), 242–64. Arias refers to a "proliferation of multiple sets of violent orders," best characterized as "violent pluralism."

24. Ibid.; Bergman, "El crecimiento del delito," 3–26; United Nations, *Millennium Development Goals,* 69–109 (for data on employment); Juan Gabriel Tokatlian, "Organized Crime, Illicit Drugs, and State Vulnerability," conference report, Norwegian Peacebuilding Center and Universidad Torcuato di Tella, April 2011; United Nations Office on Drugs and Crime, *The Globalization of Crime: A Transnational Organized Crime Threat Assessment* (Vienna, United Nations Office on Drugs and Crime, 2010), 25–36; Mark Ungar, *Policing Democracy: Overcoming Obstacles to Citizen Security in Latin America* (Washington, D.C., and Baltimore: Woodrow Wilson Center Press and Johns Hopkins University Press, 2011), 21–68.

25. Tani Marilena Adams, "Chronic Violence and Its Reproduction: Perverse Trends in Social Relations, Citizenship and Democracy in Latin America," Woodrow Wilson International Center for Scholars, Latin American Program, and International Institute of Learning for Social Reconciliation, September 2011, 1–66. See also Jenny Pearce and Rosemary McGee with Joanna Wheeler, *Violence, Security, and Democracy: Perverse Interfaces and Their Implications for States and Citizens in the Global South,* Working Paper 357 (Brighton: Institute of Development Studies, University of Sussex, 2011).

26. The Brazil scholars Teresa Caldeira and James Holston coined the term "disjunctive democracy" to refer to the ways that economic marginalization and inequality and the violence associated with them undermined citizenship rights. See Teresa Caldeira and James Holston, "Democracy and Violence in Brazil," *Comparative Studies in Society and History* 41, no. 4 (1999): 691–729, quoted by Arias, "Conclusion," 248. See also Deborah J. Yashar, *Contesting Citizenship in Latin America: The Rise of Indigenous Movements and the Postliberal Challenge* (Cambridge: Cambridge University Press, 2005), 31–53; and James Holston, "Citizenship in Disjunctive Democracies," in *Contesting Citizenship in Latin America,* edited by Joseph S. Tulchin and Margaret Ruthenburg (Boulder, Colo.: Lynne Rienner, 2007), 75–94.

27. For a recent treatment of this issue, see Kathryn Sikkink, *The Justice Cascade: How Human Rights Prosecutions Are Changing World Politics* (New York: W. W. Norton, 2011).

28. I am grateful to Tani Adams for this observation.

29. Among the first works to characterize the role of globalization in fomenting new forms of violence was Mary Kaldor, *New and Old Wars: Organized Violence in a Global Era* (Stanford, Calif.: Stanford University Press, 1999). Subsequently, the literature on economic motives in civil wars emphasized globalization's role in enhancing insurgencies' access to income from legal and illicit commodities. For a more recent treatment, see Jorge Heine and Ramesh Thakur, *The Dark Side of Globalization* (Tokyo: United Nations University Press, 2011).

Contributors

Cynthia J. Arnson is director of the Latin American Program of the Woodrow Wilson International Center for Scholars. She is editor of *Comparative Peace Processes in Latin America* (Woodrow Wilson Center Press and Stanford University Press, 1999), coeditor (with I. William Zartman) of *Rethinking the Economics of War: The Intersection of Need, Creed, and Greed* (Woodrow Wilson Center Press and Johns Hopkins University Press, 2005), and author of *Crossroads: Congress, the President, and Central America, 1976–1993* (2nd edition, Pennsylvania State University Press, 1993). She has written extensively on Colombia, Central America, U.S. policy in Latin America, governance, conflict resolution, and human rights issues. She serves on the advisory boards of *Foreign Affairs Latinoamérica,* Human Rights Watch/Americas, and the Conflict Prevention and Peace Forum of the Social Science Research Council. She received a PhD in international relations from the Paul H. Nitze School of Advanced International Studies at Johns Hopkins University.

Dinorah Azpuru is associate professor of political science at Wichita State University and associate member of the Association for Research and Social Studies (Asociación de Investigación y Estudios Sociales, ASIES) in Guatemala. Previously, she was assistant professor of political science and research coordinator of the Latin American Public Opinion Project at Vanderbilt University. In Guatemala, she was adjunct professor of political science and chair of the department of political science at the Universidad Rafael Landívar, as well as a senior researcher at ASIES. Her expertise is on democratization in developing nations, survey research in Latin America, and peace processes in Central America. She has published in *Latin American Politics and Society,* the *Journal of Democracy,* and *Orbis,* and she is coauthor of *Construyendo la democracia en sociedades posconflicto: Guatemala y El Salvador en perspectiva comparada.* She received a PhD in political science from the University of Pittsburgh and also undertook graduate studies in Guatemala, Sweden, and Switzerland.

Carlos Basombrío Iglesias is consulting director of the Citizen Security Project of the Woodrow Wilson Center's Latin American Program. He currently serves as a consultant for Capital Humano y Social SA and several other Peruvian and international organizations, and he writes a weekly political op-ed column for the newspaper *Perú 21.* From 2001 to 2004, he served in various positions in Peru's Ministry of the Interior, including vice minister of the interior, chief of the Cabinet of Advisers, coordinator of the Commission to Restructure the Police, and member of the Commission for the Modernization of the Police. He has served as director and member of the Instituto de Defensa Legal, one of Peru's premier human rights organizations, and has written extensively on issues of citizen security, democracy, peace and violence, civil-military relations, and police reform. He received a BA in sociology from the Pontificia Universidad Católica del Perú.

Ana María Bejarano is associate professor of political science at the University of Toronto. She has been a visiting fellow at the Kellogg Institute for International Studies at the University of Notre Dame and at Princeton University's Program for Latin American Studies and Woodrow Wilson School of Public and International Affairs. She is the author of *Precarious Democracies: Understanding Regime Stability and Change in Colombia and Venezuela* (University of Notre Dame Press, 2011). She also coedited (with S. Mainwaring and E. Pizarro) *The Crisis of Democratic Representation in the Andes* (Stanford University Press, 2006). Her current research project explores constitution making in five Andean nations, focusing on the politics underlying constitutional choices and the prospects for democratic deepening in the wake of constitutional change.

Raúl Benítez Manaut is a professor and researcher at the North American Research Center at the National Autonomous University of Mexico. He is president of the nongovernmental organization Colectivo de Análisis de la Seguridad con Democracia (CASEDE). He has been a Public Policy Scholar at the Woodrow Wilson International Center for Scholars and a visiting professor at Columbia University and American University. He is editor or coeditor of *Atlas de la Seguridad y la defensa de México 2009* (CASEDE, 2009); *Crimen organizado e Iniciativa Mérida en las relaciones México-Estados Unidos* (CASEDE, 2010); and *Seguridad y defensa en América del Norte: Nuevos dilemas geopolíticos,* Latin American Program Report on the Americas 24 (Latin American Program of the Woodrow Wilson Center and Fundación Dr. Guillermo Manuel Ungo, 2010).

Tania Carrasco is a specialist on issues of social development and public policy, and an ethnologist at the National School of Anthropology and History in Mexico City. She is coeditor of *12 experiencias de Desarrollo Indígena en América Latina y Exclusión Social, Estrategias de Vida de los Indígenas Urbanos en Perú, México y Ecuador,* and has written a variety of scholarly articles regarding the social integration of the poor in Mexico and Latin America. She received an MA in Latin American studies from the Universidad Nacional Autónoma de México.

Ricardo Córdova Macías is executive director of the Fundación Dr. Guillermo Manuel Ungo in El Salvador. His areas of research and teaching interests include peace processes in Central America, democratization, elections and political parties in Central America, civil-military relations, citizen security, and political culture. He is coauthor of *Cultura Poliítica de la Democracia en El Salvador: 2006* (San Salvador: Instituto Universitario de Opinión Pública, 2007) and coeditor of *Pasos hacia una Nueva Convivencia: Democracia y Participación en Centroamérica* (San Salvador: Fundación Guillermo Manuel Ungo, 2001), among other works. He received his PhD in political science from the University of Pittsburgh.

José Miguel Cruz is a visiting assistant professor in the Department of Politics and International Relations at Florida International University.

Formerly, he was director of the Instituto Universitario de Opinión Pública at the Universidad Centroamericana José Simeón Cañas in San Salvador. He has been a member of the advisory council of the Governance Program at the United Nations Development Program–El Salvador and has consulted on questions of Central American violence for the World Bank, Inter-American Development Bank, Pan American Health Organization, and United Nations Development Program. His publications on political culture, violence, and youth gangs in El Salvador and Central America include ¿*Elecciones para qué? El impacto de ciclo electoral 1999–2000 en la cultura política salvadoreña; Solidaridad y violencia en las pandillas del gran San Salvador;* and *Maras y pandillas en Centroamérica,* volumes 2 and 4.

Carlos Iván Degregori, a Peruvian anthropologist, was director of the School of Anthropology at the National University of San Marcos from 2000 to 2002, a member of the New York–based Social Science Research Council, and twice director of the Instituto de Estudios Peruanos in Lima. During his distinguished career, he was a visiting professor at Princeton University and wrote for the newspaper *Perú 21.* Between 2001 and 2003, he was a member of the Truth and Reconciliation Commission and headed the editorial committee in charge of its final report. He passed away in May 2011.

Rafael Fernández de Castro is the founding director of the Department of International Studies at the Instituto Tecnológico Autónomo de México and former senior foreign policy adviser to President Felipe Calderón. He is an expert on the bilateral relationship between Mexico and the United States as well as on Mexican foreign policy. Among his many publications are *The United States and Mexico: Between Partnership and Conflict* (with Jorge Domínguez; also published in Spanish); *The U.S. Congress: The Controversial Pivot of North America* (with Robert Pastor; also published in Spanish); and *México en el Mundo: Los desafíos para México en 2001.* In addition, he served on the Binational Panel on Migration, which published the *U.S.-Mexico Binational Study on Migration.* He was the founding editor of *Foreign Affairs Latinoamérica.*

Johanna Mendelson Forman is a senior associate in the Americas Program and the William E. Simon Chair of Political Economy at the Center for Strategic and International Studies. Formerly, she served as director for peace, security, and human rights at the UN Foundation and as codirector of a bipartisan commission on postconflict reconstruction sponsored by the Association of the United States Army and the Center for Strategic and International Studies. She also served as a senior fellow with the Program on the Role of American Military Power in the 21st Century at the Association of the United States Army. She has served in senior positions at the U.S. Agency for International Development, including as senior policy adviser for the Bureau for Humanitarian Response's Office of Transition Initiatives, where she managed the agency's policy on postconflict reconstruction, security, and governance. She also served in the World Bank's first Post-Conflict Unit. She is a scholar in residence at American University's School of International Service.

Shelley A. McConnell is assistant professor of government at Saint Lawrence University, where she teaches Latin American politics. Her research focuses on democratic governance and institution building in Nicaragua. She was previously senior associate director of the Americas Program at the Carter Center, and has monitored elections in Nicaragua since 1989. Her recent publications include "The Return of *Continuismo?*" *Current History,* February 2009; and "La evolucion incierta del sistema electoral nicaragüense," in *Nicaragua y el FSLN [1979–2009]: Que queda de la revolución?* edited by Salvador Marti I. Puig and David Close (Ediciones Bellatera, 2009). She received a PhD in political science from Stanford University.

Marco Palacios is professor of Latin American history at El Colegio de México and at the Universidad de los Andes in Bogotá. He has been a research fellow at the Centro de Estudios para el Desarrollo, National University of Colombia, and London University's Institute of Latin American Studies. Previously, he was rector of the National University of Colombia, and he has been a visiting professor at a number of universities. His extensive publications on Colombian history and politics include *Coffee in Colombia 1850–1970: An Economic, Social and Political History* (Cambridge University Press, 1980 and 2002); *Entre la legitimidad y la violencia: Colombia, 1875–1994* (Grupo Editorial Norma, 1995; in English, Duke University Press, 2006); *Parábola del liberalismo* (Grupo Editorial Norma, 1999); and *Populistas: El poder de las palabras* (Universidad Nacional, 2011). He is coauthor (with Frank Safford) of *Colombia, Fragmented Land, Divided Society* (Oxford University Press, 2002; in Spanish, Grupo Editorial Norma, 2002).

Stewart Patrick is a senior fellow at the Council on Foreign Relations. He previously served as a research fellow at the Center for Global Development, where he directed the project on weak states and U.S. national security. He also focuses more broadly on the intersection between security and development. He has served on the adjunct faculty of the Paul H. Nitze School of Advanced International Studies at Johns Hopkins University. He served as a senior official on the U.S. State Department's Policy Planning Staff, where he helped formulate U.S. policy on Afghanistan as well as a range of global and transnational challenges, including weak and failing states, humanitarian crises, postconflict reconstruction, organized crime, global health, and sustainable development. He is author, among other writings, of *Weak Links: Fragile States, Global Threats, and International Security* (Oxford University Press, 2011); and *The Best Laid Plans: The Origins of American Multilateralism and the Dawn of the Cold War* (Rowman & Littlefield, 2009).

Carlos G. Ramos is director of the Faculty of Latin American Social Sciences, El Salvador, where he has been academic program coordinator since 1999. Previously, he served as executive director of the Center for Information, Documentation, and Research Support and the weekly *Proceso* at the Universidad Centroamericana José Simeón Cañas in San Salvador. He is the author of numerous publications on security, democratic governance, local development, youth, and violence, including *El Salvador 2008: Between the Ideological Polarization and Economic Crisis; Building Democracy in Post-Conflict Societies: Guatemala and El Salvador, a Comparative Approach;* and *El Salvador: Fifteen Years after the Signing of the Peace Accords.* He studied sociology at the Universidad de Costa Rica in San José and philosophy at the Universidad Centroamericana José Simeón Cañas.

Armando Rodríguez Luna is professor of international relations at the Universidad Nacional Autónoma de México. He is a specialist on Mexican and U.S. national and bilateral security issues, with a specific focus on the Mérida Initiative and organized crime. He is the director of programs and projects at the Centro Argentino de Estudios Internacionales, a collaborator on the Program for Progressive Leadership at the Fundación Friedrich Ebert México, and an associate researcher at the Colectivo de Análisis de la Seguridad con Democracia. He is coeditor (with Raúl Benítez Manaut and Abelardo Rodríguez Sumano) of *Atlas de la Seguridad y la Defensa* *de México 2009,* and he has published several essays on security and geopolitics in various countries throughout the Western Hemisphere. He received an MA in international relations from the Universidad Nacional Autónoma de México and also studied at the National Defense University in Washington.

Victoria Sanford is associate professor of anthropology and director of the Center for Human Rights and Peace Studies at Lehman College and a member of the Doctoral Faculty at the Graduate Center of the City University of New York. She has conducted field research on human rights, child soldiers, development, gender equity, impunity, and democracy in Guatemala since 1990 and in Colombia since 2000. She has published more than two dozen peer-reviewed chapters and articles. Her books include *Buried Secrets: Truth and Human Rights in Guatemala* (Palgrave Macmillan, 2003); *Guatemala: Del Genocidio al Feminicidio* (F&G Editores, 2008); *Violencia y Genocidio en Guatemala,* (F&G Editores, 2003); and *La Masacre de Panzós: Tierra, Etnicidad y Violencia en Guatemala* (F&G Editores, 2009). She is currently working on a book on feminicide, social cleansing, and impunity in Guatemala.

Gema Santamaría Balmaceda is a doctoral student in sociology and historical studies at the New School for Social Research. She received a master's degree in gender and social policy from the London School of Economics and Political Science after completing a master's program in sociology at the New School. She has been a Chevening Scholar and a Fulbright Scholar. Her research deals with the relations between social, political, and criminal violence in Mexico and Central America.

Markus Schultze-Kraft is governance team leader and a research fellow at the Institute of Development Studies at the University of Sussex. He has served as director of the Latin American and Caribbean Program and the Colombia/Andes Project at the International Crisis Group, coordinator of human rights and international humanitarian law observation at the UN Human Rights Office in Bogotá, and lecturer in comparative politics and conflict resolution at Universidad de los Andes in Bogotá. He is the author of *Pacificación y poder civil en Centroamérica: Las relaciones cívico-militares en El Salvador, Guatemala y Nicaragua en el postconflicto* (Grupo Editorial Norma, 2005) and numerous book chapters, articles, and policy reports on diverse conflict prevention/resolution and peace-building topics. He received a degree in political science from the Free University of Berlin and an MPhil in Latin American studies and DPhil in politics from the University of Oxford.

Edelberto Torres-Rivas is a research sociologist associated with the Facultad Latinoamericana de Ciencias Sociales–Guatemala and is the head of the Departamento de Teoría del Poder y del Estado. Additionally, he has worked as a consultant and researcher for the United Nations Development Program. Previously, he was also the director of the Programa de Relaciones Internacionales at the Universidad Rafael Landívar in Guatemala. Among his numerous publications are *Barbarie o Justicia Popular: Estudios sobre los linchamientos en Guatemala* (Facultad Latinoamericana de Ciencias Sociales, 2003); and "Los Caminos hacia la democracia en América Central," in *Un Desafío a la Democracia, los partidos políticos* (edited by Diego Achard and Luis E. González; United Nations Development Program and others, 2004). He received a law degree from the Universidad de San Carlos in Guatemala, an MA in social sciences from the Facultad Latinoamericana de Ciencias Sociales–Chile, and a PhD in sociology from Essex University in England.

Index